ARABIC SPAIN:
SIDELIGHTS ON HER HISTORY AND ART

Frontispiece.

The Virgin of Rocamador, Church of San Lorenzo, Seville, a mural painting over eight feet high. Mozarabic, renovated with additions about the fifteenth century, but the original outlines respected.

ARABIC SPAIN

SIDELIGHTS ON HER HISTORY AND ART

BY

BERNHARD AND ELLEN M. WHISHAW

WITH ILLUSTRATIONS

DARF PUBLISHERS LTD
LONDON
1986

First published 1912
New impression 1986

ISBN 1 85077 101 4

*Printed & bound in Great Britain
by A. Wheaton & Co. Ltd, Exeter*

PREFATORY NOTE

THIS book is an attempt to elucidate some points in the history of Seville under the Moslems, on which the existing histories of Moslem Spain throw no light whatever. We are fully aware how little qualified we are for such a task: our ignorance of Arabic is alone a serious obstacle to an exhaustive study of the subject, and our only excuse for publishing what must necessarily be a very imperfect piece of work is that no one else has yet attempted to do it. In addition to our personal disqualifications we have been further handicapped by the entire absence in the public libraries of Seville, where this book was written, of any modern books except a few in Spanish, and of all the ordinary books of reference, Proceedings of learned Societies, etc. So defective, indeed, are these libraries, that they do not contain the monographs, often valuable, published by the Madrid Academy of History. And as it is manifestly impossible to buy all the books, reports, and so forth, to which it might be useful to refer, perhaps for a single datum, we have had to do the best we can with the materials available. On the other hand, we have the advantage of long residence in Seville, and an intimate acquaintance with many places, people, and things inaccessible to foreigners merely visiting Spain.

We have to offer our sincere thanks to Don Antonio Balleteros Beretta, Professor of History at the University of Seville, for valuable notes on the history of Seville, and especially of the Alcazar and Cathedral; to Sir George Birdwood, K.C.I.E., LL.D., etc.; Dr. A. J. Butler, F.S.A.; and Mr. Alan C. Cole, C.B., for helpful information advice, and criticism; to Don Carlos Canale, Intendant of the Royal Alcazar of Seville, for permission for private study in the palace, extending over several years; to Dr. B. Glanvill Corney, I.S.O., for much useful information, obtained at considerable personal trouble, and for assistance in correction of proofs; to M. Al. Gayet, whose private letters as well as his books have been of great value to us: to Don José Gestoso, author of *Sevilla monumental y artistica*, for permission to reproduce some of the illustrations from that and others of his works; to Mr. M. Longworth-Dames, of the Oriental and Numismatic Societies, for information on Andalucian numismatology and a translation of Ibn Hamdis' poem on the Alcazar of Seville; to Don Vergilio Mattoni, of the Seville School of Fine Arts, for permission to reproduce his painting of the death of San Fernando; to Major Nyström, of the Swedish Royal Engineers, Lecturer on Architecture to the Swedish Army, for assisting us during a whole winter in our study of the Sevillian churches; to Don Carlos Pirozzini Marti, Secretary of the Archæological Museum of Barcelona, for photographs of objects in the Museum, and permission to publish them; to the Rev. the Archdeacon of Seville, Don Luciano Rivaz, Visitor of the Diocesan Convents, for introductions to religious houses containing works of art hitherto unexamined; to the Rev. Don Manuel Serrano y Ortega, author of *Glorias Sevillanas*, who placed at our disposal a mass of local data collected by himself from sources not accessible to laymen, besides photographs of certain works of sacred art not procurable through the ordinary channels; and to the Rev. the Dean of Seville Cathedral, for admission to portions

PREFATORY NOTE

of the Cathedral closed to the general public. We also have to thank the publishers of *L'Art Copte* and *L'Art Arabe*, by M. Al Gayet, for permission to reproduce certain of the illustrations in those works; and the editors of the *Nineteenth Century and After*, and the *Burlington Magazine*, for permission to incorporate essays which first appeared in those Magazines.

SEVILLE,
  Sept., 1912.

CONTENTS

CHAPTER		PAGE
	PREFATORY NOTE	v
	INTRODUCTION	1
I.	CHRISTIANITY UNDER ISLAM	17
II.	THE SONS OF WITIZA	36
III.	THE ROYAL MUWALLADS	49
IV.	ANDALUCIA IN THE NINTH CENTURY	70
V.	ANDALUCIA in THE NINTH CENTURY (*continued*) . .	85
VI.	"KING OMAR OF TOLEDO"	100
VII.	THE INFLUENCE OF THE COPTS IN SPAIN . . .	119
VIII.	CHRISTIANS AND MUWALLADS UNDER ABDERRAHMAN III.	144
IX.	THE SUCCESSORS OF ABDERRAHMAN	154
X.	ALMANSUR AND THE CHRISTIANS I.	169
XI.	THE STORY OF HISHAM II.	180
XII.	THE ABBADITES AT HOME	206
XIII.	THE ALMORAVIDES	225
XIV.	ANDALUCIA IN THE ELEVENTH CENTURY . . .	237
XV.	SPAIN AND THE ALMORAVIDES	244
XVI.	THE BENI HUD AND MARDANISH	261
XVII.	SAN FERNANDO AND AL-AHMAR	282
XVIII.	YEMENITES AND ALMOHADES IN THE TERRITORY OF SEVILLE	303
XIX.	THE FALL OF SEVILLE	319

CONTENTS

CHAPTER		PAGE
XX.	THE PASSING OF SAN FERNANDO	334
XXI.	ISLAM UNDER CHRISTIANITY	345
XXII.	EGYPT AND THE CHURCH IN SEVILLE	357
XXIII.	THE INDUSTRIES OF ANDALUCIA UNDER ISLAM	370
	APPENDIX	381
	GENEALOGICAL TABLES	403
	INDEX	414

LIST OF ILLUSTRATIONS

FIGURE   PAGE

    The Virgin of Rocamador, Church of San Lorenzo, Seville, a mural painting over eight feet high. Mozarabic, renovated with additions about the fifteenth century, but the original outlines respected . . . . *Frontispiece*

1. Walls of the Alcázares Reales de Sevilla: the Capitol of the Romans: the palace of the Visigothic Princes: restored and refaced during the dominion of Islam in Spain. From the reconquest in 1248 until the present day one of the favourite residences of the Kings and Queens of Spain . . . . *facing*   1

2. Fragment of decoration in the Alcazar of Seville. Concealed until recent years under plaster and whitewash, and now in course of restoration. A relic of the palace of Motadid Ibn Abbad (1042–69) . . . . . *facing* 17

3. The Seville Gate at Carmona: Roman work with Moslem additions . . . . *facing* 36

4A. Coptic Church of St. George, Egypt, fourth century
4B. Mosque of Tulun . . . .   "   119
    Early pointed architecture in Egypt.

5. *Convento de la Luz* (No. 1). Copto-Arabic arches of the Central Court with fifteenth-century arcades above *facing* 142

6. West Door of the Church of San Juan de la Palma. Originally built by the Mozarabs: an existing inscription states that the tower was added in 1086 by Itimad, wife of Motamid Ibn Abbad, for her son Ar-Rashid, Kadi of Seville, the court of whose palace stands opposite, with an upper story added in the seventeenth century *facing* 144

LIST OF ILLUSTRATIONS

FIGURE   PAGE

7. Entrance to an apartment in the Alcazar of Seville, traditionally known as "The Sleeping-Room of the Moorish King and Queen," opening on to the "Court of the Ladies"; otherwise the patio of the Harem. Decorated in the style prevailing in the Moslem Court of Egypt in the late twelfth and thirteenth centuries, with some of the original tiles still existing. One of the apartments prepared by the Moorish Sultan, Yusuf Abu Yakub (the Almohade), in 1171–5, for the reception of his Yemenite bride, the Princess of Denia. (See p. 275) . *facing* 154

8. Detail of Ceiling of the Almohade period in the Alcazar of Seville, on which are superimposed, in a different and very inferior technique, the shields of Castile and Leon as borne by Fernando III. in 1248. Between the two is the shield given by him to his friend and ally, Al-Ahmar of Granada (see p. 346), a band issuing from the mouths of dragons or serpents, later adopted as the device of the knightly Order of *La Banda* . . . . *facing* 180

9. Fragment of the funeral robe of Fernando III. (d. 1252) preserved in the Archæological Museum of Madrid, with lions and castles similar to the Shields in the Alcazar of Seville. A robe of this design is depicted as worn by Alfonso X. in his *Book of Chess* . . . *facing* 206

10. *Convento de la Luz* (No. 2). Copto-Arabic pointed arches of the great Central Court . . . . . *facing* 237

11. Early pointed architecture in Seville. Church of San Roman. Mozarabic, the nave unaltered since the reconquest in 1248 . . . . . . *facing* 261

12. *Convento de la Luz* (No. 3). Arabic arches in "the modern part" . . . . *facing* 381

13. *Convento de la Luz* (No. 4). The Arabic Infirmary of the Poor Clares . . . . *facing* 398

BIBLIOGRAPHY

The following are the principal works and editions referred to in the text:—

Akhbar Majmua, Tr. EMILIO LAFUENTE (*Real Academia de la Historia*), Madrid, 1867.

ATHIR, IBN AL, *Annales du Maghreb et de l'Espagne*, Tr. E. FAGNAN, Algiers, 1901.

BUTLER, A. J., *The Arab Conquest of Egypt*, Clar. Press, 1902.

CASIRI, *Bibliotheca Arabico-hispana*, 2 vols.

CHAMBERLAIN, H. S., *The Foundations of the Nineteenth Century*, 2 vols., John Lane, 1911.

CODERA, F., *Estudios criticos de historia árabe-española*, Zaragoza, 1903.

CODERA, F., *Decadencia y desaparicion de los Almoravides en España*, Zaragoza, 1899.

CONDE, J. A., *Historia de la dominacion de los Arabes en España*, 3 vols., Madrid, 1820.

Crónica general, primera, Estoria de España que mandó componer Alfonso el Sabio, ed. R. MENENDEZ PIDAL, Madrid, 1906.

Crónica general de España, vols. VII. and VIII. by MORALES, Madrid, 1791.

Crónica general de España, vol. XIII. by SANDOVAL, Madrid, 1792.

Crónica del Rey Don Pedro, by P. LOPEZ DE AYALA, Madrid, 1799.

DOZY, R., *Geschichte der Mauren in Spanien*, 2 vols., Leipzig, 1874.

DOZY, R., *Recherches sur l'histoire et la litterature d'Espagne pendant le moyen âge*, 2 vols., Leyden, 1860.

DOZY, R., *Dictionnaire détallé des Noms des Vêtements chez les Arabes*, Amsterdam, 1845.

BIBLIOGRAPHY

Dozy, R., *Historia Abbaditarum*, 3 vols., Leyden, 1846-63.

Encyclopedia of Islam, ed. Houtsma & Seligsohn, Leyden and London (in course of publication).

España Sagrada, ed. Florez, 34 vols., Madrid, 1754-84.

Espinoza, *Historia antigüedades y grandezas de Sevilla*, Seville, 1627.

Fischbach, F., *The most important Textile Ornaments up to the XIXth Century*, Maintz, 1910.

Gayet, Al, *L'Art Copte*, Paris, 1902.

Gayet, Al, *L'Art Arabe*, Paris, n.d.

Gayet, Al, *Le costume en Egypte du 3me au 13me siècle*, Paris, 1900.

Gibbon, *Decline and Fall*, 8 vols., London, 1838.

Gudiol, J., *Nocions de Arqueologia sagrada Catalana*, Vich, 1902.

Idrisi, *Descripcion de España*, tr. A. Blasquez, Madrid, 1901.

Kuttiyyah, Al, *Histoire de la conquête d'Espagne par les Musulmans*, tr. M. A. Cherbonneau, Journal Asiatique, Nov.-Dec., 1856.

Lane-Poole, S., *The Moors in Spain (Story of Nations)*, Unwin, 7th ed., 1897.

Lea, H. C., *The Moriscos of Spain*, Philadelphia, 1901.

Lea, H. C., *History of Sacerdotal Celibacy*, 3rd ed., 2 vols., New York, 1907.

Lenormant, *Manuel d'Histoire ancienne de l'Orient*, Paris, 1869.

Makkari, Al, *History of the Mohammedan Dynasties in Spain*, tr. and ed. P. de Gayangos, 2 vols., Oriental Translation Fund, 1840.

Makrizi, *Histoire d'Egypte*, tr. E. Blochet, Paris, 1908.

Mariana, *Historia general de España*, ed. E. Chao, 5 vols., Madrid, 1848.

Marrakushi, Al, *Histoire des Almohades*, tr. E. Fagnan, Algiers, 1893.

Morgado, J. A., *Prelados Sevillanos*, Seville, 1899.

Palomo, F., *Historia de las Riadas del Guadalquivir*, Seville, 1878.

Petrie, W. M. Flinders, *Egyptian Decorative Art*, Methuen, 1895.

Pineda, *Memorial para la canonizacion del Rey Fernando III.*, Seville, 1627.

BIBLIOGRAPHY

Pons, F., *Historiadores y Geógrafos arábigo-españoles*, Madrid, 1898.
Pons, F., *Escrituras Mozárabes Toledanas*, Madrid, 1897.
Remiro, M. G., *Historia de Murcia musulmana*, Zaragoza, 1905.
Rios, Amador de los, *Inscripciones árabes de Sevilla*, Madrid, 1875.
Rodriguez, M., *Memorias para la vida de Fernando III.*, Madrid, 1800.
Schott, *Hispania illustrata*, 5 vols., Frankfort, 1603.
Serrano, M., *Glorias Sevillanas*, Seville, 1893.
Serrano, M., *Tradiciones Sevillanas*, Seville, 1895.
Sharp, Mary, *Point and Pillow Lace*, 2nd ed., Murray, 1905.
Simonet, L. J., *Historia de los Mozárabes*, Madrid, 1903.
Strabo, *Geography*, Bohn's trans., 3 vols., 1854.
Watts, H. E., *Spain (Story of Nations)*, 3rd ed., Unwin, n.d.
Williams, Leonard, *The Arts and Crafts of Older Spain*, 3 vols., Foulis, London and Edinburgh, 1907.
Zuñiga, *Anales de Sevilla*, 5 vols., Madrid, 1795.

FIG. 1.—Walls of the Alcázares Reales de Sevilla: the Capitol of the Romans: the palace of the Visigothic Princes: restored and refaced during the dominion of Islam in Spain. From the reconquest in 1248 until the present day one of the favourite residences of the Kings and Queens of Spain.

INTRODUCTION

THE history of Moslem Spain has still to be written. The material, of which there is a great quantity, is very largely in MS., and of the comparatively few Arabic texts which have been printed only a small number have been translated into any European language. Until the wealth of documents relating to Spain, now hidden away not only in the Escorial and other libraries of Europe, but also in Egypt and Morocco, has been unearthed and published, any account of this most interesting period of history must be provisional and largely conjectural.

Years ago, when we first came to live in Spain, we tried, like every one else interested in the country, to obtain books which would afford some information about the rise and development of Moslem art in Seville. We were very soon convinced of the falsity of the assertion, so often made by the local archæologists, that every trace of Arabic art previous to the occupation by the Almohades had totally disappeared from this city; while the extraordinary inconsistencies of what the same school of writers call " Mudéjar " art soon becomes evident to the least critical student of Moslem archæology and architecture.[1]

The " Mudéjarites "—if we may coin a word to describe

[1] The meaning of the word *mudéjar*, as given in the *Dict. Acad.*, is a Mohammedan who after the surrender of a place remained, without changing his religion, as a vassal of the Christian kings. It is derived from an Arabic word meaning tributary. The dictionary gives no explanation of it as a term of art.

them—have unfortunately contrived to deter serious students from making research in this part of Andalucia. No archæologist cares to waste time over, e.g. the Alcazar of Seville, when the Mudéjarites declare it to be a fourteenth-century palace built by Pedro of Castile with the assistance of "Moorish architects from Toledo," where no Moors ever set foot. Nor has any Arabic scholar thought it worth his while to examine the Kufic, Karamatic, and African inscriptions with which the whole building is covered, since the time when Amador de los Rios published his essay on the Alcazar in 1874. What interest can orientalists expect to find in inscriptions declared to have been put up by "Moorish architects" to do honour to a Christian king, a century after the Moors had been expelled from the city where these inscriptions are found? Naturally enough, serious writers on Moslem art have left Seville alone during the thirty-eight years since one of the earliest and most important Moslem buildings in Spain was damned with the name of Mudéjar.

The whole theory is based on a few inscriptions attributing the building of the Alcazar to Pedro the Cruel. Some, at any rate, of these are interpolations, one in particular of so obvious a nature that it is difficult to imagine how the most cursory glance can have failed to reveal the fact. Of these it is enough to observe that it is not a difficult matter to insert inscriptions on an outer wall, or in stucco and among scores of others in the same material. *Per contra*, there is absolutely no record, either in the archives of the Alcazar or in any contemporary or nearly contemporary chronicle or other document, of this great and costly piece of architectural work, which is supposed to have been executed by a monarch who was always in difficulties for money. Moreover, there is documentary evidence that Alfonso XI., Pedro's father, frequently lived in the Alcazar; his chronicle, indeed, mentions a winding staircase in that palace, and precisely such a staircase was discovered not long ago in the course of some alterations.

It seems strange that any doubt should be felt as to how much of the Alcazar in Seville was built by Pedro of Castile. A comparison of the apartments now known as the "Salones de Carlos Quinto" with the apses of certain ancient Sevillian churches, added, as may be gathered from the chronicle, by that monarch as penance for his sins, shows that these halls of the Alcazar, like the church apses, are of Pedro's own period, and probably were all designed by his own architect, so strong is the resemblance in style and in idea. But as we shall discuss this point at greater length in another place, we merely mention the fact here.

The truth is that the Moors in Spain had no architecture and no art of their own. All the arts and crafts and architecture miscalled Moorish are Arabic, inasmuch as they were borrowed by the Arabs of Spain (not by the Moors) from the Greeks, the Romans, the Copts, or the Persians, and their rise and decline can be traced step by step in Spain, just as they can in Syria and Egypt, which were certainly free from any Moorish influence.

It is indeed difficult to say whether "Moorish" or "Mudéjar" is the more absurd misnomer for the Byzantine and Coptic arts developed during the Moslem occupation of this country. About the Byzantine-Arabic art, of which the mosque at Cordova is the chief example in Spain, we have little or nothing to say in this book, for its history and development have been discussed by many more competent writers. But we hope that any one interested in the history and art of Andalucia, who has sufficient patience to read and weigh the evidence we offer here, will be convinced that the "Mudéjar" art supposed to have been executed by "Moorish" craftsmen to the order of their

Christian masters is, with certain easily recognised exceptions, the work of Coptic artists and artisans, or of their Arabic or Christian pupils, executed during the long period when the Southern Gothic Christians, the Muwallads, or people of mixed Gothic and Yemenite Arab descent, and the Moslems of the tribes of Yemen lived side by side in peace and amity, under the government of Muwallad or Yemenite princes who dwelt in the Alcazar of Seville—the oriental city in whose narrow streets one finds at every turn reminiscences of the florid decoration beloved of the Moors who ruled there in the latter half of the twelfth century, superimposed on the earlier and purer art of Christian Egypt, which flourished here under the Arabs of Yemen.

Very soon after we came to Spain we saw that the early (so-called) Moslem art of Seville was curiously different from the early Moslem art of Cordova. Nobody seemed able to tell us why this was so, and it has taken us some eight years of study to arrive at the conclusions which are given in this book. Hampered though we have been by our ignorance of Arabic, we have nevertheless obtained, we believe, a good many side-lights on a peculiarly unexplored by-path in the history of Spain, and we hope that our essays may be accepted as finger-posts pointing to a road full of fascination for students of early Mohammedan history and early medieval art in Spain.

Among our numerous difficulties has been the spelling of Arabic names, for in this matter every translator seems to be a law to himself. After much consideration, we decided that, as our book is primarily intended not for scholars but for the general reader, it would be best to retain as far as possible the spelling of names familiarised by popular histories of Moslem Spain, although, of course, to those who know even the rudiments of Arabic, such spellings are often hopelessly at fault. We have been obliged to refer so frequently to tribal and family names in the course of our argument, and Arabic names are at best so awkward and unattractive to the general reader, that we have felt the simplification of nomenclature, wherever possible, to be of more importance than what could be at best only relatively correct spelling. For the same reason, although naturally we are aware that Islam was divided into many sects, we have tried to avoid confusion by omitting all mention of the minor ones, broadly grouping the Moslems of Spain under the two great sects alone—the Shiites and the Sunnites. We believe that, with few or possibly no exceptions, all the Yemenite Arabs in Spain were Shiites, while all the Mudarite Arabs were Sunnites. We may be in error in drawing such a hard and fast line, but for our purposes it is necessary to define the two main parties, whose continuous hostility is the key to a good deal of the history of Moslem Spain. So we have classed as Shiites all who proclaimed allegiance to the Abbasside and Fatimite Khalifs of the East, and as Sunnites all those, not being Berbers or Africans, who were hostile to the Shiites at any given period with which we may be dealing. Our aim has not been to give details of the religious differences which divided Islam so much as to show how the Moslems of Andalucia maintained two great parties, hostile both in race and religion, and the effect that this hostility had upon the history and art of the states peopled by the Shiite Arabs of Yemenite extraction.

This point of view was not brought forward by any of the translators from the Arabic in the early nineteenth century. But when we think of the work that these men did, and of the bold plunge they made into a period of European history previously practically untouched, we wonder not at what was omitted or done amiss by those translators, but at what they accomplished. It is very well for Mr. Seybold, for instance, with the Arabic sources open to him, to write pityingly of the "unhappy times of Casiri, Conde, and Gayangos." But among all the works which he names in his article on Al-Andalus in the Encyclopedia of Islam, we find none except Conde, Dozy, and Gayangos, who even attempt to give a connected history of the Spanish Moslems for the benefit of readers unable to study that history in the original Arabic. There are, it is true, fragmentary studies of dynasties, periods, and incidents, though even these are not numerous. But the would-be student of Spanish-Arabic history from the first invasion in 711 to the final fall of Seville in 1248 has no one to turn to except the writers of those "unhappy times," who attacked the prodigious labour of collecting and translating the scattered Arabic accounts of the period.

We, who have spent many long hours trying to obtain a coherent account of some of these events and an idea of their underlying causes, have reason to admire the work done by these early historians: and although we have been forced to the conclusion that all of them have been guilty of numerous mistakes and inaccuracies, such imperfections hardly detract from the value of their work to the reader ignorant of Arabic. And it is just possible that in our own case our very deficiencies may have enabled us, notwithstanding numerous errors of detail, to put forward an aspect of Spanish-Moslem history which has escaped the less detached vision of scholars devoting themselves to the elucidation of the Arabic texts.

The nineteenth-century historians do not seem to have given any weight to the inevitable bias of the Arabic writers; and yet these are of the last importance to the discovery of the facts. How, for instance, could Ibn Hayyan, a Mudarite and a Sunnite, do justice to the part played in history by his racial and religious foes, the Shiite Arabs descended from the tribes of Yemen? He wrote the history of Spain as he saw it at Cordova, which for men of his race and religion was the only place that mattered. To him the protracted civil war of the ninth century, for instance, was merely the rebellion of "bad Moslems," "rebels," and "bandits." Makkari, a Mudarite and a Sunnite like Hayyan, naturally followed him and other writers of the same school, and inevitably their views differed *toto cœlo* from those of the Yemenites, the "bad Moslems" and "rebels" whom they so cordially hated.

Over and over again Makkari's statements contradict each other flatly. His method was to transcribe accounts of the same events as he found them in different writers, making no attempt to reconcile them when they conflicted, and merely adding the formula: "Others say so and so was the case. God only knows which is the truth."

Conde, whose *Historia de la dominacion de los Arabes* was published in 1820, adopted precisely the same method as Makkari had followed some two centuries earlier. He threw together all the material he found without making any attempt to reconcile conflicting statements, but unfortunately for his reputation, he rarely cited his authority, and omitted Makkari's formula disclaiming responsibility for what he transcribed. And he died before the whole of his work was published, and thus it lacks the notes and corrections which he would doubtless have added had he lived. Gayangos apparently did not observe the cause of a great deal of the confusion in Conde's narrative, and condemned as "ignorance" and "bad faith" in his compatriot what he commended in Makkari as honesty of purpose. Unluckily Gayangos, whose own work, though extraordinarily painstaking, is destitute of the least spark of historical insight, was immediately accepted both in England and Spain as authoritative, and his criticism of the earlier translator was taken up by the various writers who followed him, and repeated *ad nauseam,* until Conde's work has come to be described as " a book of considerable literary merit but very slight historical value, and the source of most of the errors that are to be found in later works." If there is one thing which Conde's work lacks more than another it is literary merit ; the Spanish often becomes positively uncouth through the translator's efforts to render Arabic forms of speech. But Conde, at least, never was guilty of such a mistake as to confuse Arabs with Moors, like the writer who described his work in the above words.[1]

The value of Conde's work, as we have found by experience, is that in many cases he took his account of events from Yemenite, otherwise Shiite sources, whence we naturally get a version differing radically from that of their racial, religious, and political opponents, the Mudarite or Sunnite historians who wrote exclusively from the Cordovan point of view. Moreover, Conde consulted historians inaccessible to Gayangos, who was not permitted to work in the library of the Escorial. One MS. at least was in Conde's possession which both Makkari and Gayangos lacked, and of which, according to the authorities in the British Museum, no complete copy is known to exist. This is the work of the Yemenite Al Fayyad, a portion of which was appended to Conde's copy of Al Abbar. In the body of his work Conde refers to a history of Al Fayyad " which is translated into Hebrew." Señor Pons, in his account of Al Fayyad, cites Dozy as saying that this writer is quoted in the *Kartas.*[2]

---

[1] The distinction between Arabs and Moors was clearly recognised by Fernando III. and his son Alfonso X., two Christian kings who for fifty years fought side by side with the Yemenite Amirs against their common enemy the Almohades. But after the reduction of the last of the Almohades (the true Moors) in the second half of the thirteenth century, all the Moslems who remained in the country came to be classed by Christian writers as *Moros ;* and this gave rise to much confusion.

[2] Cf. Pons., p. 138.

Thus passages in Conde's book which Gayangos dismissed as "an unfaithful and rambling version of the *Kartas*" may in fact have been taken by the earlier writer from the original author direct.

We have frequently found, by comparing names, dates, and, above all, tribal connections, as given by Conde, with narratives of the same events by other authors, in which the tribal names are omitted, that the mention of the racial relationship sheds a flood of light on what was inexplicable until we realised that a Mudarite was describing a Yemenite or vice versa.

The Sunnite Ibn Hayyan and the Cordovan historians in general suppressed, as far as possible, any recognition of the strength and importance of the elements hostile to their own party. The fact is that until the tenth century Cordova was only one, and that not by any means always the strongest, of the five states into which Moslem Spain was loosely divided. The other four were the territories restored and confirmed to the sons of Witiza by the Khalif Al Walid, and the "Land of Theodomir," afterwards known as Murcia. These, while acknowledging the more or less nominal overlordship of Cordova, hemmed it in on all sides, and were always a source of danger to it. The civil war with which the ninth century closed was not, as Ibn Hayyan represents it, a disturbance made by scattered rebels each fighting for his own hand, but a combined effort of the Andalucian states to throw off this overlordship. Toledo to the north was largely Christian down to its conquest by Alfonso VI. in the eleventh century, and gave frequent trouble to the Ommeyads even before the outbreak of the civil war in 886; Cazlona and Jaen formed the centre of the long struggle waged by Omar Ibn Hafsun (a Christian) from 886 to the accession of Abderrahman III.; Murcia was left, in the earlier times of the Moslem occupation, under the government of the Gothic Christians; while

Seville—where, as even Ibn Hayyan admits, the Beni Hejjaj, the descendants of Witiza's granddaughter Sara, "ruled like kings"—was more powerful and wealthier than any of the rest, thanks to the peaceful amalgamation of Goths and Arabs brought about by the Princess Sara's successive marriages with two Yemenite nobles.

The people of Andalucia—the Plebs, as Conde calls them in his translations from the Arabic—are still very much what they were a thousand years ago. The Yemenite Arabs brought all their racial traditions with them *via* Egypt into Spain, together with the Coptic craftsmen and artists with whom they had established relations on the banks of the Nile. Among these traditions was the memory of the material prosperity and civilisation of Yemen when their country was a world-exchange for corn, wine, and oil, fine linen and other manufactures, silver ingots and bronze and iron implements, bartered by the Phenicians for the precious stones, ivory, sandal-wood, spices, pepper, cinnamon, and cotton, which were imported by the Yemenites from India, besides incense and myrrh, laudanum, aloes, onyxes and agates, and the pearls of Hormuz, provided by Arabia herself.

We hear little of the progress of Cordova before the reign of Abderrahman III. Her brilliant period began with the tenth century, when for the first time Yemenite statesmen were admitted into the councils of her rulers. Science, art, and literature then flourished in Andalucia as nowhere else in Europe. Splendid buildings were erected, and luxury in domestic life was carried to a pitch of refinement undreamt of in the north. Women were given a place in society such as they possessed in no Christian country at that time or for many centuries later. The application of the Egyptian system of irrigation brought agriculture to a pitch never reached by Spain under Christian rule. Pottery with a gold lustre and beautiful glass were made in Seville and Murcia, and eagerly purchased abroad. Fruit of many kinds was grown and preserved for winter use. Tubular stoves were used for heating houses, and soap was regarded as one of the first necessaries of life. Most of these appliances and conveniences of civilisation existed in Seville before they were adopted in Cordova, and the indications point to their having been introduced from Egypt by the Arabs of Yemen, and developed there under what we may call the competitive civilisation of the Shiite Moslems and the Gothic nobility, who were closely connected by intermarriage and had a further bond of union in their common hostility to the Mudarites, who vainly attempted to rule the whole country from Cordova.

The city of Cordova was celebrated for its palaces and its mosque and bridge, and especially for its men of science and letters, and for the general luxury of its Court under Abderrahman III. and his successors; but nothing is said of any manufactures or industries having their head-quarters there.

On the other hand, the cities and districts peopled by the Arabs of Yemen, the Copts, the Muwallads, and the Gothic Christians, were renowned for their manufactures and their agriculture, several books on the latter subject being spoken of as currently read in the palmy days of the Khalifate.[1]

We may instance Almeria, which is recorded to have surpassed every city in the world at one time in her manufactures of silken stuffs of different kinds, including *tiraz*,[2] brocade, and damask, besides all sorts of utensils of iron,

[1] We hope to give in a future volume a full account of these places, with the names of the Yemenite tribes settled there, and the products for which they were, and in some cases still are, noted.

[2] A rich stuff with inscriptions on the edge, used in early days exclusively by royal personages.

copper, and glass; Jaen, celebrated for its culture of silk-worms; Baeza for its saffron; Murcia for silks and carpets; Valencia for its orchards and gardens, and its flowers, so plentiful as to give it the name among the Moslems of "the scent-bottle of Andalus"; and Jativa, where paper was manufactured earlier than anywhere else in Europe. As for Seville, her wine and olive oil were as great a source of wealth under the Yemenites as they had been under the Romans and as they are to-day; but while these seem to have always been her principal exports, all the fruits of the earth abounded in the fertile plain of the Guadalquivir to such a degree that a popular proverb named it as "the place to look for birds' milk" if any one wanted it. In all these districts the Yemenite Arabs and Gothic Christians were in the majority.

The Khalifate of Cordova is commonly said to have broken up in the eleventh century into a number of independent states, each under its own petty king, while the followers of the Ommeyads in vain endeavoured to restore the rule of that house in Cordova. This is the Sunnite version of the events which began with the deposition of Hisham II., the grandson of Abderrahman III. The Yemenite historians put a different complexion on affairs. It has been difficult for us to evolve a coherent narrative from the fragmentary quotations from writers cited by historians of the opposite party, who usually omit their tribal names; but we have, we hope, succeeded in collecting evidence enough to show that the last word about this period has not yet been spoken. For the Yemenite version—so far as it is at present accessible in translations—goes to show that the men described by Ibn Hayyan and his followers as kinglets [1] and persons of small importance, were in fact Governors and Amirs who ruled under the title of Hajibs of Hisham II., whom they

---

[1] In Spanish, *reyes de taifa*, which may be translated party-kings.

acknowledged as their Imam until the year 1057-58. This at any rate was no prejudiced fiction on the part of the Yemenite historians, for we have the evidence of coins struck by the Hajibs of various Yemenite states down to the time when the dethroned Khalif is said to have died in the Alcazar of Seville. The downfall of the Khalifate was due to exaggerated racial hostility. The Sunnite Arabs and the Berbers overthrew the grandson of Abderrahman III. because he leant upon Yemenite ministers and advisers, and the Yemenites rallied to protect the man whom they had accepted as their sovereign, because his grandfather was born of a Muwallad woman descended from one of their own race.

Ibn Hayyan's prejudice against the Yemenite party is nowhere more strongly shown than in his accounts of the second civil war, and he insists again and again on the base motives of those who recognised "the mat-maker of Calatrava" as the dethroned and fugitive Khalif. Even he appears to have had some doubts whether after all the "impostor" were not really the man whom the Amirs and Walis of the Yemenite states proclaimed him to be. But to admit this would have been to admit that he was the rightful monarch of Moslem Spain. And to restore Hisham to the throne of Cordova would have meant restoring the authority of the Yemenites who had saved his life and never wavered in their loyalty to him. So the Sunnites of Cordova refused to admit that their legitimate ruler had escaped two attempts at murder, although each pretender whom they set up proved more incompetent and more unpopular than the last, until at length the people themselves elected a Governor who proclaimed the sovereignty of the broken old man shut safely behind the walls of the Sevillian palace, where none of his many enemies could injure him; and then Cordova once more had a few years of comparative prosperity.

After the death of Hisham and of his protector, Motadid Ibn Abbad, the Yemenite Amirs formed a federation under the headship of Motamid Ibn Abbad of Seville. The motive of the Abbadite in urging this course upon his fellow-tribesmen was not, as the Sunnite historians assert, the desire for personal aggrandisement, for there is nothing to show that he ever called himself king of the Amirs who came into the alliance. Motamid's chief aim throughout his twenty-two years' reign was to prevail on the Moslem states to offer a united resistance to the encroachments of the Christians from the north. This policy was accepted by the Amirs who had professed loyalty to Hisham, and rejected by those who had rebelled against him. Motamid's destruction was not due, as is generally supposed, to his alliance with the Almoravide Sultan, Yusuf Ibn Tashfin, but to the intrigues of a Mudarite Arab and a Berber who had attached themselves to the Yemenite federation under the guise of friendship, and never ceased their machinations until they attained their object by bringing about war between the Shiite rulers of Africa and Andalucia.

Had Makkari given the tribal names of the actors in the tragic drama that was played in Andalucia between 1086 and 1091, the causes and sequence of events would have been a good deal clearer. But he seems on the contrary to have been at pains to conceal the bond which linked the Jodhamites of Zaragoza and Badajoz, the Beni Abi Amir of Valencia, the Beni Tahir of Murcia, the Beni al Amiri of Denia, the Bekrites of Huelva and Niebla, and the other Yemenite rulers, with Motamid Ibn Abbad al Lakhmi, who came of the same tribe as the husband of Princess Sara, and took for his queen a woman belonging to the family of the Beni Hejjaj, rulers of Seville for over a century in right of their descent from the Gothic kings.

It may seem a far cry from the "Mudéjarism" of

nineteenth-century writers to the tribal relations between the Moslem states in the eleventh century. But the artistic features which the Mudéjarites attribute to Pedro the Cruel of Castile are the connecting link. In all the provinces which were populated in the main by Yemenite Arabs when Motamid was king of Seville, may be discerned relics of what those writers call Mudéjar, but what we call Yemenite or Copto-Arabic art. And since it is not enough to assert dogmatically that this school of art dates, in Andalucia, not from the fourteenth, but from the eighth century, the only alternative is to give the historical grounds for our conclusions before we can venture to discuss survivals of the Moslem art of Seville.

The particular detail which has most misled the Mudéjarites is what we may call the Copto-Arabic arch. In their opinion the horse-shoe is the mark of "Moorish" architecture, and the pointed arch is "Gothic." Their argument may be very briefly summed up thus. There was no Christian art in the territory of Seville previous to 1248, because there were no Christians after the eighth century, so any pointed arch found here must necessarily be posterior to the reconquest. The first Christian king mentioned as having built a church in Seville (save Alfonso X., whose Church of Santa Ana in Triana is mentioned in his Chronicle) is Pedro the Cruel, who was apparently ordered by the Archbishop to expiate some of his sins by restoring certain sacred edifices. The churches mentioned in this connection have pointed arches. *Ergo*, every church with pointed arches resembling arches in those churches must have been built by Pedro the Cruel.

The critics of this school blink the fact that some of the pointed arches in the churches recorded to have been "mosques" in 1248—some of which Pedro is said to have rebuilt—are not like fourteenth-century Gothic arches anywhere else in the world. And as it has not occurred to them that there could be any relation between Moslem art in Seville and Moslem art in Egypt, they have not observed that the pointed arches which they attribute to Pedro are frequently identical with those employed by the Coptic architects, who from the eighth century onwards built in Egypt for Moslem employers, such as Amru, Tulun, and the Fatimite Khalifs. Here again we have to dive into the history of the Yemenites in Spain to learn why they employed Coptic architects to build for them in Seville, while the Mudarites of Cordova followed the Byzantine traditions of Damascus.

Thus our researches into the origin of the art miscalled Mudéjar have led us to Egypt. But indeed from Andalucia to Egypt is but a step, for as M. Franz says in a paper read before the Institut Égyptien: " Pendant ce voyage (in southern Spain) nous avons remarqué bien de choses nous rappellant l'Égypte," and the whole article is full of the resemblances which struck him.[1]

If we can convince our readers that, of the two great hostile camps into which Moslem Spain was divided, one always looked to Egypt for artistic inspiration, the special development of Yemenite or Shiite art and civilisation which is seen in what was once known as the Kingdom of Seville will appear to them as inevitable as it does to us. But to secure that conviction we must conduct them through what we fear may prove somewhat dreary paths of dry facts, among which chapter and verse references to such authorities as are accessible to us must perforce figure largely. And if any orientalist should read our " Side-lights," he will earn our gratitude by pointing out mistakes, so that we may correct them if the book should reach a second edition.

[1] *L'Andalousie et ses monuments arabes.* Cairo, 1891.

FIG. 2.—Fragment of decoration in the Alcazar of Seville. Concealed until recent years under plaster and whitewash, and now in course of restoration. A relic of the palace of Motadid Ibn Abbad (1042–69).

ARABIC SPAIN: SIDE-LIGHTS ON HER HISTORY AND ART

CHAPTER I

CHRISTIANITY UNDER ISLAM

If some of the ecclesiastical chroniclers and those who have followed them were to be believed, it would appear that the position of the Christian Church and of its members during the Moslem occupation of Spain was one long oppression and martyrdom. As a matter of fact, until the invasion of the Almohades, when there may have been a certain amount of persecution, the Christians on the whole enjoyed the fullest measure of toleration, of which the only condition seems to have been that they should pay their tribute and refrain from insulting the religion of their conquerors.

A glance at the volumes of *España Sagrada* shows beyond doubt that the Christian hierarchy, Christian worship, and Christian monasticism, continued practically without interference for something like two hundred years after the Moslem conquest; after that the record is comparatively scanty, but even in later years isolated facts point to the continued liberty which the Christians enjoyed. Thus, to take only a few instances, six bishops of Cordova are named as holding office between 850 and 988, and Morgado gives a list of thirteen bishops of Seville, extending to the middle of the twelfth century.[1] Malaga is recorded to have had a bishop in 865, and another at the end of the eleventh century. Mention is made of a bishop of Merida in the ninth century, of seven bishops of Coimbra and of nine of Viseu. An inscription records the death of a bishop of Ecija in 931, and eleven bishops of Toledo are named as occupying the See between 713 and 1077. According to Roderick of Toledo, the Bishops of Medina Sidonia, Niebla, and Marchena took refuge at Toledo in 1146 on the entry of the Almohades into Spain.[2]

In Cordova six churches are recorded as existing within the city and six others outside it, in the middle of the ninth century. In Lisbon "more than one" church was reserved for Christian use.[3] Morgado mentions an inscription recording the completion of the church of San Lucar la Mayor, between Seville and Niebla, in the year 1214;[4] this is the more interesting since the inscription proved that this church, which is still the parish church of the little town, was built during the Almohade occupation, when a certain amount of intolerance is generally asserted to have been shown. And there is an interesting notice of a church given by the Arab geographer, Idrisi, who wrote in the twelfth century. As the passage contains some curious details which we have not seen quoted elsewhere, we will give it in full.[5]

The church is called " of the crow," and is seven miles from " the cape of the Algarbe which advances into the ocean " (*i.e.* Cape St. Vincent). The writer describes it as follows—

[1] *Prelados Sevillanos*, pp. 217 ff.
[2] *España sagrada*, v. 336-84, 376-7, x. 112-4, 217, 272-87, 308, xi. 63-4, xiv. 76-90, 187, 317-21.
[3] *España sagrada*, v. 327, x. 249-60, xiv. 187 ; cf. *Crónica general*, vii. 260-1.
[4] *Prelados Sevillanos*, p. 168.
[5] Idrisi, p. 17.

CHRISTIANITY UNDER ISLAM 19

"This Church has suffered no change since the Christian domination; it owns lands, and pious souls are in the habit of making gifts to it when they go on pilgrimage. It is situated on a promontory which extends into the sea. On the roof-tree of the building there are ten crows, and no one has seen them eat or go away. The priests in the Church relate marvellous things about these crows, but the veracity of any one who repeated them would be called in question. For the rest, it is impossible to pass by without accepting the dinner which the Church gives; this is an absolute obligation, a custom which no one fails to observe, and with which one is the more ready to fall in since it is a very old one, handed down from age to age and consecrated by long observance.

"The Church is served by priests and monks (*religiosos*). It possesses extensive lands and considerable revenues, the greater part of which come from estates left to it in different parts of the Algarbe. With these they attend to the needs of the Church, of its ministers, of all those attached to it in any capacity, and of the strangers who come to visit it."

This church was built about the middle of the eighth century, to receive the relics of St. Vincent on their removal from Valencia.[1] Its continued existence, with its large estates and wealthy endowments, is in itself strong evidence of the toleration accorded by the Moslems to their Christian compatriots.

The old Gothic ritual, which was in general use in Spain until 1088,[2] is still known as the *Oficio mozarabe*. The word *mozarabe* means "a Christian who lived formerly among the *moros* of Spain, and was mixed with them."[3] Thus the very name of this old ritual proves the persistence

---
[1] *España sagrada*, viii. 187–9.
[2] Mariana, Book IX., chapter xviii.
[3] *Dict. Acad.*, s. v.

of its use through Moslem times. It is still used in one of the chapels in the cathedrals of Toledo and Salamanca, and, we understand, in the Church of La Patriarca in Valencia, which no woman may enter unveiled.

In Toledo, according to Ayala,[1] six churches were left for Christian use at the time of the Moslem Conquest, and the Mozarabic ritual continued to be used in them in 1351. We have already named a number of bishops, each of whom necessarily implies a diocese and a certain number of churches under his control. Florez quotes St. Eulogius as saying that in his time (ninth century) the Christians could build new churches, " though of rude structure." Possibly they could not afford anything better, or were unwilling to make display of wealth for fear of taxation. The same writer says that there was complete liberty of worship in Cordova,[2] that the Christians had their churches, with towers and bells, that the various offices of the Church were performed and that, " even in times of disturbance," funeral processions through the streets continued.[3]

Not only did the ecclesiastics continue to exercise their functions and the services to be held in the churches, but numerous convents and monasteries continued to flourish. Thus eight monasteries or convents are named as existing on the outskirts of Cordova in the ninth century, and various abbots are mentioned in the records of the time, one of whom, by name Sampson, presented in 875 a bell, still existing in Cordova, to the Church of San Sebastian. St. Aurea lived thirty years in a convent before she was executed in Seville in 856, and St. Theodomir, another Sevillian martyr, was a member of a monastery at Carmona. Abderrahman, or Sanchol, son of the Regent Almansur,

---

[1] *Cronica del Rey Don Pedro*, p. 63.
[2] Inter ipsos sine molestia fidei degimus,
[3] *España sagrada*, x. 246–8,

stayed for a night at the monastery called Deyr Shus shortly before he was assassinated.[1]

The epidemic of religious hysteria which occurred in Cordova in the middle of the ninth century is no doubt the reason why we have more information about the state of the Church at that date than at any other time during the Moslem rule. From the voluminous writings of Alvarus and Eulogius the editor of *España sagrada* has laboriously extracted all the facts, supplementing them from the various "acts of martyrdom" and other contemporary writings, and has thrown a good deal of light on the condition of the Church and the position of the Christians at that date.

In *España sagrada*, x. 265-6, is quoted at length an order made in 734 for the government of the Christians at Coimbra. It is doubtful whether the document from which this is taken is genuine, but the editor adduces evidence from other sources which goes to show that the enactments there cited were substantially the same as those in force elsewhere. According to this Coimbra regulation the Christians paid double the tribute exacted from the Moslems. Churches paid twenty-five "pesos" of silver, monasteries fifty, bishops a hundred pesos. The Christians were to have a "Count" of their own people, who should secure the observance of the laws [2] in accordance with Christian customs. They were forbidden to enter the mosques, or to vilify the Prophet, under pain of conversion to Islam or death. "This," says Florez, "was the most criminal offence of the martyrs of that time; so that, although they exalted the faith, the judges remained unmoved until they heard them speak evil of Mohammed or of his sect." According to the *Crónica general* [3] two "martyrs" of the

---

[1] Mariana; Book VII. chapter xvi. *España sagrada*, ix. 294, x. 255-60; An-Nuwairi in Makkari, ii. 490.
[2] "Que los mantenga en buena ley."
[3] vii. 322.

time, Rogelio and Serviodeo, entered the great Mosque of Cordova, and began not only " preaching the faith," but also " the falseness of Mohammed and the certainty of the hell to which he was guiding his followers." It is not surprising to learn that this performance cost them their lives.

Those who are interested in this epidemic of martyrdom will find the whole story set out at length in Dozy's *Geschichte der Mauren*, Vol. I. pp. 310 ff. Both the Moslem rulers and the more sensible of the Christians did their best to prevent these fanatics from throwing away their lives by deliberately insulting the religion of their conquerors, and Recafred, Bishop of Seville about 851–862, was distinguished by his common sense in the matter. He forbade Christians to seek martyrdom when their rulers did not attempt to make them deny their faith, and imprisoned " even priests" who disobeyed him. Abderrahman II. " appointed him metropolitan of Andalucia that he might do the same in Cordova," and there he imprisoned a number of Christians, including St. Eulogius and the Bishop of Cordova, doubtless to keep them out of mischief.[1]

If Morgado is correct in his statements, it would seem that the Moslem ruler of Cordova appointed Christian bishops. This is confirmed by a passage in *España sagrada* (xi. 311), to the effect that, when Valentius, Bishop of Cordova, had appointed to a living in that town a priest against whom a sentence of excommunication had not long before been passed by " the Prelates in Council," Servandus, Count of the Christians, obtained from " the Moorish king " a decree removing Valentius and appointing another bishop.

The Count of the Christians seems to have been a person of great authority and importance, though we have not been able to find any account of his precise functions. There is

---

[1] Morgado, *op. cit.*, 221–2.

CHRISTIANITY UNDER ISLAM

a letter of Alvarus addressed to " my supreme Lord Romanus, the most serene of all the Catholics." [1] This Romanus, the predecessor of Servandus as Count of the Christians, was a doctor by profession and an old friend of Alvarus, and the exaggerated terms of respect in which Alvarus addresses him, in spite of private friendship, and although he was no longer in an official position, seem to indicate the extreme importance of the post. In this letter he asks for the good offices of Romanus in a lawsuit which certain Christians had brought against him, saying that Romanus, if he chose, could counteract what the son of the Judge Gratiosus had poured into the Count's ears.[2] Felix was one of the plaintiffs in the suit, which evidently was not tried before his father, the Judge, or he would not have had occasion to address himself to Servandus. Possibly minor cases only came before the Judge, those of more moment before the Count. It will be remembered that the same official is mentioned in the Coimbra regulations. Of these Counts the names of four are recorded by Spanish writers: Romanus, Servandus, a Count Adulfus, who presented a library to the Church of San Acisclo in Cordova, and a Count Guifredus and his wife Guisinde, who was later than Servandus.[3] Ayala, the contemporary chronicler of Pedro the Cruel, says that the Christians of Toledo had their own Judge (Alcalde) and their own laws throughout the Moslem occupation.[4]

In the Arabic writers we have found several instances of the use of the title of Count. The first upon whom the

---

[1] " Serenissimo omnium Catholicorum summo Domino meo Romano," *España sagrada*, xi. 151.

[2] Quidquid vero Felix, Gratiosi Judicis filius, in auris Domini Servandi Comitis . . . immiserit, vestra Paternitas, si voluerit, tota radebit.

[3] *España sagrada*, x. 264.

[4] *Crónica del Rey Don Pedro*, p. 64.

dignity was conferred by a Moslem ruler was Artebas, son of Witiza (see p. 57). Señor Codera quotes Ibn Hayyan as saying that Artebas was chief of the Christians and collector of the tribute paid by them. This no doubt refers to the Christians of Artebas' own territory.

Abu Said Al Kumis belonged to the family of Artebas. Hejjaj Al Kumis and his son Servandus, who in 889 fled from Cordova and joined Omar Ibn Hafsun, must from the father's name have been descendants of Princess Sara, grand-daughter of Witiza (see genealogical tables). And Dozy mentions an Alphons, ancestor of Ibn Hafsun, whom Ibn Khaldun calls Count.

The Arabic *Kumis* is of course the Latin *Comes*. The evidence we have been able to collect is scanty, but it suggests that the title was bestowed by the Arab rulers upon the descendants, being heads of families, of the last legitimate king of the Goths.[1]

The Judge of the Christians is mentioned in Alvarus' letter quoted above, and another, by name Walid Ibn Khairan, is recorded by Makkari as having been present at a state reception of Ordoño of Leon by the Khalif Al-Hakem in 962.[2] The same account also mentions the presence at this function of Obeidullah Ibn Kasim, Bishop of Cordova. Gayangos remarks that it is curious that the Bishop, whether he was Obeidullah or Kasim, should have had a name so essentially Arabic, although this, he says, is not the only instance of the kind which occurs in the history of Mohammedan Spain.[3]

There was also an official called the "*Exceptor*." One

---

[1] Al Kuttiyyah in *Journal Asiatique*, 433, 469-70; Codera, *Estudios criticos*, 35-6; Makkari, ii. 415, 451-2; Dozy, *G. der M.*, i. 366 note.
[2] This Ordoño is not recognised by the Spanish chroniclers as one of the kings of Leon. Makkari, ii. 162, 465.
[3] *Ib.*, p. 471.

of these *Exceptores* is alluded to by Eulogius as a rich man, who in order not to lose his title and his right of access to the palace, denied his Christianity.[1] He is spoken of as "publicae rei exceptor," which Florez thinks means Treasurer or Administrator of the taxes. Another contemporary writer describes the man named by Eulogius as a Publicanus (*ib.*). According to Ducange, *Exceptor* means a notary. Possibly this official may have combined the functions of notary and tax collector. Dozy [2] calls him a *Katib* or secretary, and gives his name from Arabic sources.

The taxes of the Christians were collected monthly, and apparently they could evade payment by staying indoors. Those who by reason of poverty or illness remained in their houses were, says Florez, "free from all extortion." [3]

After the close of the ninth century little is recorded of the Church in Moslem Spain, and the writer of the *Crónica general* [4] attempts to account for its decay by alleging persecution. But it is open to doubt, first, whether the Christian Church really had decayed, and secondly whether there ever was any serious persecution. Dozy says that at Seville "so early" as the time of Abderrahman II. (822–52), there were so many conversions that it was necessary to build a large new mosque, and that the same thing happened at Elvira about the same time.[5] But the fact that new mosques were not required in either of these places until more than a century after the invasion seems to suggest that the conversions were few rather than many.

---

[1] *España sagrada*, x. 265.
[2] *G. der M.*, i. 331.
[3] Ut qui ex nobis ad remanentes Doctores imbecillitate corporis praepediente dirigere gressus nequiverit, aut quem inquisitio, vel census, vel vectigalis quod omni lunari mense pro Christi nomine solvere cogimur, retinuerit : saltim nocturno tempore qui necessarium duxerit, legat. Presbiter Leovogild in *España sagrada*, x. 268-9.
[4] viii. 375.
[5] *G. der M.*, i. 379, 393.

What certainly did decay after the ninth century was the use of the Latin language among the Christians, who were living on the best of terms with their Moslem neighbours, adopting their customs, their nomenclature, and above all, their tongue, both spoken and written. In the middle of the ninth century Alvarus laments the addiction of his contemporaries to Arabic studies. "My co-religionists," he says, "gladly read the history and romances of the Arabs; they study the writings of the Moslem theologians and philosophers, not to confute them, but to learn to write correct and elegant Arabic. Where is a layman to be found to-day who still reads the Latin commentary on the sacred writings? Who among them is there who studies the Gospels, the Prophets, the Apostles? ... The Christians have forgotten their own speech, and among a thousand of them one cannot find a single one who can write a correct Latin letter to a friend." Gibbon says that in 1039 "it was found necessary to transcribe an Arabic version of the Canons of the Councils of Spain for the use of the Bishops and clergy in the Moorish kingdoms."[1]

Alvarus, be it observed, does not complain that his compatriots denied their faith; he refers to their language alone. The Andalucian Bishoprics must have been in a fairly flourishing state when Alvarus could speak of "thousands" of his co-religionists, even if we make a certain allowance for hyperbole; and the Andalucian Christians certainly received no reinforcements from the North at this time. And as we shall see later, at the end of the eleventh century the Arabic writers refer to "thousands of Christians" at Granada.

Information as to the extent of the supposed numerous

---

[1] Dozy, *G. der M.*, i. 311; *Decline and Fall*, chapter li. The version in question is dated 1049, and is inscribed, "for the use of the most noble Bishop John Daniel." (Casiri, i. 541.)

CHRISTIANITY UNDER ISLAM

conversions to Islam is not forthcoming either from Christian or Moslem sources—or if it is we have been unable to find it; but the notices already given of the existence of Bishops and Churches as late as the twelfth century show that continued toleration was extended to such Christians as cared to remain faithful to their creed. This is confirmed by the accounts of the courtesy shown to the envoys of Christians from the north of Spain when they came, as they did on more than one occasion, to ask for and take away the relics of saints and martyrs buried in Moslem territory.

Thus we read in the *Crónica general* [1] that Sancho the Fat sent to Cordova to ask Abderrahman III. for the bones of one St. Pelayo; and so certain was he of getting them that he began to build a monastery in Leon, in advance, to receive the relics. Again, in 1063, Fernando I. of Castile sent a couple of bishops to ask Motadid, the Abbadite king of Seville, for the relics of St. Justa, one of the patron saints of that city, who according to the record was martyred in the third century for insulting the image of Diana. Motadid told the bishops that unfortunately he had no notion where the saint was to be found, but that they were welcome to the relics if they could discover them. While they were considering what they had best do, St. Isidore of Seville appeared to them in a vision, told them who he was and where he was buried, and suggested that they had better take him instead of St. Justa. They unearthed his body in the place the saint had pointed out, and when it was placed in the reliquary, Motadid threw on it a silk veil of marvellous workmanship, and made Isidore a farewell speech.[2] We have not been able to find any account of the removal of the relics either of St. Pelayo or St. Isidore in any Arabic writers accessible to us, and Dozy, who gives

[1] viii. 257.
[2] *España sagrada*, ix. 206–10.

the Isidore story in full, quotes Spanish authorities only. The Arabs probably did not attach much importance to the incidents.[1]

The dealings of the great Wizir Almansur with the Christians of his own household, and his respect for and gifts to Christian shrines are told at length in Chapter X. His own marriage to a Christian princess, and that of Alfonso VI. of Castile to the daughter of Motamid the Abbadite king of Seville, are related in Chapters XI. and XV. The Christian ancestry of Abderrahman III. is mentioned at p. 79.

This brings us down to the close of the eleventh century, without evidence of anything like vigorous or sustained persecution.

Certain passages in Makkari, referring to the year 1122, point to the continued existence of a powerful Christian community in the heart of the Moslem country.

Alfonso I. of Aragon had just made a kind of triumphal procession through the Mohammedan dominions, harrying one province after another for six months at a stretch, although apparently without reducing any city of importance. Continuing his account of this raid, Makkari says—

"It has been said above that the *al-Muahidin* or Christians, living in the territory of Granada, were the principal cause of Alfonso's invasion, since they had not only instigated him to penetrate so far into Moslem territory, promising him every aid and assistance in their power, but

---

[1] Tradition says that the monastery of San Isidro del Campo at Santiponce, between Seville and the buried Roman city of Italica, stands on the spot where the body of the saint was found. The monastery was endowed in 1298 by Guzman el Bueno, founder of the ducal House of Medina Sidonia, in connection with an already existing church dedicated to San Isidro. As there is no suggestion that this church was built after the conquest in 1248, nor any hint that it was a mosque converted to Christian uses, the inference is that there is a basis of fact in the tradition that it was built in the reign of Motadid, when the body of the saint was discovered. The whole structure—church and monastery—has a curiously fortress-like appearance for a religious house.

they had provided his army with every necessary, had guided him, and numbers had joined his banners. The traitors, however, did not escape the chastisement which they deserved. At the solicitation of several respectable citizens of Cordova, Seville, and other places, the celebrated Kadi Abu-l-Walid Ibn Roshd ("Averroes") crossed over to Africa, and having had an interview with Ali, explained to that Sultan the dangerous situation in which the Moslems of Andalus were, having to fight with enemies abroad and guard against traitors at home. He besought him to remedy this evil by ordering the transportation of the Christians who lived about Granada and the other districts lately overrun by Alfonso; and the Commander of the Moslems, yielding to his solicitations, issued the requisite orders, and thousands of that treacherous population were embarked and removed to Meknasah, Salé, and other towns of Western Africa."[1]

The Latin chronicle of Alfonso VII., which the editor of *España sagrada* attributes to a contemporary writer, says that in 1138 King Tashfin, son of Ali Ibn Yusuf the Almoravide, crossed from Spain to Morocco, taking with him many Christians "who had dwelt from days of old in Spain," and in 1124 the Mozarabs of Malaga are mentioned as going in numbers to Morocco.[2]

About the year 1150 a good many of the Morocco Christians returned to Spain. The same chronicle says that "many thousand Christian soldiers, with their Bishop and many of their clergy, who had been of the household of King Ali and his son Tashfin, crossed the sea and came to Toledo." Señor Codera, who quotes this passage, says that they were driven out by Almohade persecution. Be this as it may, the existence in Morocco, in the twelfth century, of a body

---

[1] ii. 306, 307.
[2] *España sagrada*, xxiii. 387.

of Christians with a Bishop and numerous clergy under the Almoravide dominion is another instance of the toleration afforded by Moslems, and especially those of the Shiite sect, to members of that faith.[1]

Again, in 1162, the Christians of Granada rose against the Almohades in concert with Ibn Mardanish, the Yemenite king then ruling over a large part of eastern Andalucia. Mardanish sent 2000 Christian cavalry from Murcia—which included the state of Theodomir or Tudmir, retained by the Gothic Christians by treaty with Abdalaziz Ibn Musa in 714—to the assistance of the rebels, and they were able to hold Granada for some months. Thus, notwithstanding the number exiled in 1122 and in 1138, it is evident that many still remained.[2] We find then that thousands of Christians were living within the borders of the Moslem dominion four centuries after the Moslem invasion, and since they certainly were not descendants of those Goths who were constantly at war with the Moslems under the legendary Pelayo and his successors, they must have been descendants of the Goths who remained in Andalucia in 711, under treaty with the Khalif Al-Walid of Damascus, by which treaty they were to pay tribute to the Khalif, but were to be governed by princes of their own blood and their own faith.

In the first centuries of the Mohammedan occupation these Goths evidently had no communion with the routed followers of Roderick, and we can understand the distrust that would exist between the two parties. Roderick's army was under the direction of the corrupt priesthood to whose intrigues against Witiza was due the overthrow of

[1] Chron. Adefonsi Imp. in *España sagrada*, xxi. c. 64. Codera, *Almoravides*, p. 119.
[2] Makkari, ii. 316; Codera, *Almoravides*, 138-40, 214; cf. Dozy, *G. der M.*, ii. 388-9. His conclusion is that after the second expulsion only a few remained in Andalucia.

CHRISTIANITY UNDER ISLAM

the legitimate royal line. The Goths who allied themselves with Musa and made treaties with the Khalifs were those who had remained loyal to the family of Witiza after that monarch's death. The first party had no real support among the rank and file of the nation, and that fact, combined with the friendly alliance of Musa and the three Princes of the legitimate line, fully accounts for the extraordinary rapidity with which the whole of the south and west of Spain submitted to or came to terms with the invaders. It was inevitable that the descendants of two parties so radically opposed at the beginning should retain their inherited hostility to and distrust of each other for some generations.

But by the beginning of the twelfth century this enmity had had time to die out. Except for their religion, and in certain cases their family names, the Goths of the south and west seem by that time to have been almost wholly amalgamated with their Yemenite neighbours and friends, through four centuries of intermarriage and alliance offensive and defensive against their common enemies; and we find these Gotho-Yemenite states and cities the first to treat with or submit to the Christian invaders from the north and east, when the Almohades or Moors, alien in religion and race alike to the Goths and the Arabs of Yemen, overran the country and endeavoured to force their sectarianism on the Moslems of Andalucia.

In this connection, although it is somewhat of a digression, it is interesting to put on record the ultimate fate of the Spanish Christians deported to Morocco in 1122.

Zuñiga gives us a good deal of information about them. St. Francis, in 1219, sent a mission of five of his friars, who preached in Seville (then the Court of the Almohades in Spain), were imprisoned in the Torre del Oro, and then went on to Morocco, where they suffered martyrdom in the following year. In 1237 Gregory IX., " becoming aware of the destitution of those Catholics," sent them a bishop, whose successor was in Seville shortly after its capture, and returned to his diocese bearing letters of recommendation from Innocent IV. to the king of Morocco.[1]

In 1386 the Christians living in Morocco sent a mission to Juan I. of Castile, asking his good offices with the King of Morocco to obtain permission for them to come and reside in Seville. The incident is thus related by Zuñiga.

" Among the Christians who lived in the kingdom of Morocco, of whom I have spoken elsewhere, were certain leading families called the Farfanes, who prided themselves on being descendants of the Goths : they desired to come to Spain, and to beg the king to admit them and ask the king of Morocco [to let them go] and Seville to receive them as residents: this year they sent one of their number, called Sancho Rodriguez, who carried back a favourable reply from this city. The letter exists in print, and one of its clauses runs—

" ' We desire to see you in this city in the service of God and of our Lord the King, we would have you know that your relative Sancho Rodriguez came to us and spoke with us on certain matters, whereby we understood his intention and yours, and he was very benevolently received by us ; wherefore be assured that if it is the will of God that you should reach this city, you will be very well received by us, and we will do with you such things as shall be to the service of God and of the King our Lord, and may God give you health.' "

This letter is dated the 8th October (1386), and is signed by the Municipal authorities and five of the *Veintiquatros*, a special class of high officials.

---

[1] Zuñiga, i. 83. In 1360 Ibn-al-Khattib visited Salé, and found the town of Rabat almost entirely populated by the descendants of the families deported in 1122. Gayangos in Makkari, ii. 515.

The necessary permission was asked by Juan I. of Abu Hasan, Sultan of Morocco, and was granted in the following terms, extracted by Zuñiga from a letter " with a long preamble, according to the custom of the Moors."

" 'Here I send thee those whom thou didst ask for, and those of thy law of great lineage, and thou hast them ; these are the fifty Christian Farfanes of the ancient Goths of thy kingdom, may God preserve them, for they are serviceable and valiant, and active, and astute, and fortunate, and of loyal counsel, and such that if thou desirest to make use of them thou wilt have benefit, they go commended to thy mercy, to the kingdoms which belonged to their ancestors, the good Goths, may God pardon them, here I send them to thee as thou desirest, and God is thy support.'

" So runs the translation which was made at the time from the original Arabic," Zuñiga continues. " They were in all fifty families, who remained settled in Seville, and in the custody of their chiefs were preserved this letter and their privileges, of which authentic copies exist and have been examined in the verification of their nobility. Some of them went later in search of the king, to whom their arrival was tragic.

" . . . he was at Alcalá de Henares, where these knights came to kiss his hand, and hearing that they were very expert horsemen he went out on horseback to the country to see them exercise, and in a short time, wishing to show his dexterity (*gallardia*) he galloped in a ploughed field where his horse stumbled, and such was the violence of the fall that the king died, so suddenly that no one heard his last cry. The unfortunate and lamentable tragedy occurred on Sunday, October 9th [1390]."

In 1394 Enrique III. granted to the Farfanes the privilege promised by his father before his sudden death, establishing them in the possession of their ancient nobility, and this was confirmed by successive monarchs down to Queen

Juana, mother of Charles V. They are described in the said documents as *Caballeros Farfanes de los Godos*. They settled in Seville, where they became owners of real estate and founded various chapels and religious houses. One of their chapels was, when Zuñiga wrote in 1680, in the parish Church of San Martin, and in the frieze of its iron screen were their arms, three green toads on a gold field. They had a deputy who was spokesman for all their lineage and upheld the maintenance of their privileges. The chapel "of those of the lineage of Farfan" was not done away with until early in the nineteenth century, when an entrance to the sacristy was made through it.[1]

It appears, therefore, that the Christian Church had a continuous, and so far as can be gathered, a vigorous existence, not only during the Moslem domination in Spain, but also in Morocco for nearly a hundred and fifty years after Islam had lost the whole of Spain except the kingdom of Granada. This fact alone shows that there can have been little or no persecution, for the sturdiest faith could hardly have survived for five or six hundred years, had any persistent attempt been made to stamp it out.

The Bishopric of Morocco is mentioned frequently in ecclesiastical records down to 1560. The last holder of the title seems to have been Don Sancho de Truxillo, Canon of Seville Cathedral, and a member of the Holy Office. The Bishopric from 1248 appears to have been, generally speaking, closely connected with Seville, the salary being provided from estates in this diocese. Don Sancho de Truxillo is mentioned as holding property in right of his see in the district of San Telmo (afterwards a naval college) and on an estate called Torreblanca in the Ajarafe. It does not seem clear at what period the Sultan of Morocco forbade

---

[1] Zuñiga, ii. 224, 232, 245 Gonzalez de Leon, *Noticia artistica de Sevilla* (1844), I. 106.

the titular bishops of that country to exercise their office there, but internal evidence points to their having done so at any rate down to 1412.[1] The present Vicariate of Morocco dates, we understand, from the establishment of Spanish colonies in North Africa in the sixteenth and seventeenth centuries.

[1] Zuñiga, iv. 16–7.

CHAPTER II

THE SONS OF WITIZA

THE history of the descendants of Witiza, the Gothic king who immediately preceded Roderick, and died shortly before the Moslem invasion in 711,[1] does not seem to have been traced by historians, whether Spanish or foreign. Yet the adventures and fortunes of these princes and their descendants form not only a romantic chapter in the history of Spain, but have an important bearing on the events of the first three centuries of Islam in the Peninsula.

Witiza, the last reigning monarch of the legitimate line, has been branded for twelve centuries with the title of

[1] Roderick of Toledo, who wrote during the first half of the thirteenth century, and whom Mariana followed, says that Roderick dethroned Witiza. But all the earlier authorities that we have been able to consult seem to agree that he died before Roderick's usurpation of the throne. The anonymous writer known as Isidorus Pacensis, who wrote about the year 754, and was therefore nearly a contemporary of the events he chronicles, suggests that Witiza died before Roderick's appearance on the scene, but does not definitely say so. The author of the *Chronicon Sebastiani*, which was written about 883, tells us that Roderick was elected king on Witiza's death; while Makkari, drawing his information from Arabic sources, says distinctly that civil dissensions arose on the death of Witiza, upon which "the Goths decided on giving the crown to a chief named Roderick." It seems on the whole probable that Roderick did not dethrone Witiza, as Roderick of Toledo says, but usurped the throne on his death. Gayangos is of opinion that Roderick dethroned Witiza, on the ground of a difference in the length of reign assigned to him by Isidore and Sebastian respectively; but this reasoning does not seem to have much weight in view of the statements made to the contrary by both Arabic and Spanish chroniclers, and of the lax ideas as to the need for accurate chronology which prevailed at the time. (Makkari, i. 254, and Gayangos' note, p. 512-3; Isidorus Pacensis in *España sagrada*, viii. 261 ff.; *Chronicon Sebastiani* in *id.* xiii. 478; Rodericus Toletanus in Schott, *Hispania illustrata*, ii. 62-3.)

FIG. 3.—The Seville Gate at Carmona: Roman work with Moslem additions.

"The Wicked." We may take, as typical of the views of ecclesiastical historians about this king, the character given him by Mariana the Jesuit, who died at an advanced age in the year 1623. According to this writer, Witiza began his reign in admirable fashion. He restored to their lands and offices those whom his father had exiled, and burnt the papers and records relating to their offences, so that no memory of them should remain. But, continues Mariana, "it is very difficult to bridle youth and power with reason, virtue, and temperance." And he goes on to tell us that Witiza was too fond of women, and treated his concubines as though they were legitimate wives. "And to give colour and excuse to this disorder he committed another grosser offence, making a law by which all were permitted to do the same, and gave special licence to ecclesiastical persons consecrated to God, to marry; an abominable and hateful law, which however gave pleasure to the majority. . . . Also he made a law denying obedience to the Holy Father, which was altogether to remove the bridle and the mask, and the straight road to the destruction of the kingdom, until then crowned with prosperity for its obedience to Rome." Further, "contrary to the provisions of the old laws," he permitted the Jews to return to Spain.[1]

---

[1] Mariana, Book VI. chapter xix. In these passages Mariana follows Roderick of Toledo, and perhaps Lucas, bishop of Tuy in Galicia, who died 1288. Both these writers treat the reign of Witiza in some detail, but neither of them give any earlier authority for their statements. Among Christian writers there seem to be only two who were nearly contemporaries of Witiza: Isidorus Pacensis, already mentioned, and the continuer of the *Chronicon Biclarense*. Their writings are now however said to be different versions of the same chronicle. From them we learn that Egica made him his heir and consort on the throne, and that he reigned mildly for fifteen years (clementissimus quindecim per annos extat in regno), recalled those whom his father had exiled, and burnt the records of their offences. Indeed it would almost appear as though Witiza, so far from being the impious profligate that he is represented by later writers, showed an almost excessive zeal for sanctity, for he urged Sindered, Bishop of Toledo, to take measures of reform which the ecclesiastical chronicler

This legislation, if it is true that Witiza was the author of it, suggests that so far from being the infamous profligate that he has been represented, he was a liberal and enlightened monarch, who attempted to check the notorious immorality of the clergy by compelling them to marry,[1] and asserted the independence of the Spanish Church; while the restoration of the Jews would probably be to the commercial advantage of the country. Unluckily we are dependent on the chance allusions of writers living long after the eighth century for our knowledge of Witiza's legislation, for the Acts of the eighteenth Council of Toledo, at which his laws were promulgated, have been lost.[2]

of his reign seems to have considered too drastic. "Per idem tempus (sc. of the Moslem conquest) divæ memoriæ Sinderedus urbis regiæ Metropolitanus Episcopus sanctimoniæ studio claret: atque longævos et merito honorabiles viros, quos in suprafata sibi commissa ecclesia reperit, non secundum scientiam zelo sanctitatis stimulat, atque instinctu jam dicti Witizæ Principis eos sub ejus tempore convexare non cessat." (Isidorus Pacensis in *España sagrada*, viii. 290.)

Of Witiza's personal profligacy, of his enforcement of marriage on the clergy, and of his quarrel with Rome, not a word is said by these earliest chroniclers, and it is impossible to know whether Roderick of Toledo had any evidence at all for his statements, or whether he, like so many other ecclesiastical writers, drew on his imagination for his facts when none were forthcoming from other sources.

The earliest notice we have been able to find of Witiza's injunction to the clergy to marry is in the *Chronicon Sebastiani*, written some time after 866. This writer does not mention the quarrel with Rome, nor the return of the Jews. (*España sagrada*, xiii. 477-8.)

[1] Or more probably by not attempting to enforce Recared's prohibitions. The Gothic clergy, like all others at that date and for some centuries after, married freely and openly. (Cf. Lea, *History of Sacerdotal Celibacy*, i. 135, and *passim*.)

[2] The dealings of the Gothic rulers and churchmen with the Jews probably had no little influence in facilitating the success of the Moslems. For nearly a century before the conquest they had been subjected to a savage persecution. And almost every Council of Toledo, from the fourth (A.D. 633) onwards, legislated against them, until the seventeenth (694) enacted that they should all be made slaves and their goods confiscated. The whole of Book XII. Tit. ii. of the *Fuero Juzgo* is filled with legislation of a persecuting nature. The Jews were forbidden to keep the Passover or their accustomed feasts and sabbaths, to marry by Jewish rites, to eat their own food, to circumcise, and, whether baptised or not, to give evidence against Christians. The result was that when the invaders came the Jews welcomed them, if they did not actually invite them over, as they were accused of doing in the reign of Egica.

THE SONS OF WITIZA

If there were any historical foundation for Mariana's account of Witiza's dealings with the priesthood and with Rome, these alone would have been sufficient cause for a conspiracy of the clergy to change the succession, and give the throne to some one more devoted to their interests. That this is what happened is suggested by a sentence in Isidorus Pacensis, to the effect that Roderick invaded the kingdom at the instigation of the Senate.[1] It is not clear what he means by the Senate; but remembering the enormous power in the State enjoyed by the Church in the Gothic Kingdom, it is not unreasonable to suppose that by the Senate Isidore means the Council of the Bishops.[2] It must also be remembered that Roderick, as Archbishop of Toledo, had access to the Cathedral archives, which possibly contained at that time, if they do not now, some record of Witiza's legislation, and that thus there may have been some basis of fact for his statements, although it is not necessary to accept his interpretation of them.

According to Makkari, Cordova, Granada, and the district of Rayah, to which Malaga belonged, were left in charge of the Jews after being taken, "and this practice became almost general in the succeeding years; for whenever the Moslems conquered a town, it was left in custody of the Jews, with only a few Moslems, the rest of the army proceeding to new conquests." Gayangos says, on the authority of Ibn Khaldun, that most of the Berber tribes inhabiting the northern shores of Africa professed the Jewish religion, and that, although the twelve thousand under Tarik's orders were said to have been previously converted to Islam, this conversion was not likely to have been so sincere as to blot out immediately all sympathy with their former co-religionists (Makkari, i. 280, 531). Lucas of Tuy says that the Jews opened the gates of Toledo to the Moslems while the Christians were attending a service on Palm Sunday at the Church of St. Leocadia *extra urbem* (in Schott, iv. 70).

[1] Rudericus tumultuose regnum hortante Senatu invasit.

[2] Ducange does not help us much here, as the only reference he gives to "Senatus," apart from the office of a Roman Senator, is to a French charter of the thirteenth century. But "Senatores," according to the same authority, was frequently used in the sense of "nobles," either the descendants of provincial members of the Senate or of those who had exercised senatorial or magisterial functions in their own cities. Whether by the "Senate" Isidore means the "nobles," those better acquainted with mediæval Latin than we are can judge.

The part played by the sons of Witiza in the Moslem invasion is described by the Christian writers as an act of treason, but a different complexion is put upon it by the Arabic historians, who relate many incidents connected with these royal personages.

Al-Kuttiyyah says, "The last of the Gothic kings of Andalucia was Witiza, who left three sons named Almand, Romulo, and Artebas. As these children were still of tender age, their mother assumed the regency and governed in their name at Toledo. Nevertheless Roderick, who was the Kaid (general-in-chief) of the armies of the defunct monarch, abandoned the child-princes; then, arrogating to himself supreme authority, he drew into his party the men of war who marched under his banners, and came to establish his residence at Cordova." [1]

Makkari quotes the accounts by various writers of the events immediately preceding the Moslem invasion, but that of Al-Kuttiyyah, which is translated much as above by Gayangos in his note, Vol. I., p. 513, of Makkari, is the most explicit. As Al-Kuttiyyah was the direct descendant of Witiza through his grand-daughter, the Princess Sara of Seville, one would *primâ facie* give more credit to his account than to any other, of the part played by the Gothic princes in the invasion, though we must remember that he wrote some two centuries after the event, and must have depended to some extent on earlier authors even for what he says regarding his own ancestors.

After relating and discussing various theories and legends touching the immediate causes of the Mohammedan invasion, Makkari goes on to say that while Roderick was staying at Cordova he invited the sons of Witiza to join him against the common enemy, and that they encamped with

---

[1] Al-Kuttiyyah in *J.A.*, p. 430.

THE SONS OF WITIZA

their forces on the opposite side of the river, until after some hesitation, due to their distrust of him, they joined him and marched against the invaders. But he adds, "Others say that the sons of Witiza did not obey the summons sent them by the usurper Roderick; on the contrary they joined Tarik with all their forces; but which of these reports is the true one God only knows. . . . Much obscurity prevails in the writings of the historians who have recorded the events of those early times." [1]

The Christian chroniclers seem to have completely ignored the fate of the descendants of Witiza. Were it not for the details of their lives given by the Arabic writers, we should hardly know that the Gothic king did not die childless. Fortunately, however, we are able to trace them for some generations under their Arabic names, and we propose to show how for a full two centuries they ruled their domains as kings, thanks to the wealth they inherited and acquired, the loyalty of a large part of the population to them, and the esteem in which they were held by their Moslem friends and connections.

It seems certain that either Witiza's sons, or envoys acting on their behalf, asked the help of the Moslems to recover their inheritance. "Ad-Dhobi and the best Arabian writers" assert this,[2] and it is confirmed not only by Roderick of Toledo and by Lucas of Tuy, for what their authority is worth, but also by the author of the *Chronicon Sebastiani*, who says that they sent envoys to ask help of the Saracens, and brought them across to Spain in ships, and by the *Chronicon Albedense*.[3]

---

[1] i. 269.
[2] Gayangos in Makkari, i. 528.
[3] Witiza's sons, "callide cogitantes, missos ad Africam mittunt, Sarracenos in auxilium petunt, eosque navibus advectos Hispaniam intromittunt." *Chron. Sebast.* in *España sagrada*, xiii. 478. Dozy (*Recherches*, i. 74 ff.) examines and rejects this statement, and argues that Tarik's expedition was originally only intended to be a raid for

Makkari's account of the events immediately preceding the decisive battle is as follows:—

"Roderick was drawing near to the Moslems, with all the forces of the barbarians, their lords, their knights, and their bishops; but the hearts of the great people of the kingdom being against him . . . in their private conversations they uttered their sentiments about Roderick in the following manner. 'This wretch has by force taken possession of the throne to which he is not justly entitled, for not only he does not belong to the royal family, but he was once one of our meanest menials; we do not know how far he may carry his wicked intentions against us. There is no doubt but that Tarik's followers do not intend to settle in this country; their only wish is to fill their hands with spoil and then return. Let us then, as soon as the battle is engaged, give way, and leave the usurper alone to fight the strangers, who will soon deliver us from him; and when they shall be gone, we can place on the throne him who most deserves it.' In these sentiments all agreed, and it was decided that the proposed plan should be put into execution; the two sons of Witiza, whom Roderick had appointed to the command of the right and left wings of his army, being at the head of the conspiracy, in the hope of gaining the throne of their father.

---

booty. Roderick gives their names as Sisibert and Eva, and says that they went to Recila Count of Tingitania. Lucas calls them Farmarius and Expulio, and says that they went to Tingitania, of which Julian was Count. Al-Kuttiyyah, as already said, calls them Almand, Romulo, and Artebas, which are the names we propose to adopt in this book; while an anonymous author of a work on the conquest of Spain calls one of them Shithibert.

In the *Chronicon Albedense*, written about 883, it is said that "per filios Vitizani Regis oritur Gothis rixarum discessio: ita ut una pars eorum Regnum dirutum videre desiderarent: quorum etiam favore atque farmalio Sarraceni Spaniam sunt ingressi." The editor of *España sagrada* says that *farmalium* means a pact or treaty; the word is not in Ducange. *España sagrada*, xiii. 478, 459. Schott, ii. 63, iv. 70. Gayangos in Makkari, i. 512-3, 523.

"When the armies drew near to each other, the princes began to spin the web of their treason; and for this purpose a messenger was sent by them to Tarik, informing him how Roderick, who had been a mere menial and servant to their father, had, after his death, usurped the throne; that the princes had by no means relinquished their rights, and that they implored protection and security for themselves. They offered to desert, and to pass over to Tarik with the troops under their command, on condition that the Arab general would, after subduing the whole of Andalus, secure to them all their father's possessions, amounting to three thousand valuable and chosen farms, the same that received after this name of *Safaya-l-moluk* (the royal portion). This offer Tarik accepted; and having agreed to the conditions, on the next day the sons of Witiza deserted the ranks of the Gothic army in the midst of the battle, and passed over to Tarik, this being no doubt one of the principal causes of the conquest." [1]

It is incredible that Roderick, who certainly had ousted the sons of Witiza from their inheritance, should have intrusted them with important commands in his army in the critical battle. Moreover, the vast extent of territory restored to them, full particulars of which are recorded, would hardly have been granted in return for the services rendered in a single battle by three youths only just old enough to sit their horses.[2] But if the whole invasion was the consequence of a treaty made by the princes and their supporters with Tarik or Musa, providing that in consideration of their influence with their vassals they should be reinstated in their possessions, the matter becomes clear. Our view is strengthened by the fact that, as we shall presently show, practically all south-west Andalucia followed their

[1] i. 270–1.
[2] Al-Kuttiyyah in *J.A.*, p. 430.

example in submitting to, or allying themselves with, the invaders in the early days of the conquest. It looks indeed as if the whole of the population in that part of Spain was loyal to the family of Witiza and readily accepted the new condition of things, the only opposition being from the small party which had supported Roderick.

The usual explanation given of the feeble resistance offered to the Moslems in the south-west of the country is that luxurious living and the benign climate of Andalucia had sapped the energy of the Goths. But that hypothesis fails when we consider the obstinate resistance made in isolated cities—*e.g.* Merida—where Roderick's party had the upper hand, and the prolonged struggle which we shall show to have been maintained later on in *la tierra de Sevilla*, as Seville and the surrounding districts were called for centuries to come. Whereas, if our conjecture as to an alliance with Tarik and Musa be correct, the surrender of strong walled cities, such as Seville and Carmona, with little or no resistance, is explained.

The whole treatment of the family of Witiza, not only by the invaders, but by the Khalif of Damascus, shows the importance attached to the good-will of those princes. Both at the time of the conquest and later, when Witiza's grandchildren visited the Syrian Court, the exalted station of the family was recognised, and its members were received not as fallen foes but as honoured guests.

Roderick of Toledo and Lucas of Tuy tell us that the Moslem conquest was facilitated owing to Witiza having thrown down the walls of most of the fortified cities. But the Moslem writers never mention these ruined fortresses, which, if the thirteenth century chroniclers spoke the truth, must have been conspicuous on all sides at the time of the invasion, some five years after the fiat of demolition is said to have gone forth. On the contrary they constantly

THE SONS OF WITIZA

allude to the walled cities which surrendered by treaty in the course of the rapid advance of the invaders, and express the admiration excited in their minds by the strength and magnificence of the great buildings, roads, and bridges, left by the Romans, which the Moslem leaders at once ordered to be repaired wherever necessary.

After their defeat at the Laguna of La Janda the scattered remains of Roderick's army retired upon the city of Assido, now Medina Sidonia in the Province of Cadiz, which dominates the plains below from a height so steep as to make any attack very difficult.[1] To quote Makkari, "Tarik's army being so considerably reinforced (by those who crossed the straits on hearing of his success) the Christians were obliged to shut themselves up in their castles and fortresses, and, quitting the flat country, betake themselves to their mountains. Tarik first marched against Sidonia, which he besieged and took by force after the

---

[1] Dozy (*Recherches*, i. 313) adopts the opinion of Florez (*España sagrada*, x. 20 ff.) that Jerez, and not Medina Sidonia, is the Roman Assido. When Florez wrote, the generally accepted site of the defeat of Roderick was on the banks of the Guadalete, somewhere near Puerto de Santa Maria. But it is now established that the battle took place on the banks of the Laguna de la Janda, near the little river Barbate, which runs into the sea somewhat to the east of Cape Trafalgar, and close to the Roman road from Algeciras to Cadiz. It is inconceivable that Roderick's defeated army, flying for refuge where they could find it, should have passed by the strong hill city of Medina Sidonia, only twelve or fifteen miles from the battlefield, to take shelter in a town in a great plain, more than twice the distance away. We believe we are right in saying that Dozy never was in the south of Spain, and therefore had no personal knowledge of the physical geography of the district. Five Roman roads lead from Medina Sidonia in different directions, one of which goes to Bejer de la Frontera on the river Barbate, whence fish was brought by a regular nightly service, continued to this day, for the lords of the Roman city.

Medina Sidonia is perched on a spur of a mountain range forming an outlying portion of the great Serrania de Ronda, and the Christians who fled there would truly be taking refuge among the mountains. But there are no mountains within ten miles or more of Jerez.

Gayangos shows how, by a series of corruptions, due to the peculiar character used by the Arabs of Spain and Africa, the Wady Barbat, also called by them the Wady Bekkeh, might have been changed into the Guadalete. (Makkari, i. 526-7.)

garrison had defended it some time. From Sidonia he proceeded to Moror (probably Moron), whence he turned towards Carmona . . . which surrendered to him immediately, the inhabitants agreeing to pay tribute. He next encamped before Ecija, and besieged it. The inhabitants being numerous and brave, *and having with them some remnants of Roderick's army* (italics ours) made at first a desperate defence. . . . No battle was afterwards fought in which the Moslems had so much to suffer." [1]

This mention of Roderick's army is significant, as is also the following sentence (p. 276)—" a few only of the principal people repaired to their capital, Toledo, with the intention of holding out resistance within its walls."

We must now return to the Gothic princes.

Immediately after the battle of La Janda, they asked Tarik for a letter to his superior officer, Musa, explaining the treaty they had made with him. This Tarik gave them, but Musa, unwilling to take upon himself the responsibility of a decision, sent them on to Damascus, where the Khalif Al-Walid received them with great kindness and granted them many favours.[2] This sounds very generous on the part of the Khalif, and his treatment of the princes would have been most liberal had they been suppliants seeking the favour of the conqueror of their country. But it may be doubted whether Al-Walid's action was disinterested. The Gothic princes were doubtless in a position to give a great deal of trouble to the would-be rulers of Andalucia if their allegiance were not secured, and the Khalif must have been perfectly aware of the fact. Already the Christians of Seville had risen against the small garrison left there by Musa, killed thirty of them, and compelled the rest to take refuge with the army engaged at the siege

[1] Makkari, i. 275.   [2] ii. 14.

THE SONS OF WITIZA

of Merida.[1] There could not have been any very large number of Moslems in the country as yet, and they were scattered over many districts, so that if the friendly Goths of the south-west had begun to suspect that the princes whom they desired to see restored to their possessions were being treated merely as petitioners for rewards, the situation was probably more serious than the Arabic writers chose to admit.

Whatever the truth of this may be, there is no doubt that Al-Walid did his utmost to conciliate the princes. He not only ratified the treaty made with Tarik, but gave each of them a further deed securing to them and their posterity all the lands specified in that treaty, and providing against any spoliation on the part of the Arab settlers.

"Almand, who was the eldest, had for his share one thousand farms in the west of Andalus, and, in order to superintend them, took up his abode in Seville. Al-Artebas, who was the second, had an equal number of estates in the centre of Andalus, for which reason he took up his residence at Cordova; while the third and youngest of all had his thousand farms in the eastern parts of Andalus and in the districts of the Thagher, for which reason he established himself at Toledo." In this manner the three brothers enjoyed undisturbed possession of their respective estates in the very heart of the Mohammedan dominions, until the eldest, Almand, died, leaving behind him one daughter named Sara, but who is better known under the appellation of Al-Kuttiyyah (the Gothic princess) and two sons of tender age.[2]

---

[1] Conde, i. 45-6. Makkari (i. 285) puts the number slaughtered at eighty. Seville capitulated after a short defence, but Musa was having a good deal of trouble with Merida.

[2] Makkari, ii. 14. For the meaning of Thagher, see p. 49. Cherbonneau's translation of Al-Kuttiyyah adds one or two small details. The deed granted by Al-Walid stipulated that the princes "should observe an absolute neutrality." The word translated in Makkari's account

Nor did the consideration of the Moslems for the family of Witiza end here; for immediately after the conquest of Toledo, Bishop Oppas, brother of Witiza, was appointed Governor of that city,[1] while Musa returned to Damascus at the command of the Khalif, and Tarik prosecuted his campaign in the north of Spain. All this, we submit, goes to show that Tarik and Musa invaded Spain as the allies of the legitimate line, who had been led to believe that the first object of the invasion was to restore their kingdom to them as the direct heirs of Witiza. The resistance encountered by the invaders was mainly from the supporters of the usurper Roderick; but the Arabic historians, intentionally or otherwise, disguised the facts and glossed over the determining cause of the invasion in order to secure all the glory of it for their own people. Such views of the duty of the historian would only be in accordance with the ideas of the time.[2]

as " farms " he gives as " villages." The two sons of Almand are named Matrubal and Oppas, the latter of whom is said to have died in Galicia. Gayangos (in Makkari, ii. 415) says that he was the Bishop Oppas who was slain at Covadonga; but this is obviously a mistake, for Witiza's son Almand was hardly more than a child in 711, while Covadonga is said to have been fought in 718.

In the *Akhbar Majmua* (an anonymous work of the eleventh century) we are told that Al-Walid received the princes with all courtesy, confirmed the treaty made with Tarik regarding the belongings of their father, gave to each one a diploma (? copy of the treaty) and conceded them the privilege of not rising when any one entered the room they were in. This account notably differs from that of Al-Kuttiyyah, which also dates from the eleventh century, inasmuch as it asserts that when the princes returned to Spain, " masters of their father's estates," " they divided them by agreement between themselves," while Al-Kuttiyyah says the division was made by the terms of the treaty. *Akhbar Majmua*, 184–5.

[1] Dozy, *G. der M.*, i. 269.

[2] It is an interesting little fact that in the Ommeyad building of Kusair Amra, to the East of the Jordan, is a portrait of Roderick in a picture representing the enemies of Islam. The other enemies there depicted are the Emperor of Byzantium, the King of Persia, and the Negus of Abyssinia. (*Encycl. Islam*, s./v. 'Amra.)

CHAPTER III

THE ROYAL MUWALLADS

THE families which sprang from the last legitimate king of the Goths are so numerous and figure so largely in the history of the ninth century in Andalucia, that we have attempted to sketch the family tree of each one in the direct line, in the tables appended to this book. The authorities on which we base our account of each individual are there given, a query being put against the names of those whose descent is presumed in the absence of any record of them that we have as yet been able to discover. We hope that with the aid of these tables the reader will be able to follow with less difficulty the complicated relations of the Muwallads (people of mixed blood) with the Spaniards on the one hand and the Arabs on the other, during an exceedingly tangled period of civil war.

Makkari says (see last chapter) that Romulo was given a thousand farms in the Thagher, and took up his residence in Toledo to superintend them.

Throughout the Ommeyad rule at Cordova the territories subject to Toledo were known as *Al-thagher-al-adani*, or the lower frontier, while those in Aragon were called *Al-thagher-al-ali*, or the upper frontier.[1] Between the possessions of Romulo in the district of Toledo, and those of his brother Artebas "in the centre of Andalus," lay the

---

[1] Makkari, i. 47.

Sierra Morena, over which the principal, if not the only, pass is that now used for both the railway and the high road from the south to Toledo and Madrid, known as the *Despeñaperros*. This pass is close to the ruins of the Castulo of the Romans, referred to by Strabo as one of the two finest cities in Oretania, near the eastern boundary of Baetica.[1] Castulo became in Arabic Kashtalah, and in Spanish Cazlona. Of the town of Cazlona nothing now remains except a farm known by that name. But the farm is strewn with Roman remains, including baths and an amphitheatre, and the road crosses the river by a stone bridge covered with Roman inscriptions, which can be read from beneath by taking a boat. And on a slightly elevated plateau, about a hundred yards outside the Roman walls, stand the ruins of the impregnable Moslem fortress mentioned by Dozy and other writers.[2]

If, as we believe, the invasion had been undertaken ostensibly or in reality with the primary object of restoring Witiza's estates to his children, we can understand that Musa may have feared lest trouble should be caused by Tarik's impetuous conduct in Toledo, a district wavering between allegiance to Roderick's party and loyalty to the old *régime*, where tact and diplomacy might secure further bloodless victories. This is more probable than that Musa tried to restrain Tarik's rapid progress out of jealousy of his success, for Musa was too renowned a general and statesman to fear being supplanted in the army by his Berber lieutenant. But the early death of the Khalif Al-Walid and Musa's degradation by his brutal successor, Suleiman, rendered the veteran commander's statesmanship fruitless.

[1] i. 228, 250.
[2] *G. der M.*, i. 453. We are indebted for this description of Cazlona to-day to Mr. George Bonsor, the distinguished archaeologist, whose thirty years' work in Andalucia has thrown so much light on obscure points in Roman-Iberian history.

Almand ruling over his possessions in the district of Seville, Artebas settled at Cazlona or Jaen, and Romulo with his uncle Bishop Oppas governing Toledo, were certainly very great men, and would be exceedingly dangerous antagonists to the Moslem rule, if they united to oppose it. But Al-Walid, or his minister Musa, doubtless foresaw the inevitable weakening of their power and influence which would result from dividing the Gothic dominions into three and arranging matters in such a manner that the brothers, while acknowledged as princes, would be forced to abandon any individual claim to the throne. The Khalif who so readily granted the restitution of their domains had a definite purpose in determining that they should all share and share alike. The wording of the deed suggests that. Each was to have "a thousand farms," neither more nor less. And this complete equality would *ipso facto* make it difficult for any one of the three to advance a claim to suzerainty over the others, such as might have been put forward had the eldest received the lion's share of the estates.

Chance did not govern the provision made for the three royal brothers. Had Musa been permitted to pursue his policy of conciliation, a couple of generations of intercourse and intermarriage might have made the Gothic states a bulwark to the Moslems against the advance of the northern Christians, who, so far as can be discovered, were captained in the early days by fugitives from Roderick's army, equally hostile to the Moslems and to the descendants of Witiza. But the wise plans of Musa and Al-Walid were not carried out, and presently we find the Muwallads or people of mixed blood, many of whom were the offspring of the three princes, heading a civil war in Moslem Spain so prolonged and so determined that it many times threatened to overthrow the rule of the Ommeyads.

Prince Almand, as already said, had his thousand farms in the south-west, in the heart of the Moslem territory, and enjoyed undisturbed possession of his estates until his death, which internal evidence shows to have occurred before 745.

After Almand's death his estates were seized, not by the Moslems, as might have been expected, but by his own brother Artebas. At least so say the Arabic authors, including Al-Kuttiyyah, although such conduct is at variance with the character of Artebas as described by Ibn Al-Kuttiyyah himself. These incidents are given by Pons [1] from an unpublished translation of Al-Kuttiyyah's history by Julian Ribera, and in view of the scanty notices which exist of the Gothic princes and their mode of life, it seems worth while to put them into English.

"They say of Artebas that Abderrahman Ibn Moawiya ordered the towns of his lordship to be confiscated, and that the cause of it was that one day, when he was going on an expedition in which Artebas was accompanying him, he made enquiries about his residence, and saw round it no small number of presents, which people were in the habit of offering him at all the stoppages that he made in the villages of his dominions, and this made Abderrahman envious. They were confiscated and given to Abderrahman's nephews, and Artebas was reduced to poverty. He went to Cordova and called on the Hajib Ibn Bokht, and said to him—

"'Do me the favour to request the Amir, whom God guard, to allow me to see him, for I have come to take leave of him for ever.'

"The Hajib asked for permission, and Abderrahman ordered Artebas to enter his presence. On seeing him come in dressed in rags, Abderrahman said—

[1] Pp. 86-7.

"'Holá Artebas! What brings thee here?'

"To which he replied—

"'Thou, thou bringest me here, who hast interposed between me and my possessions, breaking the treaties which thy fathers made with me, without any fault of mine on my part to excuse thee.'

"Abderrahman answered—

"'But what is this about desiring to take leave of me for ever? Dost thou think of going to Rome?' (*sic*) [1]

"Artebas replied—

"'On the contrary, I know that thou desirest to go to Syria.'

"Abderrahman said——

"'And who is going to let me return there, seeing that I had to leave it in order not to be killed?'

"Then Artebas asked him—

"'Dost thou propose to consolidate thy rule here, that thy son may inherit it, or dost thou only wish to enjoy that which I myself have given thee?'

"And Abderrahman answered—

"'No, by God! I not only desire to consolidate my rule, but that my son shall inherit it.'

"Thereupon Artebas clearly set forth, without circumlocutions or disguise, everything that the nation did not approve of, and Abderrahman was so pleased and grateful that he returned to him twenty of his villages, gave him splendid garments and gifts, and appointed him to the office of Count, he being the first who enjoyed this dignity in Spain.

"Ibn Al-Kuttiyyah also quotes 'the venerable Ibn Lobaba,' his master, as saying that 'God protected Artebas in his poverty, because he was a man of the most distinguished character,' and gives a long story related to him

---

[1] "Rûm." ? Constantinople.

by Ibn Lobaba, who heard it from contemporaries, of Artebas' dealings with ten Syrians of high estate. Among them entered one Maimun, ' the servant of God and ancestor of the Beni Hazan, the porters.' [1]

"When Artebas saw him in his house, he rose to receive him, embraced him affectionately, and insisted on his taking the seat which he himself had vacated, which was plated with gold and silver. The holy man refused, saying that he had no right to occupy that seat, and immediately sat down upon the ground. Artebas did the same, sitting down at his side, and said—

"'To what do I owe the honour that a man like thee comes to visit a person like myself?'

"Maimun answered—

"'When we came to this country, as we did not suppose that our stay would be long, we did not come prepared to remain in it. But our people in the East have risen against us, a thing we could not have expected, and certainly we shall not now return to our country. God has given thee great wealth, and I wish that thou wouldst give me one of thy farms to cultivate with my own hands; I will pay thee thy due, and take for myself what is right.'

"And Artebas said—

"'No, I should not be content to give thee a farm on shares.'

"He then called his steward, and said to him—

"'Give this gentleman the farm of the Guadajoz with all the cows, horses, and slaves therein; give him also the castle which is in the province of Jaen.'"

After Maimun had left, the Syrian chiefs proceeded to reproach the Gothic prince for neglecting them and showing such generosity to "that miserable person." Artebas' reply

---

[1] Gayangos in his note on this episode as related by Makkari, says he was a fakir. (Makkari, ii. 416.)

is interesting as showing how little afraid the Christians of that time were of proclaiming their own religion ; for after mentioning what "the men of his religion" had told him of the speaker, he went on to say that "the Messiah, whom God bless and preserve, said, 'Whoever honours God in one of His servants, all the world should honour him.'"

Although Cherbonneau's translation of Al-Kuttiyyah gives essentially the same account as that of Pons, it differs in certain details of interest. Thus he says that the "innumerable presents" which roused Abderrahman's jealousy, were offered by the "vassals of Artebas," and that "the confiscation of his estates compelled Artebas to seek an asylum with his nephews." This seems more probable than that the nephews referred to were those of Abderrahman, who, moreover, was the last of his line, save for various cousins, his own family having been massacred not long before by the Abbassides. Cherbonneau says that twenty of Artebas' "fiefs" were restored to him, instead of twenty villages (*aldeas*), as Pons gives it. One fief would probably contain many villages, so that the prince's rapid restoration to wealth and power would be explained.

In the same translation of the account of the visit of the Syrian chiefs we find some suggestive passages which are omitted both by Pons and by Gayangos in Makkari's relation of the incident.[1]

"After Maimun had retired and Artebas had reseated himself on his own chair [or throne, as we might perhaps more correctly call the seat covered with gold and silver], As-Somail thus addressed him—

"'What makes thee unworthy to wear the crown of thy father Witiza is that thou lettest thy benefactions fall in

[1] ii. 52-3.

the mud. What! I, a prince of the Arabs of Andalucia, I come to see thee with my friends, who are equally with me lords of the free men of the Peninsula, and thou dost not even do us the honour to offer us chairs, while before our eyes thou goest to meet this mendicant and treatest him with the greatest distinction.'

"'Abu Jushan,' replied the Christian prince, 'I have heard the Musulmans say that thou hast never been able to grasp the principles of their religion; otherwise thou wouldst not blame me so severely for the reception with which I have shown honour to a holy man.'

"As-Somail, it must be said in parenthesis, was so ignorant that he could neither read nor write.[1]

"'To you whom God has favoured,' continued Artebas, 'one only makes presents on account of your power and wealth, while as for the man to whom I have offered the tribute of my generosity, it is only to please God that I have done him a benefit. For we know that Jesus Christ said, "He who has received the benefits of God should dispense them generously to his fellows."'"

"These words reduced As-Somail to silence, as if Artebas had put a stone in his mouth. Then the visitors said to Artebas—

"'Enough of this discourse; occupy thyself rather with the object of our visit. Our needs are the same as those of the individual who has received so brilliant a token of thy munificence.'

"'But you,' replied the Gothic prince, 'are great lords, and moderate presents are not what you want.'

"Thus speaking he gave them a hundred fiefs, ten to each. Thus the estates of Torrox, of El-Fennetin, of Okbet az-Zitun, and of Almodovar came to be divided, the first

[1] That an Arab noble of the eighth century should be illiterate was sufficiently rare for Al-Kuttiyyah to comment on it.

to Abdallah Ibn Khald, and the two others (*sic*) to As Somail Ibn Hatem." [1]

The immense extent of Artebas' domains is indicated by this anecdote, for although we cannot identify Al-Fennetin or Okbet az-Zitun, a glance at the map will show how far apart are Torrox, Almodovar, Jaen, and the river Guadajoz.

Two or three points in the narrative of these incidents are worth notice.

Artebas in his interview with Abderrahman speaks of " the treaties which his (Abderrahman's) fathers had made with him." The invariable use by the Moslem writers of some such term as " treaty " in connection with the restoration of Witiza's domains to his family, supports our argument as to the immediate cause of the invasion and the position of the princes at the time. This is further confirmed by Artebas' allusion to " that which I myself have given thee." Even in his poverty Artebas must have held a leading position among his own people, for he " sets forth everything that the nation did not approve of," as one who had a right to speak for it.

Finally Abderrahman conferred on him the office of Count, " he being the first to enjoy this dignity in Spain." According to Ibn Hayyan, moreover, it was Artebas, " le Comte d'Espagne, le chef des chrétiens et le percepteur du caratch," who suggested the settlement on the State lands of the Arab troops who had been brought over about 740 to assist in quelling the Berber revolt—further evidence, not only of his importance in the land, but of the friendly relations between him and his supposed conquerors.[2]

It is not easy to believe that the hero of these incidents robbed his orphaned nephews and niece; but be that as it may, there is no doubt that Sara and her brothers were

---

[1] Al-Kuttiyyah in *J.A.*, pp. 468–72.
[2] Dozy, *Recherches*, i. 86.

unjustly deprived of their inheritance after the death of their father Almand. She tried to obtain redress from Abu-l-Khattar, the Governor of Andalucia, but without avail; whereupon she procured and fitted out a ship, and, embarking at Seville with the two boys, sailed for Syria to demand justice from the Khalif himself. She landed at Ascalon, and thence made her way to Damascus. This visit must have taken place in or about the year 745, for Abu-l-Khattar only held office during 745-6; thus it is clear that the Gothic princes had enjoyed undisturbed possession of their estates for at least thirty years after the invasion.

Sara and her brothers reached Damascus in safety, and were well received by the Khalif, Hisham Ibn Abdalmalek. She informed him of her grievance, and implored justice against her uncle, begging the Khalif to issue orders to the Governor of Andalucia to reinstate her and her brothers in all the lands belonging to their father, "as contained in the capitulation entered into with Tarik and confirmed by his predecessor the Khalif Al-Walid."

"Hisham was much pleased with Sara, whose courage and determination he greatly admired; he treated her kindly, and admitted her to his privacy; and when she expressed her wish to depart, gave her a letter for . . . the Governor of Eastern Africa [a Yemenite] intrusting him with the redress of the injury she had sustained at the hands of her uncle Artebas," the result of which was that she and her brothers were put in full possession of all their rights.

While Sara was staying at the Court of Hisham, she met his grandson, Abderrahman Ibn Moawiya, who was destined later to become the ruler of Andalucia. Before she left Hisham gave her in marriage to a noble Arab, Isa **Ibn Muzahim**, who returned with her to Spain and helped her to recover her estates. By him she had two sons, Ibrahim and Ishak, "both of whom held offices of trust at Seville, the place of their residence, and were very much esteemed and respected on account of their descent on the mother's side from the Gothic kings of Andalus."[1]

Sara's first husband died about the time that Abderrahman came to Spain (756), and soon afterwards she married Abderrahman Ibn Omar Ibn Said Al-Lakhmi.[2] Makkari says that Sara always enjoyed great favour with Abderrahman I. This he attributes to her having made his acquaintance at the Court of Hisham, when he was a cadet of the royal house, without any prospect of obtaining a kingdom of his own. But it seems more probable that the favour shown to her by Abderrahman was due to policy. His throne was anything but firmly established, and it may have seemed well to him to secure the powerful influence of Sara and her following, consisting as it did of the two elements most hostile to him—the Goths and the Yemenite Arabs. The latter especially were dangerous, for the Abbasides were in communication with their chief, Al-Yahssobi (Abu-s-Sabah). He proclaimed their sovereignty, and they sent him a black banner (the Shiite banner) on the point of a lance.[3]

According to one authority quoted by Makkari, "when Abderrahman had conquered the whole of Andalus" [which, as a matter of fact, neither he nor any of his successors ever did till Abderrahman III. mounted the throne] "Sara hastened to Cordova ... to recall herself to his memory and recommend herself to his good graces as a Christian living in his dominions."[4] This story is somewhat contradicted by

[1] Makkari, ii. 51.
[2] *Ibid.*, ii. 52, 415; and Al-Kuttiyyah in *J.A.* p. 434.
[3] *Akhbar Majmua*, 95.
[4] Makkari, ii. 51.

the account given by Al-Kuttiyyah of the negotiations for her second marriage, which Abderrahman used his influence to bring about. Her husband, Omar Ibn Said, obtained his suit against Hayyat Ibn Mulamis Al-Hadrami, a rival for her hand, through the intervention of Thaleba Al-Jodhami, who interested himself on Ibn Said's behalf. If Sara was of so little importance as to be anxious to recommend herself to Abderrahman, merely because she was a Christian, it would hardly have been necessary for her Moslem suitor to call in the aid of an ex-Governor of Andalucia and a great noble, as Al-Jodhami was, to secure the support of the Amir.

As a matter of fact, Abderrahman is shown to have treated Sara throughout as a friend and equal. He granted her the privilege, reserved only for persons of the highest rank, of entering the palace at all hours. And, says Makkari, "he continued bestowing on her new honours and distinctions, going so far as to grant her leave to visit his harem and see his wives and daughters without their veils on." No greater marks of confidence than these could have been shown by Abderrahman, for to this day in aristocratic Sunnite houses where strict etiquette prevails, it is usual to send a servant some hours in advance to announce the visit of one woman to another, even though related to the family.[1]

Abderrahman would not have gone out of his way to honour a Christian woman merely because he had been acquainted with her in his youth. But it is easy to see that the Moslem ruler, whose tenure of the throne was precarious, recognised the immense importance to himself of standing well with a princess who ruled as a queen over precisely that portion of the mixed Christian-Moslem community

---

[1] Cf. *Le Jardin fermé* by Marc Helys, p. 140.

THE ROYAL MUWALLADS

which would be, if offended, most capable of overturning the throne on which he was trying to establish himself.

When Yusuf Al-Fehri, the Governor of Andalucia,[1] heard of the arrival of the Ommeyad prince in Spain, he consulted As-Samil, a leader of the Mudarite tribes, as to the wisest course to pursue.[2] As-Samil recommended an immediate attack on Abderrahman, before he had time to strengthen himself. "For," said he, "I strongly suspect that the Yemenite Arabs will go over to him, owing to the hatred they openly bear to us, the Beni Mudar."[3]

This was what happened, and the small amount of dependence to be placed on such support, given to a racial and religious antagonist, was very soon shown.

Yusuf Al-Fehri, instead of following As-Samil's advice, waited to give battle to Abderrahman near Cordova, when the Ommeyad prince won a brilliant victory. The Yemenite Arabs fought on Abderrahman's side, but apparently in a half-hearted fashion, and after the battle was over their leader, Abu-s-Sabah of Seville, proposed to his followers that as they had (in their own belief) annihilated the party of Yusuf and As-Samil, they should complete the work by putting Abderrahman to death. "If we do," he said, "the empire is ours, and we may then appoint one of ourselves to the command of this country, and be for ever rid of the Beni Mudar."[4] His advice was not acted upon; on the contrary, his words were reported to Abderrahman, who about a year later had Abu-s-Sabah executed.

Whatever may be the exact truth as to the details of Abderrahman's acquisition of the supreme power in Cordova, there is no doubt that bitter hostility existed then, as it had

---

[1] He, like Abderrahman, was of the tribe of Koraish.
[2] This As-Somail or Samil was the Syrian to whom Artebas gave an estate.
[3] Makkari, ii. 67.
[4] *Ibid.*, ii. 72.

existed long before the Hegira, between the Yemenite Arabs and the various tribes of the race of Mudar, and it looks as though some powerful influence must have been brought to bear on the Yemenite nobles of Seville before they would have taken the field in support of the enemy of their race. The only person in a position to exercise such influence was the Gothic princess, who owed all that she possessed to Abderrahman's grandfather. The cordiality of her relations with Abderrahman after he was settled in Cordova would be explained if he was indebted to her and the pretender to her hand for support in the first days of his arrival in Andalucia. The Arab tradition of hospitality must also have weighed with her, for she had been an honoured guest of his family, and had eaten of their salt, together with her first Arab husband, in Syria.

We have referred to one Ibn Mulamis Al-Hadrami as a rejected suitor of Sara's when she became a widow in 756. It would seem as though Abderrahman wished to do away with any ill-feeling that might have been created by his support of Al-Hadrami's rival, for about 760 the Amir paid a visit to a member of the family in his house at Seville, " which he gave up to the king with all that was in it, and King Abderrahman accepted his generous offer in order not to offend him." Conde adds that this Ibn Mulamis died not long after, and that Abderrahman commemorated him in some elegant verses, in which he praised his hospitality, munificence, and other noble qualities.[1]

There can be no doubt that Abderrahman's host at Seville was the Ibn Mulamis mentioned by Makkari as having come over with Musa in 712, while the Princess Sara's rejected suitor was his younger brother, or some other near relative. After the death of the elder man, Hayat Ibn

---

[1] Conde, i. 178–9.

THE ROYAL MUWALLADS

Mulamis rose (Makkari says in 772) in [the territory of] Seville with the recently settled Syrians from Emesa,[1] supported by Abdul-Jafar Al-Yahsobi, whom we may take to be a son of the murdered Abu-s-Sabah.

Among those who went out with Abderrahman in the campaign against them were three Sevillian Yemenites, Malhab Al-Kelbi, and Ibn Al-Hejjaj and his son.[2] The Beni Hejjaj must have been closely related to Omar Ibn Said Al-Lakhmi, Sara's second husband, for one branch of her descendants, of whom we shall hear a great deal as we go on, bore that name.

Makkari records, between the years 758 and 779, eight distinct risings against Abderrahman, in most of which Yusuf Al-Fehri or his friends and relations, and some at any rate of the Yemenite Arabs, took part. As the Fehrites and Yemenites belonged to different and exceedingly hostile races, Gayangos' suggestion that most of these revolts were due to the inveterate feuds between the tribes of Mudar and Yemen[3] is not convincing. Both the Ommeyads and the Fehrites were of the race of Mudar, and the fact that some of the Yemenites joined with the Fehrites against the Ommeyad Amir, proves that this prolonged rebellion was political, not racial.

Our view is that the nobles of Seville who are spoken of as having welcomed the young Ommeyad were the Christians and such of the Yemenites as were open to the influence of Sara through her Arab husbands. We have not been able to find any information as to the tribe to which belonged the Arab Isa Ibn Musahim, to whom the Khalif Hisham married her at Damascus. He can hardly have been a Syrian, for his descendants were completely amalgamated with the

---

[1] These are stated to have been few in number. (*Akhbar Majmua,* 92.)
[2] *Akhbar Majmua,* 100.
[3] Makkari, ii. 421.

Sevillian Yemenites in succeeding generations, and were either attached to the Shiite sect or retained the Christian religion of their royal ancestress, as many of them certainly did. But there is no question about Omar Ibn Said. He belonged to Abderrahman's racial and religious antagonists, and in the natural course he would have fought on the side of his own people.

Yet, as we have seen in the passage quoted above, members of his family are specially mentioned as being with the Ommeyad Amir against a party led by Yemenites. It may be argued that gratitude to Abderrahman for his good offices with the Gothic Princess was the motive of this allegiance among the Seville Lakhmites; and no doubt the personal equation had something to do with the conduct of that generation. It is not until about 130 years later that we find the descendants of Sara implicated in riots or rebellions against Cordova, for from the arrival of Abderrahman I. in 756, to the accession of Abdullah, in 888, these families are never mentioned in connection with the slight and easily quelled disturbances which occasionally broke out in Seville at the instigation of more or less unimportant malcontents.

If, as we believe, the Princess Sara and her husband made a treaty of neutrality with Abderrahman I. at the same time and on the same terms as the Christians of Kashtalah (see p. 67), this policy on their part is accounted for. Whatever the true cause, the result was singularly beneficial to the internal prosperity and progress of the territory ruled over by this Gotho-Yemenite stock, who had become enormously powerful an hundred years later.

It was the policy of Abderrahman to attach the discontented to his person by forgiving them on the first sign of repentance, and appointing them to high offices in the state. True, it is not always easy to trace the favours he conferred on the Yemenites, for Ibn Hayyan and his seventeenth century successor Makkari, both being Sunnites, never mention the tribal name, if they can avoid it, when recording honours bestowed on Shiites. But here and there we find suggestive hints as to what really took place—*e.g.* in Makkari's account of the above-mentioned rebellion of Ibn Mulamis and his friends. Although he states positively that they were defeated with awful carnage and all the leaders remained dead on the field, yet, he adds, "there are not wanting historians who assert that they escaped from the slaughter, and were some time afterwards pardoned by Abderrahman." And Ibn Hayyan relates that after the final defeat of Al-Fehri, "for several days the palace of Abderrahman was crowded with governors and chiefs, who came to swear fealty to him; and Abderrahman would receive them with great affability on appointed days, and after confirming them in their respective offices and land tenures, he would converse with them and address them in words which delighted them and attached them to him." [1]

It is to be wished that Ibn Hayyan had given us only a few names among these "governors and chiefs" who, as they came to swear fealty, must have been of the opposite party, as he would certainly have done had they been on his own side. But the Court historian of the Ommeyads did not think it well to chronicle the importance of his master's enemies, even when they had been forgiven.

One incident recorded of this Amir points to his strong sense of justice and determination to punish those who had behaved dishonourably, even though closely connected with himself.

It appears that when Abu-s-Sabah, the chief of the Yemenite Arabs, revolted, he gave as a reason that certain

---

[1] Makkari, ii. 84-5, 88.

terms agreed to by the Wizir Ibn Khaled in Abderrahman's name, previous to his arrival in Spain, had been violated by Abderrahman (who may not have been in possession of the facts). After the capture and execution of the Yemenite chieftain, Abderrahman removed Ibn Khaled from his office, and swore never to employ him again as long as he lived. Accordingly, Ibn Khaled "passed out of memory at the court, and remained without taking any part whatever in the affairs of the Government." [1]

Makkari adduces this incident, among others, as showing how little gratitude Abderrahman showed towards those who had helped to raise him to the throne. But it may equally well be read as evidence of his determination that those who committed dishonourable acts in his name should suffer for it.

"One of the historians of the West," whose name is not given, says that Abderrahman "was a man of very sound judgment and quick perception : he was deeply learned . . . slow and prudent in his determinations, but firm in carrying them into effect. . . . He was exceedingly liberal, and well versed in the science of government ; he always dressed in white, and wore a turban of the same colour.[2] He used to visit the sick and attend funerals, saying his prayers in the mosque in common with the people on Fridays and other festivals ; he harangued his troops himself, and raised the banners with his own hand." Ibn Hayyan adds that "he issued orders that all who came to him with petitions should be admitted to his audience room without delay, that he might attend to their cases and listen to their complaints, and that numbers of poor distressed people ... would flock to the Amir's hall on the days of public audience, when they invariably obtained the redress of their wrongs." [3]

[1] Makkari, ii. 90–1.
[2] The Sunnites wore white ; the Shiites black, in token of their perpetual mourning for the murder of Ali.
[3] Makkari, ii. 88–9, 93.

THE ROYAL MUWALLADS

The only charge which Makkari brings against Abderrahman is that already mentioned—his ingratitude to those who had helped to place him on the throne ; but of this fault he only cites two instances besides the one given above, while there are numerous stories of his kindheartedness and readiness to forgive and show mercy. Indeed, the reception he gave to those, whether Mudarites or Yemenites, who had struggled against his rule, when they offered submission, proves how little he permitted personal feeling to interfere with the broad liberality towards his enemies which evidently was the guiding principle of his life.

Whatever his own preferences may have been, it is clear that as long as he lived, Abderrahman I. loyally observed the terms of the treaty made by the Khalif Al-Walid, so far as the Princess Sara was concerned. As for Artebas, the account of the seizure of his property is so unconvincing and so contrary to all that we know of Abderrahman's character that we should be inclined to treat the whole story as an invention, but for the terms in which the act of restitution is narrated. No Moslem writer would have been likely to invent this ; nor, indeed, is it at all probable that Ibn Hayyan, in view of Sara's connection with the Yemenites, would have alluded to the treaty with Tarik, had it not been too notorious for omission. Probably the whole affair was the result of an intrigue on the part of some enemy of the Goth, and Abderrahman's conduct on discovering that he had been misled into an act of injustice was inspired by the same motives as those which caused him to degrade the Wizir Ibn Khaled.

Conde has an illuminating paragraph on the subject of treaties entered into in the time of Abderrahman I. He says—

"King Abderrahman rejoiced greatly at the news of this victory [over Yusuf Al-Fehri] hoping that the miserable death of the leader would put an end to the vain attempts of his party. At the same time King Abderrahman settled with the Christians of Castilla [1] the tribute which they were to pay him, and the letter of protection and safeguard which he granted them read as follows : ' In the name of God, the clement and the merciful. The magnificent King Abderrahman to the Patricians, Monks, Nobles, and other Christians of Spain, to the people of Castela (*sic*) and to those of the districts who follow them, grants peace and safety, and promises on his soul that this compact shall be stable, and that they are to pay ten thousand ounces of gold, and ten thousand pounds of silver, and ten thousand head of good horses, and as many mules, with a thousand coats of mail and a thousand swords and the same number of lances each year for five years : written in the city of Cordova on the third day of the month Safar of the year 142.' " (June, 758.)[2]

It is worth noting that Conde, although, as his note shows, he was perfectly aware of the confusion between Castilla and Castela or Castulo, made by the writer he was translating, copied the treaty as he found it. Thus we are indebted to the careful transcript of this much-abused author for an important piece of evidence as to the wealth and power of the Christians ruled over by the descendants of Witiza in the eighth century. It is quite clear that the Christians of Galicia are not here referred to, for there is no record of any tribute paid by Fruela to Abderrahman. On the contrary, the only mention of Fruela in Makkari refers to his conquests and his increasing strength.[3] Nor is there any suggestion of

---

[1] *Sic.* But Conde has a note to the effect that this must be a mistake because at that date the country on the other side of the Guadarrama was not called Castile, but Galicia. Clearly Castela (Kashtalah) is meant. Gibbon refers to this treaty, which he read in Casiri's version, and notes the anachronism in the use of the word Castile. (Chapter li. *ad fin.*)

[2] Conde, i. 173-4.

[3] ii. 85.

a tribute in the *Crónica general*. We think, however, that Conde, or the writer he was translating, was mistaken in attributing this treaty to the year in which Al-Fehri was killed. We can find no record that the Christians of Cazlona supported him, and it seems more probable that the treaty was made soon after the Ommeyad obtained the throne of Cordova.

Casiri (ii. 104) prints the treaty with a Latin translation, in which "Castella" is given for Kashtalah. Perhaps Conde took his version from that writer's *Bibliotheca Arabico-Hispana*.

CHAPTER IV

ANDALUCIA IN THE NINTH CENTURY

THE immediate successors of Abderrahman I. on the throne of Cordova followed his methods in attaching the Christians and Yemenite Arabs to their own persons. Frequent references are made to their appointment to high offices, and Abderrahman II. gave the post of Kadi of Cordova to a Lakhmite, and had a man of Christian family, Obeidallah Ibn Carloman, as his private attendant and intimate friend. That he was on good terms with Seville is shown by the help he gave the city when it was attacked by the Northmen, and by his repairing the walls and mosque after the damage done by them.[1]

This policy of conciliation was successful, for until the year 888 Seville remained loyal to her over-lords at Cordova. But on the death of the Amir Al-Mundhir in that year, a complete change in their relations was brought about, though what was the determining cause there is little to indicate, unless it were the dismissal of a Lakhmite Kadi of Cordova by Abdullah as soon as he ascended the throne.[2] The fact

---

[1] Conde, i. 268, 283; Makkari, ii. 116. Dozy, in his *Recherches*, has collected all the evidence available about the various invasions of the Spanish Peninsula by the Northmen. Of these the only one in the course of which they reached Seville was that of the year 844-5, when according to Al-Kuttiyyah, the earliest writer who relates the story, they destroyed the walls and attempted, without success, to set fire to the mosque. Abderrahman defeated them and drove them away, and "built the great mosque" of Seville.

[2] Makkari, ii. 459.

ANDALUCIA IN THE NINTH CENTURY

is stated by Ibn Hayyan, without comment. And then suddenly the whole country seems to burst out into civil war, and from that year until he died, in 912, Abdullah is found constantly contending with the great Yemenite faction, headed by members of Muwallad families sprung from the Princess Sara and her two Moslem husbands.

Chief over them all at that time was Abdullah Ibn Hejjaj Al-Lakhmi, lord of Seville and Carmona, who ruled like a king in Seville.[1] Hayyan tells us that in 888 Ibn Hejjaj kept princely state in Seville, although he nominally acknowledged the Sultan Abdullah as his over-lord. He had, says Hayyan, a bodyguard of five hundred horsemen, used the royal robes called *tiraz*, with his names and titles woven into the border, which were exclusively reserved for those of kingly birth, appointed the Kadis and public officers all over his dominions, and was fond of science and liberal towards the poets who visited his Court.[2]

Dozy, relying it would seem mostly on the writings of the Beni Hejjaj's own kinsman, Al-Kuttiyyah, largely expands Hayyan's brief account.

From the time of the Visigoths, he says, Seville had been the seat of Roman learning and civilisation, and the Arabic invasion hardly brought about any change in the social conditions of that city, where resided the wealthiest and noblest of the Gothic families.[3] The Princess Sara made it her Court from the time of her return from Damascus with her first husband, Isa Ibn Muzahim, and her descendants, both by him and by her second husband Omar Ibn Said Al-Lakhmi, succeeded her in her dominions and in the esteem and respect of the Sevillians. The Beni Hejjaj were now at the head of the united families.

[1] Ibn Hayyan calls him Ibrahim, but internal evidence points to his having given the name of the younger brother by mistake.
[2] Ibn Hayyan in Makkari, ii. 439.
[3] *G. der M.*, i. 392.

Abdullah Ibn Hejjaj and his brother Ibrahim were the descendants at the third or fourth generation of Sara and her second husband, while their historian Al-Kuttiyyah descended at perhaps one generation more from her and her first husband. It is a fair assumption that the advanced condition of Seville towards the close of the ninth century was due to the amalgamation of the Gothic nobility with the Arabs of Yemen, who in their turn had behind them the tradition of centuries of luxury and refinement in Arabia Felix previous to the Persian occupation which drove them out of their beloved Yemen into what was to them the "wilderness" of Egypt.[1] Indeed, until the reign of Abderrahman III., who as we shall see was of Yemenite-Christian, otherwise Muwallad, descent on the mother's side, Seville was decidedly in advance of Cordova in certain respects, especially under the Beni Hejjaj and their contemporary the Sultan Abdullah.

Hayyan and Al-Kuttiyyah, as quoted by Dozy, differ in the dates they assign to the respective reigns of Abdullah Ibn Hejjaj and his brother Ibrahim, both of whom ruled over Seville between the accession of Abdullah Ibn Ommeya at Cordova in 888, and that of his grandson Abderrahman III., who succeeded him on the throne in 912. We may assume, however, that Abdullah was dead in 895, for several authorities name Ibrahim, the younger brother, as prince or king of Seville in that year, after which there was a truce in the bitter civil war between Syrians and Berbers on one side, and Yemenites and Muwallads on the other. So we will take Dozy's description of Ibrahim's Court at that period as applying equally to that of his recently deceased brother.

A severe battle had taken place at Carmona (of which particulars will be found a few pages further on), and

[1] Lenormant, Book VII.; cf. Butler, *Arab Conquest*, pp. 147-8.

according to the Cordovan Court historians, Abdullah Ibn Hejjaj had been taken prisoner and strangled by the Sultan's son Al-Motref, while his party had been almost annihilated. Nevertheless, his successor's position in the same year was still that of an independent prince paying tribute to Cordova, and within his own boundaries wielding absolute power. Ibrahim had his own army, which he paid as the Sultan paid his; and he appointed (as Hayyan says his predecessor had done in 891) all the Government officials in the kingdom of Seville, from Kadis and Prefects downwards.

Nothing of inherited kingly state was lacking to Ibrahim Ibn Hejjaj; neither the family bodyguard of five hundred horsemen, nor the royal robes of brocade upon which the Prince's names and titles were woven in gold. At once Prince and merchant,[1] a learned man and a patron of science, he often received in the same ship gifts from rulers across the sea and tissues from the manufacturing cities of Egypt, learned men from Arabia and female singers from Bagdad. The beautiful slave Kamar, whose talents had been reported to Ibrahim, and whom he had purchased at a great price, and the Bedouin Abu Mohammed Odhri, a linguist from Hedjaz, were the brightest jewels of his Court. Odhri, when he heard an incorrect phrase or an unsuitable word, was wont to exclaim aloud—

"Oh, ye town-dwellers, what have ye done with the language?"

He passed for an oracle in all connected with purity of speech and elegance of language.

The talented Kamar united with her gift for music natural eloquence, poetical aptitude, and a noble pride. In one of her improvisations she said that if a woman must be ignorant in order to attain Paradise, she would prefer to go

[1] Compare Lenormant's account of the development of commerce in Yemen previous to the Persian invasion.

to Hell.[1] In the tenth century we hear of numerous female poets, musicians, and learned women at Cordova, but they are not mentioned before the reign of Abderrahman III., it may be therefore conjectured that the fashion of employing educated women about the Court was introduced at Cordova through the influence or example of the Yemenites of Seville.[2]

On one occasion a satirical poet named Kalfat, who could not make a living at Cordova owing to Abdullah's penurious dealings with members of his profession,[3] read to Ibrahim some verses full of bitter jokes upon the Ministers and courtiers of Cordova. Ibrahim heard him to the end, and then said—

"Thou errest in believing that a man like me can take pleasure in hearing such vulgar abuse."

And Kalfat returned empty-handed to Cordova.

It is easy to understand that such a man as is here depicted would struggle to prevent his country from falling under the bloodthirsty misgovernment of Abdullah Ibn Ommeya, or rather of his son Al-Motref, who was Commander-in-chief of the Cordovan army, and Abdullah's evil genius throughout his reign.

The whole religious tradition of the Sevillians—the Yemenite or Muwallad party—was opposed to indiscriminate bloodshed, and, above all, to the subjection of non-combatants to the horrors of war. The Yemenite Arabs were, with rare exceptions, followers of Ali, the nephew and son-

---

[1] Dozy, *G. der M.*, i. 444–5.

[2] Conde (i. 455, 482) mentions several at the Courts of Abderrahman III. and Al-Hakem : others are recorded by Pons (p. 513) and Makkari (i. 161, 162) : the tribal names of several of those mentioned show that they were Yemenites : others were certainly Mozarabs. Cf. Lenormant, Bk. VI. 347, on the position of women in Yemen.

[3] This is Dozy's version of the story (*loc. cit.*), but Conde (i. 337) relates some dealings of Kalfat's with regard to Ibrahim which suggest that he had gone to Seville in the capacity of a spy in the interest of the Sultan.

ANDALUCIA IN THE NINTH CENTURY 75

in-law of Mahomet, whose murder by the Merwan party (from which dynasty the Ommeyads sprang) brought about the division of Islam into the two hostile sects—the Sunnites, who approved of the murder, and for forty years afterwards daily cursed the name of Ali in the public prayers; and the Shiites, who regarded him as a martyr, in many places wore black garments and bore a black banner in token of perpetual mourning for him, and everywhere worshipped his memory as that of their patron saint.

Hence the eternal hostility between the Yemenite families, whose capital was Seville, and the Syrians and Berbers, who acknowledged the Ommeyads of Cordova as their rulers. The differences in their modes of life and thought, and above all, in their principles of warfare, were irreconcileable. The Shiites in this matter followed the "Instructions" of Abu Bekr, which his successor in the Khalifate, the murdered Ali, had adopted as his own counsel of perfection. Ibn Hayyan and his fellows among Sunnite historians naturally say little or nothing, in their narratives, of what has been called the "Law of Ali"; but Conde, writing here—perhaps unknown to himself—from the Yemenites' point of view, refers to this tradition in plain words several times. We also find echoes of the "Law of Ali" here and there in passages from Ibn Said, Ibn Al-Ghalib, and other Shiites, not only in Conde, but in transcriptions by other writers, while it is made clear later on that the last great Yemenite dynasty, the Nasrites of Granada, built up their kingdom on the observance of that law.

Conde gives us a version of the whole of the "Instructions" in the early part of his history.[1] From this we abstract some of the most striking portions of Abu Bekr's address to his army when he sent them out against the Syrian hosts.

[1] i. 8–10. See also Gibbon, chapter li.

To the leaders :—

"Be careful not to act hastily, rashly, or without judgment. Be just with all, for he who is not just and exact will not prosper."

To the troops :—

"Follow and obey your leaders; do not yield or turn your backs on the enemy; as you are fighting in God's cause, let not other base desires move you; thus fear not to go into battle, nor let the excessive numbers of your adversaries daunt you. If God gives you the victory, do not stain your swords with the blood of those who submit, nor with that of children, women, and weak old men. When marching through the enemy's country do not cut down trees, nor destroy his palms or fruit trees, nor ravage or burn his fields or dwellings, but of them and of his cattle take only what you may require. Destroy nothing without necessity; occupy the cities and fortresses, and only destroy those of them which may give shelter to your adversaries. Be merciful to the vanquished and humiliated, and God will be merciful to you. Deal harshly with the proud and rebellious, and with those who do not observe your conditions. Let there be no falseness or double dealing in your treaties and dealings with the enemy, but be always faithful, loyal, and honourable, and keep your word and your promise. Do not disturb the peace of monks or hermits, nor destroy their dwellings; but put to death the enemy who resists under arms the conditions imposed on them."

In others of the numerous versions of Abu Bekr's address there is an additional paragraph after that relating to monks and hermits. It is to the effect that there will be found another class of men of religion, who may be known by their shaven crowns. These are to be put to death without option of surrender. The allusion evidently is to the Christian secular clergy, but we doubt whether Abu Bekr himself was responsible for this order, which looks like a sectarian interpolation of later date, and is out of keeping with the broad principles of humanity and justice which characterise the " Instructions " as a whole.

The attitude taken by the Sunnites towards the law so reverenced by the Shiites is illustrated by an appeal of Al-Motref to his nephew, Abderrahman III., in the course of a campaign against Ibn Hafsun in 917, for leave to extirpate the rebels " without regard to considerations of ill-understood gentleness and humanity," [1] referring, as Conde says in a note, " to the maxims and customs of war called those of Ali, which prohibited . . . the killing of fugitives beyond the field of battle, and forbad cities to be rigorously besieged for more than a few days " ; the implication being that Abderrahman had ordered their observance.

This incident alone is enough to show how hopelessly at variance were the two sects in their most elementary principles, and helps to explain the constant strife between a ruler whose policy was conducted " without considerations of ill-understood gentleness and humanity," and those whose religion included the strict observance of such conditions.

Incidentally we may observe that the marked difference of principle between the two sects in their method of warfare explains much that is otherwise incomprehensible in the history of Islam in Spain, and clears up many otherwise inconsistent accounts of savage murder and bloodshed alongside of instances of chivalry and charity worthy of the highest civilisation.

Compassionate treatment of the defeated, of noncombatants, and of the religious orders, and regard for the interests of agriculturists and farmers, are to be observed in the history of Abderrahman III., of his son Al-Hakem, and

[1] Conde, i. 367.

his grandson Hisham (or rather of the latter's great Yemenite Wizir Almansur), and of Motamid, the Abbadite king of Seville, all of whom had Yemenite blood in their veins. The three last Cordovan Khalifs must have adopted the tradition from their Seville ancestry, for no other Ommeyads displayed such sentiments. And that it formed the basis of the most successful methods of government in Moslem Spain is shown by the brilliancy of the reigns during which it was carried out, for at no time was Moslem Spain so powerful, rich, prosperous, and contented as under the rulers just named, all of whom acted more or less in accordance with the Law of Ali.

Soon after Abdullah came to the throne of Cordova, in 888, his son Mohammed was Governor of Seville, although it is not clear whether he owed his appointment to his father or to his father's predecessor, Al-Mundhir. No explanation is given of his position in a city where, as Ibn Hayyan says, the Beni Hejjaj ruled as kings.[1] But it may be suggested that the Cordovan Governors so often mentioned as appointed to this or that city which we know to have been peopled and ruled by adherents of the other great party in the State, were in reality functionaries who did little more than represent the nominal over-lord in regard to the collection of the tribute paid by the Muwallad princes. As we have explained, practically all the south-west of Andalucia was dominated by the descendants, more or less direct, of Witiza, with whom the Shiite families were as a rule on friendly terms, if not actually connected by marriage. Yet there are many stories of quarrels between the " people " and the Governors appointed by the Sultan Abdullah, and a distinction is generally, if not invariably, drawn between the gentlemen (*caballeros* or nobles) who supported those Governors and

[1] Dozy, *G. der M.* i. 398, Conde, [i. 327; Gayangos in Makkari, ii. 460–1, quoting Ibn Hayyan.

ANDALUCIA IN THE NINTH CENTURY

the inhabitants of the place. We take this to mean that although the Governor and his entourage might be loyal to the Ommeyads, the mass of the people disliked and often disobeyed them.

The accounts given by different writers of Prince Mohammed's part in the events which followed his father's accession, and especially of his course of action at Seville, are so hopelessly contradictory that no coherent narrative can be obtained from any one writer, and least of all from Ibn Hayyan or Gayangos. But by piecing together fragmentary allusions to names, places, and dates in passages taken from different authors, we have managed to extract a fairly convincing explanation of the causes and results of the tragedy of this young prince, whose fate Ibn Hayyan and other Sunnite historians seem purposely to have left in obscurity, regardless of the great part played by his son in the history of their nation.

Mohammed, although endowed with learning, prudence, and courage, was on bad terms with his father and with the other members of his family, apparently on account of a love affair with a Christian girl named Mary, whom he married some time between 888 and 890.[1]

---

[1] Conde, i. 327, 358; Casiri, ii. 35. It appears that Mohammed himself was a Muwallad, for the author of the *Crónica general* says that he found " in a very old book " in the library of St. Isidore of Leon, a copy of which is in the Escorial, a genealogy of Abderrahman III., tracing his descent, on the female side, from King (or Duke) Iñigo Arista of Navarre. Iñigo had a son Garci Iñiguez, he had a daughter Iñiga, who married the Sultan Abdullah *en secondes noces*, and was the mother of Mohammed. Makkari tells us (ii. 127) that in 861 the Sultan Mohammed raided the territory of Pamplona, and carried back with him Fortunio, one of the sons of Garci Iñiguez, king of Navarre, who remained in captivity in Cordova for twenty years. The author of the *Crónica general* finds independent confirmation of this story in Roderick of Toledo's History of the Arabs, and in " ancient documents," and plausibly conjectures that when Mohammed carried off Fortunio, his sister Iñiga went with him. He adds that when Garci Iñiguez was killed in 885, there was an interregnum in the kingdom of Navarre, until Fortunio was released, after the death of Mohammed and Al-Mundhir, by his brother-in-law Abdullah. (*Crónica general,* viii. 102–4.)

It is easy to understand that if Mohammed, the son of a Christian, had fallen in love with and married a Christian, the fact would be likely to cause friction with the orthodox Sunnites of his family. There is no doubt that Mohammed's wife Mary belonged to Princess Sara's family, for some fifty years later we find a long account of the dealings of his son Abderrahman III. with "his cousin Ahmed Ibn Ishak," who was of Christian parentage, and a descendant of Sara by her first husband. And we are inclined to think that she may have been the daughter or niece of " King " Abdullah Ibn Hejjaj himself, from the careful suppression of her father's name by Makkari, who calls her Moznah *tout court*.[1]

When Mohammed reached Seville, the city was in a turmoil on account of a quarrel between the Muwallads and the clients of Abdullah, the details of which we may omit. The contending parties had already sent messengers to lay their respective sides of the case before the Sultan at Cordova, and Mohammed had been charged by his father to pacify the disputants. After hearing both sides, he sent to request Abdullah to delay his decision on the case, as about to be laid before him by messengers on the road, because the matter was complicated and demanded careful consideration. But Abdullah, influenced by Al-Motref, who always put forward the view inimical to Mohammed, ignored his eldest son's advice and even treated it as evidence of disloyalty, for no better reason than that Mohammed had meanwhile permitted Ibn Ghalib, one of the persons concerned, to return provisionally to the castle of which the Ommeyad party were endeavouring to deprive him.

The Muwallad party rejoiced, regarding the young

[1] Makkari, ii. 145. Arabic scholars would know whether " Maria " could become " Moznah " through copyists' errors. The necessary change seems to be only an alteration of points. Cf. Pons, *Escrituras Mozarabes*, p. 67 note.

ANDALUCIA IN THE NINTH CENTURY

prince's kindness to their friend as evidence of his sympathy with themselves. But Abdullah was highly incensed, had Ibn Ghalib seized and put to death, and sent another member of the royal family, named Omeya, to replace Mohammed as Governor of Seville, whereupon that prince threw in his lot with the Muwallads and Yemenites, and remained with them till his death.[1]

When Abdullah heard that his own brothers Al-Kasim and Al-Asbagh, as well as his son Mohammed, had joined the rebellious leaders of Lucena and Estepa, and those of Elvira, Rayah, and the Serrania of Ronda, and found that many of the ostensibly loyal Wizirs and citizens refused to obey his orders to make war on the people and district of Jaen, he grew anxious lest his son Mohammed should raise the banner of rebellion in the district of Jerez and (Medina) Sidonia also. For the Governors of those cities were his uncles (Al-Kasim and Al-Asbagh), and had always favoured him. He therefore sent Al-Motref to Seville, hoping that his prudent counsels might soothe " the restless and proud spirit " of the elder brother, while he himself went to besiege Toledo, a stronghold of the Christians, which for years past had been disputing the Moslem rule.

Mohammed, however—who must have had a just grievance to account for his father's evident desire to placate him—refused to make terms or even to enter into negotiations with Al-Motref. That prince wrote to Abdullah that he was not allowed to enter Seville, and that Mohammed declined to reply to his letters. Possibly Mohammed knew

---

[1] Perhaps Mohammed feared that if he fell into his father's hands his life would not be safe. Apparently, too, he was now married, and would have been separated from his wife had he left Seville. No information whatever is given by the Sunnite historians of the Ommeyad dynasty (so far as we have been able to procure translations of their works) as to the proceedings of the heir to the throne after he was superseded as Governor of Seville, and Gayangos says that he could find no more on the subject than we have quoted here.

by experience how little he could depend on his brother as an intermediary.

Many rebels had joined him, and were urging him to attack Cordova, and his allies had already roused the whole district of Jaen, where lay the estates of the descendants of Artebas. Indeed, the situation appeared so serious to Al-Motref, who seems to have been a competent soldier, that he recommended the Sultan to leave the siege of Toledo to his officers, and return immediately to Cordova.

On this Abdullah hastened back, and arranged a plan of campaign with Al-Motref, which included making war upon Mohammed until he should be driven out of Seville and taken prisoner, while the country should be quieted by the punishment of the rebels. Little did either Abdullah or Al-Motref imagine that it would take over a quarter of a century to accomplish this.[1]

For the next five years Mahommed was one of the leaders, if not the supreme chief, of the Muwallads. While Omar Ibn Hafsun carried on continual war in the district of which his fortress of Bishter was the centre, Mohammed and the ruler of Seville, Abdullah Ibn Hejjaj, held their own without difficulty in the territories of Seville, Niebla, and Carmona; Al-Motref fought with varying fortune against his brother at Sidonia, Jerez, Estepa, and Carmona, while Ibn Hejjaj, with his guard of five hundred horsemen, protected the environs of Seville.

A glance at the map will show that this long civil war ranged over, and was practically confined to, the territories owned by the Gothic princes in the eighth century, and their allies the Yemenites; a fact which goes far to show that, whatever Ibn Hayyan chose to call it, it was in reality a prolonged and determined effort to overthrow

[1] Conde, I. chapters lx.-lxii.; Gayangos in Makkari, ii. 460-1; Dozy, *G. der M.*, i. 398 ff.

ANDALUCIA IN THE NINTH CENTURY

the Cordovan dynasty in favour of a ruler descended from Witiza.

Whether the Muwallads had intended to offer the throne to Mohammed himself, in right of his wife, it is impossible to say, for any such scheme, if formed, was nipped in the bud by the premature death of the young prince, after five years of fighting side by side with his Sevillian connections. It was during those five years (Dozy says in 891) that his only child was born, he who afterwards became the great ruler Abderrahman III. Abderrahman was twenty-one when he came to the throne in 912, and his father Mohammed was in the Seville district from 888 or 889 to 895.[1]

In 895, when Abdullah returned to Cordova from the siege of Toledo, he sent his cavalry to reinforce the army with which Al-Motref was pursuing the rebels. Conde says that on this occasion Al-Motref took both Seville and Carmona, but the account given by Ibn Hayyan does not imply this. He tells us that Al-Motref halted at a place called Tarbil, on the banks of the Guadaira, two miles from Seville, and from there went on to Carmona, where, although Ibn Hayyan does not mention it, took place a battle in which Mohammed and his uncle Al-Kasim were wounded and taken prisoners.[2]

[1] *G. der M.*, i. 449 note.
[2] Conde, i. 338-9; Makkari, ii. 454. The "Tarbil" mentioned in Ibn Hayyan's account can only be Tablada, two miles from Seville on the vast plain by which that city is surrounded, and lying in an angle formed by the junction of the Guadaira and the Guadalquivir. It is now a recreation ground, where horse racing, pigeon shooting, polo, aviation, and other sports take place. Many times in history Seville's enemies got as far as Tablada, which has always been open to attack, but they seldom got any nearer. The Northmen reached Tablada, but it is doubtful whether they ever got inside the city; and Fernando III. was encamped there for eighteen months in 1247-8, before he was able to enter Seville, although he had all the forces of Christian Spain at his back. Possibly many incidents described as "the taking of Seville" by historians unfamiliar with the ground refer actually to the occupation of Tablada. On this assumption several puzzling contradictions of historical fact would be cleared up.

In this battle the Muwallad forces were completely routed after hard fighting on both sides. Prince Mohammed made a brave stand, as did his knights and all his people; but his horse was killed under him, and he himself, "so full of wounds that he could not move," was carried into the presence of his brother Al-Motref. His uncle Al-Kasim, in much the same case, was also taken before Al-Motref, who ordered that both the wounded princes should be guarded and their wounds attended to. Al-Kasim recovered, and we hear of him again in Seville some years later. But Mohammed died in prison at the age of twenty-eight. Some say that he was poisoned by order of his brother, others say by order of his father; others, again, say that he died of his wounds and his despair. The general opinion is that he was murdered, and the name given to his son commemorated the fact. The child Abderrahman, then aged four, "was called at court the son of Mohammed Al-Maktul (the assassinated)."[1]

[1] Conde, *loc. cit.*: cf. Gayangos in Makkari, ii. 460-1, and Dozy, *G. der M.*, i. 449, quoting Ibn Adhari.

CHAPTER V

ANDALUCIA IN THE NINTH CENTURY (*continued*)

THESE events occurred in 895. Ibn Hayyan tells us that on Al-Motref's return to Seville from the campaign in which the battle of Carmona took place, "he gave orders that Ibrahim Ibn Hejjaj, Khaled Ibn Othman Ibn Khaldun, and Abdalmalek of Sidonia, and their followers, who were kept as hostages in his army, should be brought into his presence. Three days after he ordered them all to be strangled." Conde, however, puts the execution of Ibrahim Ibn Hejjaj in the year 910–911,[1] after another skirmish, the place of which is not given; but if we may assume that Ibn Hayyan (or his copyist) by a slip of the pen wrote Ibrahim for Abdullah, the events which followed will be more intelligible.

No hint is given by Ibn Hayyan as to what became of the infant Prince Abderrahman after the death of his father Mohammed. We think it likely that he was living in Seville under the protection of his mother's relatives until several years later, and that it was in the court of Ibrahim Ibn Hejjaj, who on our hypothesis succeeded his brother Abdullah in 895, that he was given the name of the "son of the assassinated." No one would have dared to give the child such a nick-name within hearing of the Sultan Abdullah or his son Al-Motref, at whose hands Mohammed had died, whereas in Seville it would be a title of honour, since his

---

[1] Conde, i. 350; but as to the date, see note, p. 88. Ibn Hayyan in Makkari, ii. 454.

father would there be regarded as a martyr to the cause of the Muwallads and Yemenites, of whom Ibn Hejjaj was the "king." And certainly the story could only have been chronicled by a writer of that party.

If we may assume that Conde is correct in postponing the death of Ibrahim Ibn Hejjaj until several years later than the date given by Ibn Hayyan, and, further, that the Ibn Hejjaj executed by Al-Motref was not Ibrahim, but Abdullah, his account becomes somewhat less inexplicable, for there is little indication given by Hayyan or any other writer that Seville had really been conquered or pacified by any member of the Cordovan party, while the evidence that the Beni Hejjaj still ruled there is strong.

Conde says that in 902 the Sultan Abdullah, instead of yielding to the "fanatics" who urged him to come to terms with Ibn Hafsun and declare war against the Christians, sent his general, Obeidallah Ibn Gamri, to treat with Alfonso III., King of Galicia and Leon, and that Ibn Gamri succeeded in making terms with him, and getting him to agree to "make ceaseless war on the rebels who reached his frontiers."[1] The alternative to this treaty seems to have been peace with Ibn Hafsun. These negotiations are said by the authority from whom Conde took this chapter of his work, to have offended "the austere Moslems of Andalucia" to such an extent that in some cities they omitted Abdullah's name from the Khotba or daily prayer for the king, as though he were a bad Moslem or excommunicated. But the suggestion thus offered that it was a religious and not a political dispute is negatived by the next sentence. The Yemenites never were "austere and very religious" in the Sunnite sense, as the people who omitted Abdullah's name are said to have been. On the contrary, they are often spoken of by

[1] Conde, i. 344-5.

the Syrian writers as careless and negligent of the stricter laws of Islam. So when we learn that it was especially in Seville, the capital of the Yemenites and Muwallads, that this public insult was offered "with the greatest audacity" to the Cordovan ruler, and that these "insolent opinions" were encouraged there by Al-Kasim, Abdullah's brother, we know that the trouble was not religious but political.

In a previous chapter, we are told that Abdullah had desired to win Al-Kasim back to his allegiance by giving him the Governorship of Seville after the fight at Carmona, in which he and his nephew Mohammed were defeated, but that Al-Motref had opposed his father's desire, so that Al-Kasim was left "forgotten as if in prison." Apparently he had escaped in the interval, or perhaps Abdullah had for once acted in defiance of Al-Motref's advice, since in 902 we find Al-Kasim once more influential among the Sevillians.

When reports of what was going on in Seville came to the ears of Abdullah, he sent one of his Wizirs, presumably in disguise, to find out the facts. The Wizir, who was an astute and brave man, found out that what had been communicated to the king was true, and that instead of his name they put in the public prayer that of the "Khalif of the East,"[1] while Al-Kasim publicly said that the *azaque* ought not to be paid to Abdullah, because he was a bad Moslem and an unbeliever, who used the tithe against the Moslems.[2] Thereupon Abdullah had him seized and poisoned in prison.[3]

Probably the real ground of the offence taken by the

[1] The Abbasside, who as a Shiite and a descendant of the murderer of the Ommeyads was the racial and religious foe of the Cordova party.

[2] The *azaque* was the proportion of their goods which the Moslems were supposed to devote to the service of God—a sort of tithe.

[3] Conde, i. 344-6. It is not clear how Al-Kasim, who apparently was in an almost independent position in Seville, should have been so easily captured by Abdullah. Probably the Wizir caught him by a stratagem.

Yemenites and Muwallads of Seville against Abdullah, with whom they appear to have been more or less at truce from 895 to 902, was his treaty with Alfonso III. against their own ally Ibn Hafsun (see next chapter), who, although himself a Christian, was bound by ties of friendship and relationship with numerous families belonging to the tribes of Yemen.

At this crisis, however, the relations between the Beni Hejjaj and Abdullah suddenly entered upon a new phase. Dozy says that Abdullah became friends with Ibn Hejjaj, and since Seville was the focus of the rebellion, once he had disarmed the hostility of this chief of the rebels, Niebla and all the other centres of disaffection down to Algeciras followed suit. He explains the change by a long story, of which we shall presently give the gist, about Abdullah holding Ibn Hejjaj's son as a hostage, and inducing the father to submit by restoring the lad to him.[1]

Conde tells us that in the year 910–911 Al-Motref surprised the Muwallad troops, and that in order to save their own lives they handed over their leader Ibrahim Ibn Hejjaj, and Al-Motref cut his head off.[2]

In this same year, says Conde, the general Obeidallah Ibn Gamri, who had won so many victories over the rebels, found that Al-Motref was persuading his father to retire him (Ibn Gamri) from his military command and his governorship of the Province of Merida, on the ground that his advanced age required him to repose after the fatigues of the last war. Abdullah objected, but Al-Motref pressed the

---

[1] *G. der M.*, i. 441-7.
[2] Conde, i. 350. The date here given by Conde (H. 298, A.D. 910–1) is obviously erroneous, for we are informed elsewhere that for the last nine years of his reign Abdullah was at peace with the Beni Hejjaj. By reading H. 289 (A.D. 902) instead of H. 298, however, we get something like chronological sequence in the incidents recorded by different writers, and in order to do this we make the necessary alteration in Conde's date.

matter, the real reason being that he wanted Ibn Gamri's appointment for himself. When this came to Ibn Gamri's ears, he adopted the dignified course of voluntarily resigning his position in favour of Al-Motref, on the excuse that he wished for long leave in order to make his pilgrimage to Mecca. The pilgrimage, however, seems to have been abandoned, for when he came to Cordova on his retirement, Abdullah made him captain of his guard of Slavs, " who were foreign orientals, much respected for their courtesy and courage, and great faithfulness. They were the guards of the interior of the palace, and bore a two-handed sword, a shield, and a mace."

Al-Motref being away, beheading or spearing all the rebels he could lay his hands on, and making himself feared by friends and foes alike for the severity of his military discipline, Ibn Gamri took the opportunity of revenging himself upon this prince by introducing to Abdullah his grandson, who would be the natural heir to the throne were he in Abdullah's good graces. He declared himself the protector of the young Abderrahman, son of Mohammed the assassinated, and contrived to win the heart of the king and the affection of the Sheikhs, Walis, Wizirs, and other influential personages on behalf of the lad. Abdullah suppressed all outward show of favour for fear of annoying his son Al-Motref, but in private he heard with much complacency the praises of his grandson, whose gentleness and amiable qualities made him the delight of Cordova.[1]

This passage (evidently taken from a Shiite writer) shows that Abdullah was afraid of his son, who was believed by many to have determined on obtaining the succession for himself, as would have been natural enough had both Mohammed and his son been dead. It also suggests that

[1] Conde, i. 351-2.

owing to Al-Motref's jealousy the young Abderrahman had hitherto been kept carefully out of sight.

Let us now look at Dozy's story of the "son" of Ibn Hejjaj in the light thrown upon it by Abdullah's care to conceal his affection for his Muwallad grandchild "in order not to cause uneasiness" to Al-Motref. His account of the pacification of Seville is very long; it may be summarised as follows :—

In 899, Ibrahim Ibn Hejjaj saw a letter written to the Sultan Abdullah by Khaled Ibn Khaldun, from which he learnt that Ibn Khaldun was plotting against him. He reproached Khaled and his brother Koreib with their treachery. Khaled attacked and wounded him, whereupon he summoned help and killed them both. From now on, says Dozy, he was the sole lord of the Province of Seville, but as he felt that he must justify his conduct to the Sultan, who still had his son in his power,[1] he wrote to him that he could not have acted otherwise than he did, that the Khalduns had continually urged him to rebel, that at the bottom of his heart he had never shared their views, and that if the Sultan would appoint him Governor of Seville, he would bear all the expenses of the public service, and would pay in addition 7000 ducats a year. The Sultan accepted the offer, and sent "a certain Kasim" to Seville as joint ruler; but Ibrahim soon gave Kasim to understand that his services would not be needed.

It certainly seems strange that Ibn Hejjaj, if he could humble himself as described in order to obtain favours of Abdullah, should have entirely omitted to include among these the restoration of his son, while offering such liberal terms in return for his appointment as Governor of the district of which we are informed he was already sole lord.

[1] This seems to be the first mention of this son of Hejjaj, whom we presently find to be named Abderrahman.

Having secured his Governorship and got rid of " a certain Kasim," Dozy tells us that he now demanded the return of his son; he asked for him several times, but Abdullah obstinately refused to surrender him, although Ibrahim endeavoured to secure his object by threatening to withhold the tribute, and to make an alliance with Omar Ibn Hafsun.

The curious result of Ibrahim's threat was a treaty of peace between Ibn Hafsun and the Sultan, not between Ibrahim and the Sultan, or Ibrahim and Hafsun, as we should have expected.

The truce was short-lived; it was agreed upon in 901 and broken in 902, when Ibn Hafsun attacked the Cordovan troops under Ibn Gamri and defeated them. Directly Abdullah heard the news of this reverse, he had three of Ibn Hafsun's hostages executed, the fourth being spared on swearing allegiance.

"Then came the turn of Abderrahman, son of Ibrahim Ibn Hejjaj," which suggests that Ibn Hejjaj was out with Ibn Hafsun on this occasion, unless we are to take it that Ibn Hejjaj's alliance with Ibn Hafsun—entered into as a defiance of the Sultan—involved him in the truce made the previous year between Abdullah and Ibn Hafsun. It will be seen that Dozy's own statements are sometimes difficult to reconcile one with another.

Abdullah had ordered the young Abderrahman to be taken out and executed, when the slave Bedr, who was friendly with Ibn Hejjaj, pressed some common sense upon the incensed monarch.

Ibn Hejjaj, he reminded him, had promised to submit to his rule when his son was restored to him. If the lad were now put to death, Abdullah would not only have to contend with Ibn Hafsun, who, being a Spaniard, would never forgive the execution of his hostages, but also with the undying enmity of the ruler of Seville. He was an Arab, and it was not yet impossible to win him over to the Sultan's side as matters stood, but if the young Abderrahman were killed, Hafsun and Hejjaj would be bound together in lasting hostility to the Sultan.

Abdullah wavered when this aspect of the case was put before him. Bedr proceeded to assure him that he could answer for the loyalty of the Sevillian chiefs, once the son of Hejjaj was set free; and eventually Abderrahman was sent back to his father, after having been six years absent from Seville.[1]

If these events occurred, as Dozy says, in the year 902, this young Abderrahman must have fallen into the hands of Abdullah about 895, the year of Prince Mohammed's defeat and death.

Afterwards, says Dozy, for the last nine years of Abdullah's reign, Ibn Hejjaj kept the peace, and paid his tribute so punctually that there was no need to send troops into the district. And this desirable state of things being the result of the good advice of Bedr the Slav, Abdullah made him a Wizir, and treated him with so much confidence that he became Prime Minister in fact, if not in name.[2]

This Abderrahman is not mentioned again until 913. During the interval Ibrahim died, and was succeeded, says Dozy, on what was practically the throne of Seville by his son Abderrahman. In or about the year when Abderrahman III. succeeded his grandfather Abdullah at Cordova, the other Abderrahman (Ibn Hejjaj) died, and his place was taken by his brother Mohammed, who swore allegiance to the new Sultan.[3]

Setting aside now once for all the attempt to reconcile

[1] Dozy, *G. der M.*, i. 438–44.
[2] *Ibid.*, i. 447.
[3] *Ibid.*, i. 456.

different versions of the story, we will offer that which we have deduced from Dozy's narrative of the hostage Abderrahman, and Conde's account of the youth of Abderrahman III., premising that we hold the two Abderrahmans to have been one and the same—namely, the son of Prince Mohammed and his wife Mary, and that the inextricable confusion in the accounts of the hostages and the various executions of the different members of the Beni Hejjaj is due to the suppression of the truth by the Sunnite historians, who regarded it as a political if not a religious duty to obscure the events of this long period of defeat and disgrace. We do not pretend to say that our story is the true one; but we think we may say that it has more plausibility than any other version of the same occurrences.

When Prince Mohammed died, in 895, his child was at Seville with his mother. The Sultan Abdullah, who really loved his eldest son, notwithstanding all that had come between them, would have taken the little orphan under his own protection, but was dissuaded by Al-Motref, who had no desire whatever to see the natural heir to the throne growing up under his grandfather's care. The Beni Hejjaj at the moment were disheartened by the loss not only of their young commander, but still more so by the murder of their own chief, Abdullah Ibn Hejjaj, who had been taken prisoner at Carmona, together with Prince Mohammed, Prince Al-Kasim, Khaled Ibn Khaldun, and other Yemenite and Muwallad leaders. Abdullah Ibn Hejjaj had been retained as a hostage by Al-Motref, who soon afterwards had him strangled, for reasons which Ibn Hayyan, who relates the fact, does not give.

The Seville party were not long in recovering from their reverse, for in the same year Abdullah's brother and heir, Ibrahim Ibn Hejjaj, made terms with the Sultan Abdullah for the sole control of his own dominions. The lever which he used to obtain his appointment as Governor of Seville,[1] was the guardianship of Prince Mohammed's child. The conditions upon which Abdullah agreed to Ibrahim's demands were the following, secretly imposed in order to avoid protest from Al-Motref, and, therefore, unknown to the Sunnite writers, upon whom Ibn Hayyan depended, though currently known among the Seville party and their historians.

The greatest care was to be taken with the up-bringing of the little prince from the time that he was weaned, which was about the period of his father's death. He was to be given the most famous masters, who were to instruct him in the learning most suitable to his age and position. He was to have the Koran read to him, and to learn its doctrines by heart; and as soon as he was eight years old, he was to be taught the Sunna and the Hadith, grammar, poetry, and Arabic proverbs, lives of princes, the science of government, and all other human wisdom. He was also to be taught to ride and to manage his horse in the complicated exercises usual among good horsemen, to use the bow and arrows and the lance, and to be expert in all the arms and stratagems of war. In short, he was to be given an education which should fit him to become a ruling monarch.[2]

Ibrahim, having agreed to educate the child Abderrahman on these lines, a truce was made between him and the Sultan, which left Ibn Hejjaj as much king in his own country as his brother had been before him. And that the Beni Hejjaj honourably fulfilled the conditions is proved by the brilliant success of their pupil, when he came to man's estate, in all the arts and accomplishments of which the foundation had been laid by his Seville masters.

The truce was kept between Seville and Cordova until

---

[1] This event Ibn Hayyan puts in the year 889 (Makkari, ii. 451); Dozy in the year 899 (*G. der M.*, i. 438-9).
[2] Conde, i. 355-6.

901 or 902, when the Sultan's alliance with Alfonso III. of Leon against Ibn Hafsun, a relation of the various Muwallad families of which Ibn Hejjaj was the chief, produced such ill-feeling as to lead to the omission of Abdullah's name from the Khotba, where, as over-lord, he should have been prayed for daily. And in the course of the campaign which followed between Ibn Hafsun and the Sevillians against the forces of Abdullah, a party of Muwallads belonging to the court of Seville were surprised by the vanguard of Al-Motref, and, on his threatening to put them all to the sword, they gave up, not Ibrahim, but the young Abderrahman, now eight years old, as a hostage for the rest.[1]

That same year Ibn Gamri, who had hitherto been loyal to Al-Motref, even while disapproving of his bloodthirsty methods of dealing with the rebellion, was arbitrarily removed from his position as Governor of Merida and Commander-in-Chief of the army in that territory, by Al-Motref, who had some ground of quarrel against him—possibly too great a sympathy with the son of his dead brother, Mohammed. Ibn Gamri thereupon retired to Cordova, where Abdullah, evidently not sharing his son's views in the matter, gave him the captaincy of his own bodyguard, whose station was within the royal palace.

Then Ibn Gamri came forward openly as a protector of the young Prince Abderrahman, and used his position in the palace to gain the Sultan's private ear. He played his cards so well that he succeeded in winning the favour, not only of Abdullah, but of the Wizirs and all the principal persons at Court for his *protégé*. Soon Abderrahman's charm of manner (*gentileza, gentillesse*) and amiable qualities became the delight of Cordova. But Abdullah did not show his affection publicly for fear of offending Al-Motref,

[1] Conde, i. 350. As it will be seen, we are taking great liberties with various authors in order to make our story coherent.

although he heard with much complacency in private the general praise bestowed on his grandson.[1]

Ibrahim Ibn Hejjaj, although he was doubtless glad to learn that the young prince was gaining ground with his grandfather, of whom he would, if all went well, be the natural heir, had no confidence in the honour of Al-Motref, who had already frequently shown his indifference to the rights of non-combatants and hostages. He, therefore, made many efforts to obtain the restoration of Abderrahman, whom he appears to have represented as his own son, for fear that if the boy's identity were known he might fall a victim to the jealousy of Al-Motref. But Abdullah refused all overtures in this direction, and Conde's account of his increasing attachment to the lad makes it easy to understand why he would not give him up.

When Al-Motref was due to return from the Merida campaign, Ibrahim, growing ever more anxious as to what would befall the boy, turned from entreaties to threats. Unless Abderrahman were returned safe and sound to Seville, Ibrahim would ally himself with Ibn Hafsun against the Cordovan party, and would pay no more of the 7000 ducats a year which had been the price of his little kinsman's life when he was captured.

At this juncture Al-Motref returned to Cordova, and immediately discovered not only the negotiations with Seville, but the identity of the boy whose interests Ibn Gamri had been so zealously advancing.

We may now take up the story as Dozy wrote it, for by reading " Prince Abderrahman " for " Abderrahman, son of Hejjaj " and " Al-Motref " for " Abdullah," we get ample motives for the attempted murder of the boy.

Hafsun appears to have broken the truce, and if this were so, perhaps the execution of his hostages was justified. But

[1] Conde, i. 352.

to include the hostage of Ibn Hejjaj in the general condemnation, when he had as yet done no more than threaten to go to war if the boy were not restored, suggests that this hostage was a person whose death was desired by the person ordering the death penalty; for Abderrahman was to be killed forthwith, notwithstanding that Ibn Hejjaj had offered to submit to his over-lord once the boy were back in his own keeping.

When all seemed to be lost, and Abderrahman was just about to be executed, the Slave Bedr obtained audience of Abdullah, and implored him to forbid the murder, on the ground that if Abderrahman were slain the Sultan would never overcome the hostility of the Sevillians, whereas they would undoubtedly submit if their young kinsman were restored to them.

Abdullah, who probably had been kept in the dark as to Al-Motref's intentions—for there seems no doubt that he was aware by that time of the boy's birth—not only acted on Bedr's advice, but rewarded him for it by making him a Wizir, and thenceforward gave him so much confidence that Bedr was his Prime Minister in all but name.

After this the Beni Hejjaj kept peace with the Sultan as long as he lived; no doubt because the young Abderrahman remained at the Court of Cordova, where he would form a bond of union between the relatives, who, though opposed in politics, were agreed in their love for him.

Abdullah evidently took courage to acknowledge his affection for his grandson after so nearly losing him for ever, for we read that when the boy was eleven years old he freely played about the gardens of the palace with other lads of his own age, while his grandfather watched him, lost in delight. On one of these occasions night fell without Abdullah observing it, and when his Wizir, Ibn Gamri, warned him of the hour, he improvised a set of verses excusing his abstraction on the ground of the young Abderrahman's charms.

In 911 the Sultan's mother died, and Abdullah, who had loved and honoured her all his life, bitterly mourned her death. He sank into a profound melancholy, became convinced of his own approaching end, and ordered a second sepulchre for himself to be made beside the magnificent one he had erected for her interment in the palace or garden called the Rusafa.

Early in the year 913, feeling that death was near, he called together his Wizirs and Walis, and declared his grandson Abderrahman his successor on the throne, charging Al-Motref to protect and guard him as if he were his own son.

During those nine years of peace Ibrahim Ibn Hejjaj had died, and had been succeeded by his son Mohammed. And among the first of the many formerly rebellious chiefs of the Yemenites and Muwallads who proffered allegiance to the Muwallad monarch of Cordova, was this Mohammed, now Lord of Seville. He died in 915, and the Beni Hejjaj then ceased to play a leading part in Andalusian history,[1] although we meet with a daughter of the house (by birth or adoption) sharing the throne of Seville a hundred and fifty years later.

We give this conjectural version of their history for what it is worth, and our readers will form their own conclusions. As for our theory that the incessant fighting which darkened the twenty-four years of Abdullah's reign was due to the policy of his son Al-Motref rather than to his own, it is supported by one of the unnamed authors quoted by Conde, who sums up Abdullah's character thus:—

"He was a good king, who maintained his courage in the midst of disturbances and discords in every province of Spain, an excellent commander of his troops in war, politic and honourable in observing his compacts; for that he was

[1] Dozy, *G. der M.*, i. 456, 460.

censured by the fanatics as a bad Moslem, for not making continual war on the Christians." [1]

The Christians here referred to must have been the Muwallads, for Abdullah's wars with those of the North were few. The allusion would seem to be to the peace concluded with the Beni Hejjaj during the last decade of his reign, and the "fanatics" who blamed him probably included his son Al-Motref, whose aim was to extirpate the party which protected the young Abderrahman, destined, notwithstanding all his uncle's efforts to get rid of him, to succeed Abdullah on the throne.

In the *Akhbar Majmua* we find some remarks not quoted elsewhere touching the troublous reign of Abdullah. When he came to the throne the forces which had been under his brother Al-Mundhir at Bobaster mutinied and departed, each division to the district and tribe to which it belonged, regardless of the Amir's commands that they should remain where they were, and he was compelled to fly before an attack of his enemy, Omar Hafsun. There were dissensions among the officers in Cordova. Money was scarce, for, owing to the whole of the provinces being in rebellion, the taxes notably diminished. Abdullah economised in every direction, not excepting the pay of his soldiers and personal servants. Meanwhile, he devoted himself to asceticism and manifestations of devotion. It was perhaps hardly surprising that under such conditions disorder increased on every side.[2]

[1] Conde, i. 358.   [2] *Akhbar Majmua*, 131.

CHAPTER VI

"KING OMAR OF TOLEDO"

EXCEPT for the dealings of Artebas with Abderrahman I., already referred to, we find no direct mention of any branch of the Gothic royal family, except Sara's, until the reign of Al-Mundhir (886-8). But although no record of them survives, it would seem that they were meanwhile multiplying in numbers and increasing in wealth, for when we meet with them again, we find the head of the family in a position to hold his own against the whole strength of the Cordovan Amir, while ruling as a king over his own people, as his distant relative, Ibrahim Ibn Hejjaj, was doing in Seville at the same time.

This was the celebrated Omar Ibn Hafsun, who aimed at, and almost succeeded in, re-establishing the Gothic supremacy in Andalucia, while the Christian kings of Galicia and Navarre were endeavouring to throw off the Moslem yoke in the north of the Peninsula.

Omar's descent has been made the subject of much discussion, for Ibn Hayyan and others of his school not unnaturally recorded every tradition they could find derogatory to the dignity of the man who very nearly broke the power of Islam in Spain. One writer, indeed, goes so far as to say that he was a Berber from the Moghreb.

But Ibn Khaldun, Ibn Adhari, and Ibn Al-Khattib, all carry back his genealogy to one Alfons, whom Ibn Hayyan calls "Count," while Al-Kuttiyyah says that he was descended from Romulo. "As to Romulo . . . he had chosen

Toledo for his capital. Among his descendants one observes Hafs, son of Al-Borkadi, the Stranger."[1]

Dozy (*loc. cit.*) gives various particulars of the immediate parentage of Omar. The names of the son, grandson, and great grandson of Alfons are Gothic or Latin, although badly mutilated by copyists. The name of Omar's father was Hafs (the Ibn Al-Borkadi of Kuttiyyah), but "he was so beloved and honoured by his neighbours that instead of calling him Hafs they called him Hafsun; a termination which is equivalent to a title of nobility." Conde[2] gives his grandfather's name as Giafar, and his great-grandfather's as Arius. Dozy places the family estate, "which had been theirs for a hundred years," in the neighbourhood of Malaga, but there is ground for suspecting the complete accuracy of his account of Omar's rise to fame.

Ibn Hayyan says very little about Omar's genealogy, but he never suggests that he was other than a Christian, and mentions that in 893 "the infidel dog" tried to prevent Al-Motref from destroying a church which his father had erected close to his castle of Bishter.[3] We may take it that the family church would be built on the family estate, and this incident alone goes far to prove that they were people of importance and of old standing, while it contradicts any idea that Omar did not respect his father, or the work by which his father had gained the esteem of his neighbours.

Dozy's account of his early years is very briefly as follows. A quarrelsome youth, he killed one of his neighbours

---

[1] Dozy, *G. der M.*, i. 366 note ; Al-Kuttiyyah in *J.A.*, 432–3. The word which M. Cherbonneau translates "stranger" is "*ajem*," which Gayangos translates as "a Christian not subdued." It is a fair assumption that the "Hafs Ibn Al-Borkadi" of Al-Kuttiyyah was Omar's father; otherwise one cannot understand why Al-Kuttiyyah should have singled him out for special mention. Dozy calls Omar a renegade, and says that renegade and Muwallad were interchangeable terms. (*Ib.* i. 278.)

[2] i. 295.

[3] Makkari, ii. 453.

in a fight, and his father, to save him from the gallows, fled with him from the family estate to the Serrania of Ronda. There the young Omar became a highway robber, fell into the hands of justice, was flogged, and turned out of the house by his father. He left Spain for Tahort, in Africa, but returned after a few weeks in consequence of a prophecy of his future greatness, uttered by an unknown old man. He established himself at Bishter or Bobaster, which Dozy places near Antequera (see p. 106), got together a number of like-minded spirits, and started a career of brigandage about the year 880 or 881. His operations were so successful that in a very short time he was able to put to flight the Governor of the Province, who had attacked him, but nevertheless he was soon afterwards compelled to yield and to go with his whole band to Cordova. The Sultan, " who recognised him as an excellent leader, and his men as good soldiers," took him into his service.

Very soon after this, in 883, he fought well for the Sultan in a campaign against Leon, but on his return he quarrelled with the Prefect of Cordova, and returned with his men to Bobaster " to take up again the adventurous and free life of the woods." He stormed the castle of Bobaster, which had been greatly strengthened, and was held by the Sultan's troops, and forced the garrison to fly in such haste that they left behind the mistress of their commander, whom Omar married (884).

"From this moment," says Dozy, " he was no longer a robber chief, but the head of all the Spaniards in the south," whom he gathered round him by offering to free them from the Moslem yoke. For two years Mohammed, Sultan of Cordova, took no serious steps against him, but in 886 he was badly defeated and wounded by Al-Mundhir, the heir to the throne. In the moment of victory Al-Mundhir had to return to Cordova in consequence of the death of his

"KING OMAR OF TOLEDO" 103

father. Omar invited the lords of a large number of castles to make common cause with him, and " from this moment he was in truth the king of the south." [1]

Dozy's account is principally drawn from Ibn Adhari, a Moroccan historian who wrote in the thirteenth century. It is on the face of it improbable. No plausible explanation is suggested of how a young outlaw, with a following of only a few freebooters, should have contrived in four years to make himself the head of all the Spaniards in the south, and in two more practically their king. Dozy does not mention his descent from Romulo, which would of itself account for his acceptance by the Spaniards of the south as their leader, and Ibn Adhari, writing some four hundred years later, was not likely to be well informed as to Omar's relations with his fellow countrymen.

Conde's account of his early days is very different. He mentions the possession of the " robber " castle of Bobaster or Bishter, which, he says, " is one of the various accounts that there are in Spain of the beginning of his rebellion," and goes on to say that being driven out of Andalucia, he went " with his bandits " to the frontiers of Afranc (France) and settled in the fortress of Rotalyehud (Rottat al Yahud, now Roda, near Zaragoza), where he was joined by the Governor of Lerida and the Christians of the mountains of Afranc. After an unsuccessful campaign, Mohammed took Roda, and drove him out, and he took refuge " in the mountains of Arbe " (the Sierra de Sobrarbe, north of Huesca). In 876-7, Hafsun, who had taken shelter with the Christians of Afranc (he seems to be lost sight of between 864 and now), " offered them homage and tribute, and to deliver them to the frontier fortresses, and with their help he occupied the forts on the Segre (a tributary of the Ebro) and they called him king, and he paid them tribute, and he

[1] Dozy, *G. der M.*, i. 366-73.

sold the cities to the enemies of Islam." In 882 he was defeated by Al-Mundhir,[1] and in 883 he is again found raiding in the district of Borja, near Lerida, coming down from the mountains of Jaca (near Lerida and Fraga; *see* Idrisi, p. 11) : " they called him king of those parts," and he defeated a force sent against him by Al-Mundhir.[2]

On the death of Mohammed, in 886, Hafsun " again came out of his mountains," got possession of Zaragoza and Huesca, advanced to Toledo, fortified the castles on the Tagus, together with Ucles and Huete, Alarcon and Cuenca,[3] and, by means of a stratagem, entered Toledo.[4]

Makkari does not help us much. He mentions the campaign of 881, in which Hafsun was defeated by Al-Mundhir. This expedition, Gayangos says, was directed in the first place against Zaragoza. The royal troops under Al-Mundhir laid waste the environs of that city, and took by storm the castle of Roda. From thence the army went to Borja, then to Lerida, and lastly to the district called Birtannieh (in the present province of Huesca, of which Barbastro was the strongest fortress: *see* Makkari, ii. 265), from whence they penetrated into Castile and Alava.[5]

---

[1] Conde says that he died of his wounds, and that a son of his carried on the war, but this is an obvious error.

[2] Señor Codera refers to Conde's account of Hafsun's campaigns in the North, which, he says, " does not merit the honour of discussion." But he says that the Arabic writers mention, with numerous though obscure details, the campaign of Al-Mundhir in 882, with allusions to several of the place-names referred to by Conde. (*Estudios*, 231–2.)

[3] These all lie to the east of Toledo, in the present province of Cuenca.

[4] Conde, i. 295–321.

[5] Makkari, ii. 436, quoting An-Nuwairi. The storming of Roda, which Makkari and Gayangos assign to the year 881, Conde puts in 870, but his dates are frequently wrong. The word translated by Gayangos as " Castile " should probably be " the Castles." It is very doubtful whether the present Castile was known by that name to Arabic writers until a good deal later, and in Makkari (ii. 127) " The Castles " are twice named in connection with Alava in the account of Mohammed's campaigns.

Señor Codera, in his *Decadencia de los Almoravides*, has savagely attacked Conde for his account of Hafsun's adventures in the

"KING OMAR OF TOLEDO"

Omar comes very much to the fore in 886, on the accession of Al-Mundhir. That Amir's reign, says Makkari, was of short duration and mostly spent in war with Omar Ibn Hafsun, "a man of Christian origin, who rose during the lifetime of Al-Mundhir's father Mohammed, and whose craftiness and perfidy are demonstrated sufficiently in the histories of that time. . . . With this man Al-Mundhir had to fight many pitched battles, and after defeating him in several partial encounters, Al-Mundhir fell a victim to his own intrepidity, and was killed in a skirmish near Yobashter (Bishter) in 888, after a reign of barely two years." [1]

Before going further we must say something about the situation of Bishter, or Bobaster, for that strong fortress was almost always the centre of Hafsun's operations.

Al-Homaidi mentions a castle in the district of Rayah, called Yobashter, and a strong fortress near Malaga, called Bobashter, which are probably one and the same.[2] Conde and Ibn Hayyan both mention a place of the name in Rayah, and Conde further mentions a Yebaster belonging to the Beni Idris of Malaga, which seems to be the place

north. Conde, he says, mistook Bobaster or Bishter, the centre of Hafsun's operations, for Barbastro in Aragon, and therefore transferred the whole scene to Barbastro, altering the names of the surrounding places accordingly. This, as Señor Codera admits, is a charge of deliberate falsification, in which he persists, although he admits the possibility that Conde had before him some Arabic MS. containing the account of these wars as he gives it. Had Señor Codera read Conde before bringing these charges, he would have seen that in the only mention made of Yabaster, as Conde spells the name of Hafsun's stronghold, it is distinctly stated that it was in Andalucia. "He and his followers fortified themselves in Adherwera in the castle there known as Calat-Yabaster. . . . In the year 250, being driven out of Andalucia, he went with his bandits to the frontiers of Afranc." (i. 295-6.) The only mention of Barbastro in Aragon that Conde makes in his account of Hafsun's adventures in those parts is at page 297, where he says that Hafsun offered Mohammed to turn his arms against those of Afranc, and asked to be given the Governorship of Huesca or Barbastar. The acrimony and injustice with which Conde is attacked both by Señor Codera and by Gayangos, his fellow-countrymen, are inexplicable

[1] Makkari, ii. 130-1.
[2] Bishter, Bobaster, and Yobashter are practically identical in Arabic, with the variation of a single point.

referred to in the extracts from Al-Homaidi printed in Makkari. Gayangos is convinced that this castle, in the district of Rayah, of which Malaga was the capital, is the Bishter of Ibn Hafsun. Neither Bishter nor Yobashter are now to be found on the map, but Gayangos mentions a small hamlet called Abistar, in the Axarquia of Malaga, which he thinks might be the Bishter of the Arabs.[1]

Dozy has examined the question at great length in his *Recherches*[2] and concludes that Bishter was on the site of a Roman fort, the Municipium Singiliense Barbastrense, about a mile west of Antequera. Idrisi (p. 10) mentions a town Bobastero (*sic* in the Spanish translation) in the province of Rayah, a district which would include the site assigned by Dozy. And this situation fits in more or less with the brief accounts of some of the campaigns against Ibn Hafsun, given by Ibn Hayyan. Thus, in 891, Abdullah fought Hafsun at Hisn Belay, near Cabra, defeated him, and pursued him to Archidona and Bishter.[3]

But Conde, in his notes to the geography of Idrisi, says that Bishter is what is now the small town of Vilches, between the Guadalen and the Guarizaz, tributaries of the Guadalimar in the north of the province of Jaen. This, Gayangos says, is erroneous, because the province of Rayah never extended beyond what is now the province of Malaga.[4] The position, however, agrees with the account of another campaign, which the Antequera site would make unintelligible. In 897, says Hayyan, an army went from Cordova to chastise "the rebel." After giving the outward route, which includes Tarifa and Algeciras, besides several other places which we cannot trace, he goes on: "Thence the army returned to Kasr Bineyrah (Pineira), and the next march

---

[1] Conde, i. 295, ii. 16; Makkari, ii. 456, 438, App. B., p. xviii.
[2] i. 323-7.
[3] Makkari, ii. 451-2.
[4] Makkari, ii. 438, where Conde is quoted.

took them to Wady Beni Abderrahman . . . opposite to Bishter. After besieging the rebel in his castle, and doing all possible harm to the districts which obeyed his rule, the army returned by the Alpujarras and Jaen to Cordova." [1]

To go from Antequera or its neighbourhood to Cordova, viâ Jaen, would involve an immense detour, which cannot have been necessary when the army had done its work, and was going home. But Jaen hardly lies off the direct road from Vilches to Cordova, and a visit to that city may have been necessary for some military purpose, such as victualling the troops.

The Alpujarras, mentioned frequently during these wars, is usually supposed to be the mountain range of that name on the coast-line between Malaga and Almeria; but Idrisi distinctly states that Alpujarras was a province, of which Jaen was the capital. He does not as a rule give the points of the compass, but he mentions that the province of Farmera, which contains the town of Baeza, borders on that of Alpujarras, which, he adds, contained a great number of castles.

Vilches is near the ruins of Cazlona, which in Omar Ibn Hafsun's time was a great fortress in the possession of Ibn Ash-Shaliyyah, a connection by marriage of Omar. Thus the pass over the Sierra Morena to Toledo was completely controlled by the leader of the Christians and Muwallads during the civil war, as long as he and his friends held the two fortresses.

Near Vilches there is still a little town called Guarraman, which might well be named from the Wady Beni Abderrahman of Hayyan, if we accept Conde's identification of Vilches with Hafsun's Bishter.[2]

In the life of Argentea, daughter of Ibn Hafsun (see

---

[1] Makkari, ii. 455.
[2] Dozy identifies this river with the Guadaljorce; for no reason, apparently, except that there is a river of that name near the site which he assigns to Bishter. (*Recherches, loc. cit.*)

below), we are told that she was born in the " city " (*urbs*) of Bishter. A fortress perched on the top of an almost inaccessible rock, which is how Bishter is described by Dozy, could hardly be accounted a city. Idrisi, it is true, speaks of a town of Bobaster in the province of Rayah, but of this no trace remains, unless it be Gayangos' " Abistar in the Axarquia of Malaga," the situation of which does not in the least agree with Dozy's identification of Bishter with the Roman Singilis. The alternative is Conde's suggestion of Vilches.

It is not possible to reconcile all the statements made about Bishter with any of the sites assigned by Dozy, Gayangos, or Conde, and the only satisfactory solution is that there were two places of the same or similar names, one on the site of the present Vilches, the other, as Dozy says, near Antequera. In this case we may suppose that the Vilches Bishter was the " city " where Argentea was born, and of which her father was " king," and the Antequera Bishter a rock fortress where he occasionally took refuge when hard pressed. Except on this assumption the identification of Bishter is an insoluble problem.

In the life of Hafsun's daughter Argentea, already referred to, we are told that she was nobly born in the city of Bibister, her father being Samuel, a king, and her mother Columba. She became a nun, and asked her father to turn his castle into a convent for her.[1] Dozy, in relating this, says that Hafsun was baptised in his old age under the name of Samuel, and that Bishter then became a focus of fanaticism as determined as that which obsessed the monks of Cordova sixty years earlier.[2] It is worth noting that so late as the

---

[1] Vita b. virginis Argenteæ, in *España sagrada*, x. 564 ff. The writer is unknown, but the Editor of the collection says that from internal evidence it was written in Cordova in the middle or towards the end of the tenth century.

[2] *G. der M.*, i. 452–3.

middle of the tenth century the lord of Bishter was accounted a king by the Christian chronicler, as well as by the Moslem writers. That Omar ever was a Mohammedan is disproved by every incident in his career, from his care of the church built by his father, to his death as the leader of the Christian party in Andalucia; while throughout the civil war his fortresses were a refuge for men of that faith. We may instance as an example, Count Servandus, or Sherbil, the son of Count Hejjaj, referred to on p. 24. Fearing for his life in Cordova, Servandus fled in 889 to Omar, who gave him the command of part of his forces. Dozy has a long account of this Servandus, drawn mainly from the writings of the Spanish abbot Sampson, who exhausts a copious vocabulary of abuse to characterise Servandus' treatment of the Christians of Cordova at the time of the martyr epidemic, during part of which he was in high official position as Count of the Christians. But it may be doubted whether Servandus Count of the Christians was, as Dozy tells us, the man whom we find nearly forty years later flying from Cordova to take refuge with Ibn Hafsun. If he was, he must have been a very old man, and his father, Count Hejjaj, who is said to have been executed with him by the Sultan Abdullah, well over a hundred years of age. Be this as it may, it seems clear that one Servandus, or Sherbil, a Christian, took refuge with Ibn Hafsun, when he was threatened with death by the Moslems of Cordova. In another passage, Ibn Hayyan says that the refugee was the son of Count Servandus, which seems more probable.[1]

In Dozy's account of this episode we get a valuable side light from Ibn Hayyan upon the condition of Andalucia when Servandus joined Omar. He incidentally mentions that outside of Cordova the Sultan was powerless, and that Hafsun had possessed himself of all the strongest fortresses

[1] Dozy, *G. der M.*, i. 414–6 ; Makkari, ii. 451–2.

to the south of the Guadalquivir,[1] that Abdullah no longer offered to any one the empty titles of Governor of Elvira or Jaen, and that practically all Andalucia had submitted to Omar.

The twenty-four years of Abdullah's reign were taken up with continuous civil war, and Andalucia is usually represented as being at that time torn to pieces by the various conflicting parties—Arabs of Spain and Syria, Yemenites and Mudarites, Berbers and Spaniards, each fighting for his own hand; but although no doubt here and there a lesser chief lost his life at the hands of those who had been, or should have been, his friends, it generally proves—if it be possible by comparing names and dates to arrive at any clear conclusion as to the cause of the execution—that treachery, or the suspicion of an intrigue with the common enemy, was the motive, rather than a quarrel brought about by personal ambitions or private offences. Indeed, the whole course of events shows that the Christians, Muwallads, and Yemenites had in the main the strength that can only be found in unity. A number of petty nobles, each fighting for his own hand, could hardly have stood out for so many years against the whole strength of the Cordovan ruler.

Gayangos, in his translation of Ibn Hayyan's history of the civil war, summarises the different classes of persons mentioned by that historian as enlisted under the banner of the Muwallads.

First we have the *Ahl-adh-Dhimmah*, or "Christians paying tribute," and the *Ajem*, who were "Christians who had never been subdued." There certainly had been no

---

[1] This supports our contention that Hafsun's dominions lay in the centre of Andalucia. The province of Rayah would hardly be described as "to the south of the Guadalquivir." An-Nuwairi mentions "the mountain of Ibn Hafsun" in the neighbourhood of Cordova, a fruitful and well-watered district. (Makkari, ii. 494.)

influx of Christians from the north into Andalucia between 711 and 888, when Abdullah came to the throne. These then must have been the descendants of the Gothic Christians, who had maintained their own religion for nearly two centuries in what we have been taught to regard as the heart of the Moslem territory.

Then we have the *Muradiin,* or Moslems who had deserted their faith ; a curious element in the population, if indeed Mohammedanism was the religion of their effective conquerors. And lastly we have the *Mosalimah,* or Christians converted to Islam, in whom, if Gayangos be right, loyalty to their race must have been stronger than their attachment to their religion.[1] " Over all these motley groups waved the banner of the Muwallads," notwithstanding that, according to Dozy and Gayangos, the Muwallads were renegades, despised and treated as outcasts by the proud Arabs, because they were people of mixed blood.

The situation, as described by Ibn Hayyan and Gayangos, appears an impossible one. The numbers of the different classes named are not in any way indicated, but it is safe to assume that the *Muradiin*—the Moslems who had deserted their faith—cannot at any time have been numerous, unless indeed the Muwallads were so powerful as to make it politic for the common people to gain their protection by professing Christianity. As for the *Mosalimah,* if they were indeed Christians converted to Islam, it is impossible to understand why they should have attached themselves to a party in which their change of religion could only prejudice them in the eyes of their leaders, when they would have been welcomed by the tottering forces of Cordova.

The probability is that the bulk of the forces led by the Muwallads (and we must not forget that Abderrahman III.

[1] Makkari, ii. 458.

himself, and apparently his father Mohammed also, were of this caste) belonged to the first two classes described—the *Ahl-adh-Dhimmah*, or Christians who had been paying tribute since about 711, in order to retain the rights and privileges, the religion and property, secured to them by the treaty with Al-Walid; and the *Ajem*, or "unsubdued Christians."[1] The *Muradiin* and the *Mosalimah*, if they were renegades from their respective faiths, cannot have been numerically of much importance.

The "bad Moslems" who are mentioned by various Sunnite writers, but are not included in any of the above groups, were probably the Shiites or Yemenites connected by marriage with the Muwallads, but true to their own religion, of whom large numbers fought under Ibn Hafsun, as well as under Prince Mohammed. As we shall presently show, these "noble Arabs," as writers who are not Sunnites frequently call them, were always liberal and broad-minded in their dealings with the Christians. The Ommeyad dynasty, with some exceptions, treated the Christians of Cordova well, even endeavouring to protect them from their own fanaticism, as in the epidemic of martyrdom already referred to. But in their case, it seems probable that expediency often, and even necessity sometimes, dictated generosity, whereas the Yemenite kings of Seville in the eleventh century were so completely masters of their large domains that they needed no such motive to induce them to show courtesy and kindness to the Christians at their court. And as we shall see, the conduct of Motamid, the Yemenite king of Seville in the eleventh century, and the relations between Fernando III., the conqueror of Seville, and the Yemenite kings of Granada, Niebla, and Baeza in the thirteenth, show that the Yemenites as a race were men of

[1] It will be remembered that, according to Al-Kuttiyyah, Omar Ibn Hafsun's father was an *Ajem*. See p. 101.

high purpose and broad views of their duty towards their subjects and those of their allies.

It appears to us by no means impossible that the term Muwallad was applied in the ninth century only to the descendants of the Princess Sara, who by that time had become numerous. Omar Ibn Hafsun, for instance, is never called a Muwallad, so far as we can discover, while the Christians of Toledo were known as Mozarabs, a term which never seems to have been applied to the inhabitants of the territory of Seville, whether of Gothic or mixed descent. We have found the term Muwallad applied many times to members of the families which sprang from the marriage of Sara and Omar Ibn Said, not only in and around Seville, but in Niebla and the Algarbe ; and the individuals referred to always figure as leaders of the party opposed to Cordova, and owners of castles and fortresses. If this was the case, Sara, the Gothic Princess, was nothing less than the foundress of a ruling caste, although the offspring of other Christian women marrying Moslems were at once absorbed into their father's race. The point seems worth the attention of Arabic scholars.

Who Omar Ibn Hafsun's mother was, we do not know. But it seems probable that the Hafs family must have been united by ties of blood to some of the Yemenite families, otherwise these would hardly have been so loyal to Omar after the death of Prince Mohammed.

Between 886, when the Sultan Mohammed died, and the accession of Abderrahman III., in 912, Hafsun was continually at war with Cordova, with varying fortunes, inclining on the whole, so far as can be made out, in favour of the Christians. In the year 901, according to Ibn Hayyan, there was a brief respite from hostilities, when Hafsun made proposals for peace, and sent hostages to Cordova. In the following year he is said by the same historian to have broken the treaty he had made, three out of his four hostages being put to death in consequence.[1] In 905, a poet named Soleyman was imprisoned for having written satirical verses about Abdullah. When the Sultan pardoned him and had him released, he threw himself on the ground, and, with his face on Abdullah's feet, informed him that Ibn Hafsun was concealed in Cordova. He was promptly sent back to prison, lest he inform Omar's friends that he had made his presence known; but they, having had previous experience of the poet's machinations, urged Omar to disappear. The Wizirs arrested many persons suspected of disaffection, and some of them were put to the torture. But all that could be discovered was that Omar certainly had been in Cordova, and that he had departed in the guise of a beggar, asking for alms from door to door.[2]

For a long time he was so powerful that he was able to hold the castle of Aguilar (Poley), although this was only a day's journey from Cordova. His cavalry spread themselves round about the capital, and every day, morning and night, advanced as far as the ruins of Secunda [3] and the defile of Almeida, without meeting with any resistance. Things came to such a pitch that one day one of the most adventurous of Omar's knights made an incursion to the defile which dominated Cordova, passed the bridge, and threw his lance at the statue which was over its gate (*Bab-as-Sora*), afterwards returning to rejoin his companions. It was not until twenty-five years later, according to this authority, that Omar was compelled to abandon the Castle of Aguilar

---

[1] Makkari, ii. 456. See p. 91.
[2] Conde, i. 347.
[3] A Roman town on the Guadalquivir opposite Cordova, which had been reduced to a village by the time of the Moslem invasion. The Gothic princes are said to have encamped there when called upon by Roderick to join the forces preparing to resist Tarik, on the ground that they distrusted him too much to enter Cordova. Under Abderrahman III. it recovered importance as a suburb of the city.

"KING OMAR OF TOLEDO"

by Abdullah's general, Abi Abdah (Ibn Gamri), who, as we have seen, constituted himself the guardian of Prince Abderrahman before he was recognised at the Court of Cordova.[1]

The end of the protracted civil war, and the final disappearance of the Hafsuns from history, are told by Dozy as follows—

Immediately on Abderrahman's accession, he resolved to attack the insurrection at its centre, the Serrania of Regio or Rayah, where Islam had almost disappeared. His expectation was that many of the Christians would have sufficient confidence in his justice to submit voluntarily.[2] His expectations were not disappointed, many of the lords of the castles in the Serrania asked for and obtained amnesty; but one of them, Tolox, which Ibn Hafsun was defending, he was unable to take.[3]

---

[1] *Akhbar Majmua*, 131–2. There is a range of hills called Cerro de Aguilar, near Cordova.

[2] Dozy here relates on the authority of Al-Khoshani, a writer who died in Cordova in 971, an interesting instance of Abderrahman's equitable treatment of a Christian, which, though it has nothing to do with Hafsun, is worth relating. It appears that some Christian lord who had submitted in the previous year, and was living in Cordova, had a Moslem woman as his concubine. She appealed to the Kadi to free her from this position, on the ground that she was of free descent, and that it was not lawful for a Moslem woman to live in that connection with a Christian. The Hajib Badr hearing of her appeal, sent to the Kadi to remind him that the Christian had yielded by capitulation, and that every agreement must be conscientiously observed; therefore, that he must not set the woman free. The Kadi's reply showed that he intended to grant the woman's petition, to which Badr answered that he had no wish to interfere with the course of justice, and that all he demanded was that the rights of the Christian secured by agreement should be allowed due weight, for, he said, "thou knowest that it is our duty to treat Christians with equity and great consideration." Dozy adds that on one occasion Abderrahman wished to appoint a "renegade," whose father and mother were Christians, to the highest magisterial office, that of Kadi of Cordova, and was only dissuaded with difficulty by the Faquis. (*G. der M.*, i. 458.)

[3] Dozy here quotes Arib as saying that Abderrahman at this time took several ships which were bringing provisions from Africa to Ibn Hafsun. One wonders where Hafsun could have been, to be accessible to ships, unless "Tolox" is a misprint for Torrox on the coast a little to the east of Malaga. (*Ib.* p. 459.)

Three years later, in 917, died Omar Ibn Hafsun, unconquered to the last. He left four sons—Jaafar, Soleiman, Abderrahman, and Hafs, none of whom seem to have inherited either the genius or the courage of their father. Soleiman entered the Khalif's service the year after his father's death; a few years later he seems again to have been in rebellion, and was slain in 927. Abderrahman, who was more addicted to literature than to war, went to live a student's life in Cordova. Jaafar (according to Dozy) was slain by his own soldiery in consequence of his declared intention to become a Moslem. Hafs was besieged in Bobaster, which fell in 928, and then he entered Abderrahman's service.

The complete pacification of the country soon ensued. Some of the rebel towns and fortresses capitulated at once, others after a short siege, and the fall of Toledo, in 932, made Abderrahman the undisputed master of the whole of Andalucia.[1]

Conde, as usual, adds some details. On his accession, Abderrahman took the field against Toledo, and Ibn Hafsun, fearing to meet this large army, retired to the east of Spain to seek reinforcements, leaving his son, Jaafar, to defend Toledo. Al-Motref, who was in command, did not stay to lay siege to Toledo, but marched to meet Ibn Hafsun, whom he defeated on a great plain, apparently not far from Toledo. Hafsun retreated to "Hisn Conca" (? Cuenca, a Yemenite stronghold) and other fortresses of that district, and Abderrahman was horror-struck at the sight of the battle-field, "seeing so much Moslem blood poured out, as though Islam had not enemies in Spain, and as though there were not on the frontiers blood still unavenged. He ordered that the wounded of both armies should be treated with the same care."

[1] Dozy, *G. der M.*, i. 456, 460-3, 467, 469.

"KING OMAR OF TOLEDO" 117

In 917, Zaragoza, where Hafsun had many supporters, opened its gates to Abderrahman, and while he was there Hafsun sent him proposals for peace. The Khalif's answer was to the effect that he would not treat with a rebel, and that he gave Hafsun a month to submit unconditionally, adding that he only did not nail the messengers to stakes because they were envoys. This reply is so contrary to Abderrahman's usual attitude towards repentant enemies, that we have no hesitation whatever in attributing it to his uncle Al-Motref, who was with him in the campaign, and remained in Zaragoza to continue the war on the frontier.

In 918, Jaen and other strong places in the Alpujarras surrendered, and Ibn Hafsun died, Conde says, in Huesca.[1]

In 925 or 926, orders were given to begin the attack on Toledo, where Jaafar Hafsun was, and three years later the siege was begun in earnest. Jaafar, finding resistance useless, advised the inhabitants to surrender, and it was decided that three or four thousand of the defenders should try to cut their way out, after which the gates should be opened. This was done, and Jaafar and his troops escaped, while the city surrendered, and was well treated by Abderrahman (927).[2]

Jaafar asked the help of the Christians of Galicia, and there was some fighting as far south as Talavera, in which the troops of Abderrahman were finally victorious. After this we find no further mention of Jaafar and the family of Ibn Hafsun.[3]

One other detail of the pacification of Andalucia may be added. Soon after Abderrahman's accession, Obeidallah Ibn Ash-Shaliyyah, whose daughter had married Jaafar

[1] Dozy, quoting Arib, puts Hafsun's death in 917, and does not mention the place.
[2] Dozy puts the fall of Toledo five years later.
[3] Conde, i. 364–82.

Hafsun, and who was holding Cazlona, volunteered his submission, and was appointed Wali of Jaen.[1]

All we get out of Makkari is that, some time between 924 and 933, Abderrahman " had to contend against some of his own subjects, who had revolted against him and sought the assistance of the Christians." This, says Gayangos, probably refers to Jaafar Ibn Hafsun, who about this time held Toledo.[2] But Makkari throughout says as little as possible about the long and obstinate resistance made by Ibn Hafsun and the Muwallads to the domination of Cordova.

With the fall of Toledo and the final pacification of the whole country, we lose sight of the family of Ibn Hafsun, the Spanish hero who frequently made the ruler of Cordova to tremble, and failed by very little to drive out the alien conquerors and to re-establish a Gothic dynasty in Spain. The Beni Said, the Beni Moslemah, and the Beni Hejjaj, who sprang from a Gothic-Yemenite alliance, gave to the world men of letters as well as men of war. The Hafsuns depended for their eminence on their military qualities alone, and when they could no longer fight, they disappeared from history. But their story shows as plainly as does that of the descendants of Sara, that the surrender of Spain in 711 was due to other causes than the decay of the old martial spirit of the Goths, since the descendants of the men who at the beginning of the eighth century gave way almost without an effort to the invader, were able, in spite of another two hundred years of the supposed enervating influences of the Andalucian climate, to offer so prolonged, so obstinate, and so nearly successful a resistance to their conquerors.

---

[1] Conde, i. 364 ; cf. Ibn Hayyan in Makkari, ii. 439.
[2] Makkari, ii. 135, 462.

FIG. 4A.—Coptic Church of St. George, Egypt, fourth century.   FIG. 4B.—Mosque of Tulun.

Early pointed architecture in Egypt.

CHAPTER VII

THE INFLUENCE OF THE COPTS IN SPAIN

We have said that the amalgamation of the Roman-Gothic and Yemenite traditions of culture and civilisation helped to place Seville in advance of Cordova previous to the accession of Abderrahman III. But there was a third influence at work here, the existence of which seems to have been overlooked even by students fully aware of the importance of the race in question in another country under the rule of Islam. This was the Egyptian, otherwise the Coptic influence, which reflection on the relations of Islam with Egypt will show to have been inevitably at work in Andalucia, in the districts where the Arabs of Yemen predominated.

Gibbon's statement that in the conquest of Egypt by Amru, lieutenant of the Khalif Omar, the Copts received the Moslems more as deliverers than as enemies, is controverted by Dr. Butler, who shows that their supposed chief, Al-Mukaukas, was the Patriarch Cyrus, Viceroy of Egypt, and that he practically betrayed the Egyptian Christians to the invaders. But Dr. Butler, like Gibbon, makes it clear that after the surrender to Amru the Christian religion was allowed free play under certain conditions laid down by the conquerors, and tells us that " in the novel atmosphere of religious freedom the Coptic Church revived, and soon proved its claim to be considered the Church of the nation." [1] The Coptic writings describe " a time of peace and safety after

[1] *Arab Conquest of Egypt,* 439-40.

the troubles and persecutions caused by the (Greek) heretics," and speak of the people as "rejoicing like young calves when their bonds are loosened and they are set free to suck their mother's milk."[1] In the sermon delivered by Amru in Easter week, A.D. 644, in the mosque which still bears his name, the following passage occurs, "And take good care of our neighbours the Copts. Omar, the Commander of the Faithful, told me he heard the Apostle of God say, 'God will open Egypt to you after my death. So take good care of the Copts in that country, for they are your kinsmen and under your protection. Cast down your eyes therefore, and keep your hands off them.'"

Another version of the same story is that Mohammed on his death-bed said three times, "Take care of the men with curly hair," explaining his words thus:—"The Copts of Egypt are our uncles and our brothers-in-law. They shall be your allies against your enemy and your helpers in your religion. . . . They shall relieve you of the cares of this world, so that you shall have leisure for religious worship."[2]

Mohammed himself had taken an Egyptian woman named Mary as his concubine, and we may assume that she was one of the two Coptic maidens sent him as a gift before the conquest. With them went two female servants, an eunuch, an alabaster vase, an ingot of pure gold, oil, honey, and the fine white linen of Egypt, besides a horse, a mule, and an ass, all admirable of their kind.

Gibbon comments satirically on the amours of the Prophet with this Mary, and the descent of the Angel Gabriel with a special chapter of the Koran authorising his relations with her; but there is a touch of human interest in the statement that she was endeared to him by the birth of a son, whom he named Ibrahim, and whose premature death at

[1] *Arab Conquest of Egypt*, 445.
[2] *Ib.* 435–6 and note 2.

THE INFLUENCE OF THE COPTS IN SPAIN 121

the end of fifteen months once more left him without a male heir.[1]

We cannot doubt that the Moslems, when they established themselves in Egypt, speedily followed Mohammed's example in marrying or taking concubines from among the Coptic women. Their leaders certainly did, for Makrizi mentions that the brother of the Khalif Harun ar-Rashid, when he was Governor of Egypt at the close of the eighth century, restored to the Copts the privileges granted to them by Amru, thanks to the ascendancy which his Coptic mistress obtained over that prince.[2]

As for the relief from the cares of this world, which Mohammed had promised his followers if they treated the Copts kindly, the meaning of this becomes clear when we see the part the Egyptian Christians played in the domestic economy of Islam as soon as the two races settled down after the conquest; for the accounts of the industrial and artistic conditions prevailing in Egypt in the seventh century show how invaluable the Egyptians must have been to the Moslem warriors, who as yet—with the exception of the Yemenite Arabs—had no conception of domestic luxury or comfort. The researches and excavations of Mons. Al. Gayet and others have produced material evidence that the descriptions of the historians were not exaggerated, so marvellously fine and delicate are the woven and handworked fabrics found in the sepulchres of Copts and Moslems, all bearing the impress of their Egyptian origin, though they may have been influenced in design by contact with Persia and Byzantium.

In textiles there was a large trade and a great variety of fabrics. Linen probably finer than anything wrought in the looms of ancient Egypt was made, and silk had come into common use, while fabrics of both materials were often adorned with beautiful embroideries. Drawn-thread work,

[1] *Decline and Fall*, chapter li.   [2] *L'Art Arabe*, p. 47.

netted and pillow laces, knitted foot-gear, and fine woollen cloths have been found by M. Gayet in the coffins of Arabs, Egyptians, and, at Damietta, of European crusaders of the thirteenth century ; all of the characteristic Coptic technique, whatever influence may have guided the designers of the garments. Dr. Butler remarks that in the Egyptian textiles dating from about the end of the fifth to the beginning of the tenth centuries, " the political changes which passed over the country are reflected as in a mirror," and M. Gayet in his *Costume en Égypte du 3me au 13me siècle* carries on the same parallel to the period of the Crusades. Gauzes, brocades, striped silks, velvets, damask, cloth of gold and tissue of silver, tapestries, worked leather, carpets, rugs, and curtains are named as made at various places in Egypt, nor was it only in textile fabrics that this nation excelled during the Middle Ages. In goldsmith's work, in enamelling, in ceramics, painted and lustre-glazed, in glass work, metal work, wood and ivory carving, in inlay of fine woods, ivory, mother of pearl, and precious metals, in sculpture, painting, and architecture—in short, " in every province of design and construction, it was the Copts who kept alive the artistic traditions of the country." [1]

To the Arabs of Yemen most, if not all, of these luxuries were already familiar by tradition if not in fact, for not only had Yemen under ancient Egypt been in a high state of civilisation, but during the Persian occupation Chosroes had brought refinement and luxury there, and especially in the capital city of Sana, to a height not exceeded elsewhere in his time. The Yemenites, of whom large numbers had been converted to Christianity previous to the rise of Islam, were almost all Monophysites, like the Copts themselves, and the description of the Cathedral built for

[1] Butler, *Arab Conquest*, chapter viii., *passim*; Gayet, *L'Art Arabe, L'Art Copte*, and *Costume en Égypte*, *passim*.

THE INFLUENCE OF THE COPTS IN SPAIN 123

Christian worship at Sana suggests various features still found in Coptic churches in Egypt. It was built in the sixth century, but, like the Egyptian churches to-day, the choir was divided off by a screen of carved wood, and the doors were overlaid with panels and plates of metal. At Sana, the screen, the plates, and the panels, were of ebony inlaid with ivory, gold, silver, and precious stones, while in the Coptic churches poverty forbade any such lavishness. But the woodwork inlaid with ivory, *e.g.* in the Monastery of St. Sergius and in the Church of Mohallakah [1] show what was done by the Egyptian Christians by sheer manual skill, when they could not procure gold or jewels to adorn their places of worship. At Sana crosses of gold with a red jacinth in the centre stood in relief in the panels of the doors, and in the Church of Mohallakah metal crosses were sunk in the columns, on which figures of the Apostles were sculptured in high relief. The many-coloured enamels of Sana are represented here by ivory inlaid with other ivory, dyed red or black to produce extraordinarily intricate designs. The Cathedral of Sana was basilican in form, and lofty columns of precious marble divided the nave from the aisles. The Coptic churches too were basilican, and tall columns or piers, not of marble but of masonry, marked the line of the nave. Indeed the great height is what one first notices in these Coptic buildings. The walls of the Sana Cathedral were adorned with paintings and mosaics in gold and colours, and in some of the Coptic churches excavated by M. Gayet in Egypt, there are traces remaining of painting and other decoration, which covered the walls from floor to roof. In short, whatever we can learn of the Christian Cathedral of the Yemenite Arabs appears to have existed in a more or less relatively humble form in the Coptic churches in Egypt from the fourth to the eleventh century, while certain

[1] *L'Art Copte*, Plates I., III. and IV.

resemblances can be observed even in those of the present day.

Communities of Christian Arabs, moreover, survived the Moslem conquest of Palestine, and there was a bishop of the Christian Arabs as late as the eighth century.[1]

Probably it was these ties of religion that Mohammed had in mind when he spoke of the Copts as "brothers" of the Moslems. The Arabs of Yemen, until recently Monophysite Christians like the Copts, are not likely to have lost all memory of the religious bond in the few years that had elapsed since their conversion to Islam. Thus it was only natural that this important section of the Moslem invaders should fraternise with a nation with whom they had such strong sympathies, and it is not surprising to find that numbers of official posts were soon filled by Copts, and that for a long time practically the whole business of the state was managed by them. Mohammed doubtless had taken all the conditions into account, and desired to conciliate the Yemenites—recent and perhaps not very convinced converts to the new faith—when he urged gentle treatment of the Copts, with whom those Arab tribes were so closely connected by a common religious tradition.

We have dwelt at some length on the relations between the Copts and the Arabs of Yemen in Egypt previous to the Moslem invasion of Spain, because it is necessary to show why the Coptic influence was so strong in south-west Andalucia and other places settled by Yemenites, from the beginning of the eighth century down to the end of the

[1] Butler, *Arab Conquest*, 147-8, 151, n. 3; Gayet, *L'Art Copte, L'Art Arabe, passim*. The glories of Sana never faded from the traditions of the Arabs of Yemen, and their poets in Andalucia, as in Sicily, would refer to their ancient capital as their highest analogy for beauty and delight. Schack in drawing attention to this feature in the writings of *e.g.* Ibn Hamdis (who like Al-Lebbanah, after enjoying the hospitality of Motamid Ibn Abbad at Seville, followed him into exile in Africa) speaks of the tales of the splendour of Sana as hyperbole, but Dr. Butler and others make it clear that such traditions had a solid basis of fact.

THE INFLUENCE OF THE COPTS IN SPAIN

eleventh, when the last of the Yemenite princes of Seville was dethroned and died in an African prison.

Musa Ibn Noseir, about whose parentage the Mudarite writers give so many contradictory accounts, was of a Yemenite tribe. Even his enemies admit that, although they represent him to have been a slave or bondman adopted by a Yemenite chief. At the time of the conquest of Spain he was Governor of Africa, having been appointed to that post by Abdalaziz, Governor of Egypt and brother of the Khalif Abdalmalek, with whom Musa had taken refuge when he was in trouble with the Khalif. Musa's first duty there was to complete the subjugation of Africa, which had been begun by his predecessor, Hossan, and the force employed for that purpose seems to have included a large number of Egyptian troops. In the year 702, when Musa was engaged in his campaign against the Berbers, his son joined him " with the van of the Egyptian army ; " and although we need not suppose that this Egyptian army consisted wholly or chiefly of Copts, who were not a fighting nation, it is practically certain that troops from Egypt would bring in their train a number of Copts as servants, camp-followers, etc. There is a history of Musa in an anonymous MS. attributed by Gayangos to the first decade of the ninth century, translated in Makkari. In this account we are told that in 703 or thereabouts " the Egyptian fleet " sailed for Sardinia in defiance of Musa's advice, and that about 708 Abdullah Ibn Marrah " arrived with a body of men from Egypt," and that Musa " gave him the command of the sea." [1]

The early Moslems were no sailors : indeed Ibn Khaldun says that the Khalif Omar forbade their putting to sea because they were so unaccustomed to that element and so unfitted for navigation, and that this prohibition continued in force until the reign of Moawiyah (661–79), when the

[1] Makkari, i. app. E. lxvi.–lxvii.

Moslems began to employ foreign navigators and pilots until they had gained sufficient knowledge to build and sail ships for themselves. After this their progress was rapid; and within the first century of the Hegira they not only had numerous ships in the Syrian ports and in Alexandria, but also at Tunis on the newly conquered African coast, where Musa built a dockyard and organised a considerable fleet.[1]

The references to the Egyptian fleet and sailors show that Musa drew on that country for the manning of his navy. Since the remaining Greeks and Romans had been practically exterminated or driven out by Amru, and the Copts *en masse* were now under Moslem protection, we can only conclude that this Egyptian fleet must have been manned by Copts under the now increasing body of Arabs competent to take command of their own ships. When the Arabic writers speak of the Egyptians, they must be taken to refer to the Copts, who at that time were the only Egyptians: and thus the frequent mention of them in connection with Musa seems to prove that his expedition contained numbers of the race so useful, if not indispensable, to the Moslems in North Africa at that time, as indeed Musa's own antecedents would lead us to expect.

According to Conde, the garrison which Musa placed in Tangier under his son Merwan, after his conquest of that city in 705, consisted of 10,000 men, "all Arabs and Egyptians."[2] Gayangos accused Conde of "invariably" misreading "the tribes of Misr" for those of Mudar;[3] but in the passage from the *Akhbar Majmua* referred to below the text distinctly reads Misr, although in a note the Spanish editor gives Mudar as an alternative reading.

In this particular passage it is unlikely that the Mudarites

---

[1] Ibn Khaldun in Makkari, i. app. xxxiv. ff. and anon. in *id.* lxvi.
[2] i. 23.   [3] In Makkari, ii. 402.

were meant, for although the Fihrites not unnaturally struggled to the last against Abderrahman I., he was, generally speaking, accepted by those of his own race.[1] When he came to set up a kingdom in Spain, there was, according to the *Akhbar Majmua*,[2] a *jond* (troop or militia) of Egyptians at Beja, who rose under a Yemenite leader opposed to the rule of the Ommeyads. Ocsonoba, Beja, and the territory of Tudmir (Theodomir) were settled by the Egyptian troops when the tribes and regiments were distributed about the country after the disturbances of 742.[3]

We have found the Egyptian influence in textile design and technique stronger in the Algarbe and the neighbourhood of Beja (now in Portugal) than in almost any other part of Andalucia except Seville. So much so, indeed, is this the case that we have known travellers fresh from Egypt single out a specimen of antique lace from the district of Ocsonoba as "pure Egyptian" in design. Tudmir was a part of what is now the province of Murcia, and under the Moslem occupation the silks manufactured there were celebrated all over Spain, and were so good as to be largely exported to Egypt and the East.

We think, therefore, that there can be no doubt that the Arabic writers who spoke of "the Egyptians" and "the militia of the Egyptians" meant the Copts who came over under the banners of Musa and other leaders. In other passages Conde speaks of the discords caused by the factions of "Yemenites, Egyptians, Syrians, and Alabdaris,"[4] in consequence of which the "most noble Kahtanite Arabs and some Egyptians" elected a ruler by common consent.

---

[1] The Ommeyads were Mudarites of the tribe of Koraish. The Fihrites were also Mudarites, but opposed Abderrahman because he overthrew the Fihrite Governor of Andalucia.
[2] P. 95.   [3] Dozy, *G. der M.*, i. 169; Conde, i. 112.
[4] i. 109, 121.

The Abdaris, according to Gayangos,[1] were a tribe of Mudarites; so that in this paragraph we have Yemenites, Mudarites, and Syrians, besides the Egyptians,[2] and there seems no alternative but to accept the Egyptians as a race apart from all three.

Two hundred years after the invasion, Abderrahman III. mentions the Copts by name in a letter written to one of his Seville relatives (see p. 148). It is not clear from the translation that the Khalif meant to imply that the actual family of his cousin belonged to the despised race, although his remark about Ahmed Ibn Ishak's mother is suggestive. But the verses he quoted would have had no point had there not been Copts resident in the country at the time, while to call Ahmed's mother "the witch Khamduna" was significant, in view of the occult powers claimed by the Egyptians throughout history.

In Makkari's account of the Moslem conquest of Santiago in 997, taken verbatim from Ibn Hayyan, he mentions that the church dedicated to St. James was held in great estimation by pious Christians, who repaired to it "from the most remote parts, from Nubia, from the land of the Kobts, and from other distant countries."[3] It will be remembered that the Coptic Christians took the name of Jacobites from James Baradæus, who revived their church when it had been nearly destroyed by persecution. Gibbon says that the history of this man is obscure, and that "the Jacobites themselves had rather deduce their name and pedigree from St. James the Apostle."[4] Thus a church dedicated to St. James the Apostle would have a peculiar sanctity in Coptic eyes.

[1] In Makkari, ii. 402.
[2] The Syrians here mean the Syrian troops who came over with Balj, and were dispersed about the country afterwards in the interests of peace, the various groups being separated as widely as possible on the advice of Artebas. See p. 57.
[3] Makkari, ii. 195.   [4] Chapter xlvii.

THE INFLUENCE OF THE COPTS IN SPAIN

It seems hardly likely that Nubian and Egyptian Christians should have made pilgrimages to the north of Spain from their respective countries, but it is not impossible that Coptic Christians from Andalucia and Christian slaves or fighting men brought to Spain from Nubia should have been allowed to do so, for at that time great consideration was shown to members of their religion, especially by Almansur, the conqueror of Santiago (see p. 174).[1]

During the reign of Abderrahman III. the political disturbances in the East reacted upon the commerce of Spain. In or about 955 the Khalif ordered a great ship to be built in Seville for the Egyptian and Sicilian trade, but on its first voyage this ship fell foul of an African vessel carrying letters from Moizz-ad-Daula, Wizir of Bagdad, to the Wali of Sicily, and there was a fight near the island,

[1] We find little mention of Nubians in Seville after this indirect hint of their presence in Moslem Spain, until the fourteenth and fifteenth centuries, when they are said to have been numerous. In 1475 the Catholic Kings had a negro porter named Juan de Valladolid, who was appointed Mayoral (administrator) of the community in Seville with the title of the Negro Count. A street in the city still bears the name of El Conde Negro in memory of him. Among the various institutions supported by the negroes was a religious Confraternity, founded in 1400, and still existing in 1852, with its own chapel in the parish church of San Roque. Over one of the altars in this chapel there were two antique paintings, one of which represented San Elesban (*sic*) King of Ethiopia, and the other Santa Efigenia. The legend of this saint relates that she was baptized by St. Matthew, when he was preaching in Ethiopia, and when the convent in which she shut herself up with two hundred maidens, was set on fire by Hitaco (*sic*), St. Matthew appeared in the air and put out the flames. This was the incident represented in the picture of Santa Efigenia (*Glorias religiosas de Sevilla*, 381–99). Their choice of subjects for pictures strongly suggests that the negroes of Seville claimed descent from the Nubians, otherwise they would hardly have depicted a king of Ethiopia and an Eastern Saint named Iphigenia. Thus they form a connecting link with the Nubians who worshipped at the shrine of Santiago in the tenth century. There is still a negro race at Niebla, in the province of Huelva, with the crisp black curly hair, the large liquid eyes, and the blueness under the finger nails which we associate with the negro type, but without the thick lips of the African black. In complexion they are not darker than the average Gitano (Egyptian) of this region, but the type is entirely distinct. They are called *negritos* by their neighbours. In the course of a few hours' stay in the town we saw at least a dozen children of the *negrito* race.

K

in which the Andalucians came off conquerors. They took the Wizir's ship with all that was in her, continued their voyage to Alexandria, sold their merchandise there and took in a cargo of Egyptian products, and set out to return to Spain. But when Moizz-ad-Daula heard what had occurred, he sent out armed ships from the Egyptian ports and from Sicily, which overtook the Seville vessel in the port of Almeria, seized her with all her cargo, burnt various small boats in the harbour, and fled satisfied with their vengeance and their prize. The Hajib Ahmed Ibn Said (we are not told his tribe, but the name suggests Gotho-Yemenite parentage:—see genealogical tables) offered to Abderrahman to make reprisals, and opened a campaign against merchants trading in the Moghreb under the protection of Moizz-ad-Daula, which produced enough booty to satisfy both the Khalif and the troops.[1]

Moizz-ad-Daula was an upstart who had possessed himself of Bagdad by intrigue, if not by actual force, imposed himself as Wizir on the feeble Abbasside nominally reigning there, and reduced the authority of the ostensible head of Islam to a shadow. He tried to replace the name of the Abbasside in the Khotba by that of the Fatimite Abu Tamim, and was only restrained by the objections of his own troops. And he placed his own men in the government of Irak, so that the Khalifate was in fact, if not in name, deprived of all its possessions.[2]

The interest of the incident to us lies in the indication that Abderrahman had been previously trading with Egypt peacefully, since his vessel was taken by surprise by the envoy of Moizz-ad-Daula, bearing the letters to the Sicilian Government announcing his advent to power.

Altogether there seems to be a fair amount of more or less direct evidence that Copts came to Andalucia in sufficient

[1] Conde, i. 444 ff.   [2] Makrizi, *Hist. Egypt,* 80-1.

THE INFLUENCE OF THE COPTS IN SPAIN

numbers to take to a large extent the same part in the domestic economy of the Moslem state as they did in Egypt; while undeniable evidence is found of Coptic influence in the art and architecture of Andalucia, wherever the Yemenite Arabs preponderated.

The most noteworthy instances of this influence are seen in the churches which, according to sixteenth and seventeenth century writers, " were formerly mosques." There are a large number of these churches in and around Seville, and in the neighbouring provinces of Cadiz and Huelva, and some in Murcia and elsewhere, which obviously have never been entirely rebuilt since their foundation. How they could ever have been mosques does not appear; certainly they were not originally intended for that purpose, for many of them are older than the eighth century. It is in these churches — one at least of which retains its dedication to an early saint no longer to be found in the Spanish calendar—that traces of the Egyptian tradition are most apparent. They are all of the basilican form, some indeed of a very early style, but almost invariably the roof seems to have been heightened—often very greatly so—by the addition of pointed arches to the masonry piers dividing the nave from the aisles. The fondness of the Copts for lofty buildings is shown clearly enough in M. Gayet's illustrations to the section " Architecture " in *L'Art Copte;* and the basilican churches in Seville show that this predilection was shared by those who altered the primitive churches here. The Arabic influence, on the other hand, is seen in the roofs. These are always covered with tiles, of the style used in this part of Spain from Roman if not from pre-historic times. They are not ceiled or vaulted within, but show the wooden beams. And these beams are decorated with *artesonado,* which is the untranslatable name for a special kind of Arabic woodwork, richly carved, and pierced and inlaid in geometrical designs. In some of the oldest of the rural churches near Seville may be seen really splendid examples of this *artesonado*.

To the basilican ground plan, with the pointed Coptic arches rising above the archaic masonry piers and the Arabic woodwork under the tiled roofs, another addition has been made in the majority of cases. This consists of three doors, on the west, north, and south sides, more or less handsomely decorated with what would elsewhere be called Lombardic sculpture, and with pointed arches. Some of these arches (*e.g.* that of the College of San Miguel, which is recorded as being a relic of the primitive cathedral of the Goths), although pointed almost like the " Gothic " arches, lack the characteristic " Gothic " splay, the opening being cut square into the wall; others are splayed, with little columns varying in number from one to seven, but projecting from the wall, not built into it as in the northern Gothic. To connect this projection with the wall at the top, a deep cornice is superimposed, supported as a rule, in the case of Seville, by lions' heads, and in the country churches by simple corbels, all of more or less Oriental inspiration.[1]

If it were not evident at first sight that these porches are a later addition to the main fabric, it would be proved by comparison with the great gates of Carmona, Ronda, and Medina Sidonia, where horse-shoe arches with just such cornices and corbels are built on outside the Roman gateways in the city walls. The actual date of the arched porches may vary, and it is not difficult in some cases to form a guess at the time which elapsed between the building of one and another. But the obvious addition to the original construction is the same in all, and it is essentially not that of the thirteenth century Gothic which we see, *e.g.* in San Gil

[1] The lion and the eagle were the idols of heathen Yemen.

and Santa Ana in Seville, work which we know to have been done under Alfonso X., in 1261 and 1282. There the advance in method and design is so marked as to be in itself proof of the considerably later date of Alfonso's work, although the conditions that prevailed for many years after the reconquest make it practically certain that the actual craftsmen were Moslems or Mozarabs native to the soil.

At the west end of these basilican churches we find circular windows with Arabic stonework, sometimes of the most primitive kind. The side chapels resemble the mausoleums of great men attached to early mosques in Egypt. Arabic decoration, still in excellent condition, has been revealed beneath a ceiling of plaster and whitewash in Santa Marina in Seville, through the fortunate accident of a fire. Such mausoleums may be recognised by the sixteen-sided dome resting on an octagon, which again stands on a quadrangle, the whole having a lantern light at the top. This peculiar feature can only be derived from Egypt, since the earliest instance of such a scheme of construction is found in the Coptic monastery of Akhmim, built A.D. 550.[1] In Seville these polygonal chapels are always placed one at each side of the east end of the aisles, and generally opposite each other. The light falling from above through the lantern is employed with good effect in the display of the images which now stand in these erst-while Mohammedan monuments. In the apses of almost all such churches we find northern Gothic work in the lancet windows and the graceful vaulted roofs, which prevailed in the thirteenth and fourteenth centuries here as in other European countries. Here we are on firm ground, for in several instances we have the records of this last addition. It is true that the chroniclers of the fourteenth century often loosely say, as their Moslem predecessors did before them, that such and such an

[1] Gayet, *L'Art Arabe*, p. 82.

edifice was " rebuilt " by such and such a personage, but in these cases they can only refer to the apse, for that alone is of the period in question. It is indeed curious to see, *e.g.* in the Church of San Andrés in Seville, which presents all the features above described, Hathor-headed capitals supporting fourteenth century vaulting, and conventional " lotus " corbels under graceful lancet windows in the apse, the latter enlarged and altered, but not newly made, in the fourteenth century. And when we see a gorgeous baroque reredos, all gilding and red paint, cutting across and hiding half the Gothic apse, while the basest late eighteenth century pictures in distemper disfigure the ancient basilica walls, then indeed the story of the Church in Spain is complete ; and we may say of these buildings, as Dr. Butler says of the textile fabrics in Egypt, that in them " the political changes which passed over the country are reflected as in a mirror."

There was no distinct line of demarcation between the Coptic and Arabic schools of design in Egypt down to the fall of the Fatimites.[1] The Copts made no distinction between the mosques they built to order and their own churches, employing the same ideas for both alike. Thus we may see, in Copto-Arabic and Copto-Christian art in Egypt, a cross figuring in the middle of a geometrical design, and a polygonal medallion surrounded by a border containing the mystic hare, the hieroglyph for Oun, the symbol of Osiris as protector of the dead, and so on *ad infinitum*.[2]

We find the same strange combination of symbolism and geometrical design in Seville and some of the neighbouring places, and especially in such districts as that of Huelva

[1] We refer of course to the school which sprang from the employment of Coptic artists and architects by the early Moslem rulers, as *e.g.* Amru, Abdalaziz, Al-Walid, Tulun and so on down to the Fatimites. Even as late as the fourteenth century Hassan I. employed a Coptic architect whose signature is on Hassan's mosque. (Gayet, *L'Art Arabe*, pp. 27, 39, 41–42, 49–50, 121.)

[2] *L'Art Arabe*, p. 30 ; *Costume en Égypte, passim.*

THE INFLUENCE OF THE COPTS IN SPAIN 135

(the Ocsonoba of the *Akhbar Majmua*) where an Egyptian *jond* was settled in the eighth century. Moreover, we find these designs applied here even now to materials similar to those named by Makrizi as in vogue at the Fatimite Court, *i.e.*, fine linen, transparent muslin, and rich silk. The methods, too, are precisely those employed to adorn the garments taken by M. Gayet from Coptic and Arabic tombs, dating from the third to the thirteenth centuries;—silk, linen, and muslin, with the pattern drawn from the thread and embroidered; and embroidery on netted lace, formerly called here *red de pez* (fish-net) and now known as *malla*. Extraordinarily fine and complicated work is still produced in Andalucia by both these processes, and even in modern times we meet with the Svastika, the Kha, and endless geometrical and symbolical animal designs, produced for their own purposes by peasant women. We have seen an example of such work on home-spun and home-woven linen, with a most curious reminiscence of the Kha, made by drawing the threads, the figure being that of a woman whose hands ended not in fingers but in a cross, precisely as in a Kha figure on a lamp in the Cairo museum. It came from a remote hamlet in the Sierra de Huelva, where certainly no one knew anything about Egyptian or Coptic symbolism a hundred years ago. But the traditional designs are so carefully preserved from one generation to another even in the twentieth century that one understands how such ideas would persist in remote places where no later artistic influence ever stepped in to disturb them.[1]

---

[1] Sun symbols and sun designs, still popularly described as *el sol* or *dibujo de soles* (pattern of suns) are exceedingly common in the districts referred to. These and other survivals of symbolism will be discussed at length in a future volume. We must, however, mention a bronze door-handle in our possession consisting of an Egyptian head with two serpents springing from it. It is Seville work of the fifteenth century, but visitors at first sight always say that it is evidently Egyptian, and ask why it figures in a collection of Andalucian products.

Of Copto-Gothic or Copto-Arabic pottery, woodwork, ivory carving, jewellery, armour, and furniture, we must treat later, for we have already digressed too far from the history of Andalucia under Islam. But we have, we hope, shown that if Seville was more advanced than Cordova before the reign of Abderrahman III., it was because of the art and culture brought about by the combination of the three elements which met and amalgamated here. First, the survival of Roman traditions preserved by the Gothic nobles whose centre and capital was Seville. Secondly, the traditions of culture and luxury maintained by the Arabs of Yemen, of whom Seville was the capital throughout almost the whole of the Moslem occupation of Spain. Thirdly, the Egyptian traditions of arts, crafts, and industries, fostered by the Yemenite Arabs here as in Egypt, and in no way hampered by the prohibition of representations of animate life which were observed by the Sunnites of Cordova.

While the sources of information at present available give no indication that Greek artists were ever employed in Seville (as they are recorded to have been employed at Cordova on at least two occasions), it is nevertheless undeniable that a strongly Christian influence is visible in all the early art of Seville under Islam. It is impossible that this should be due to the Goths who dwelt, however amicably, alongside of the Moslems in southern Spain, for if they had made a permanent impression on Andalucian art in the course of the five centuries during which no Christian influence could have entered here from outside, the art and architecture of Seville under the Moslems would have continued as Roman in style as it was when they came. How strongly the Roman tradition then persisted may be seen at Medina Sidonia, where a Visigothic hermitage still exists.[1] This

[1] The primitive nave remains unchanged, with a Visigothic inscription dating from the seventh century on one of the massive

little building, with its disproportionately large columns and its low barrel roof, is as unlike the basilican churches of Seville as it is possible to be. Nor is this the only one of the kind in this part of Spain, for at Puerto de Santa Maria there exists, beneath the castle restored by the Guzmans in the fourteenth century, another such church, also with Roman columns, evidently appropriated from some building in the neighbourhood. Here they are sunk deeply in the ground, without either bases or capitals, and the arches spring from a kind of rude moulding, without anything in the nature of an abacus. Pelayo Quintero y Atauri in the article referred to on p. 385, suggests that the church was built by Mozarabs previous to the occupation of the Almohades, and we fully agree with him, for while the most primitive work reflects the Roman influence, there are later arches of the Coptic form, and horse-shoe arches leading to what are obviously additions to the original fabric. The little church has a curious flavour of the great mosque of Cordova about it. It is not basilican in form, which indeed it hardly could be if from the first it were designed to be the basis of a castle built above it. A perspective of transverse arches opens from right and left of the nave, while the very low vaulted roof is of the same height all over; not raised as usual above the central nave. If one pictures the Cordova mosque as it was when the Moslems first shared it with the Christians—before the upper tier of arches was added by Abderrahman II. to give more air to the crowds of people who began to flock to Cordova in his reign—one sees that this little Christian church has the same ground-plan in miniature. The horse-shoe arches in the transepts add to the impression. In the midst of the space before the high

pillars. No alteration seems to have been made in this building until the sixteenth century, when the Guzmans, Dukes of Medina Sidonia, renovated the walls with faience of the period, and somewhat enlarged the tiny sacristy.

altar which in a Christian church would be wrapped in a dim religious gloom, the favourite lantern-light of the Almohades lets in a flood of sunshine upon the Roman columns and the seventeenth century decorations of the ruined altar (chancel there is none) pointing to the truth of the local legend that the image of the Virgin found by Alfonso X. in the castle-moat was hidden there by the Christian community because the Moors took possession of their church. Doubtless it was they who built on the transepts, to obtain the square or rectangular form convenient to their purposes of worship, and thus gave the little church its suggestion of the great mosque of Cordova.

Further search among the remoter villages is revealing other such relics of the Visigothic dominion, the existence of which seems to be unsuspected by most archæologists.

It is clear that most of the Christian churches in Andalucia escaped all interference, whether for good or evil, throughout the whole period of the Moslem rule, down to the time when San Fernando conquered the Moors and restored to Christian worship all of them that had been alienated to other uses. On the other hand, it seems clear that where restoration or rebuilding took place, previous to the invasion of the Almohades, Coptic artists or their pupils were employed in the Christian churches, just as Coptic architects were employed by the Shiite Moslems in Egypt to restore or rebuild edifices which they had adapted to their own purposes. The use of the pointed arch proves that some influence other than Byzantine was prevalent in this region, as elsewhere where the Yemenite Arabs predominated. Nor is it only in actual construction that this Coptic form is found in early Arabic work in south-west Andalucia: it is also frequent in the plaster and stucco work used for decoration, and is seen in the *almenas* (battlements) copied in cut tiles from the battlements of

THE INFLUENCE OF THE COPTS IN SPAIN 139

Arabic castles. The *almenillas* (diminutive of *almena*) which were introduced under the Almohades are of a different form. It is interesting to notice how constantly the early pointed *almena* accompanies the style of decoration miscalled Mudéjar in this region, while "Moorish" work is invariably finished off with the much later and less artistic *almenilla*.

Unfortunately little now remains of the textile fabrics, goldsmith's work, glass, or pottery, which according to Ibn Said had reached so high a degree of perfection under the rule of the Yemenites in Seville, Murcia, and elsewhere during the eleventh century, when the Coptic school of art touched high-water mark both in Spain and Egypt. By that time it is certain that the Yemenite Arabs had attained as much skill in these productions as their Egyptian teachers, and fine craftsmanship seems not to have been limited to the industrial classes, for one of the most celebrated examples of goldsmith's work of the eleventh century bears an inscription stating that it was made by a Yemenite prince for Motamid of Seville, who was his grandfather.[1]

Yemenite counsellors helped to govern Seville even under the Almohades, and to their influence with the Moorish rulers may be ascribed the Arabic feeling which prevails over the Moorish in the tower so well-known under the name of the Giralda. The resemblance between the decoration on the tower and that of the lower part of the façade of the Alcazar (which is probably a relic of the palace built by Motamid Ibn Abbad), will not be overlooked by students of the subject,

[1] See genealogical tables. The inscription is translated into Spanish by the Academician Fernandez y Gonzalez, and may be Englished as follows : " . . . the work of Mohammed Ibn As-Seraj . . . in none of the parts (which receive fame) of the artificers, nor in the Eden of God (will there be) any one who works more notably then Abu Hassan (when he does it) by order of the Amir. The Amir Mohammed desired that I should make it for his second wife, Al Badr (the moon) herald of the peace of Eden." (*Museo Español de Antiguedades*, i. 67.) The casket is in the Madrid Museum.

the contrast between this dignified work and that of the Moorish portion of the palace façade being clearly marked. The Arabic work in the façade has been badly defaced by the insertion of the shields of early kings of Castile and Leon (previous to the supposed builder, Pedro I.), but the outlines are both of one school.

In the injury inflicted on this fine decoration by the heraldic artists of the Christian kings we obtain a clue to the disappearance of most of the Copto-Yemenite or Copto-Gothic works of art which were found in Seville and elsewhere when the Almohades were expelled. How fine and rich and elegant were the glass, the furniture, the draperies, and so on, which the Castilians adopted as their own, may be judged from the illuminations to the works of Alfonso X., where the domestic life of the period is represented with faithfulness and close attention to detail not exceeded by those of the Bayeux tapestries. That the fabrics preferred by the Castilians were those of Arabic manufacture and design is shown by the mortuary robe of San Fernando, a fragment of which is preserved in the Madrid Museum. The design of this robe consists of chessboard squares of red and white, on which are woven ingenuous little castles and Coptic-looking lions, reminiscent of those in the woodwork of the mosque of Al-Azhar, and also of the lion on the *renk* of Beibars Al-Bukhari, as was remarked to us by M. Al. Gayet in a private letter relating to the "Coptic" lions of Seville. In Alfonso's *Book of Chess* there is a portrait of the king himself wearing just such another robe, and fragments of his children's dresses, also in the National Museum, have Arabic inscriptions woven into the stuff together with their names—a possibly unique instance of the *tiraz* being used for Christian royal robes.

There is no doubt that the Christians of Castile fully appreciated the luxuries and beauties of Moslem life in Seville in the thirteenth century; so much so, indeed, that before long their kings began to legislate against too lavish indulgence in these things. But, as always, familiarity bred contempt, and it did not occur to any one that the artistic glass, silver, and faience, or the exquisite embroideries and woven stuffs which adorned the mosques and palaces of the conquered people were worthy of careful preservation by the conquerors, any more than the beautiful pierced stone and stucco of the façade of the Alcazar. In the course of nine years' investigation we have, however, found what we believe to be an almost perfect example of the carpets in use in Seville before the reconquest, and we are not without hopes that even yet some relics of the vanished silks, damasks, and brocades may be discovered in remote country churches, where such things are looked on as no better than rags.

The one exception is the magnificent piece of work known as the *Paño de la Monteria* (the hunt-carpet) in Seville Cathedral. Although something like a third of it has been cut off, besides the border, which may have been of considerable size and probably contained an inscription, enough remains to be extremely heavy for one man to handle. This, we suppose, is the reason why the custodians of the Cathedral flatly refuse to show the carpet to inquirers. We are told that we are the only foreigners who have as yet been allowed to study it, and this we owe solely to the kindness of our friends the Dean and the Archdeacon of the Cathedral, and their sympathetic interest in our study of Andalucian art. It is of red velvet, extremely hard and short in the pile, of which hardly a square inch is left visible, so closely is it embroidered with the mystic "hunt" of strange denaturalised animals, all pursuing or being pursued. These are always in pairs, and many of them are mounted one on the back of another, tearing more or less savagely at each other's vitals. This singular idea, prominent in the textiles of the Sassanides, is seen on quite a large proportion of the few relics that remain of the art-work of those days. It figures on the fountain of Almansur, made in Seville in 988 A.D., in this case in the form of eagles with jackals under their claws: in the casket of Abdalmalek, son of Almansur, dated 1005; and, as already said, in the *Paño de la Monteria*, the animals in this last case being winged in a singular fashion, very like the winged Lion of Pisa, which, according to M. Gayet, is Fatimite work of the tenth century.[1] Makrizi declares the Fatimite representations of animals to have been so life-like that at a distance they might have been taken for real, but no one who has seen these mystic creatures, with wings that might be serpents and tails that might be leaves or flowers, would agree with him. As for the origin of the device of the two creatures mounted one on the other, we may find this also in Egypt. M. Gayet gives an illustration of a symbolic Coptic group in the Egyptian Museum in Cairo. In this a bird, supposed to be a dove, is standing on and apparently clawing at a jackal, with an ape, a gazelle, and two lions below, all enclosed between the arms of a cross amid a mass of foliage. This was sculptured several centuries before the fountain of Almansur, yet while the technique of the later work is far better, the design hardly varies, except that in the Seville fountain-head the bird is an eagle—the ancient idol of Yemen—and the lions are eagle-headed like that at Pisa, and have wings like those of the dragons in the Seville *Paño*. The inspiration we take to have come from Persia, *via* Yemen, before the days of Islam. The attitude of the lions in the Coptic group is almost absurdly like that of the lions in the San Fernando mortuary robe. And, as showing the persistence of this idea, we find in a great fifteenth century woven carpet, also in Seville

[1] *L'Art Arabe*, p. 189.

Fig. 5.—*Convento de la Luz* (No. 1). Copto-Arabic arches of the Central Court with fifteenth-century arcades above.

THE INFLUENCE OF THE COPTS IN SPAIN 143

Cathedral, bearing the F and the Y of the Catholic Kings, a modernised and conventionalised imitation of these Sassanide groups, in the self-same attitude as those of the *Paño* and the casket of Abdalmalek, but flanked by a couple of fighting bulls such as one sees to-day on picture postcards of Seville. We have found the same idea in other Arabic work previous to the twelfth century, but space forbids further details here. We have shown, we hope, the close links in symbolism and technique that connect these several works of art, so widely divided in point of time from each other and from the Copto-Arabic school of Fostat, which gave birth to the Seville school.

In the future we propose to offer illustrations of these and other designs, showing the persistence of the Persian-Egyptian influence in the art of Andalucia. For the moment enough has been said, we hope, to prove that such an influence existed and made an ineradicable mark on the artistic ideas of the districts in which the Copts, owing to their skill and experience, took the lead in the decorative art and architecture of the Yemenites, Goths, and Muwallads whose capital was Seville.

CHAPTER VIII

CHRISTIANS AND MUWALLADS UNDER ABDERRAHMAN III

ABDERRAHMAN was not yet twenty-two when he ascended the throne, fair and blue-eyed, as might be expected of his Gothic ancestry, and as handsome as a prince should be. But even more winning than his physical beauty was the goodness of his heart and his virtuous spirit. He was clever, learned, and prudent beyond his years. All these excellent qualities being generally recognised, the satisfaction of the people at his accession was universal, and the Khotba was read for him in all the principal mosques.

His uncle, Al-Motref, now displayed a fatherly love for him; he was the first to swear allegiance, and Abderrahman received his oath with demonstrations of affection and respect, which brought tears to the eyes of those who witnessed it.[1] Perhaps those who wept recalled how this same Al-Motref had brought the young king's father to the grave some eighteen years before. Be this as it may, we may assume that Al-Motref was loyal to the oath sworn that day, for we hear after this of his fighting his nephew's battles on more than one occasion.

One of the most noteworthy features of the reign of the greatest of the Ommeyads was that the long feud between Seville and Cordova was at once allayed. Dozy attributes this to the weakening of the Muwallad and Yemenite rebels by old age or death, and it is a fact that the Seville party, whose chief, Ibrahim Ibn Hejjaj, had died and had been

[1] Conde, i. 359.

Fig. 6.—West Door of the Church of San Juan de la Palma. Originally built by the Mozarabs: an existing inscription states that the tower was added in 1086 by Itimad, wife of Motamid Ibn Abbad, for her son Ar-Rashid, Kadi of Seville, the court of whose palace stands opposite, with an upper story added in the seventeenth century.

succeeded by his son Mohammed before Abderrahman's accession, accepted their new over-lord without protest, nor do we find any serious revival of trouble here during his long reign. But the Muwallads and Christians do not seem to have been materially weakened by the twenty-five years' ceaseless warfare, for we find Omar Ibn Hafsun, now their acknowledged leader, more persistent than ever in his attempts to carve out a kingdom for his own people. The truce with the Seville party was personal to Abderrahman.

Immediately on Abdullah's death, Mohammed Ibn Hejjaj took the oath of allegiance, and the other Yemenite leaders shortly followed his example. Abderrahman undoubtedly did his best to make these acts of submission as easy as possible to those who had stood aloof from his grandfather. He used every means in his power to heal old enmities and quarrels, settled blood feuds between certain families, and by his gentleness and prudence gained the hearts of many who had grievances : he ameliorated the condition of all his subjects by suppressing many illegal taxes which had been imposed by his predecessor, while by causing justice to be fairly and impartially administered, and by encouraging agriculture and trade, he laid the foundations of that national prosperity which before his death had placed Cordova in the foremost rank of the civilisation of the time.[1]

How could all this have been accomplished, and accomplished apparently almost immediately on his accession, but for the ties of blood between the young ruler and his Yemenite and Muwallad subjects ?[2] The whole mental attitude of a race or faction does not immediately undergo a radical change because a handsome and amiable young man

[1] Dozy, *G. der M.*, i. 456-7 ; Conde, i. 359 ; Makkari, ii. 134.
[2] The inextinguishable racial feud between the tribes of Yemen and those of Mudar must be borne in mind. The Ommeyads belonged to the latter great division of the Arab peoples.

reigns in place of an old one, no matter how unpopular the latter may have been. It must have been Abderrahman's Christian mother, Mary, who wrought the miracle. Whether she was alive or dead when he assumed the reins of government, we are not told. Possibly she was yet living, for she is named in connection with his accession, and when the Khalif's mother—who was always treated with the greatest respect—had died before he mounted the throne, the fact is as a rule mentioned. But Conde [1] is the only writer who mentions Mary, and he tells us no more than we have said. If she still lived we may imagine how she would use her influence alike with her son and with her Seville relatives to bring about a lasting peace. That Abderrahman honoured her family for her sake, if not for their own, is made clear by many incidents recorded during his long reign.

One of his first acts was to reappoint a Yemenite, degraded by his grandfather, as Kadi of Cordova, and to restore the aged Ibn Gamri to a command in the army, of which Abdullah had deprived him.[2] Throughout his reign Abderrahman's policy always was to receive with open arms any rebels who showed signs of willingness to submit, at once offering them employment in his service. And such was his sympathy with his mother's religion that he not only gave orders that the Christians were to be treated with the greatest consideration, but on one occasion wished to appoint a man whose parents were both Christians to the highest magisterial office, that of Kadi of Cordova, and only desisted owing to the opposition of the Faquis.[3]

[1] The silence of the Sunnite writers and especially of Ibn Hayyan, in regard to the birth and up-bringing of this greatest of all the Ommeyad Kings of Spain is too remarkable to be accidental.
[2] Conde, i. 359–60.
[3] Dozy, *G. der M.*, i. 458–9. Dozy adds that at this time Mohammedanism had almost died out in the mountain ranges where Ibn Hafsun held sway, and there are many other indications that Christianity was far more widely extended than is commonly supposed over all the south-west of Andalucia.

His relations with the Beni Ishak [1] were intimate, for he seems to have submitted to be almost domineered over by his contemporaries of that family, and Dozy relates a curious incident in this connection. But he has overlooked the Gothic descent of the Beni Ishak, who are mentioned to have been of Christian origin, and, presumably because Abderrahman acknowledged him as a cousin, describes Ahmed Ibn Ishak, the hero of the affair, as " a prince of the blood," assuming that as he was a relative of the Khalif he must be of the royal family of Ommeya. The relationship was, of course, through Abderrahman's Christian mother, Mary, and the royal descent of Ahmed Ibn Ishak was Gothic not Ommeyad. It thus appears that as late as 937, the date of the incident about to be narrated, the royal blood of Sara's descendants was still acknowledged, for we cannot suppose that Dozy should call a man a prince of the blood unless the author he quoted gave him some authority for doing so.

In 915 or 916 Abderrahman appointed the head of the Beni Ishak one of his Wizirs, and presently we find Ahmed Ibn Ishak, the son of the Wizir (now dead) Commander-in-chief of the cavalry in a campaign against the Christians of the north, Governor of the upper frontier, and entrusted with the siege of Zaragoza (the Tojibite Governor of which had rebelled and was treating with the King of Leon), while his brother Ommeya had been made Governor of Santarem. Dozy tells us that in 937 Ahmed had grown so presumptuous that he actually requested the Khalif to appoint him his heir, and we read of his execution not long after, because he was discovered plotting to advance his pretensions. Dozy translates at length a letter written by Abderrahman to Ahmed in reply to his request to be named heir apparent, which, as throwing a side-light on the manners of the time, is not without interest. It should be premised that Ahmed

[1] Descendants of Pirncess Sara's son Ishak by her first husband.

shortly before had roused Abderrahman's anger by his want of vigour in the conduct of the siege of Zaragoza.

The letter of Abderrahman is as follows:—

"Since we only wished to do that which was pleasing to thee, we have always treated thee hitherto with the most extreme benevolence; but now we are convinced that it is impossible to change thy character. That which alone is fit for thee is poverty; for as formerly thou knewest not wealth, it has now filled thee with intolerable pride. Was not thy father one of the meanest horsemen of Ibn Hejjaj, and hast thou forgotten that thou thyself wast in Seville nothing but a donkey-dealer? We have always taken thy family under our protection when they begged for it; we have helped thee, have made thee rich and powerful, we conferred on thy late father the dignity of a Wizir, and have appointed thee the commander of our cavalry and Governor of the greatest of our border provinces. And nevertheless thou hast despised our commands, hast paid no attention to our interests, and to fill the measure full, thou now demandest that we should name thee our heir! What merit, what title of nobility canst thou plead? To thee and thy family the well-known verses may be applied:—

"'Ye are people of base origin. How can hemp compare itself with silk? If ye are Koraishites, as you declare, take wives of that renowned tribe; but if you are Copts, your pretensions are ridiculous.'

"Was not thy mother the witch Khamduna? Was not thy father a simple soldier? Was not thy grandfather a door-keeper in the house of Hauthara Ibn Abbas? Did he not make ropes and mats in the vestibule of that lord? May God damn thee, thee and thine, who laid a trap for us when they advised us to take thee into our service! Contemptible, leprous son of a dog and a bitch, come and humble thyself at our feet."

CHRISTIANS AND MUWALLADS 149

After this vigorous remonstrance Ahmed and his brother Ommeya entered into an intrigue which had for its object an alliance with Ramiro, King of Leon, and was designed to overthrow Abderrahman and hand Spain over to the Fatimite Khalifs of Egypt. Abderrahman, discovering the plot, banished Ahmed from his court. Then, as he continued intriguing, he was taken prisoner, tried, and condemned as being a Shiite, or, according to another version, "for some civil offence." [1]

Whatever may be the truth of this, Ahmed now disappears from history, and we must follow the thread of the family fortunes in his brother Ommeya.

"No sooner did Ommeya Ibn Ishak hear of the fate that had befallen his brother, than he left Santarem and fled with a handful of followers to the Court of Ramiro II., the King of the Galicians, whose service he entered, guiding his armies to the defenceless points of the Mohammedan frontier and to the passes and fords at which he could best assail the territories of Islam. However, whilst Ommeya, who had all the time retained possession of Santarem, was one day enjoying the amusements of the chase, one of his own slaves, who had remained in charge of the fortress, rose and took command of the place, shut the gates against Ommeya, and sent a messenger to Abderrahman apprising him of what had occurred, while Ommeya again fled to his ally the King of Galicia, who received him with the greatest kindness, and appointed him his Wizir. This was the motive of Abderrahman's expedition." [2]

There seems to be something wrong here, as Ommeya could hardly have gone backwards and forwards from Santarem to Ramiro's court at Leon, as this story implies. Probably he did not go there at all until after Abderrahman's

---

[1] Dozy, *G. der M.*, ii. 34–6; Makkari, ii. 136.
[2] Makkari, ii. 136.

party, by some stratagem, had succeeded in shutting him out of the city.

The next event in the story was the battle of Zamora, which Makkari thus describes.

"Abderrahman having led his army against Zamora, which he beseiged, Radmir (Ramiro II.), King of the Galicians, hastened to its relief and encamped in the neighbourhood. . . . A contest soon ensued between the two armies, in which the Moslems came off victorious, this being in the month of Shawwal, 327 (July or August, 939), three days after the eclipse of the sun which happened the same month. The garrison of Zamora having made a sally were repulsed by the besiegers, who pursued them sword in hand beyond the moat within the walls of the city. But, as the Moslems were preparing to follow up their advantage, the Christians fell suddenly upon them and killed fifty thousand of their number.[1]

"The city of Zamora was enclosed between seven walls of wonderful structure, the work of one of the early kings. The space between the walls was occupied by ditches and wide moats filled with water.[2] The Moslems succeeded in

---

[1] Gayangos says that this battle took place at Simancas, July 19, 939 (Makkari, ii. 463). The *Crónica general* (viii. 220) also places it at Simancas, in the year 938.

[2] Gayangos adds the words "of Galicia" after "of the early kings" in the text, but this must be conjecture.

Zamora had been taken several years before by Alfonso III. of Leon, and in 893, according to Ibn Hayyan, he rebuilt and repeopled the city and repaired the fortifications, the architects being people from Toledo. Toledo was at that time frequently if not continuously under the control of Omar Ibn Hafsun, which may account for Alfonso being able to obtain architects from a city nominally subject to Cordova. (Makkari, ii. 453; Conde, i. 319, 342.) We have seen an ancient castle in Andalucia, rebuilt in the fourteenth century, and recently restored on the old lines, with two dry moats, one above the other, and the Castle of Badajoz has three such moats, of which the lowest still contains outlets for the water which once filled it from what now serves as the town reservoir. We believe this system of fortification to be pre-Moslem. If Zamora was fortified with six of these dry moats, rising one above the other, and protected by water in the lowest of them, it is easy to understand that the Moslems found themselves at the

CHRISTIANS AND MUWALLADS

forcing their way through the two first enclosures, but when they came to the third they were furiously assailed on all sides by the Christians, who put to death every Moslem they could overtake. Upwards of forty thousand men, others say fifty thousand, were drowned in the moats. This was doubtless one of the most signal defeats ever inflicted on our brethren of Andalus, either by the Galicians or the Basques; and the victory would have been still more complete had King Ramiro pursued the remnant of Abderrahman's army, which, panic-stricken as it was, he would have had no difficulty in annihilating. But by alarming Ramiro with the fear of an ambush, and alluring him with the rich spoil left behind by the Moslems in their camp, Ommeya Ibn Ishak prevented him from following up the victory." [1]

Conde, who dates the siege in 938, thus agreeing with the *Crónica general*, gives a long account of the campaign, which is in substantial agreement with that of Makkari.[2] The only additional facts of interest that we find in his version are that Al-Motref commanded the vanguard of the Moslem army, and that Ibn Ishak and his followers wore plate mail like the Christians.[3]

Perhaps the most remarkable feature in this affair is the small effect it seems to have had upon Abderrahman's affection for his relatives the Beni Ishak. It is generally agreed that it was Ommeya Ibn Ishak's military skill which alone enabled Ramiro to hold his own against the Khalif: yet Ommeya some time after applied to his cousin for a safe-conduct, and, having received it, left the Court of

mercy of the Christians when they had rushed the outer defences and were received by the besieged, shooting from their secure entrenchments behind the parapets of the successive dry moats above.

[1] Makkari, ii. 136-7.
[2] Conde, i. 419-24.
[3] Makkari and Conde both took their accounts of the siege from Al-Mesudi, who wrote in Egypt and died about 946 or 947.

Ramiro and went with perfect confidence to Cordova, where he was graciously received by Abderrahman.[1]

Conde adds some further particulars. He places Ommeya's submission only a year later, in 940, after another campaign which ended with the fall of Zamora and San Esteban de Gormaz [2] to the Moslem arms. Ommeya Ibn Ishak, having quarrelled with Ramiro because that king had lost confidence in him (which is perhaps hardly surprising), wrote to Abderrahman asking to be restored to favour, and excusing his previous conduct by explaining that he believed himself bound in honour to avenge the death of his brother. "Now he was convinced that Ahmed had not been unjustly executed, and prayed to be allowed to give his services to prove his loyalty and show that he was a good Moslem. And Abderrahman not only accepted his excuses, but took him back into favour and reinstated him in his dignity as Wizir and Commander of the frontier." [3]

Another member of the family, Yahya Ibn Ishak, was one of Abderrahman's physicians. He was very skilful and excelled in the knowledge of medicines. Abderrahman made him a Wizir and gave him the government of Badajoz. Ibn Abi Ossaybiah, who gives these particulars, adds that his father was a Christian.[4]

Another descendant of Sara to whom Abderrahman showed especial favour was Ismail Ibn Badr Ibn Said, known as Abu Bekr, whom he made Wali of Seville about 940. The family were Muwallads, the first of the name who rose to prominence being the son of a Christian named Zadlaf. This was Yahya Ibn Zadlaf, who built a strong fortress with iron-lined gates at Santa Maria del Algarbe,

[1] Makkari, ii. 137.
[2] This stronghold, with its Arabic castle and watch-towers, is a conspicuous feature of the landscape on the railway line between Valladolid and Ariza.
[3] Conde, i. 429–30.
[4] Makkari, i. 187, 464.

in the district of Ocsonoba. His son Bekr was granted the Governorship of Silves in the Algarbe, but nevertheless he continued to support the Christians and Muwallads until he died at the beginning of the reign of Abderrahman III.[1] The Beni Said were the direct descendants of Jilbab or Habib, Sara's only son by her second husband, as were the Beni Hejjaj, the Beni Moslemah, and the Beni Jorj. Thus Karis Ibn Abbad Ibn Said al-Lakhmi, Imam of the great Seville mosque and progenitor of the brilliant dynasty of the Abbadites of Seville, must have had a strain of the royal Gothic blood in his veins, although none of the Sunnite writers allude to it.

There seems no room for doubt that their descent from the Gothic kings was one reason for the high place this race of mixed ancestry held in Abderrahman's esteem, apart from his mother's connection with them. And it is equally safe to assert that their personal connection with the son of the Ommeyad prince who died at the head of the Seville army, and of his Gothic-Christian wife whom he married in Seville, was the true cause of the magical disappearance of the Yemenite and Muwallad hostility to the rule of Cordova, when the son of Mahommed and Mary, and the grandson of the Christian Iñiga, ascended the throne of their racial enemies.[2]

[1] In many cases the so-called "grant" of such Governorships was undoubtedly the Sunnite euphemism for possession by inheritance or force of arms on the part of their opponents the Yemenites or Muwallads. In the case of the Beni Said this was certainly so, for we find them there generation after generation, and always in opposition to the Sunnite rulers.
[2] Conde, i. 425; Makkari, ii. 250, 440, 503; Al-Kuttiyyah in *J.A.* 434.

CHAPTER IX

THE SUCCESSORS OF ABDERRAHMAN

MAKKARI sums up the character of Abderrahman in the following words :—

"He has been described by the historians of the age as the mildest and most enlightened sovereign that ever ruled a country. His meekness, his generosity, and his love of justice became proverbial: none of his ancestors ever surpassed him in courage in the field, zeal for religion, and other virtues which constitute an able and beloved monarch; he was fond of science, and the patron of the learned, with whom he loved to converse, spending those hours which he stole from the arduous labours of the administration in literary meetings, to which all the eminent poets and learned men of his court were admitted. The histories of the time are filled with anecdotes which show his love of justice and his respect for the learned." [1]

It is clear that Abderrahman was a ruler in whom the noblest attributes of Christian and Moslem were combined. This alone accounts for the extraordinary brilliance of his reign, and for the success of his efforts to bring peace within the borders of a country previously distracted by strife between opposing religions. It is not necessary to seek explanations in the decay of martial spirit or the decline of race antagonism. The unity brought about by this great monarch was due to personal causes. It endured as long as his son sat on the throne and conducted the affairs of state

[1] Makkari, ii. 147.

FIG. 7.—Entrance to an apartment in the Alcazar of Seville, traditionally known as "The Sleeping-Room of the Moorish King and Queen," opening on to the "Court of the Ladies"; otherwise the patio of the Harem. Decorated in the style prevailing in the Moslem Court of Egypt in the late twelfth and thirteenth centuries, with some of the original tiles still existing. One of the apartments prepared by the Moorish Sultan, Yusuf Abu Yakub (the Almohade), in 1171–5, for the reception of his Yemenite bride, the Princess of Denia. (See p. 275.)

on the same broad lines of justice and generosity, and also while a strong minister governed in the name of his grandson ; but the old inextinguishable hostility broke out again when the controlling hand was removed, and burnt more fiercely than ever fifty years later, not to be cooled even by the dismemberment of the empire which Abderrahman had built up on what seemed so secure a foundation.

His son Al-Hakem, who succeeded him, was like himself a wise and enlightened ruler, just, generous, and liberal-minded. His strict observance of religious duties, and his enforcement of the precepts of the Sunna made him popular with the orthodox party, while his erudition and devotion to literature, in addition to his parentage, won the regard of the cultivated Yemenites, among whose leading families literature flourished from an early date. Al-Hakem surpassed every one of his predecessors in love of learning, and is described as having converted Andalucia into a great market whither the literary productions of the whole Moslem world were brought for sale. Indeed, so much stress is laid by all Arabic historians on this feature of his reign that we might suspect a desire to withdraw attention from less laudable characteristics of it, were it not that we find him maintaining internal affairs in a peaceful and prosperous condition, and confining his military operations to resisting aggression from the Christians of the north.

Even with these Christians he was on good terms during much of his reign, receiving embassies from the rulers of Galicia, Castile, Navarre, Barcelona, and Tarragona, and showing in his every action that he, like his father, preferred negotiation to force.

That he had good common sense is shown by his action in regard to the practice of drinking wine, which had become general in Andalucia, owing, Makkari says, to the tolerance or negligence of former Sultans. Possibly this remark was aimed at the sympathy of Abderrahman III. with the Yemenites, who never pretended to obey the injunctions of the Sunna in this respect, any more than in the prohibition of representations of animate life.

Be that as it may, Al-Hakem desired to check the abuse of wine, and to that end ordered that all the vines in the kingdom should be rooted up. According to Makkari, one of his wisest counsellors told him that any such action would ruin the vine-growers, who were poor men. He also pointed out that if people were bent on drinking wine they would procure it from the Christian countries—where no edicts against drunkenness existed—or make it themselves of figs or other fruits from which alcohol could be extracted. Al-Hakem, convinced by this reasoning that his contemplated action would not only be unjust but unpractical, recalled the order, permitting sufficient vines to be cultivated to provide grapes for eating, either fresh-plucked or in the form of raisins, and to make the extract of grape juice and other wholesome and lawful drinks.[1]

Conde gives further details of the reasons for this reform. " Owing to the bad habits and licence introduced into Spain by the people of Irak and other foreigners, the use of wine had become free and was regarded as lawful, so that common people and even Faquis drank it, and it was allowed at wedding and other feasts with scandalous liberty. King Al-Hakem, who was religious, abstinent, and learned in the approved explanations of the Koran, called together his Alimes and Faquis, and asked them what could be the origin of the general abuse going on in Spain, where not only was *ghamat* or red wine drunk, but also *sabha* or white wine, *nebid*, date wine, or that made of figs, and other strong drinks which were intoxicants. They replied that since the reign of King Mohammed it had become the accepted opinion that, as

[1] Makkari, ii. 171.

the Moslems of Spain were continually at war with the enemies of Islam, they might use wine, because that drink increased the courage and spirit of the soldiers in battle, and thus its use on all the frontiers was lawful in order to have more strength for fighting. The King reprobated these opinions, and in his hatred of the abuse, he ordered all the vines in Spain to be plucked up, save only the third part," which he permitted to remain for the purpose described above.[1]

As was only natural under the protection of so literary a monarch, the histories of Al-Hakem's reign are filled with the names of celebrated writers, among which we find those of many Yemenites and Muwallads.

The following anecdotes are quoted from Conde, as throwing a little light on the domestic manners and customs of the time, a subject about which not much is known.

"A savant named Ibn Safaran El Xeibani[2] lived in Cordova, on the bank of the river by the fountains; and one day the Kadi, having been caught in a storm of rain when riding past the house, drew his horse for shelter into the *patio*[3] of El Xeibani, who came out and insisted on the Kadi dismounting and coming in. After the guest was seated on the couch of honour, and the usual compliments had been paid El Xeibani said—

"'I have in my house a girl belonging to this city, with the sweetest voice it is possible to hear. If it please thee she shall sing a passage from the book of God, or a few verses.'

---

[1] Conde, i. 465–6.
[2] We have not been able to find mention of this man elsewhere, and have only Conde's spelling of his name.
[3] The *patio* is the open courtyard round which houses in Andalucia are always built. Probably the Kadi entered, not the *patio*, but the vestibule or entrance now called the *zaguan*, which is open to the street in the day-time, and where passers-by frequently take shelter. The access to the *patio* proper is closed by an iron grille.

"The Kadi replied, 'I have come in a fortunate hour.'

"The maiden appeared, the most lovely one that human eyes ever beheld. El Xeibani told her to read, and then she sang several verses. It all pleased the Kadi very much, and without being seen he took out a purse and put it beneath his seat. When the rain was over he thanked El Xeibani and took his leave. El Xeibani went out to see him depart, and when he returned he found a purse with twenty pieces of gold under the couch of honour."[1]

Of Ahmed Ibn Said al-Ansari of Toledo,[2] a learned Faqui of that city, rich and respected, it is related that "he used to collect in his house as many as forty friends devoted to *belles lettres*, not only from Toledo, but from Calatrava[3] and elsewhere. In the months of November, December, and January, they met in a large room, the pavement of which was covered with silken and woollen carpets and cushions, and the walls draped with tapestries and embroidered hangings. In the middle of the room there was a large tube as high as a man, full of burning charcoal, and everybody sat round it at the distance they pleased. While they read a portion of the Koran or recited verses and discussed them, musk and other agreeable perfumes were brought to them, and they were sprinkled with rose-water. Then a table was served to them, with the meat of tender kid and mutton, and a variety of dishes cooked in olive oil; then followed milk curdled and whipped, butter, and different sweetmeats, dates and other fruits. In the shortest days of the winter they passed most of the day at table. These meetings

---

[1] This story is related on the authority of "the Kadi Jonas," who from the name would appear to have been a Christian.

[2] The Ansari were Yemenites, established in the eighth century all over Andalucia, and were especially numerous in and around Toledo. (Makkari, ii. 25.) From this tribe sprang the great Nasrite dynasty of Granada in the thirteenth century.

[3] Another district populated chiefly by Arab families from Yemen of the tribe of Jodham.

continued until the end of January, and took place every year. No one else in the city was as hospitable as this Faqui, although there were others who were very rich. The King appointed him head judge of the city, and out of envy and jealousy of his fame and popularity the Kadi of the same district brought about his murder. The assassin went into his house, where he was well known, and found Ibn Said reading the Koran.

"'I know for what thou hast come,' he said; 'do that which thou art commanded. God is in heaven and sees and knows all.'

"And the assassin strangled him, and pretended that he had died a natural death."[1]

During Al-Hakem's reign the hostility between Syrians and Yemenites continued to slumber, and indeed Al-Hakem seems to have gone out of his way to show equal favour to the men of both races, for although the Mudarite Arabs were numerous at Cordova, the most famous among the several masters whom he procured for his only son, afterwards Hisham II.; was Al Zobaidi, a Sevillian of a well-known Yemenite family. He was the most learned man of his time in the Arabic grammar and language, and his especial charge was the instruction of the young prince in these two subjects. Al-Hakem made him Prefect of the Court of Justice of Cordova, and when Hisham came to the throne he, or his Prime Minister, appointed Al Zobaidi Kadi of Seville, and gave him other exalted posts.[2]

Al-Hakem was a great lover of peace, and contrived to keep it even with the Christians during most of his reign, notwithstanding the belligerence of some of the Governors of his own frontier towns. It is said that the lessons that he gave to his son Hisham always concluded with these words:—

[1] Conde, i. 483–5.
[2] Conde, i. 485–6; Pons, p. 90.

"Do not go to war without necessity. Keep the peace for thy own felicity and that of thy people. Do not draw thy sword except against the unjust. What pleasure is there in invading and destroying towns, ruining states, and carrying ravage and death to the confines of the earth? Keep thy people in peace and justice, and be not beguiled by the false maxims of vanity. Let thy justice be like a lake, always clear and pure. Moderate thy imaginations, restrain thy desires, trust in God, and thou shalt reach in peace of mind the appointed end of thy days." [1]

The wealth of Moslem Spain at this period was immense, and although it was partly derived from gold and silver mines,[2] and to some extent from those of precious stones, yet the chief riches were those produced by agriculture. During the reign of Al-Hakem the great irrigation systems of which we still see the remains, were developed in the vegas of Granada, Murcia, Valencia, and Aragon, reservoirs being constructed for the purpose, and every kind of fruit and vegetable suitable to the climate and the land was brought into cultivation. Al-Hakem also spent great sums in building mosques, asylums for the poor, hospitals and colleges, and he added baths, inns, fountains, and markets to many cities in his dominions.[3]

Some two years before his death Al-Hakem appointed a Yemenite Wizir, promoting him to that office from the position of Kadi of Cordova, to the evident indignation of the Sunnite historians, some of whom—*e.g.* Ibn Hayyan—devote so much attention to what they represent as the Wizir's intrigues to obtain power, that they seem hardly able to appreciate his extraordinary statesmanship.

This was Mohammed Ibn Abi Amir, of the tribe of Maafer,

[1] Conde, i. 486.
[2] Probably the gold was washed out in some of the rivers: gold-mines are not known to exist in Spain.
[3] Makkari, ii. 172; Conde, i. 487.

a descendant of one of the Arab nobles who came to Andalucia at the time of the invasion, and destined to become known to all the world by his surname of Almansur, or "the victorious."

Makkari asserts that Mohammed Abi Amir—or Almansur, to use the more familiar name—obtained his titles and honours in the Court of Cordova by currying favour with Prince Hisham's mother, who introduced him to Al-Hakem and induced the Khalif to bestow on him a lucrative appointment.[1] The improbability that a jealous Oriental should show favour to a handsome young man with whom his own wife was on terms of undue intimacy, is too obvious to need comment. Nor need we waste time over the same author's suggestion that one of Almansur's chief holds over the Khalif consisted in his talent for astrology and divination. Al-Hakem, himself an intelligent and able man, was quite capable of recognising the exceptional promise of the young Yemenite, and we may safely assume that he gave him increasingly important appointments because he saw that he could not find a better man for the purpose.

Hisham II. was only a child when his father died, and Al-Hakem as death approached no doubt foresaw that unless his son were provided with a competent administrator from the moment of his accession he would have small chance of retaining the throne. Indeed it is said that the loyalists found it necessary to get rid of Al-Mugheyrah, his uncle, before the child-ruler could be proclaimed, owing to the existence of a strong party in Cordova who preferred him to the rightful heir, on account of his age and experience, and probably because he did not favour the Yemenites. Almansur is accused of having put Al-Mugheyrah to death with his own hands two days after the death of Al-Hakem, and of having plotted to get the young Khalif into his power

[1] ii. 178.

in order to usurp his authority, and we are given in this connection various instances—which fail to carry conviction—of his malice and cruelty not only towards individuals, but to whole families whom he suspected of endeavouring to undermine his influence with Hisham. But it seems clear that Almansur had for some time to contend with antagonism to Hisham at Court, and probably if we knew both sides of the story we should find that he had very good reason, as a loyal servant of the crown, to take severe measures against the persons described by Hayyan as the innocent victims of his unfounded hatred.[1]

Having, according to Makkari, got rid of every one who opposed his ambitious designs, Almansur usurped all authority and ruled with absolute sway. He "sat on the throne of the kings," letters, proclamations, and commands were issued in his name, he ordered a prayer to be offered for himself after the usual one for the Khalif, he obliterated the rights and insignia of the Khalifate, and nothing remained to Hisham except his name on the coins and on the skirts of the royal robe called *tiraz*. Even these, says our author, Almansur enjoyed concurrently with Hisham, for he caused his own name to be struck on the coins and woven into the *tiraz*.[2]

Almansur and the mother of the young Khalif, Sobha or Sobeya,[3] are accused of secluding Hisham within the harem

---

[1] Makkari, ii. 175-6, 183.

[2] *Ib.* 187. Gayangos says that he has seen coins inscribed with Almansur's name, some with the addition of "Hajib," others without. *Ib.* 477. The *tiraz* may have been merely a gift from Hisham, for it was by no means unusual for the Khalifs to present a robe of ceremony from their own wardrobe to those whom they wished to honour. This could easily have been magnified by persons inimical to the Hajib into an infringement of the royal prerogatives. But not long after it became the common practice of the nobility to use the *tiraz*, if indeed it had not already become the vogue.

[3] She is said to have been the sister of the Slavonian eunuch, Fayik, chief of the royal guard instituted by Abderrahman III., but this seems doubtful. (Makkari, ii. 175, 186, 477.)

for their own evil purposes, and of deliberately treating him as of weak intellect until he became next door to an idiot. But when we remember what a child he was when his father died in 976 (Makkari says he was only nine years old), and when we note the many indications of conspiracy against his rule, we see that his Hajib and the Queen Mother may have had excellent reasons for placing a careful guard about his person.

Makkari quotes Ibn Bassam (whom Dozy also apparently follows in his account of the events immediately following the death of Al-Hakem)[1] to the effect that Fayik and another Slavonian eunuch plotted to set the child Hisham aside and give the throne to his uncle Al-Mugheyrah. Al-Mushafi, the Chamberlain of the late Khalif, pretended to enter into their conspiracy, and immediately sent Almansur with some soldiers to put Al-Mugheyrah to death, thereby frustrating the scheme.[2] This, if true, suggests that Makkari's statement of the relationship between Hisham's mother and Fayik, the chief of the eunuchs, is incorrect, since Fayik would hardly have conspired to oust his own nephew, a child under whose nominal rule he might expect to maintain and increase his power, in favour of a man of mature age.

Makkari says that Almansur, immediately after Al-Hakem's death, expelled the Slavonian body-guard from the palace, and employed, in the protracted intrigue which followed, a Shiite general born in the Andalucian quarter of Fez, and therefore called "the Andalucian," to carry out his plans against those who resisted his authority.[3]

Conde puts forward the more human and natural explanation of the seclusion of Hisham at this time, and it is noteworthy that more than once in his account of Hisham's reign he quotes Al-Fayyad, the Yemenite historian whose

[1] *G. der M.*, ii. 84 ff. [2] Makkari, ii. 176–8.
[3] *Ibid.*, ii. 176, 475.

work was not accessible to Makkari, Gayangos, or Dozy. His account is as follows.

When the funeral ceremony of Al-Hakem was over, his son Hisham was proclaimed at the age of ten years and a few months. He was the only son of Al-Hakem, and his mother was the Sultana Sobeya. This Conde says in a note means Aurora, the name which Dozy always gives her.

The Queen Mother had so won the heart of Al-Hakem by her discretion and beauty that for more than ten years (evidently since she had given a son to the hitherto childless monarch) nothing great or small, whether in the house of the king, in the Court, or in the provinces, had been done without consulting her, and her lightest suggestions were sovereign orders to be obeyed without excuse or delay. The secretary of the Sultana was Mohammed Ibn Abi Amir, whose courtesy, refinement, courage, and consummate prudence had won the esteem and confidence of the King as well as the Queen, and respect and consideration from all the Walis, Wizirs and Governors.

Not long after his arrival at Cordova, the Queen Sobeya made Ibn Abi Amir her secretary and majordomo, and later on, having regard to her son's tender years, she entrusted the government to Almansur, and named him High Chamberlain,[1] to be guardian of the Khalif's person and first Minister of State and War. Every one approved of this choice except the former Chamberlain, Al-Mushafi, who looked upon it as a slight to himself, and whose secret resentment was shared by his sons.

Meanwhile Hisham, as was natural at his tender age, thought of nothing but his games and innocent pleasures, and never left his palaces and delightful gardens, nor wished for other amusements than what he found there, while his companions were little slaves of his own age, who lived shut

[1] Su primer Hajib; cf. Makkari, ii. 175, 187.

THE SUCCESSORS OF ABDERRAHMAN 165

up with him, and were not allowed to communciate with anybody.[1] Such precautions were but natural if there was a long continued intrigue at work to dethrone or murder the little Khalif, as seems to have been the case.

We think, however, that the real explanation of Hisham's seclusion, prolonged until the death of Almansur twenty-six years later, was the desire, perhaps the imperative necessity, to conceal from the people that he was weak in intellect. True, the lessons recorded as given him by his father (p. 160) do not suggest imbecility in the pupil, unless the mention that the advice was frequently repeated means that Hisham's memory was faulty. But even could we place implicit reliance on the account of any one historian, uncorroborated by others, it would not follow that the prince who appeared to develop normally up to ten years old necessarily continued to develop when he approached adolescence. Conde [2] says " he had no other will than that of his servants " (*que no tenia mas voluntad que la de sus siervos*) referring to the period of revolution in 1009.

More than ten years after his accession, when he was certainly twenty (authorities differ as to his exact age when his father died) the Queen Mother was still acting as regent, if we may judge from the fact that there was an inscription on a reservoir at Ecija, existing as late as 1820, to the effect that it was erected " by the order of the mother of the Prince of the Believers, Hisham the favoured of God, son of Al-Hakem," with the date 377 (A.D. 987).[3]

Instances are found of the mother of the heir to the throne being commemorated in work done by her order on mosques which were called hers; [4] but we doubt if important public works such as the conduit and reservoir here referred to

[1] Conde, i. 491–493.
[2] *Ibid.*, i. 558.
[3] *Ibid.*, i. 496.
[4] *E.g.*, the Church of San Juan de la Palma in Seville.

would have borne the mother's name had the reigning monarch been capable of attending to affairs of state himself.

Dozy quotes Makkari as saying that Al-Zobaidi found Hisham remarkably clever and quick to grasp ideas,[1] and argues from this that his mother and Almansur deliberately laid themselves out to enfeeble his mind after he became Khalif.

Al Zobaidi's testimony would have greater weight if we could find further evidence of Hisham's intellectual activity. But although he may have been quick-witted as a little child (and no great amount of talent is needed to make a Crown Prince appear clever in the eyes of his father's courtiers) he seems undoubtedly—so far as can be judged from the data accessible in translations—to have been deficient in adolescence and manhood. When we remember that his father was about fifty-two years old when Hisham was born, and that he had no other children either by his wives or concubines, possibly his son's mental weakness may be accounted for. As for Hisham himself, he never had a child at all.

But whatever the cause of the Khalif's deficiencies may have been, his reign, thanks to those very disabilities, was almost as glorious as that of Abderrahman III., as long as his kingdom was under the rule of the Yemenite whom his mother wisely selected for his first Minister immediately on his father's death.

The warlike enterprise and invariable success of Almansur are familiar to all who have read any of the popular histories of Moslem Spain, and we will not repeat what is so well known, but will instead relate some incidents showing another side to his character.

Conde gives us an interesting anecdote illustrating his

---

[1] *G. der M.*, ii. 110. We have not been able to find the passage in Gayangos' translation.

stern sense of justice and disregard for influential family connections, which we have not found related elsewhere.

A young lad of seventeen named Maron (Merwan) son of Abderrahman Ibn Maron and grandson of Abderrahman III., loved a maiden who was a captive slave belonging to his father. They had been brought up from infancy together, and as they grew in years so grew their attachment. The father of Maron, unaware of this, separated the two when it appeared convenient to him, but parting only increased their passion.

One night the impetuous youth, unable any longer to restrain his ardour, furtively entered the gardens where his father's slaves were amusing themselves, and there, screened by the myrtle bushes, he saw the maiden.

"There is no time for speech," he told her. "We must do quickly that which we have to do."

She, only anxious to please him, followed him out of the garden and they fled together from the spot, to be met at the outer gates by Maron's father Abderrahman.

Maron, mad with passion and excitement, did not recognise his father, nor paused to remember that the man who tried to stop his flight in such a place and at such a time could be no other. He drew his sword and ran him through.

At the cry uttered by Abderrahman his servants rushed up. Vainly Maron tried to cut his way through them. The maiden fell fainting in his arms, and while he turned to support her he was disarmed and taken prisoner.

In the absence of Almansur, the Kadis, at the queen's order, inquired into the affair, and taking into consideration Maron's youth, sentenced him only to as many years' imprisonment as the years of his age, a decision which was confirmed by the Queen Mother and the Khalif.

Now comes the detail which suggests that Hisham was not regarded by his Chamberlain as entirely without responsibility.

When Almansur returned from the campaign on which he had been absent, and heard what had taken place, he told the Khalif that he had judged the offence from the point of view of a youth and a lover, not as the father of a family. Which comment, if it means anything at all, means that Hisham was expected by his Minister to administer justice with impartiality, even though the offender were a youth and one of his own house. And this hardly looks as if the speaker regarded Hisham as deficient in intellect. On the other hand it must be noted that the Queen Mother gave the order for the offence to be brought to trial, and she as well as the Khalif confirmed the sentence.[1]

On the whole it appears that Hisham, if not actually weak-minded, was easily influenced by persons who had won his affection, and entirely lacked decision to come to a resolution and courage to meet dangers and difficulties. If this was the case—and his general conduct after the death of Almansur certainly points to it, the desire of his mother and the Prime Minister to keep him and his deficiencies hidden from the critical eyes of his enemies in the State was fully justified.

In an attempt to obtain a coherent idea of persons and events of which flatly contradictory accounts are given by different historians, it is permissible to assume that when two versions of a man's conduct are given, the probability is that that which is most in accordance with his general character is most likely to be the true one. The whole weight of evidence in regard to Almansur is that he was not only a great administrator, but a just and generous ruler, and we may therefore conclude that he would not have treated the son of the man to whom he owed everything, with the brutality of which he is accused by the enemies of his race.

[1] Conde, i. 499-500.

CHAPTER X

ALMANSUR AND THE CHRISTIANS

ALTHOUGH Almansur was continually sending expeditions against the Christians who invaded the Moslem frontiers, and although he frequently commanded those expeditions in person, his personal conduct towards them, both as individuals and as a community, was exceedingly liberal.

The Christian writers themselves admit this, and before quoting examples from the Arabic historians we will give two or three instances of the great Yemenite's consideration for the Christians as related by themselves.

In an account of a siege of Leon in 984, it is said that "Almansur's courtesy and good treatment of all, and the great offers he made them, resulted in many 'bad Christians' deserting their own cause and following his banners without shame." [1]

In Makkari's account of this expedition he says that Almansur invested and took Leon, putting the inhabitants to the sword, and that he attempted to demolish the fortifications, but desisted owing to the thickness of the walls and the time the operation would be likely to take.[2]

When Christian and Moslem writers disagree so markedly about the treatment of Christians by Moslems, it is safe to accept the Christian version if, as in this case, it testifies to

---

[1] *España sagrada*, xxxiv. 303.
[2] Makkari, ii. 189. Abdalmalek, son of Almansur, is said to have destroyed Leon and razed it to the ground (*ib.* 222, 486). As to the destruction of the city it is enough to say that the Roman walls are still standing.

the good treatment of the Christians. No one who has read the Spanish chronicles of the Moslem occupation of Spain needs to be reminded that they do not err on the side of charity to their conquerors.

A writer in *España sagrada* gives a curious picture of the credulity of his time (1753) which may be worth translating.

In the course of one of his victorious campaigns Almansur was proposing to ride his horse into the Church of the Holy Martyrs, Saints Claudio and others, in Leon. It was a favourite church for the celebration of marriages, and on the very day when Almansur was about to commit his sacrilegious act, no less than twelve Christian nobles, with their twelve equally noble brides, had gone there to be married. Almansur, having been informed of this, came to the church door with the barbarous intention of sacking the church and taking the newly married couples prisoners. But a wonderful miracle prevented the commission of his projected sin. On the very threshold of the entrance (*atrio*) his horse suddenly fell dead. This caused Almansur to inquire what was taking place within (notwithstanding that, according to the writer, he had come because he knew of the twelve weddings) and he was so impressed by the piety of the Leonese that instead of carrying out his wicked intentions he made offerings to the saints to whom the church was dedicated.

Almansur did apparently make an offering to the church in question, for the writer says he saw the record in the *Leccionario antiguo*, and that Almansur's gift consisted of a hanging with his insignia, and twelve copes of valuable cloth, "which to-day are in the tower of St. Claudio." [1]

The accounts of the taking of Santiago by Almansur are, as usual, contradictory. Ibn Hayyan tells us that—

"All the public buildings were very solid and of wonderful

[1] *España sagrada*, xxxiv. 360.

structure, yet they were so completely destroyed that no one could have imagined (to see the flat surface) that they had stood there only the day before." [1]

Mariana's account is very different. He says, as though he were relating a crime—

"Miserable was the state of affairs, and great the insult to the Christian religion. Galicia was very ill-treated by the attacks and arms of the barbarians: even the city of Compostella was taken and one wall of the temple of Santiago thrown to the ground. They did not touch the sepulchre of the Apostle: the reason of this is not known. . . . Almansur himself . . . being told by a certain man that one of the disciples of the Son of Mary was buried there, determined to abandon that undertaking" (*i.e.* his campaign, apparently).[2] This hardly suggests that Santiago was so utterly destroyed that not one stone was left upon another.

Even Ibn Hayyan admits that Almansur respected the sepulchre assigned by tradition as the burial place of St. James. He says, "the tomb only of St. James was preserved, Almansur having appointed people to take care of it and prevent any profanation." And again, "they say that the Moslems found no living soul in Santiago except an old monk who was sitting on the tomb of St. James. Being interrogated by Almansur as to himself and what he was doing in that spot, he answered, 'I am a familiar of St. James.' Upon which Almansur ordered that no harm should be done to him." [3]

In connection with the statement in *España sagrada* that Almansur won to his cause many "bad Christians," who fought with him against their own people, it is interesting to note that Ibn Hayyan gives the following information:—

[1] Makkari, ii. 195.
[2] Mariana, Book VIII., chap. viii.
[3] Makkari, ii. 195-6.

"On his (Almansur's) arrival at the city (capital) of Galicia he was met by a considerable number of the Christian counts, who acknowledged his authority, with their respective forces, all mounted and equipped (for war). Having joined the Moslem troops, all together crossed the Christian frontier."[1] Dozy also mentions the "needy, money-loving, bad patriots" among the Christian Spaniards, who, according to him, deserted the Castilian, Leonese, and Navarrese armies for the sake of the gold offered by Almansur.[2]

Ibn Hayyan tells us that when Almansur, on his return from Santiago, arrived at the districts of the allied Counts who were in his army, he ordered his soldiers to desist from further ravages, and passing rapidly through their territory, he arrived at a castle called Beliko, which he had reduced on a former occasion. This Gayangos suggests to be Vallecos near Ciudad Rodrigo, and consequently not far from Coria, where Almansur had entered the enemies' territory at the outset of his campaign. Having there assembled the Christian Counts who had assisted in the enterprise, he rewarded each man according to his rank, distributing dresses of honour among them and their followers, after which he dismissed them to their respective countries. "In this campaign Almansur gave away to the Christian princes and others who had shown themselves friends of the Moslems, two thousand two hundred and eighty-five pieces of the silken stuff called *tiraz*, of various colours and patterns; twenty-one dresses of seal-skin; two dresses of the stuff called *anbar;* eleven of scarlet cloth; fifteen *marishat* (a word which Gayangos cannot translate); seven horse-cloths made of brocade; two dresses of the same stuff manufactured in Greece; and two others lined with weasel-skin."[3]

[1] Makkari, ii. 194.   [2] *G. der M.*, ii. 115.
[3] Makkari. ii. 194–6, 480–1.

ALMANSUR AND THE CHRISTIANS

We can find no hint anywhere as to who these Christian Counts were. Their territory, which was traversed peaceably, seems to have lain in the south of Leon or the north of Estremadura. It is possible that they were the descendants of the Christians who, under Romulo the son of Witiza, had settled in the neighbourhood of Toledo and had lived there in practical independence for some two hundred years, until they capitulated to Abderrahman III., about fifty years before the date of Almansur's campaign. It will be remembered that when Toledo opened her gates to Abderrahman, Jaafar Hafsun escaped with some thousands of his followers, and we are not told where he went. If among these Counts were the descendants of Romulo and of Hafsun, it is possible that they may have preferred the Moslem alliance to absorption in the growing powers of the north, who were continuing the traditions of Roderick. But this is pure conjecture.

In 995 or 996 Almansur took prisoner Garcia, son of Sancho, "king of the Christians of the mountains," who was so seriously wounded that he died a few days afterwards, notwithstanding all the care which Almansur lavished on him. He commanded the body of the king to be placed in a well-carved coffin, and wrapped in a beautiful covering of scarlet and gold, with fine perfumes, in order to send it to the Christians ; and when some knights of Garcia's army came to ransom the corpse, Almansur gave it to them and refused their gifts.[1]

In 997, when Abdalmalek, Almansur's son, wrote to tell his father of the success of his arms in Morocco, where he had won the city of Fez, Almansur not only gave alms to

[1] Conde, i. 532-5. Conde in a note to this passage says that this was Count Garcia Fernandez of Castile, who, however, according to Mariana, died ten years later, in 1006 (*Lib.* VIII. chapter x.). According to Watts (*Spain*, p. 308), Garcia Fernandez died in 995, which agrees with the date assigned by Conde.

beggars and paid the debts of many poor and honest persons, but set free fifteen hundred captives and three hundred female Christian slaves, in token of his gratitude to God for such great mercies.[1]

Dozy says, on the authority of the Monk of Silos, that when there was a dispute between a Christian and a Moslem, Almansur always favoured the Christian. Makkari tells us, on the authority of an anonymous history of Almansur, that Sunday was a day of rest for Almansur's household, who were always on that day allowed some relaxation from their duties, the reason according to Gayangos being that his household was composed of Christian slaves.[2]

The consideration, acknowledged on all hands, with which Almansur treated the Christians, throws great doubt on the oft-repeated story of his making the Christian captives of Santiago carry the bells of their church from that city to Cordova on their backs; and the improbability of the tale is increased by Ibn Hayyan's statement that all the inhabitants of Santiago had fled before Almansur got there. (See above, p. 171.) It is not likely that a man who was so generous and broad-minded as to respect the tomb of a Christian saint, and to consider the religious and physical well-being of his Christian slaves, should have murdered women and children of that religion, sacked their houses, and destroyed their churches, as Almansur is represented by Ibn Hayyan to have done. The most plausible explanation of his narrative is that he depicted the Shiite as doing what he, a Sunnite, would have thought it right to do in his place.

Numerous stories of Almansur's charity, benevolence, astuteness, and sense of humour are related. Most of these we must leave aside, as foreign to our subject. We cannot, however, resist the temptation to show the lighter side of

[1] Conde, i. 539.
[2] Dozy, *G. der M.*, ii. 115; Makkari, ii. 215, 485.

ALMANSUR AND THE CHRISTIANS

the great Minister's life, by translating one or two passages from Conde which are not so well known as the records of Almansur's conquests.

There was a famous man of learning from Bagdad named Abulola,[1] who came to Cordova and won his way into Almansur's good graces, for the Hajib was as devoted an amateur of literature and learning as Al-Hakem himself had been. Almansur showed him much honour, and supplied the cost of his living from the funds set aside for litterati, although owing to Abulola's extravagant way of living, the allowance was all insufficient for his needs.

One day he entered the presence of Almansur wearing a vest of drawn thread (*deshilado*) so thin that the under dress was seen through it. Almansur noted it, and asked him—

"What is this, Abulola?"

And he replied in a humble and pitiful tone—

"This was a gift of our Sovereign, whom God guard and repay. I have no finer garment, and for that reason I have put it on to-day."

Almansur replied—

"Thou hast done well, and in order that thou shouldest preserve it we will send thee to-morrow other garments to take its place, so that this may be taken care of as it deserves."

Another day, when Abulola visited the Hajib, Almansur was reading a book on the cultivation of gardens, which had just been presented to him by the Governor of a certain town, in which were mentioned the terms for the inequalities of the land before being sown. Almansur called Abulola and said—

"Perhaps thou hast chanced to see this book in Bagdad, among the many which have passed through thy hands?"

And Abulola replied—

"Yes, my lord, I saw it in Bagdad, in the handwriting

---

[1] Cf. Makkari, i. 461.

of Abu Bekri Ibn Daweid, in writing like ants' legs,[1] and it had such and such marks on the cover."

And Almansur answered—

"Art thou not ashamed to tell such lies, Abulola? The book was written in such a place, by such an author, and treats of such a subject, and that is the truth."[2]

Evidently Almansur, far from being offended, enjoyed turning the tables on the learned impostor.

To Conde also we are indebted for a description, which he attributes to Ibn Hayyan, of the hospitality offered to Almansur by the Kaid of Murcia, during one of his military expeditions.

For thirteen days this generous host entertained the Minister, his gentlemen, and his servants. They were not accommodated in his own house, but every day the Kaid sent to them at their *posada*,[3] an abundance of bread, meat, and fruit, all at his own expense, while to Almansur himself and his officers he had served every day different splendid meals, with preserves and fruits of marvellous kinds.

When Almansur learnt that the Kaid was doing all this without making any charge for it, he thanked him in the King's name, and when he returned to Cordova he proposed to Hisham that the Kaid and his family should be relieved from all taxes and dues from thenceforth, which was done.

In another version of the same story, also quoted by Conde, it is said that the Kaid added to the other luxuries daily baths of rose-water, and beds with beautiful coverings of silk and gold.[4]

---

[1] "*En letra de zanca de hormiga*," which for all we know may have been the name of a particular style of handwriting.

[2] Conde, i. 525–6.

[3] In Spain there are to this day the three classes of hostelry used by the Moslems; the *Fonda*, which is an ordinary hotel, providing food, attendance, etc.; the *Posada*, which provides rooms without food, and the *Parada*, which is merely a rest house for man and beast.

[4] Conde, i. 511–3.

We have also an interesting account of the wedding festivities of Almansur's eldest son Abdalmalek, who was married in the spring of 986 to Habiba, daughter of Abdullah Ibn Abi Amir (a member of Almansur's family) and his wife Boriha, Almansur's own daughter. Marriage between an uncle and niece was not unusual among the Moslems of Spain, and indeed in a community where one man—or at any rate one king—sometimes had a hundred children by a number of different wives, it may not have been always easy to find a bride unrelated to her husband. The prohibition of such marriages among the inextricably confused relationships of the sixteenth century, and the declaration that they were incestuous and their offspring illegitimate, was one of the many cruel details of the persecution of the Moriscos by the Inquisition.

The wedding took place in the gardens of the Almeria, close to the palaces of Az-Zahira, which gardens the Khalif Hisham presented to his Minister when he asked permission to celebrate the wedding there. Great festivities and public rejoicings marked the event, and the whole nobility of Cordova attended the entertainments given in honour of the young couple.

"The lovely bride was conducted in triumph through the principal streets by all the maidens who were friends of the family, preceded and followed by the Kadi, the witnesses, the lords, sheiks, and gentlemen of the city. The maidens, armed with rods of ivory and gold, guarded the entrance to the bride's pavilion all day, until the bridegroom, accompanied by the noble youths of his family, and protected by the gilded pikes of his friends, succeeded at nightfall in forcing his entrance, notwithstanding the bold defence made by the damsels.

"The whole of the gardens were illuminated, and from all the thickets, from the fountains, and from the boats on their limpid lakes, resounded sweet music, praises of the bride and bridegroom forming the theme of the songs. Music and singing continued until daybreak, and the rejoicings went on all next day.

"Almansur signalised the occasion by presents of arms and robes to his guards, gave much money in alms to the poor of the *Zawiya*,[1] dowered and married poor orphan girls from his Aljama,[2] and gave handsomely to the talented persons who praised his son and his grand-daughter. Never were greater days seen in Cordova, nor more splendid wedding feasts."[3]

In conclusion we will quote Makkari's summing up of Almansur's character and career, in which for once he let his pen run freely, forgetting the Shiite in the man, whom after all he found worthy of honour.

"Among the meritorious actions of Almansur, the following are particularly recorded. He wrote with his own hand a Koran, which he always carried with him on his military expeditions, and in which he used constantly to read. He collected and kept all the dust which adhered to his garments during his marches to the country of the infidels, or in his battles with them. Accordingly, whenever he halted at a place, his servants came up to him, and carefully collected the dust in kerchiefs; until a good-sized bag was filled, which he always carried with him, intending to have it mixed with the perfumes for the embalming of his body.[4] He also took with him his grave-clothes, thus being always prepared to meet death whenever it should assail him. The winding sheet was made of linen grown on the lands inherited from

---

[1] The *Zawiyas* were shelters for professional beggars. Each house had its majordomo to attend to the comfort and discipline of its inmates.

[2] Apparently the schools attached to a mosque which he supported.

[3] Conde, i. 519–20.

[4] The explanation of this curious custom will be found in a future volume.

his father, and spun and woven by his own daughters. He used continually to ask God to permit him to die in His service and in war against the infidels, and this desire was granted. He became celebrated for the purity of his intentions, the knowledge of his own sins, his fear of his Creator, his numerous campaigns against the infidels, and many other virtues and accomplishments, which it would take us too long to enumerate. Whenever the name of God was mentioned in his presence, he never failed to mention it also ; and if ever he was tempted to do an act which might deserve the chastisement of his Lord, he invariably resisted the temptation. Notwithstanding this he enjoyed all the pleasures of this world, which make the delight of kings, with the exception only of wine, the use of which he left off entirely two years before he died." [1]

[1] Makkari, ii. 220.

CHAPTER XI.

THE STORY OF HISHAM II.

THE racial feud between the Mudarites on the one side and the Yemenites and Christians on the other, which had been in abeyance for nearly a hundred years under Abderrahman III. and his successors, burst out again with all its old bitterness shortly after the controlling hand of the great Yemenite Wizir was withdrawn.

But now an extraordinary reversal of the earlier conditions took place.

In 886 the Yemenites and Muwallads rose against the rule of their racial and religious enemies the Ommeyads, who were Sunnites of the race of Mudar, and continued the struggle until a prince combining the blood of the two opposed peoples ascended the throne, when they at once submitted to him. But in 1009 it was the Mudarites who rose against a monarch of their own race, the last of the direct line of the Koraishite kings of Cordova, and it was the Yemenites and the descendants of the Muwallads who protected and supported him. It is explicitly stated that the dethronement of Abderrahman's grandson was brought about by the Mudarite Arabs, because of their jealousy of the Yemenites. Thus we have the singular spectacle of the hereditarily hostile tribes maintaining their loyalty to a ruler who was three generations removed from their own blood, because his father and grandfather had treated them well, while his own people rejected him and did their utmost to secure his death.

Almansur died in August 1002. When the Khalif was

Fig. 8.—Detail of Ceiling of the Almohade period in the Alcazar of Seville, on which are superimposed, in a different and very inferior technique, the shields of Castile and Leon as borne by Fernando III. in 1248. Between the two is the shield given by him to his friend and ally, Al-Ahmar of Granada (see p. 346), a band issuing from the mouths of dragons or serpents, later adopted as the device of the knightly Order of *La Banda*.

THE STORY OF HISHAM II.

informed of the fact he summoned to his presence a number of civil functionaries in order to announce to them the sad news, but such was his grief that he could not utter a single word, and he stood speechless, endeavouring to explain to the assembly the fatal occurrence he had to communicate.

Abdalmalek, Almansur's eldest son, who was in Cordova at the moment of his father's death, returned to Medina Celi to find that Almansur had been buried in his palace there. After some days he went back to Cordova, and the singing women of Almansur's harem put on hair-cloth sacks and coarse blankets instead of the silk and brocade which they had been accustomed to wear.

Hisham treated the son as he had the father: he himself clothed him with a *khilah* or dress of honour, and signed his appointment to the office of Hajib. This was not done without some opposition among the eunuchs of the palace,[1] but at last "the ill-disposed became loyal, and things took their right course." Abdalmalek followed in the footsteps of his father; "his administration lasted seven years, which were to the Moslems a succession of festivals."[2]

Abdalmalek, unhappily for Hisham and for Andulucia, died young, after one of his brilliant campaigns against the Christians, and his younger brother, Abderrahman, who succeeded him in the administration, was incompetent to control the growing hostility of the Sunnite party in the State.

The immediate cause of the rebellion which led to the downfall of the Cordovan Khalifate was that the childless

---

[1] An-Nuwairi says that the opposition was not only among the eunuchs, but from the people of Cordova generally, and that it was only quelled when Abdalmalek went out in person at the head of his guards and charged the mob with great slaughter. We must read this in the light of An-Nuwairi's consistent hostility to the Beni Abi Amir and all their doings.

[2] Makkari, ii. 221-2, 486. As Makkari says that Almansur died in 1002 and Abdalmalek in 1008 or 1007, this period of seven years is an obvious mistake.

Hisham publicly declared young Abderrahman as his successor on the throne. We may imagine how such an announcement would irritate the various elements opposed to the Beni Abi Amir. For two hundred and fifty years the throne of Cordova had been in the possession of the Ommeyads, a branch of the tribe of Koraish, and belonging to the race of Mudar. Now it was proposed to bequeath this throne to a member of the hated race of Kahtan, a Yemenite, and not only that, but to a man who was not even of pure Arab blood.[1]

Makkari quotes; from "an author of those days," the deed by which Hisham nominated Abderrahman or Sanchol, as he is usually called, being the diminutive of Sancho, his maternal grandfather's name. In this document, after recapitulating Sanchol's brilliant natural gifts and qualifications for the office, he goes on to say that "Another no less weighty consideration has moved the Commander of the Faithful to take this step, namely that while perusing works on the occult sciences . . . he has discovered that he was to be succeeded by an Arab of the race of Kahtan, respecting whom there exists a well-authenticated tradition ascribing the following words to our Prophet : ' The time shall come when a man of the stock of Kahtan will drive men before him with a stick.'" [2]

Dozy says that the text of the proclamation is given by Makkari, Ibn Bassam, Ibn Khaldun, and An-Nuwairi, but curiously enough his version of the prophet's prediction is worded quite differently from Makkari's and runs—

---

[1] His mother was a Christian, the daughter of one Sancho. According to Ibn Al-Khattib (quoted by Dozy), " The chief of the Rûm feared Almansur to such an extent that he was desirous of allying his own house with him, and offered him his daughter. She became the favourite wife of Almansur, and surpassed all the others in piety and virtue." (Dozy, *Recherches*, i. 209-10.) Dozy thinks she was the daughter of Sancho Garcia, Count of Castile, with whom Almansur was on friendly terms at the time of the marriage, which Dozy places in or about 985.

[2] Makkari, ii. 222-4.

THE STORY OF HISHAM II.

"The last day shall not come until a man of the stock of Kahtan wields the sceptre."[1]

Dozy and Makkari are agreed that the proclamation of Sanchol brought about the downfall of the Amirides, but we obtain different ideas from these two historians as to the causes of the hatred with which the new heir to the throne was regarded.

Makkari says that the Beni Ommeya and the Koraishites were the most opposed to his nomination: "they detested the rule of Abderrahman; and moreover they were much afflicted at seeing the power of the Koraishites and the rest of the Beni Mudar in the hands of their enemies the Yemenites. They therefore . . . entered into a conspiracy . . . deposed Hisham II., and appointed in his room" a descendant of Abderrahman III.[2] Dozy attributes the destruction of the Beni Abi Amir principally to the fact that Sanchol was obnoxious to the priests, on account of his birth, and because he was a wine-bibber and said to be irreligious.[3]

Conde says that the rebellion of the Mudarites broke out before the deed of nomination had been made public.

"King Hisham had no son to succeed him in his kingdom, although he was not yet so old as to be without hopes of having one.[4] The Hajib Abderrahman, without thinking of that, or of the relatives of the king, consulting only his own foolish vanity, and confiding in the insecure liking of the populace who loved and blessed him from a blind devotion to his father's memory, ventured to propose to and to persuade the king to declare him successor to the throne, this declaration being put off until after his first expedition against the Christians, which he hoped would be fortunate. Although these things were spoken of secretly in the halls

---

[1] *G. der M.*, ii. 166. [2] ii. 224–5.
[3] *G. der M.*, ii. 164. [4] He was then about 43 years of age.

of the Alcazar, they did not fail to get known, and excited the indignation and hate of all the Merwans, and especially of a cousin of King Hisham's named Mohammed Ibn Abd-al-Jabbar Ibn Abderrahman An-Nasir, a young man of much merit who expected to succeed to the throne in default of sons to King Hisham." [1]

Sanchol started for the field of war, but had hardly left Cordova when he learnt that his enemies had seized the Alcazar, taken possession of the person of Hisham, and proclaimed his own deposition. He hurried back, expecting that his appearance would put an end to the rebellion, but he found that matters had got far beyond his control. There was a sharp fight, and he fell, severely wounded, into the hands of his rival Mohammed, who ordered him to be crucified.

"This was done instantly, and Abderrahman, the son of the great Almansur, and brother of the illustrious Abdalmalek, expired nailed to a stake. And still there are people who trust in the ungrateful and changeable populace . . . He who a few days since was admired and blessed by the people, now in a moment was accursed: his property was confiscated, his name only mentioned in terms of contempt, and his friends did not dare to appear in public for fear of the general disquiet." [2]

There are various other accounts of the murder of Sanchol which it is not necessary to transcribe. An-Nuwairi says that he was accompanied on his journey to the seat of war by a Christian Count named Ibn Aumas,[3] who, when the news of the rebellion came, advised Sanchol to take refuge in his (the Count's) dominions until the storm should have

---

[1] Conde, i. 559–60.   [2] *Ibid.* 561–2.
[3] Gayangos suggests that this name is a copyist's error for Ibn Kumis; Dozy, on the authority of Sandoval, says that he was Count Carrion of the family of Gomez, one of his Leonese allies. (*G. der M.*, ii. 171.)

blown over. This Sanchol refused to do, trusting in the affection of the people of Cordova, so the Count accompanied him to the Monastery called Deyr Shus, where Mohammed's men took them and put them both to death. Sanchol's body was taken to Cordova and exposed, nailed to a stake, and beside it was stationed the captain of his guard, who had to cry aloud—

"This is Sanchol Al-Mamun; may the curse of God fall on his head and mine!"[1]

Makkari says that Mohammed, who now assumed the name of Al-Muhdi or Al-Mahdi, having secured the reins of government, shut Hisham up in his palace, and himself assumed the titles of Khalif and Imam. One of his first acts was to seize and put to death as many of the chiefs attached to the party of the Amirites as he could find. An-Nuwairi adds that he burned Az-Zahira, Almansur's palace outside Cordova, and sacked and gutted the houses of the wealthy partisans of the Beni Abi Amir, from which he obtained immense spoil.[2]

Thus the luckless Hisham, after some thirty-three years of peaceful retirement under the strong government of his Yemenite Ministers Almansur and Abdalmalek, suddenly found himself in peril not only of his throne, but of his life.

Conde tells us that one Wahdeh Al-Amiri, a body servant of Hisham, saved his life. When Al-Muhdi determined to assassinate him, Wahdeh dissuaded him, representing that it was unnecessary to kill the King, who lived in seclusion and was so well guarded that there was no fear of his injuring the usurper's interests. He convinced Al-Muhdi that Hisham might safely be allowed to live, and promised that he would give him in charge to a trustworthy person.[3]

[1] Makkari, ii. 489-90.   [2] *Ibid*. ii. 225, 488.
[3] An-Nuwairi says that Wahdeh was a freedman of Almansur, and about this time was Governor of Medina Celi. It is impossible to reconcile the different stories: the essential points are that Hisham's

A man was then found resembling Hisham in age, height and features, who was strangled and placed in the king's bed. It was given out that Hisham was dangerously ill, and that by his order Mohammed Al-Muhdi was proclaimed his successor. The supposed Hisham was then buried with great pomp in the first patio of the Alcazar, and Mohammed Al-Muhdi reigned in his stead.[1]

Dozy relates the same story, but says that the substitution was made, not by Wahdeh or the friends of Hisham, but by Al-Muhdi, who feared that he might be a rallying point for all parties, and therefore determined, not to kill him, but to give out that he was dead. The substituted Hisham was not some unfortunate, knocked on the head for the purpose, but a Christian resembling him, who had just died; the real Hisham was left imprisoned in the palace of one of Al-Muhdi's Wizirs.[2]

Cordova was in a state of chaos. Another pretender to the throne appeared in the field, in the person of Suleiman, also a descendant of Abderrahman III., and he, Al-Muhdi, and the Berbers, between them sacked Cordova, massacred the inhabitants, and devastated the surrounding country. Before long Al-Muhdi was murdered; three years later Suleiman met the same fate at the hands of one of his captains, who in his turn was murdered by some of the Slavonian pages who were formerly attached to the Ommeyad household.

The anarchy lasted for several years, during which Cordova was sacked more than once, with the usual accompaniments of murder and rapine, the Shiites being always the special sufferers in these outbreaks. Az-Zahra, the

life was preserved at this time, and that Wahdeh, although ostensibly giving Al-Muhdi some support, was faithful to Hisham, knew where he was concealed, and took the earliest favourable opportunity of producing him. (An-Nuwairi in Makkari, ii. 491, 494.)

[1] Conde, i. 563-4.   [2] *G. der M.*, ii. 176.

THE STORY OF HISHAM II.

beautiful suburb built by Abderrahman III., was destroyed, as was also that of Az-Zahira near by, where Almansur and his wealthy supporters had raised palaces and country houses. Makkari mentions the case of a distinguished poet, who was in Cordova by chance on one occasion when it was sacked: he was killed by the Berbers, and his body, after lying in the open court of his house for three days, was at last privately buried without any funeral service; and Conde adds that the body was thrust into the grave without being washed or arrayed in clean linen, in Moslem eyes the greatest insult that could be offered to a corpse.

During all this time Hisham seems to have been kept in safe custody. On one occasion, in 1010, he was produced by Wahdeh, who seated him on the throne and invested him with the royal insignia. Al-Muhdi, informed of what was going on, hastened into the throne-room and attempted to seat himself by the Khalif's side, but was dragged out and killed. For a time Wahdeh seems to have been able to maintain the supremacy of Hisham, but in 1013 Suleiman and his Berbers took Cordova, and in Makkari's words, " a general massacre ensued, the houses of the inhabitants were sacked and profaned, women and children insulted, wealthy families reduced to poverty, and magnificent buildings razed to the ground."

In the whole annals of Moslem Spain we can find no episode in which the Yemenites behaved with any approach to the savagery of the troops led by these Mudarite princes and nobles. Nor was their brutality exhibited on one occasion only, for Cordova was sacked and pillaged by each claimant to the throne in turn, always to the accompaniment of rapine, murder, and an absolute disregard of anything like military discipline.[1]

[1] See Dozy, *G. der M.*, ii. 174 ff.; Makkari, ii. 225 ff.; and An-Nuwairi's account, *ib.* pp. 491 ff.

What became of Hisham then no one knows. In 1016 Suleiman was defeated by the Pretender Ali Ibn Hammud, and taken prisoner. On being asked by Ali what he had done with Hisham, he replied that Hisham was dead, whereupon Ali ordered that the body should be disinterred and examined. This was done, and no signs of violence were found upon it.[1] Doubtless the body examined was that of the substitute who was buried under Hisham's name in 1009. As the corpse had been in the grave some seven years, any real identification must have been out of the question.

Conde gives a somewhat different version of the incident. He says that it was the father of Suleiman who was asked by Ali what he had done with Hisham, and that he denied any knowledge of his fate. Ali killed Suleiman with his father and brother, and had a thorough search made in Cordova for Hisham, " so that not a room or vault in the palaces and the houses of the city was not visited "; but no trace of Hisham could be found, so his death was publicly announced, " which gave rise to gossip and stories on the part of the common people." [2]

The story of Hisham's ultimate fate is told by Dozy as follows:—

Disappearing from Cordova during the reign of Suleiman, he wandered about in Asia, and remained in Jerusalem for some years working as a mat-maker. He returned to Spain in 1033, was seen in Malaga and Almeria, and in 1035 went to Calatrava, where he remained.[3]

This story, Dozy continues, was blindly believed by the people, but seems (in his opinion) to have no foundation. What is true, he says, is that there was at this time in Calatrava a mat-maker named Khalaf, who bore a striking

---

[1] An-Nuwairi in Makkari, ii. 497.
[2] Conde, i. 592, 593. Dozy, quoting Ibn Hayyan, tells the story rather differently. (*G. der M.*, ii. 197.)
[3] *G. der M.*, ii. 197, 242-5.

THE STORY OF HISHAM II.

likeness to Hisham. As he so often heard how remarkable the resemblance was, he gave himself out as the Khalif, and his fellow-citizens believed him, and even rose against their over-lord, Ismail Ibn Dhinnun, on his behalf. This Khalaf, it should be said, was not a native of Calatrava, a fact which, according to Dozy, contributed to his acceptance by the town as the vanished Hisham. We are not told how long he had lived in the town, nor where he came from.

The tale of Hisham's wanderings in Asia we may at once dismiss as legendary, but there is nothing improbable in his having escaped from Cordova some time during the long-continued confusion, and taken refuge at Calatrava. In this town and district were settled numbers of Arabs of the tribe of Jodham, which was closely allied by descent with that of Maafer, to which Almansur belonged,[1] and thus would be willing to give shelter to the ruler whose fall was immediately due to his affection for and dependence on the Beni Abi Amir. All the historians that we have been able to consult, agree that he was reported to have been concealed at Calatrava.

The story of the mat-maker is on the face of it incredible. We must recollect that Hisham had lived since childhood in the closest seclusion, hardly ever appearing in public, and that his features even were not known to the great majority of the citizens of Cordova.[2] How then should the peasants and citizens of Calatrava recognise in a chance arrival in the town the Khalif whom they had never seen? We are given no hint as to where this strange mat-maker came from, or who first called attention to his likeness to the King whose lineaments were unknown outside Cordova. Dozy suggests no reason for his acceptance as Hisham by his fellow-citizens of Calatrava, beyond the fact that he was not a native of the town. How could a humble labourer, by the mere force

[1] Makkari, ii. 27.   [2] Dozy, *G. der M.*, ii. 136.

of reiterated assertion, so impress himself upon the people of a whole city, that they should have risen against their over-lord on his behalf? It is only on the hypothesis that the Calatrava mat-maker really was the vanished Khalif, that the story becomes in the least credible.

But before continuing it, we must make a digression into the history of the family which gave him a refuge on his expulsion from Calatrava when Ibn Dhinnun laid siege to the city ; or when, perhaps, he elected to leave it in order to spare his adherents the horrors of a siege which could have only one termination.

The Abbadites, who became the rulers of more than half of Moslem Spain after the downfall of the Cordovan Khalifate, and made their capital, Seville, as great a centre of civilisation in the eleventh century as Cordova had been in the tenth, were intimately connected with the closing years of the unfortunate Hisham II.

The first member of the family of whom we hear—apart from their progenitor Ittaf, who came over in 741—is Karis, who, according to Ibn-al-Khattib was captain of the middle guard of Hisham, and was afterwards appointed by that king to be Imam to the principal mosque in Seville. His son, Ismail, became Judge of the Criminal Court under Hisham, and was also Imam at Seville.[1]

The Abbadites prided themselves on their descent from Himyar, like the other families of the Lakhmite tribe. Ismail, however, had gifts, apart from his birth, which raised him above his fellows. He was very wealthy, and both before and after the civil wars which followed on the deposition of Hisham in 1009, he maintained his authority in Andalucia, and lived in almost regal luxury and magnificence. No other private gentleman of Spain could be compared to

---

[1] Makkari, ii. 250, 503 ; cf. Ibn Khaldun in Makkari, i. App. xxxii. Dozy, *G. der M.*, ii. 237–8.

THE STORY OF HISHAM II.

him in these respects. He possessed great herds of cattle of all kinds, had many servants, and was extremely liberal and generous. His house was the asylum for all the illustrious knights (*caballeros*) exiled from Cordova in the civil discords,[1] and his frankness and liberality, united to his wisdom, sagacity, and seeming candour, won the hearts of all and advanced his schemes of aggrandisement.[2]

When Ismail died, his son Mohammed, following in his father's footsteps, continued to keep open house for persons who got into trouble at Cordova; among those he entertained being Abu Bekr al Zobaidi, the grammarian, who as we have seen was one of Hisham's tutors in his youth. Al-Kasim Ibn Hammud, brother of the Ali Ibn Hammud who killed Suleiman to avenge the supposed murder of Hisham, appointed Mohammed Ibn Abbad to be Kadi of Seville, and out of gratitude for this favour Mohammed received Al-Kasim in his palace when that prince had to flee from Cordova. During the rule of Al-Kasim's nephew, Yahya, in Cordova, Al-Kasim remained in Seville, where he was joined by his black slaves, as well as by all the Berber and Andalucian officers who were opposed to his nephew. This was in 1019, and Al-Kasim remained in Seville till 1023, when Yahya had to fly in his turn, and his uncle returned to Cordova.[3]

After this Al-Kasim and his nephew continued fighting for the supremacy at Cordova, and a third party appeared, who wished for the restoration of the Ommeyad dynasty. Their plans, however, did not then meet with success, and Al-Kasim ordered a most scrupulous search to be made throughout his dominions for any surviving members of

---

[1] This refers to the revolts which began with the deposition of Hisham in 1009.
[2] Conde, ii. 7. The author quoted by Conde, who is clearly a Sunnite, seems to have found it difficult to reconcile his admiration of Ismail's qualities with his racial dislike to speak well of a Yemenite.
[3] The epitaph of one of Al-Kasim's officers is in the Seville Museum.

the family of Ommeya, who in order to avoid his persecution had been compelled to fly to the provinces and take refuge in farms and country-houses under various disguises.[1]

We may now take up again the story of Hisham II., as related by Ibn Hayyan.

"Among the best known stories about Abdul-Kasim (Mohammed Ibn Abbad) is that he turned his eyes to those followers of the Merwanides who survived: then a message was brought to him about that supposititious man who resembled Hisham Ibn Hakem in appearance, and who now made no secret of having escaped from the hands of Suleiman, his oppressor, of having remained hidden for a long time in the east, and of then having returned to Spain. Then this story struck root in men's hearts, for there had been talk of that man (Hisham) before, and doubts were expressed about his death, since Suleiman, his slayer, had neglected to show his corpse, as was the custom of the servants of kings, if they deprived them of empire: which is to be explained either because Suleiman held in contempt those whose noblemen he now ruled over by force, or that, by the will of God, a mistake had been made (*i.e.* that some one else had been killed in place of Hisham, and he escaped. Dozy's note). . . . Some of his attendants announced that he was dead, but at the same time stories were told about this matter which are alien from the truth and originated among the women and eunuchs of the palace of Cordova: these (stories) clove as it were to men of greater dignity among the attendants of the Merwanides, who asserted that he had escaped safe and decided that he was still living. . . . The story of this man who resembled Hisham did not cease to spread in men's hearts as fire spreads in coal: then Ibn Abbad thought of those things which were said of this man, and relying upon

[1] Makkari, ii. 238–9; Dozy, *Abbadites*, ii. 32, *G. der M.*, ii. 200; Conde, ii. 7.

THE STORY OF HISHAM II.

them devised a trick: for the least advantage that might thence redound to him was that he would be able to withdraw himself from the unpleasant rule of Ibn Hammud and excite all men to wage war against him. He therefore declared that Hisham had come to him: he collected all the women surviving at Seville who formerly had belonged to the palace or the harem, many of whom recognised that man and saw that he was the same as Hisham: for Ibn Abbad had hinted to those of them in whom he trusted, what sort of declaration he expected from them concerning him (Hisham); wherefore it was done, as they did not wish to contradict him, but on the contrary desired to gratify him. Thus then Ibn Abbad interposed a cause for the war which he was endeavouring to wage against Ibn Hammud. He withdrew that man Hisham from men's eyes, but informed all the noblemen and princes by letters of his presence, and urged them to strain every nerve for this hidden Khalif, by freeing slaves, feeding orphans, and waging a sacred war in his name. Then many in Spain threw themselves headlong into the business: the Cordovese wished to appoint him Imam of the whole people (of Spain), and sent delegates to see whether that man really was Hisham: then firm witness was given concerning him: Ibn Jehwar and others published testimony about this matter, although they very well knew what the truth of it was. . . . But Ibn Jehwar soon retracted and confessed that he had affirmed a falsehood, in which confession he remained for the rest of his life." [1]

Dozy, who tells this story on the authority of Ibn Hayyan, Ibn Bassam, Al-Athir, and An-Nuwairi, says that Ibn Hayyan and the historian Ibn Hazm always protested against this story as a gross deceit, " although it would have been in their interest to recognise the so-called Hisham." He adds that Abul-Hazm Ibn Jehwar (the father of the writer) who

[1] Dozy, *Abbadites*, i. 229–32; iii. 82–3.

was then "President of the Republic of Cordova," was not deceived, but "saw the impossibility of resisting the will of the people: he understood how necessary was the union of the Arabs and Slavonians under one head, and feared that the Berbers might attack Cordova. Therefore he did not oppose the wishes of his fellow-citizens, and allowed Hisham II. again to be reverenced."[1]

Makkari's version is as follows:—

"As there remained (in 1031) no other member of the house of Ommeya to whom they could offer the throne, the people of Cordova met together and determined upon giving the command to Abul-Hazm Jehwar Ibn Mohammed, a man of much wisdom and experience, who had once been Wizir of the Beni Ommeya under the administration of the Beni Abi Amir [Almansur and his son]. Jehwar at first assumed no other title than that of Wizir of the Beni Ommeya. It appears even that with a view to reduce to obedience the petty rulers of Andalus, he pretended that Hisham Al-Muyyed-Billah [Hisham II.] was still living; and having caused prayers to be said in his name, he wrote to the Kadi Ibn Abbad, King of Seville, to Al-Mundhir, King of Zaragoza, and to Ibn Dhinnun, King of Toledo, inviting them to send in their allegiance to Hisham, and to acknowledge Cordova as the capital of Andalus. None, however, listened to his words; upon which Jehwar, perceiving that his stratagem produced not the desired effect, published that Hisham was dead, and usurped the royal power."[2]

Al-Homaidi, who wrote about 1068, gives us the following particulars about Jehwar's administration:—

---

[1] *G. der M.*, ii. 242–5. The second volume of Dozy's collection of extracts referring to the Abbadites, which contains the passages from Al-Athir, An-Nuwairi, and others, is not translated.

[2] Makkari, ii. 249.

"It must be said of Jehwar that although he administered the government and provided for the security of the capital, though he assumed in every respect the authority of a supreme ruler, he took none of the insignia of the Khalifate, but ruled as none of his predecessors had done, declaring that he held the command until one more deserving of it, or having better titles to the empire, should make his appearance, when he would immediately resign all authority and power into his hands. He thus ordered that the palaces of the Beni Ommeya should be kept in the same state as they had been under the regular government, and that the door-keepers, the servants and guards, should be stationed about the gates of them as in former times. He himself never inhabited them, but resided at his own private house in the city."

After speaking of the excellent government of Jehwar, Al-Homaidi adds the following paragraph:—

"In the meantime Hisham Al-Mutad, [also called Hisham III.], who had been in confinement, found means to escape, and took refuge with Ibn Hud at Lerida, where he remained until the time of his death in 427 (1035). Hisham having left no male children, the family of Merwan was entirely extinguished, and their empire abolished for ever. It is true that while Yahya Ibn Ali Al-Hasani was besieging Seville, the inhabitants of that place, and such as followed their party in the neighbouring districts and dreaded the rule of that prince, gave out that Hisham (II.) Al-Muyyed-Billah, the son of Al-Hakem, was still living and among them: and they accordingly went through the usual ceremonies of taking the oath of allegiance to him, and proclaiming him their sovereign, their example being followed by most of the people of Andalus. But all this was a stratagem devised by Ibn Abbad, the ruler of Seville, as we have shown elsewhere. At last, when it was close upon the year 450 (1058) the same people who had proclaimed Hisham gave out that he was dead; and thus did the *khotbah* for the Beni Ommeya cease from the pulpits of the mosques in all the provinces of Andalus until the present moment, when it has not yet been re-established."[1]

We have given the various accounts of the resuscitation of Hisham at perhaps tedious length, because we wish the reader to have before him all the materials on which to form an opinion.

The first point to notice is that Ibn Abbad, who produced Hisham, was a Yemenite, and Ibn Jehwar, who according to Ibn Hayyan first recognised him and then withdrew his recognition, had been in the service of the Yemenite Minister Almansur; whereas all the historians quoted belonged to the Mudarite or Sunnite party. In their eyes Hisham would hardly count as an Ommeyad, so completely overshadowed had he been by his great Hajib, with whose family he had been bound up to such an extent that the downfall of the Beni Abi Amir brought about his own instant deposition.

Dozy lays stress on the fact that Ibn Hayyan and the historian Ibn Hazm refused to recognise the alleged Hisham, although it would have been to their interest to do so. We cannot see how it would have been to their worldly interests, and it would certainly have been against their principles to acknowledge as Khalif the man, even though he were of the royal stock, who was so inextricably linked with the Yemenites during his reign, and whose reappearance on the scene was due to another of that hated race. When we remember that the Mudarites deliberately plunged the nation into anarchy through their hatred of the Yemenite government under which Moslem Spain had reached her culminating point of glory, we see how little feeling of unity there was, how little patriotism counted in comparison with race-

[1] Makkari, ii. App. pp. xvi.–xvii.

hatred, and thus how impossible it was for Sunnite writers, such as Ibn Hayyan, Al-Homaidi, and Makkari, to give a fair and unprejudiced account, especially of events occurring during their lifetime.

Ibn Hayyan, who lived through all the troubles of the eleventh century (he was born in 987 or 988, and died in 1076), is looked upon as a final authority on the events of his time; but in the nature of things he must have depended upon second-hand information for all he wrote about the Abbadites and Hisham, after the disappearance of the latter in 1013, and there is small doubt that he was not over-careful to verify the truth of reports that reached him, provided they reflected discredit on the men and the party he detested. As to Al-Homaidi, his statement that Ibn Jehwar after proclaiming Hisham announced that he was dead when he found that the other rulers did not listen to him, is contradicted not only by the facts (for, as we shall see, his invitation to acknowledge the Khalif was largely accepted), but by Al-Homaidi's own statement that public prayer was continued for Hisham in the mosques till 1058. Jehwar himself died in 1043, and was succeeded by his son Abul-Walid, "who followed his steps in the administration of the government until he died." [1]

Ibn Hazm is the other historian whose refusal to recognise Hisham Dozy considers as final. With regard to him, Señor Pons says, "Had so respected a man as Ibn Hazm recognised the impostor, his example would have been followed by many legitimists, and that party would have renewed its vigour by an alliance with Ibn Abbad; but Ibn Hazm was a man of too great integrity to lend himself to a fraud, even when it might have redounded to his own advantage and that of his party."

But the Beni Hazm, according to the same writer, were

[1] Al-Homaidi in Makkari, ii. App. p. xvi.

clients of the Ommeyads, and this very man had been a Wizir under Abderrahman V., the sixth of the pretenders to the throne of Cordova who sprang up between the years 1009 and 1024. The family were of Gothic descent, and the grandfather of the historian was the first of them to embrace Islam. His father, Ibn Jehwar, had been, as already said, in the service of Almansur and his son Abdalmalek, and was therefore allied by interest if not by blood with the Yemenite party. But Ibn Hazm himself admitted no such ties, having indeed repudiated his own family; and as a client of the Ommeyads and the servant of one of the claimants to the throne, would hardly have been disposed to recognise the Khalif whose reappearance would so greatly redound to the credit of the Yemenite ruler of Seville. As for his respectability, on which Señor Pons lays some stress, it is perhaps enough to say that his patron Abderrahman V. was overthrown by the people of Cordova, on the ground that he "neglected the affairs of Government and passed his time with literary men and poets, as his low inclinations prompted him." And among these poets and literary men is especially mentioned Ibn Hazm, "well known for his satirical and controversial writings against the Ulemas of various religious schools." Eventually his schismatic opinions brought him into such disfavour with the orthodox Faquis that he had to fly for his life.[1]

Thus we see that the evidence of Ibn Hayyan and Ibn Hazm, the only two persons whose names are given as having declared against the identity of the refugee from Calatrava with the missing Hisham, is not to be trusted in a matter affecting the good faith of their enemies, the Yemenites; on the other hand we have the "unshaken testimony" of the

[1] Notwithstanding that he had forsworn his father's family and denied all connection with them, in his peril he sought and found a refuge in Montelixam in the province of Niebla, where his Christian ancestors had lived. (Makkari, ii. 242; Pons, 131–2.

THE STORY OF HISHAM II.

delegates from Cordova, mentioned by Ibn Hayyan; the recognition of the Khalif by the women of his harem; and his acknowledgment as their Imam by the rulers of all the Yemenite states in Spain.

The recognition by the women Ibn Hayyan gets over by asserting that Ibn Abbad had told them what to say; but how are we to account for the presence of these women in Seville some twenty years after Hisham had vanished from Cordova? Ibn Hayyan does not suggest that they were impostors, produced *ad hoc* by Ibn Abbad: on the contrary he says that Ibn Abbad "collected all the women surviving at Seville who had formerly belonged to the palace or the harem." The only explanation is that when Hisham was driven out of Cordova they must have escaped—protected no doubt by some of the adherents of the Beni Abi Amir—and taken refuge in the city and with the man known to be devoted to the Khalif's cause.

And there may have been another and a closer tie between the Abbadites of Seville and the grandson of the great Muwallad Khalif Abderrahman III. The Abbadites were of the tribe of Lakhm, and it appears (cf. p. 153) that their progenitor was more or less closely related to the Yemenite second husband of Princess Sara. Abderrahman III. was, as we know, related to the Beni Ishak, whose Christian father was a descendant of Sara's son, Ishak, and thus there may have been actual ties of blood-relationship between Hisham, through his Christian great-grandmother, and Mohammed Ibn Abbad.[1] In the case of Princess Sara, as we have already pointed out, so much value was attached to descent from her, either by her first or second Moslem husband, that Ibn al-Kuttiyyah, "the son of the Gothic Woman," assumed

---

[1] The number of generations lying between the related progenitors and the individual in question weighed nothing with the Arabs, who were used to trace their descent to the parent stock in Yemen.

the name as a title of honour during the century before that of which we are writing.

If there was an actual relationship, however remote, between Hisham and the Abbadites, they would have a strong reason for protecting him if he were indeed the real man, while it would make it even more improbable that they should insult their family and the Yemenites generally by asking their allegiance to an impostor who was not even of gentle birth.

The Abbadites continued to shelter the poor helpless Hisham, now becoming an old man, for many years, always acknowledging him as their Khalif and over-lord and placing his name first in the Khotba. Nor were they the only great men loyal to him.

"Although," says Ibn Hayyan, "he was withdrawn in the darkness from the eyes of all and appeared neither to the courtiers nor to the people; nevertheless his authority was always acknowledged by the Amirs of the eastern part of Spain" (all the south-west being under the dominion of the Abbadites).

If he were the real Hisham, it was no wonder that he dreaded the light of day, and desired nothing better than to live in peaceful seclusion, accustomed as he was from childhood to a life of complete retirement, and shaken and terrified as he must have been by the events preceding his flight from Cordova. But if, as Ibn Hayyan says, he was an impostor produced by the Abbadites for their own purposes, why should either they or he adopt a course certain to give rise to suspicion? They could have had no motive for hiding a man so like Hisham as to have been accepted as Hisham, not only by his own women but by the delegates from Cordova. On the contrary, the more the impostor appeared in public, the better, it would seem, for their schemes, if only to accustom the people to the idea of his presence among them. Few in Cordova were at all familiar with his appearance.[1] As for Seville, he certainly had never been seen in that city until he fled there from Calatrava in terror of his life.

The description of Hisham's existence, even at the height of his glory as monarch of the great nation administered by Almansur, suggests a man suffering from a chronic nervous disease which caused him to shun the eye of the world. Probably the first (unrecorded) attempt on his life was made when he was a little child. Dozy says that schemes to set him aside were afloat the moment Al-Hakem was dead. If the conspirators—and it must be remembered that the head and front of them was his uncle, who naturally had the *entrée* to the palace—went so far as to terrify the little prince with any form of physical violence, it may well be that permanent injury was done to his constitution. We are told that Wahdeh had to bring him out of his confinement and place him on his throne on one occasion (see p. 187), whereas a normal man would have forced his own way out the moment that restraint on his movements was removed. We are not told that he shunned the world during his father's lifetime. The rigorous confinement of the child-monarch within his palace walls, where no one was ever admitted to see him save by special permission of his mother or his Prime Minister, dated from the frustrated conspiracy which cost the life of the chief conspirator, his uncle Al-Mugheyrah.

Assuming that Hisham, as a child, was terrified into a state of chronic nervous timidity, which would be aggravated rather than alleviated by the seclusion in which he lived, it

---

[1] Conde tells us that even when as a young man he attended public prayers in the great mosque on festival days he did not leave the *maksurah*, the raised tribune surrounded with gilded rails set apart for the Khalifs during religious offices, until the whole congregation had left the mosque, and then he came out surrounded by his suite and his guards, and returned to the palace, which was close by, hardly visible to the people. (i. 509-10.)

is easy to imagine the condition to which he must have been reduced by the events of the twenty years following on the murder of Sanchol. The horrors of the successive sacks of Cordova, in the midst of which he must have been, the threats of his various captors, his several imprisonments, his flight to Calatrava and long concealment there, and finally the attack upon his place of refuge by the ruler of Toledo, were enough to crush any small remnants of courage that he may have possessed, and probably nothing short of force on the part of the Abbadites could have dragged him from the retirement of their Alcazar, once he found himself within its protecting walls.

Such conduct, if he were Hisham, is entirely consistent with what we know of his previous life. But nothing is more unlikely than that an impostor, who originally pretended to be the Khalif out of vanity and ambition, should have voluntarily renounced all the outward glitter and show which were his to take and enjoy, once his imposture was accepted, in order to hide himself in the palace of the Abbadites, and thus increase the difficulty of convincing the sceptical that he was indeed Hisham.

The "imposture," as Ibn Hayyan and Dozy call it, was kept up until the year 1059, when, according to the former, " messengers came several times to us, dwelling in Cordova, to say that in none of his dominions should the Imam Hisham Ibn Hakem be more commemorated in the sacred prayer, for he was dead who had always been remembered in the Khotba since the time when Mohammed Ibn Abbad had assumed the empire until the end of this year." He adds that Motadid (the son and successor of Mohammed Ibn Abbad) called together the principal men of Seville and announced to them that Hisham had died some time before of paralysis, but that, as he was then at war, " the Amirs of Spain " (*i.e.* those who had acknowledged Hisham) had

THE STORY OF HISHAM II.

dissuaded him from announcing his death and holding a public funeral. Now, however, that peace prevailed, it was necessary to proclaim the truth openly.[1]

Ibn Hayyan here says that Hisham had been publicly prayed for "since Mohammed Ibn Abbad had assumed the empire." If he is to be depended on for this fact, and if by the assumption of the empire he means the time when Mohammed succeeded his father Ismail, the mention of Hisham's name in the Khotba antedated his reappearance by some twelve years, for Mohammed succeeded his father in 1023. This strengthens our theory that the Abbadites never lost sight of him, and only waited for a convenient time to make his existence generally known.

However this may be, we have it on the authority of Ibn Hayyan and Al-Homaidi that Hisham continued to be prayed for until the year 1058 or 1059. Motadid succeeded his father Mohammed Ibn Abbad in 1042, and certainly at the time of his accession, if not before, the power of the Abbadites was too firmly established to need any prestige or support which might have accrued to them by acting as Ministers of a shadowy Khalif, concealed from every eye within their palace walls. Even if Mohammed, having for his own purposes produced a fictitious Khalif, did not afterwards think fit to disavow him, there was not the slightest reason for Motadid to continue the imposture. He could easily have had the man killed or locked up, and have announced that he was dead. Why should he have taken the trouble to keep this mat-maker masquerading as a king in the bosom of his family when he was of no further use to him? Far from disowning or removing the alleged impostor, Motadid, when his father died, succeeded him "under the title of a Hajib or Prime Minister" of Hisham,[2] and when he announced his death

[1] *Abbadites*, i. 277–8.   [2] Dozy, *G. der M.*, ii. 273.

to the nobles of Seville, " it is said that at the same time he gave letters to the Amirs of Spain who acknowledged the authority of this Hisham who was detained like a captive, announcing his death, and inviting them to substitute another (Imam) for him." [1]

To the very last Motadid showed his reverence for the poor feeble old man whose supremacy he had acknowledged. He buried Hisham with all the honours due to a king, and himself followed the funeral procession on foot, walking behind the coffin, without his *tailesan*, " according to the custom of the Hajibs of monarchs." [2]

The question whether the "mat-maker of Calatrava" was really the missing Khalif or a vulgar impostor has to be decided, if decided it can be, on a balance of probabilities. We may briefly sum up the case in his favour.

It is quite certain that his fate was unknown in Cordova, where he was said to have been killed and resuscitated several times.[3] The question is whether the Yemenites and the friends of the Beni Abi Amir knew or did not know all through that he was still living. Ibn Jehwar, an old servant of Almansur, from the moment that he obtained supreme power in Cordova, ruled as vice-gerent for one with a better title than himself, as did his son after him, and, according to Makkari, himself proclaimed Hisham. When Ibn Abbad

[1] Ibn Hayyan in *Abbadites*, i. 278.
[2] Dozy, *G. der M.*, ii. 294 ; and *Dictionnaire des vêtements*, p. 280.
[3] Ibn Bassam, copying Ibn Hayyan, gives the following reports current at one time or another about him : " He was put to death by Al Muhdi and publicly interred as if he had died a natural death. He was next restored to life by Wahdeh the Slavonian, who declared that it had all been a stratagem of that usurper, and that Hisham was still alive. Suleiman had him strangled when he took Cordova, and privately buried ; but many years after the dethronement of Al-Mutad (Hisham III.), in 420 (1029–30), the Wizir Jehwar pretended that he was still alive, and caused the Khotba to be recited in his name in all the mosques of Cordova. . . . Lastly Abul-Kasim the Kadi of Seville, wishing to extend his sway to other provinces of Spain, announced that he had found Hisham in a dungeon of the castle of Calatrava." (Makkari, ii. 503.)

THE STORY OF HISHAM II.

produced the alleged Hisham, he was recognised by delegates sent from Cordova for the purpose, and by the survivors among his own women, while the Abbadites, father and son, continued to rule in his name until his death, even when their position cannot have been at all strengthened by acting or pretending to act as his deputies. Against this we have only to set the bare assertions of Ibn Hayyan and other Sunnite writers whose racial prejudices always led them to misrepresent the Yemenites in every possible way. If the man was an impostor, the conduct of Ibn Abbad, Ibn Jehwar, and the various other rulers who recognised him as the Khalif, is unintelligible ; if on the other hand he was the real man, their recognition of and respect for him, until the day of his death, was perfectly natural, having regard to the loyalty and affection shown to his line by the Yemenites from the accession of his Muwallad grandfather Abderrahman III.[1]

[1] Ibn Al-Athir quotes Al-Fayyad as saying that the inhabitants of Calatrava recognised the authority of Hisham on his arrival there, but were forced to send him away for fear of Ibn Dhinnun. Alluding to the story of his supposed death and fraudulent resuscitation by Ibn Abbad, he remarks satirically on the absurdity of suggesting that an impostor should have been accepted as Khalif and made the ground of bloody wars, twenty years after the death of the true Hisham. (Ibn Al-Athir, 438–40. This passage seems to have been overlooked by Dozy.)

CHAPTER XII

THE ABBADITES AT HOME

ABBAD, usually called Motadid, the second of the Abbadite dynasty of Seville, has been represented to the world as a savage barbarian who took delight in decorating his garden in the Alcazar of that city with the skulls of his enemies stuck on sticks to represent growing plants and flowers. Where this story originated we have not been able to discover. Every Sunnite historian tells it, but no two versions are the same. One says the skulls were converted into beautiful vases adorned with gold, jacinths, emeralds, and rubies. Another says that a large enclosure before the palace doors was filled with them. A third says the skulls were kept in cupboards, in carefully sealed jars. And yet another attributes this singular taste for a garden of skulls on sticks to the usurper of the Cordovan throne, Mohammed Al-Muhdi, who died in 1010, before Motadid of Seville was born.

No doubt the Abbadites, like all their predecessors, contemporaries, and followers, received occasional trophies of victory consisting of their enemies' skulls preserved in camphor. Such offerings were continually made to victorious princes. Thus the camphorated head of Abdalaziz was presented, in the presence of his father Musa, to the Khalif Suleiman, early in the eighth century, and the camphorated head of the usurper known as the Red King was offered to the rightful monarch of Granada by his friend Pedro of Castile in the second half of the fourteenth, these two gifts being

FIG. 9.—Fragment of the funeral robe of Fernando III. (d. 1252) preserved in the Archaeological Museum of Madrid, with lions and castles similar to the Shields in the Alcazar of Seville. A robe of this design is depicted as worn by Alfonso X. in his *Book of Chess*.

connected by many other such during the intervening 650 odd years. So that if Motadid, King of Seville from 1042 to 1069, did accept preserved skulls from his friends, he must not be written down a savage because he acquiesced in the custom of his age.

Apart from this tale, we have found nothing to suggest that any of the Abbadites who, whether as Walis, Hajibs, or kings, ruled Seville for nearly three quarters of a century, differed from the rest of their race and religion in their humane and kindly treatment of those under their sway.

We have already referred to the Law or Instructions upon which was based the character and conduct of the Shiites (see p. 75); and have shown what was the reputation of the founder of the Abbadite dynasty, and how consistently the family and race traditions of hospitality and loyalty was maintained by his successors, Mohammed and Motadid, in their dealings with old Hisham II. when he threw himself upon their protection.

Of the private life of Motadid little is said. The Sunnites assert that he was savage and blood-thirsty, but do not bring forward any evidence, except the skulls story, in support. We learn that his family affections were unusually strong, and that he was a great believer in astrology. We are also told, by Ibn Hayyan, that even in his father's lifetime he kept a harem of seventy slaves, which was increased to eight hundred on Mohammed's death. This has been put forward as evidence of exaggerated sensuality; but a harem of seventy was nothing out of the common at that time, even for persons of less importance than Motadid. The increase to eight hundred when he came to the throne is probably Hayyan's imagination, for he could never have set foot inside the palace of the Abbadites, if indeed he ever went to Seville, and could only have repeated the gossip of his own friends at Cordova, by whom every action of the

Sevillian princes was distorted to their discredit. Whatever the number of women in the Alcazar of Seville during Motadid's time, we may discount a good many as being those of the Khalif Hisham, who as we have shown lived there as if it had been his home.

Notwithstanding the dimensions attributed to his harem, Motadid is recorded to have been devotedly attached to his wife, the Princess of Denia, daughter of Mujahid, and although he is said by the Sunnites to have married her from political motives alone, he never took another wife. When his son Motamid was born, his father, Mohammed, had the infant's horoscope cast. It foretold greatness and prosperity, ending in great misfortune—a prophecy which seems seldom to have been absent from the mind of its object after he had reached maturity.[1]

Motadid was highly cultivated, like all his race, and an excellent poet, although surpassed in this art by his son. And Makkari comments upon the splendour and magnificence with which these kings of Seville surrounded their Courts, the boundless liberality with which they rewarded authors and poets, and the love and enthusiasm which they themselves showed for the sciences.[2]

Motadid's love for his children was such that, according to Conde, his death was hastened by grief for the loss of a daughter.

"It happened [in 1068] that Taira, daughter of the King of Seville, whose grace and beauty were beyond compare, fell ill of a burning fever and died in the flower of her age, in the arms of her father, who loved her devotedly. Such was the pain and grief that Motadid experienced that he too was attacked by a fever, and became desperately ill. He fell into a lethargy, and the doctors feared his death. They applied stimulants, and he appeared better. But he desired

[1] Conde, ii. 24.   [2] *Ibid.* ii. 250.

THE ABBADITES AT HOME

to see the splendid funeral of his daughter: the principal ministers of the royal house carried the coffin, and Motadid ordered that the princess should be interred at the entrance of the Alcazar. It was at the end of March, and notwithstanding the warnings of the physicians, Motadid placed himself at a window to see the procession, and this increased his illness. He became rapidly worse, until there was no hope of his life, and a week after the death of Taira, God decreed his release from his sufferings; the fever increased and he lost the power of speech, and his spirit went to the mercy of God at midnight. At that hour there arose a sorrowful lament in his palace, and throughout the town was heard the wailing of his slaves and his family."

The next day obedience was sworn to his son Motamid. He was proclaimed and taken on horseback through the streets of the city, accompanied by the principal ministers and military commanders, who gave him various names of good omen. Then he commanded that his father should be buried with great magnificence along-side of his sister Taira, at the gate of the Alcazar, "in the evening of the day after Motadid had given an account to God of his sins."[1]

The story of Motadid's wholesale murder of the Berber princes from Ronda is told by Dozy,[2] and like the tale of the skulls, has been taken as conclusive evidence of sheer savagery. It is as follows.

In 1052 the Berbers of the south were at peace with Motadid, and had recognised his over-lordship, "or rather that of the so-called Hisham II." Motadid resolved on paying them an unexpected visit, with the intention, says Dozy, of setting them altogether aside and taking possession of their states. Accordingly, accompanied by only two servants, he went to visit Ibn Abi Korra, the lord of Ronda, and Ibn Nukh, the lord of Moron, without giving them any

[1] Conde, ii. 47-8.   [2] *G. der M.*, ii. 286 ff.

notice of his intention. Dozy comments on the rashness of this proceeding on the part of Motadid, who " knew how the Berbers hated him," and explains it by saying that, in spite of his own faithlessness towards everyone, for his own part he trusted the uprightness of others. If this is a correct explanation, all we can say is that it is the first time we have heard of a treacherous man being so confiding. He was well received by both princes, found in both places an Arab population eager to rise against their Berber rulers, and succeeded, says Dozy, in corrupting many of the Berber officers without raising the suspicions of their masters.

At Ronda Ibn Abi Korra gave a feast in his honour, and when it was over Motadid expressed a desire to rest. He was taken to a couch, apparently in the banquetting room, and when he was (as they imagined) asleep his hosts began discussing the expediency of murdering him. All the gold in Andalucia, they said, would not have brought him into their fastness against his own will, and now that he was there of his own accord, it would be well to make an end of him once for all. " When this devil is dead," they said, " we shall have no one to dispute with us the government of this country."

One voice only was raised in Motadid's favour. Moad Ibn Abi Korra, a youthful relative of the lord of Ronda, urged the sacred duties of hospitality, and declared that they would be shamed for ever in the eyes of their tribal brothers if they murdered a guest who had trusted to their honour. His persuasions prevailed, and Motadid left next day, without betraying any knowledge of the conspiracy, or of his debt to the young Moad.

Six months later, however, he took his revenge. According to Dozy, he invited the rulers of Moron and Ronda to visit him in Seville, in return for their hospitality to him, and also sent an invitation to Ibn Khazrun, the Berber lord of Arcos and Jerez. All three accepted, and on their arrival with their suites Motadid offered them a bath. Some sixty of them, including the chiefs, entered the bath house, and when they were safe inside, Motadid locked the doors, closed the ventilating apparatus, and turned on the steam. The only one left alive was young Moad, whom Motadid had detained from going with the rest. To him the king spoke of what had passed at Ronda, and of his gratitude for Moad's part in the affair. He rewarded him with a palace in Seville, various magnificent gifts, and a command in his army with a handsome salary; and whenever he discussed state affairs with his Wizirs, he gave Moad the place of honour.

Al-Kortobi mentions "an experienced general named Muad Ibn Abi Korra" as being in command of forces sent by "Ibn Abbad" to aid Ibn Hud in one of his wars with Aragon. This seems to have been a campaign dated by Conde in 1068, and if this is correct, this Muad might be the man mentioned in Dozy's story: on the other hand, Al-Kortobi's account implies that the campaign took place soon after 1033.

Dozy tells the story (apparently) on the authority of Ibn Bassam and An-Nuwairi: it is not alluded to in Makkari or in Conde, and as related offers several difficulties.

The Berbers, if they spoke Arabic at all, spoke it as an acquired language. Their own tongue was unintelligible to the Arabs, and it is most unlikely that Motadid, a pure-blooded Arab, would have troubled to familiarise himself with what his race would regard as a barbarous jargon, unworthy of the notice of an educated man. Nor is it to be supposed that the Berbers, discussing treason among themselves, should have done so in a foreign tongue. How, then, could Motadid know what they were plotting? Setting this aside, it is impossible to believe that a Yemenite Arab should completely disregard, as Motadid is said to have done, all his racial traditions of the sacredness of the guest, and should voluntarily brand himself with that shame of treachery to invited guests, which even the Berbers of Ronda had flinched from incurring. It is true that when, according to the story, he murdered them, they had not yet broken bread in his house; but even so we may reasonably hesitate to credit the tale, in the absence of better evidence than that adduced.

The description given by Dozy of Motadid's bath-house is interesting, because it tallies to a surprising extent with that known to-day as " the bath of Maria Padilla " in the Alcazar of Seville. The details in which it differs from Motadid's bath date from the sixteenth century, when, as Rodrigo Caro tells us, several radical changes were made in the garden on either side of the building, with its vaulted roof and skylights, so that the level of the ground was raised to the top of the roof, doing away with the semi-subterranean orange grove which had existed outside the bath-house until then. But even now, although the great tank is empty, and the artificial ground above conceals the historic apartment, the curious observer may see, behind a hedge of privet, the lights or ventilation shafts along the vaulting, and if he examines the passages leading from it under the palace by the light of a lantern, he will find the remains of the heating pipes which, according to Dozy, were used to suffocate sixty Berbers some eight hundred and fifty years ago.

Notwithstanding the wholesale slaughter of the Berber chiefs, Motadid still had to do some heavy fighting before he could conquer Ronda, Finally, however, he became master of the place, and built himself a beautiful palace, in which he established a family to keep it in readiness for his visits. And when, later on, evil days fell upon his race, his grandson Ar-Radi, or Radila, gallantly defended Ronda

THE ABBADITES AT HOME

against one Kasur, a commander of the Almoravides, and was speared by that same Kasur after his surrender, in defiance of justice and his treaty of capitulation.[1]

Motamid, son of Motadid, was only twenty-nine when he ascended the throne: he was high-spirited, yet prudent, magnificent in his way of life, but so liberal to those who served him and were faithful to him, that he won all hearts; and alike in prosperity and in the hour of victory he was moderate and self-restrained. He was not very religious, and drank wine, especially in time of war, and he allowed all his people to do the same when they were fighting. He was an excellent poet, and competed in that and in his patronage of learned men with his friend Moizz-ad-Daulah, King of Almeria.[2] Abdul-Jabbar says of him, " Such were his brilliant qualities that though his praises are in everybody's mouth, yet enough cannot be said of him to do him justice." [3]

Motamid's first marriage was a pretty romance. One evening he was walking on the banks of the Guadalquivir, among a crowd of towns-people, all enjoying the pleasant river breezes. He was accompanied by his greatest friend, Ibn Ammar,[4] a poet like himself, and the two were improvising verses about the rippling stream, when suddenly a girl passing by chimed in with so apt a line as to attract the prince's surprise and admiration. The girl was extremely pretty, and Motamid (according to Ibn al-Khattib), when he found that she was a slave, purchased her of her master and married her, giving her the name of Itimad, owing to its grammatical affinity with his own, both being derivatives of the same verb.[5]

[1] Dozy, *G. der M.*, ii. 290; Conde, ii. 25, 167.
[2] Conde ii. 47-9. Conde is wrong in the name: the writer he is quoting referred either to Motamid's cousin Ali of Denia, or more probably to Ibn Somadeh (Motassim), King of Almeria.
[3] Makkari, ii. 252.
[4] Afterwards one of his greatest enemies.
[5] Makkari, ii. 512.

Itimad was first known as Romaikiyyah, from the name of the man, Romaik Ibn Hejjaj, from whom Motamid is said to have bought her. Dozy says that she was a slave girl, employed as a donkey driver, but neither Makkari nor Conde gives a hint of this, and we suspect from the fact that Motamid asked her to be his wife instead of taking her for his concubine, that she was a relative instead of a servant of Ibn Hejjaj, whose name proves him to have been of royal Muwallad descent.[1] The family, of which we heard a good deal in the ninth century, still existed in Seville. An Ibn Hejjaj is mentioned by Dozy as having been chosen, among others, by Mohammed Ibn Abbad as his colleague when, some time before 1027, "the patricians of Seville offered him the supreme power," and he refused to rule alone.[2]

Throughout his life Motamid treated her with the utmost affection, which was heartily reciprocated, for she accompanied him in his exile, and they were buried in the same grave. Several anecdotes are told of his devotion. Thus on one occasion he planted a whole hill-side above Cordova with almond trees, because Itimad once saw and admired a snow-storm on the Sierra Morena, and thought she would like to repeat the experience. Snow does not often fall in south-west Andalucia, so the poetical king supplied almond blossom as a substitute.

Another act of gallantry on the part of the king seems to us less romantic than the snow-storm of almond petals.

One day, not far from her palace in Seville, Itimad met some country women selling milk and walking up to their ankles in mud. On her return she said to her husband, "I wish I and my slaves could do as those women are doing!"

Whereupon Motamid ordered a room in the palace to be

---

[1] Makkari, ii. 299; Conde, ii. 169.
[2] *G. der M.*, ii. 238.

strewn with a thick paste made of ambergris, musk, and camphor, dissolved in rose-water. He then had vessels imitating milk-skins slung on ropes of the finest silk, and with these on their arms Itimad and her maidens splashed in the aromatic mud to their hearts' content.

It is related that one day when some angry words passed between the king and queen, Itimad, whose pride was wounded, exclaimed—

"By Allah! I never saw any good come from thee!"

"Not even the day of the mud?" said Motamid, meaning that in one day he had spent an immense sum of gratify her merest whim. And Itimad (who evidently had some common sense) blushed and kept silence.[1]

Makkari ends his history of Motamid as follows [2]:—

"The histories of Andalus are filled with the praises of this monarch. 'Al-Motamid,' says Ibn-al-Katta, 'was the most liberal, high-minded, and munificent of all the rulers of Andalus, owing to which circumstance his court became the meeting place of the learned and his capital the resort of poets and literary men: so much so that there never was a king at whose court a greater number of eminent men were assembled.'

"He was himself an excellent poet, as appears from the many elegant verses which Al-Fath, Ibn-al-Hijari, Ibn Said, and above all Ibn Lebbanah cite in their works. The last-mentioned writer, who was one of Motamid's Wizirs and visited that prince in his confinement [in Africa, after his deposition in 1091] made a collection of all his verses, as well as those of his father and grandfather. . . .

"'No poet,' says Ibn Bassam, 'ever equalled him in tenderness of soul, and in the sentiment which prevailed throughout his verses. Wishing upon one occasion to send the women of his harem from Cordova to Seville, he went

[1] Makkari, ii. 299; Dozy, *G. der M.*, ii. 318–9.   [2] ii. 300–2.

out and travelled part of the road with them from night till sunrise of the ensuing day; he then took leave of them, and returned to Cordova, repeating extempore verses, of which the following two form part :—

"I accompanied them when night had spread her impervious veil, so as to conceal from sight the traces of the travellers,

"I stopped and took leave of them, and the hands of morning stole from me those bright stars.'

"Among the singular and extraordinary circumstances connected with Motamid," continues Makkari, "one is that when he was buried at Aghmat, and the funeral service read over his tomb, the prayer of the stranger was chanted, as if he had been an adventurer, without having regard either to the nobility of his birth or to the extension of his empire, or the splendour and magnificence of his court; or to his having ruled over Seville and its districts, Cordova and its Az-Zahra. Such, however, are the ways of the world.

"We might fill volumes with anecdotes respecting this prince. . . . Suffice it to say that the memory of that illustrious Sultan is still alive in the west, and that his tomb at Aghmat is well known and much frequented by travellers. . . . We visited the tomb of Motamid and that of Romaikiyyah, the mother of his children, when we were at Morocco in the year 1010 (A.D. 1601). We arrived at Aghmat, and not knowing where that prince was buried, we proceeded to inquire from such of the inhabitants as we chanced to meet. . . . At last an old man, bent with age, showed us the place, saying—

"'Here lies a king of Andalus, and by his side she whom his heart loved tenderly.'"

Strange to say, a memorial to her "whom his heart loved tenderly" exists to this day in Seville, although the passionate love and tragic fate of Motamid are unknown even to a thousandth part of those who now dwell in the city over which he ruled some eight centuries ago.

Conde (ii. 169) speaks of an inscription referring to "Said Cubra" (another of the names by which Itimad was known) on a mosque built by her in 1085. This inscription remained until the close of the eighteenth century on that mosque, now the Church of San Juan de la Palma, when in consequence of the restoration of part of the ancient building it was removed to the Seville Museum. It is to the effect that "the royal lady, mother of Ar-Rashid the son of Motamid, caused this minaret to be added to her mosque in the year 1085."[1] It has often been referred to by old and modern writers as one of the "Moorish" remains in Seville, regardless of the fact that this royal lady was no Moor, but an Arab queen, despoiled, dethroned and done to death in a Moroccan prison.

Itimad went into exile with her husband, but she soon fell ill. The celebrated Ibn Zohr, who had been their court physician and owned property in Morocco, hastened to Aghmat at Motamid's appeal, but his art was exercised in vain, and Itimad died in prison. Her daughters went barefoot, performed all the domestic offices, and spun linen to earn their own and their father's living. Yet the poet Ibn Labbanah was able to sing when he visited them,

"Aghmat holds the secret of the heavenly world,"

for in the midst of all their misery, the majesty of undeserved affliction nobly borne irradiated the countenances of the royal personages, among whom love played so large a part.

Motamid soon followed his wife to the grave. He died, still in confinement, in 1095, only four years after leaving Seville. And Ibn Al-Abbar wrote of him some hundred and fifty years later:

[1] *Inscripciones Arabes*, p. 106.

"Every one loved Motamid, every one pitied him, and to-day people weep for him still." [1]

Many incidents related of him by enemies as well as friends show that the last of the Abbadites was a man of lofty sentiments and noble character.

When Al Ammar, in prison for treason, sent to his patron verses making an appeal to his well-known magnanimity, Motamid remarked—

"God has taken from him all feeling of generosity, yet has left him all his fine and penetrating intelligence."

Even at the last moment Ibn Ammar nearly succeeded in obtaining pardon, for Motamid could not forget his former services, and when, upon being admitted to his presence, the poet flung himself at his feet and embraced his master's knees, Motamid uttered words which indirectly implied forgiveness. Unfortunately for the traitor, he straightway wrote to Prince Ar-Rashid that Motamid had pardoned him. Ar-Rashid received the letter when he was in company with persons who strongly disapproved of Ibn Ammar, and they divulged to the king what he had written to Ar-Rashid. Thereupon Motamid asked Ibn Ammar if he had told any one of what had previously passed between them. Ibn Ammar denied having spoken of it. The king then asked—

"Of the two sheets of paper which were given thee, one served to write the poem addressed to me. What has become of the other?"

"It was used," said Ibn Ammar, "for the rough copy of the verses."

"Then," said Motamid, "show me the rough copy."

The traitor this time had nothing more to say, and Motamid, suddenly becoming furiously angry, seized an axe and killed him.

Yet even then, convinced though he was of the poet's

---

[1] Al-Marrakushi, 124; Conde, ii. 170; Dozy, *G. der M.*, ii. 400, 404.

THE ABBADITES AT HOME

treachery, he seemed to regret what he had done when he came to himself, for he ordered the corpse to be washed and prepared for burial, and himself read the funeral prayer over Ibn Ammar's grave in the Alcazar of Seville.[1]

One can understand that a man who found it so hard to believe evil of one who had once been his friend, and so difficult to refuse forgiveness until angered past control, would be betrayed again and again by persons of less honourable character; and indeed Ibn Ammar's was by no means the only case in point.

Al-Marrakushi says—

"This prince resembled Harun Al-Watek billah the Abbasside in the subtlety of his intelligence and his vast literary knowledge: his verses unfolded themselves like rich hangings, and poets and men of letters crowded round him, in numbers greater than had ever before been seen in any court of Spain. Of the various forms of human knowledge he cultivated literature and the allied arts alone; add to that he had every kind of personal good quality, courage, generosity, modesty, discretion, and other similar virtues: briefly, I do not know a praiseworthy human trait with which God had not liberally endowed him. Of all the benefits which Spain received from her conquest down to this day (1224) Motamid is certainly one of, if not the greatest."[2]

The siege of Seville by the Almoravides seems to have begun with the machinations of a group of mal-contents who plotted a revolt. Motamid was informed of their actions and objects, and when he was convinced of their evil designs, "he was urged to publish their shame and shed their blood, to give up their wives to dishonour and to uncover the faces of their daughters. But his racial honour and wisdom and the general loftiness of his character forbade his yielding to this advice; as much as did the sincere faith,

[1] Al-Marrakushi, 108-9.   [2] 86-7.

the sane good sense, and the true religion which he owed to Divine generosity." He took no steps against them, and they escaped from the city. Soon after, "with the aid of some God-forsaken wretches," they rose in revolt. " Motamid left his palace clad only in his tunic, without shield or cuirass. At one of the city gates he met one of the assailants, a knight renowned for his courage and strength, who struck at him with his short-handled, sharp-pointed spear; [1] but the weapon was entangled in his tunic and passed under his arm-pit, thanks to the Divine favour and protection." Motamid returned the stroke with a sword-thrust, which killed his enemy on the spot.

This seems to have been the beginning of the final attack on Seville; Al-Marrakushi proceeds as follows:—

" The enemy were put to flight and those who had scaled the walls retreated, so that the Sevillians thought that they could breathe. But on the afternoon of the same day the attack recommenced, and then the town defence gave way on the river side, and there was no further hope of holding it there; his (Motamid's) haters and detracters saw their hopes realised, thanks to the fire which destroyed his galleys, drove away hope, reduced to silence, took away all power of resistance." [2]

The rising within the city must have been made in combination with the Almoravides, for Al-Marrakushi now gives the names of Yusuf's commanders who reduced the town on the land and on the river sides respectively. Nevertheless, he continues, " the situation remained uncertain a few days, until the arrival of Seyr Ibn Abu Bekr Ibn Tashfin," Yusuf's nephew, bringing large reinforcements. Then the terrified

---

[1] Qui lui frappa de sa lance, à la hampe courte et nerveuse, au fer long et aigu.

[2] The " galleys " were no doubt the bridge of boats between Seville and Triana, which according to Conde, Motamid had shortly before strengthened. (ii. 163.)

people "tried to escape by road, to swim across the river, to creep through the sewers, and to leap down from the walls, hoping to escape death. But those who were loyal to their duty and firm in their love for Motamid, resisted until Sunday the 21st of the month Rejeb of the said year (1091), when the terrible event, the great overthrow, took place on the appointed day, when the breach was too great to be repaired. They entered the city by the river, and after a desperate struggle, citizens and peasants found death.

"As for Motamid, he fought with a courage, stubbornness, and disregard of death which have never been surpassed or even equalled. This is what this prince wrote on the matter, when later on he was groaning in an African prison:—

"'When my tears were dried and my broken heart had regained calm, "surrender" they said to me, "it is the wiser course." But it would have seemed to me sweeter to swallow poison than to submit to such shame. If fate takes from me my kingdom, if my troops desert me, my breast has not yet given up the heart it contains. My noble character remains to me, for who can deprive a man of race of his honour? The day I was attacked by my enemies I chose to meet them without cuirass, and I threw myself on them with no more protection than my shirt; I exposed myself to death while I made the blood of my adversaries flow. But my hour had not come, and I remained unhurt, notwithstanding my ardent wish to escape humiliation and shame. I never threw myself into the mêlée with the hope of return. These are the traditions of the ancient Arabs, of whom I am: as is the tree, such are the branches.'

"The town was given up to pillage," Al-Marrakushi goes on, "and the Berbers deprived the inhabitants of everything they possessed: the palaces of Motamid were most shamefully robbed, and he, reduced to captivity, was forced to write to his two sons, Motadd billah and Radi billah, Governors of the well-known fortresses of Ronda and Mertola, that no one would join them if they attempted resistance. Their aged mother united her prayers to his, and both of them implored their pity, not concealing from them that the life of the whole family depended on their submission. At first they refused thus to degrade themselves, scorning to recognise any authority after that of their father; then, touched by pity they acknowledged the rights, derived from nature and from God, of their parents. Both of them, obeying the divine precepts, renounced worldly advantages, and surrendered their strongholds under treaties and capitulations of the most binding description. Motadd was forthwith despoiled of all he possessed by the officer to whom he surrendered, while Radi, as soon as he emerged from his fortress, was treacherously assassinated and his corpse spirited away." [1]

To the last Motamid never wavered in his pride of race. He wrote of some begging poets who importuned him for alms at Aghmat—

"All the poets of Tangier and the Moghreb have met from all sides in the region of the west, to ask of a captive what it would be difficult for him to grant, for his need is greater than theirs. Was anything stranger ever seen? Were he not withheld by shame and by the profound respect due to the honour of the Lakhmites, he would beg like them. Formerly when an appeal was made to his liberality, he gave without counting the cost, and when a cry for help sounded at his door, he immediately threw himself on his horse." [2]

No wonder that Motamid's subjects, when they saw their monarch and his family taken from them, wept and mourned.

[1] Al-Marrakushi, 119–22; cf. Makkari, ii. 298.
[2] Al-Marrakushi, 123.

Ibn Lebbanah describes the scene as follows, in a poem written after Motamid's death.

" Would that I could remember nothing but that morning when, like the dead in their tombs, they sailed down the river in their boats, while the people, covering the two banks, were astonished to see these pearls borne by the foam of the water. The women had all taken off their veils, and were tearing their faces as they would have done with a coloured dress.[1] They were stupified by having to separate and cease the common life, they who had grown up together. When the moment came to say farewell, men and women cried aloud at the idea of losing those beloved beings. The vessels disappeared, followed and accompanied by sobs, which might have been taken for the chant of the camel-driver urging on his beasts. How many tears then went to swell the river! How much sorrow did those boats bear away!"

And again—

"In the refuge where they dwelt unhappiness has entered, in spite of the lions and serpents who challenged its entry."[2]

"In this holy temple, which was peopled by so many hopes, there is now neither dweller nor guest! . . . The light goes out when the source of its production is exhausted, the flower withers after having sweetly lived.

---

[1] We cannot explain this, unless it is that the Shiite women, as a rule, wore black.

[2] The lion in Seville bore a double significance. It was the symbol of force, and the Fatimites of Egypt had it sculptured " as the emblem of their power " over the doors of their palaces (cf. *L'Art Arabe*, 279). The lion and the eagle were also the idols of ancient Yemen (*ib.* 186). Thus the presence of sculptured lions' heads, markedly Egyptian in style, on many of the Mozarabic churches built or added to under Islam in Seville, is accounted for. As for the serpents referred to by Al-Lebbanah, we need only recall that the serpent was the hieroglyph for royalty in ancient Egypt, to understand why the Copto-Arabic artists of Andalucia placed representations of it at the entrance of the palaces they built. The idea still persists wherever the Copts and Yemenites settled in this region, although it has long degenerated into something more resembling a capital S than a serpent.

Know, oh guest, that the house of benefactions is empty: take thy baggage and collect what thou hast left of provisions. Oh thou who didst hope to dwell in their valley, know that the servants have left, that the crops grow no longer. Thou art deceived, traveller, by this well-known road of benefits: seek another, for on this thou wilt no more find a guide." [1]

A monarch who expressed and who inspired sentiments such as are recorded of Motamid Ibn Abbad, must have been as lovable in character as he was exalted in position. Of few kings can it be said, when they have lain for an hundred and fifty years in a despised and neglected grave—

" To-day people weep for him still." [2]

---

[1] Marrakushi, 125.

[2] Not only the Arabs but also the Christians of Seville had cause to grieve for the fall of Motamid, for he protected them throughout his reign and allowed them the free exercise of their religion. Numbers of Mozarabic churches were rebuilt or restored during the eleventh century all over the south-west; and Motamid even employed Christians about his person; *e.g.* Ibn Al Margari, one of his favourites, who was a Christian of Seville and a distinguished poet. (Simonet, 660.)

CHAPTER XIII

THE ALMORAVIDES

On few points connected with the history of Moslem Spain is there more difference of opinion than on the origin of the Almoravides. Some writers say that they were barbarous Africans or Berbers whose chief ambition was to destroy the " noble Arabs " with whom they came in contact : others that they were themselves of Arabic descent. Some hold that they were fanatics whose conquests were undertaken for the propagation of their religion, while others again tell us that they were a gentle and kindly people who thought more of developing their own civilisation than of interfering with their neighbours.

Certain facts stand out among all these contradictory accounts. The Almoravides as a nation were attached to the Shiite form of Mohammedanism, prayed for the Abbasside Khalifs of the East in the *khotba* in every mosque in their dominions, and wore black like the most devoted followers of Ali.[1] And whatever may have been the origin of the numerous tribes which were eventually united under the banner of Yusuf Ibn Tashfin, he himself claimed descent from the Arabs of Yemen, and was described in a poem by Abd-al-Jalil as " born of the tribe of Himyar." The passage occurs in an address to the Almoravide king, which says that the tribes of Yusuf and of Motamid were " united like sword-belts joined together," because Yusuf was born of

[1] *Encyc. of Islam*, s./v. " Almoravides " ; Conde, ii. 157 ; Al-Marrakushi, 79, 232.

the tribe of Himyar and Motamid of that of Lakhm.[1] The poet thus confirms Conde's account of the genealogy of the Almoravides, which is as follows:—

"They were the descendants of another more ancient tribe called Lamtuna, who came of a man named Lamtu, relative of another called Gaddala and of a third called Mustafa, progenitors of the tribes of the same names. All three prided themselves on their descent from another older and nobler tribe called Sanhajah, of the ancient blood of Homair (Himyar) one of the first kings of Yemen or Arabia Felix. . . . The Sanhajah left Yemen for the deserts on account of certain wars in which they were compelled to fly in order not to mix with the barbarians and fugitives in Africa : and being poor they used a simple sort of clothing which enveloped and cloaked them, and from this dress, which is called Lamt, some try to show that they got their name, although it appears more certain that they owed it to their progenitor in unknown times."[2]

Makkari says that their name was derived from their use of shields covered with the skin of the *lamt,* which in the text Gayangos translates as hippopotamus, but elsewhere he says that the lamt was a kind of antelope.[3] There is no reference to these shields in any other account of the Almoravides.

Lenormant tells us that when he wrote, in 1869, one of the districts colonised by the descendants of Joktan—a name altered by Arabic tradition into Kahtan—whose king Himyar founded, in the first century B.C., the dynasty bearing his name, was still inhabited by the great tribe of the Beni Lam, who dwelt in what that author calls "the cradle of the Joktanides," including Meshalik (the Mesha of Genesis), the Hedjaz, Hadramaut, and Yemen.[4] It

[1] *Abbadites,* i. 116.
[3] i. 408 note ; ii. 273.
[2] Conde, ii. 73-4.
[4] iii. 248, 251, 283.

seems therefore more likely that the Lamtunites of Africa took their name from their progenitors in Arabia Felix than from using shields made of hippopotamus or antelope hide.

The account of the Almoravides in the *Encyclopedia of Islam* says nothing about their manners and customs, dealing only with their religion and their conquests. We will therefore add a few particulars from Conde.

The first we hear of the Almoravides is in connection with one Yahya Ibn Ibrahim, chief of the Sanhajah, who early in the eleventh century, after a pilgrimage to Mecca, induced a man of letters to return with him to instruct his tribesmen in religion and the learning of the schools. This was Abdullah Ibn Yasin al Juzuli, a professor who had studied for seven years in Andalucia, but whose origin is not mentioned either by Conde or the *Encyclopedia*. He established a *ribat* or monastery [1] on an island in the Niger or the Senegal, with the support of a few followers, among whom were two chiefs of the Lamtuna, Yahya Ibn Omar and his brother Abu Bekr, who, says Conde, were of the old blood of Himyar, and speedily obtained a great number of adherents, for the Lamtunites " were not so barbarous and ferocious, but that they desired to learn both letters and religion, for they were naturally very kind and humane, amid all their primitive customs."

Here Conde's account diverges somewhat from that of the *Encyclopedia,* for it attaches more weight to the desire of the people for civilisation, and less to the religious factor.

[1] Conde (i. 619, note) says that these *ribats* were in the nature of religious settlements of fighting men, very like the Military Orders of the Christians. La Rabida, the monastery from which Columbus sailed, is the survival of one of the Moslem *Ribats* on the borders of the kingdom of Niebla, the boundary between which and the principality of Saltis is still marked by Palos de la Frontera. Idrisi (p. 14) mentions a Rabida Rota near Cadiz, where there was a mosque so sacred as to be the object of constant pilgrimages. (Marrakushi, 270.) The little town he refers to is still called Rota, but the " Rabida " has dropped out of the name.

Both agree, however, as to the veneration in which the teacher was held and the power he obtained over the chiefs, "seventy of the most noble of whom at once joined his classes." Eventually Ibn Yasin collected about a thousand warriors and chiefs in his *ribat*, and called them *Murabitun*, which became in Spanish *Almoravides*.

Yahya Ibn Omar having died in battle, Ibn Yasin appointed his brother Abu Bekr in his place, but not long afterwards he himself was killed in a fight with a tribe of Berbers whom he proposed to convert to his doctrines at the point of the sword. Abu Bekr, who had been little more than a figure-head to the masterful Yasin, now took command in earnest, and set about developing the country within as well as extending its borders without.

A considerable increase of population accrued to him from the arrival of people from the desert, and by the year 1068 " they were multiplying so much that the immigrants were pressing on the natives and there was hardly room for them in the land, the natives not agreeing well with the foreigners " : wherefore Abu Bekr, at the request of his people, founded the city of Morocco. This took place, according to Conde, in the year 1070. But while Abu Bekr was busy building his new capital, news came that his relatives of the tribe of Lamtuna were in trouble and in fear of destruction at the hands of hostile neighbours unless he came to their aid. He appointed his cousin, Yusuf Ibn Tashfin, who, like himself, was "of the ancient blood of Himyar," to act as regent in his absence, and hastened to the help of his family.

When he returned a year later he found Yusuf completely master of the situation, having enormously increased the prosperity of the new kingdom. Whether he voluntarily resigned his throne or whether Yusuf deprived him of it seems uncertain. Yusuf remained at the head of affairs,

THE ALMORAVIDES

and Abu Bekr returned to his original home in the desert, and died in the Soudan in 1087-8.[1]

Yusuf Ibn Tashfin had all the Yemenite fondness for building, and under his auspices the new capital of Morocco rapidly attained importance. When the Almoravides first settled there they found nothing but a valley in a forest, with lions, tigers, wild goats, ostriches, and the like for its sole inhabitants, but the place had many natural advantages, such as plenty of sweet cool water and abundance of pasture land in a favourable position. Abu Bekr had begun to plan streets and public places before he was called away, and when Yusuf Ibn Tashfin took the government he walled the city, built a mosque, and added a fortress in which to store arms and treasure. He himself worked among the other labourers with his own hands at the construction of the mosque, "giving to all an example of zeal and humility. May God pardon one who built thus!" "This is now the noble city of Morocco," concludes the author from whom Conde extracted his account, "in a delightful situation, with abundance of pasture, fruit, and water, so that wherever a well is sunk at a little depth is found sweet pure water.[2]

Yusuf, who ended by ruling over Andalucia as well as all western Africa, united a generous soul to many bodily advantages; he was prudent in the government of his people, skilled and courageous in war, always attentive to the security and defence of his states, very careful of his frontiers, fond of war, which he conducted with much intelligence and good luck, extremely liberal, serious and austere. Careless of dress and adornments, but very clean, abstemious and moderate in his pleasures, gentle in his manner and conversation; in every way he showed himself fitted for the great destiny for which God had created him, which was to

[1] *Encyc. Islam*, s./v. "Almoravides"; Conde, ii. 73-81.
[2] Conde, ii. 84-5.

conquer a great part of the world for Islam. His dress was of wool, and he never used any other material; his nourishment barley-bread and camel-meat and the flesh of other robust animals, but in small quantities; he was never in his life heard to complain of the flavour of his repasts, nor of the quantity nor quality of them; in this he was always consistent. In his whole life he never had an illness save the one which God sent to convey him to the prizes and recompenses of the other life.

He administered his states with justice, but although he was so just, he was gentle and friendly with his subjects. He made treaties of peace with the infidels whom he conquered, and the tribute they paid in accordance with those treaties amounted to so great a sum that on his death 300,000 arrobas of silver and 5040 arrobas of gold were found in his treasury.[1] He was very clever and good-natured, but modest and retiring. "It seemed," says his biographer, whose intimate acquaintance with the details of Yusuf's domestic life suggests that he was a contemporary, " that in him all the virtues were united."

It is said that Yusuf bought a large number of slaves who were sold to him by certain merchants who traded with Guinea in a city called Gasza, far in the desert, and that these negroes were formerly Christians, but through contact with the Berbers, or through the evils and violence of war, or owing to some other cause which is not known; they ended by losing their religion.[2] These negroes were sent to the coasts of Andalucia and exchanged for captive Christians who were bartered by the Andalucians. Yusuf had these young men from Andalucia instructed in the law, mounted and armed, and trained in the mastership of arms

---

[1] The Spanish arroba now is about 25 lbs.
[2] Those who are acquainted with the early history of Guinea will know whether there is any foundation for this curious statement.

and horses, and of them he had as his own guard two hundred
and fifty picked and skilled men. Besides this Andalucian
troop, he had a guard of two thousand trained negroes.[1]

He had a gold coinage, and his horses were caparisoned
with gold, and his swords had hilts of gold and silver. Dresses
of linen and of fine kidskin were in use at his Court, besides
the shawls or blankets of scarlet and white wool, peculiar
to the Lamtuna. His people also knew how to make a kind
of fine cloth which was waterproof. They used the aromatic
sandal-wood, very sweet and fragrant, musk, camphor,
amber, and civet. And these refinements were in vogue in
Morocco at an early period of the Almoravide rule, for many
of them are mentioned in an account of the gifts made to
Abu Bekr when he was induced to resign the dominion to
his cousin.[2] The luxury here suggested is hardly that of a
barbarian, nor does the general description of Yusuf's
character and modes of life and thought indicate religious
fanaticism. True, he is said to have helped to build a mosque
with his own hands, but Abderrahman I. of Cordova did
as much before him, and certainly religious fanaticism was
not one of the leading characteristics of that ruler.

Before Yusuf Ibn Tashfin died his empire extended from
Algiers to Tangier on the north, and included all the Moghreb
and the city of Fez. Conde's account of his development
of the last named throws an important side-light on the
origin and rapid advance of the Almoravide civilisation.

The first thing Yusuf did was to throw down a wall which
separated " the Andalucian quarter " from that of the people
of Kairwan within the city. He then proceeded to enlarge
and improve Fez in every direction, making the inhabitants
take part in the work.[3] This was in 1070.

These Andalucians had made their mark on the city long

---

[1] Conde, ii. 82–6 ; cf. Codera, *Almoravides*, 30 note.
[2] *Ibid.*, ii. 88–90. [3] *Ibid.*, ii. 93.

before Yusuf Ibn Tashfin became its master. In Fez there are still standing ancient buildings containing inscriptions in the peculiar form of the Kufic character which was so largely used in Andalucia in the tenth and eleventh centuries. These would date from the time of Almansur, when Fez was subject to Cordova, and Almansur's son Abdalmalek, as representative of the Khalifate, built a mosque there. One of the inscriptions in this mosque, bearing the date 985 (H. 375) is reproduced in an engraving in Conde.[1] It is identical with inscriptions reproduced in the same work from tenth and eleventh century buildings in Andalucia, and with inscriptions in the Alcazar of Seville, and on *objets d'art* and sculptures preserved in various museums, which bear dates of the same period. Although many years had passed since Fez emancipated herself from the Spanish over-lordship, yet Yusuf found a colony of Andalucians in the city in 1070, numerous enough to have had a quarter of their own, and sufficiently skilled in building for him to pull down the dividing wall in order that they should be amalgamated with the rest of the inhabitants in the work which he set on foot for the improvement of the place.

How did the Andalucians come to be settled in Fez in such considerable numbers? There was no colonisation under Almansur, whose occupation of the country was purely military and of brief duration.[2]

We get the clue from Ibn Ghalib, an eleventh century writer largely quoted by Ibn Said, who in his turn is transcribed by Makkari at great length in his chapters on the domestic economy of Spain under the Moslems.

Ibn Ghalib, who appears to have died in 1044,[3] says—

"Africa may be said to have derived its present wealth and importance, and its extent of commerce, from Anda-

---

[1] Conde, i. 517. [2] *Ibid.*, i. 514 ff., 521–2.
[3] Makkari, i. 310, 332.

lucians settling in it. For when God Almighty was pleased to send down on their country the last disastrous civil war [*i.e.* the war which began with the deposition of Hisham II.] thousands of its inhabitants of all classes and professions sought a refuge on these shores,[1] and spread over the *Moghreb al aksa* (the Far West) and Africa proper, settling wherever they found comfort or employment. Labourers and country people took to the same occupations which they had left in Andalus, they formed intimacy with the inhabitants, assisted them in their agricultural labours, discovered springs and made them available for the irrigation of their fields, planted trees, introduced water-mills and other useful inventions; and in short they taught the African farmers many things they had never heard of, and showed them the use of excellent practices whereof they were completely ignorant. Through their means the countries where they fixed their residence became at once prosperous and rich, and the inhabitants saw their wealth increase rapidly, as well as their comforts and enjoyments.

"The [Andalucian] inhabitants of cities being for the most part well-educated people, and being versed in all the branches of learning and polite literature, soon made themselves conspicuous and known at court, or in the chief towns where they settled. They filled posts of distinction in the state, and were appointed to the charges of Wizirs, Katibs, governors of provinces and districts, tax-collectors, and other offices under government, so that there was no district in Africa wherein some of the principal authorities were not Andalucians.

"But it was in the class of operatives and workmen in all sorts of handicrafts that Africa derived most advantage

[1] These were the Andalucian Shiites, who were the especial objects of rapine, pillage and slaughter by the armies of the usurpers, whether Berbers or Sunnite Arabs; cf. Makkari, ii. 225–30; An-Nuwairi in Makkari, ii. 488, 496, and *passim*.

from the tide of emigration setting towards its shores. It is well known that before the arrival of the Andalucians many of the trades which are now [*i.e.* in the first half of the eleventh century] in a flourishing state were hardly known in Africa, and that in activity and dexterity the emigrants ranked far above the native workmen. For instance, if they undertook the building of an edifice they completed it in the shortest possible time, and finished everything so beautifully and with such perfection of design, that they won the hearts and affections of their employers, and their reputation grew immense among the people: these being notorious facts which none but the ignorant or ill-intentioned could deny." [1]

Not only did the Almoravides appreciate and profit by the civilisation and skill of the Andalucian exiles who had fled to Africa to escape the excesses of the Sunnite and Berber soldiery of Spain, but there is evidence that the Almoravide rulers valued the Yemenite culture, and employed Yemenite poets and men of letters in their Council and about their person. Among Yusuf's secretaries was Abu Bekr Ibn al-Kasira, who had been in Motamid's employment, and Ali, Yusuf's son and successor, employed in the same capacity Ibn Abdun of Evora, a well-known poet, and also, according to Conde, one of Motamid's own sons.[2] The Almoravide rulers, it is clear, retained enough of their racial instincts and traditions to be able and willing to avail themselves of the Yemenite-Andalucian civilisation which they found at Fez and elsewhere.

Before leaving this subject we must add that the Almoravide coinage was perfect in design and execution and abundant in quantity before Yusuf invaded Spain. Señor Codera remarks upon this as a curious fact, explaining it by the

---

[1] Makkari, i. 118–9, quoting Ibn Ghalib from Ibn Said.
[2] Marrakushi, 138–9; Conde, ii. 193.

THE ALMORAVIDES

assumption that the art of engraving gold was then cultivated in all nations of importance, and that the reform of the coinage was not a chance and isolated development, but in accordance with a fixed method proceeding from a central power. Señor Codera presumably had not observed Ibn Ghalib's account of the Andalucian influence which was so strong at that period in Africa, otherwise he would have found no difficulty in understanding how the Almoravides learnt to produce their beautiful coinage. He calls attention to the material prosperity indicated by such a coinage both of gold and silver. The gold coins are especially notable on account of their uniform weight. The gold coinage of Andalucia had not possessed this quality, and it would appear that laws compelling a fixed weight were introduced here under Yusuf Ibn Tashfin. For minor commercial transactions the Almoravides divided the dirhem into halves, quarters, eighths, and sixteenths, which also seems to have been an innovation, although the last Kings of Badajoz, the Beni-Al-Aftas, tried to introduce these small coins. And the artistic level of the coinage is maintained also in another class of inscriptions, namely those in stone. Here the ancient Kufic characters cease to appear, the elegant cursive writing replacing them: while the inscription as a whole is framed in graceful ornamentation.[1] A little of the beautiful writing referred to by Señor Codera is to be seen in the Alcazar of Seville, generally placed in the carved frame-work of the great doors, between the sternly simple Kufic and the florid African style favoured by the Almohades.[2]

Such was the monarch and such the people who were invited to come to the aid of the Moslems of Spain in the

[1] Codera, *Almoravides*, 218 ff.
[2] The coinage in the eleventh century was in the "Seville" Kufic script, which ceased to be used after the fall of Motamid.

year 1086, in order to resist the encroachments of the Christians. The internal relations of the Spanish Moslems and the reasons which decided them to take a step, the final result of which was the loss of their own independence, must be examined in another chapter.

The "Andalucian quarter" (*Barrio de los Andaluces*) still exists in Fez, and one district in it is still called Triana, after the Potters' suburb in Seville. Here stands the mosque of the Beni Idris, who ruled North Africa, from Fez to Biserta, in the tenth century. In 973 the last of the Beni Idris submitted to the over-lordship of Hisham II., and Almansur built a chapel for the adornment of this mosque, and presented a pulpit of richly carved ebony to its *Aljama* (Conde, i. 472, 514-6).

When the discontented tribes besieged Fez under the French Protectorate in May of this year (1912), their first thought was to force their way into the Andalucian quarter and possess themselves of the sacred banner of the Beni Idris, which is preserved in the ancient mosque. This they succeeded in doing, in spite of the efforts of the French artillery, their intention being to proclaim the "Holy War" under the ancient banner of the Fatimite rulers of Morocco.

AS-R

Fig. 10.—*Convento de la Luz* (No. 2). Copto-Arabic pointed arches of the great Central Court.

CHAPTER XIV

ANDALUCIA IN THE ELEVENTH CENTURY

THE following is a brief sketch of the political conditions prevailing in the eleventh century, when the states governed by men of Yemenite descent, or by their clients, were united in a loose federation under the Imamate of the Khalif Hisham II. until his death in 1058, and then continued their federation under the over-lordship of the Abbadites of Seville.

BADAJOZ.—The government was assumed in 1009 by Shabur, a freedman of the family of Almansur, who coined money under the title of Hajib (of Hisham II.). His tombstone was discovered in 1881 in pulling down a house in the Calle de Abril in Badajoz. The inscription gives the name of Shabur the Hajib, and the date of his death, 1022.[1] He was succeeded by the Beni-Al-Aftas of the tribe of Tojib, who also coined money as Hajibs of Hisham. They were literary men, and seems to have remained loyal to the last to their alliance or vassalship under Motamid after the death of Hisham.

Minor states eventually incorporated with Badajoz, or, as it came to be called, the Algarbe, were Niebla, Santa Maria de Algarbe, Saltis, Huelva, Gibraleon, Ocsonoba, and Silves, many of which had been ruled for centuries by

[1] See an article by Amador de los Rios in the *Revista de Archivos* for February, 1909, p. 48. The writer speaks of Shabur as "presumably one of the many unknown kinglets of that period." Makkari and Gayangos differ as to the date of his death, and neither gives the one inscribed on his monument.

Christian or Muwallad families connected with the descendants of the Princess Sara. All were loyal to Hisham, and later to Motamid. The daughter of the Amir of Niebla was one of Motamid's wives. References are made by both Christian and Moslem writers to the continued existence of churches and monasteries in this district, and these Mozarabic edifices are still to be seen all over the country.

ZARAGOZA.—A Tojibite family governed this state—the most northerly settlement of Arabs at the time of the invasion, and those chiefly Yemenite—until 1044, and coined money as Hajibs of Hisham. In that year the Beni Hud, who were Jodhamites, replaced them. They too coined money as Hajibs of Hisham as late as 1082. Why they continued to do so for many years after his death has not yet been explained, but the fact cannot be disputed, for coins thus dated are in existence. Minor states also ruled by members of the Hud family were Calatayud and Tudela, where also money was coined by them as Hajibs of Hisham. Calatayud, Daroca, and Huesca were peopled by Yemenites, and in early days were governed by Tojibites, who were generally found united with other Yemenites or with the Gothic Christians against the Sunnites of Cordova during the first civil war. There are certain striking resemblances between the earliest Arabic art surviving in Zaragoza and that of the same period in Seville.[1]

DENIA and the BALEARIC ISLES were governed by the Beni Al-Amiri, descendants of a freedman of Almansur's younger son, Abderrahman (Sanchol). They coined money down to 1075 as Hajibs of Hisham, and then as Hajibs without the name of any Imam. Motadid of Seville married one of the daughters of Mujahid, the founder of this family. Another daughter was married to Abdalaziz of Valencia, son of Abderrahman (Sanchol). Thus the King of Seville

[1] There was a Bishop of Zaragoza from 1040 to 1063.

ANDALUCIA IN THE ELEVENTH CENTURY

and the Amir of Valencia in the succeeding generation were first cousins, and they loyally stood by each other to the last. Abdalmalek, son of Abdalaziz, was dispossessed by Mamun Ibn Dhinnun of Toledo in 1065. Some twelve years later the Valencians rose and restored the Beni Abi Amir in the person of Abdalmalek's son Abu Bekr. Unfortunately for himself Abu Bekr entered into an alliance with Yahya, son of Mamun Ibn Dhinnun, and by way of consolidating it, married his daughter. When Toledo surrendered to Alfonso VI., in 1085, Yahya went to Valencia, and with the help of Alfonso assumed the government of his son-in-law's dominions.[1]

VALENCIA was governed by the Beni Abi Amir, a family founded by the grandson of Almansur, Abdalaziz son of Sanchol. Their coinage bears the name of Hisham as Imam down to his death. A later member of the family struck money as Hajib of the Abbasside Khalif Abdullah.[2]

TORTOSA, although a very small and unimportant state, had its own coinage with the names of its governors as Hajibs of Hisham II.

LERIDA had a coinage with Hisham's name as Imam.

CORDOVA was ruled from 1031 by the Beni Jehwar as Hajibs of Hisham II. until, the city being besieged by the Berbers in 1058 (the year of Hisham's death), Abdalmalek

[1] The relations of the Beni Al-Amiri with the Christians of their country were remarkably friendly. A curious document of 1058 is extant, by which Ali, son of Mujahid, made over all the churches of his kingdom, including the Bishoprics of the Balearic Isles, Denia, and Orihuela, to the Bishopric of Barcelona, ordering all the clergy, presbyters, and deacons of those dioceses to be ordained by and in every way subject to, the Bishop of Barcelona and no other. The right of the King of Denia to do this was recognised by the Bishop of Barcelona and three other Bishops, who assisted at the consecration of the new cathedral of Santa Cruz and Santa Eulalia in 1058; and according to some authorities, by the Pope also. It would appear from this that Ali took the title of king on the death of Hisham in that year.

[2] The Beni Abi Amir also protected the Christians, and we read of a Bishop of Valencia in 1089.

Ibn Jehwar appealed to Motadid of Seville for help, and handed the government of the city over to him. Cordova from that time formed one of the federation of states under Yemenite rule. No coins of the period have yet been traced.

MURCIA was governed by the Beni Tahir, a Yemenite family, from 1038 to 1069, as Hajibs of Hisham II. Coins have not been traced. The Beni Tahir were overthrown by an intrigue between the Mudarite Ibn Rashik and Motamid's Wizir and false friend Ibn Ammar. Ibn Ammar, who had been sent by Motamid to inquire into disturbances in which the Beni Tahir were unjustly represented to have been supporting the Berbers of Toledo against the federated states, planned with Ibn Rashik to secure Murcia for themselves. Ibn Ammar was recalled by Motamid to give an account of what was taking place, and although on his return the Beni Tahir submitted to him under the impression that he was acting for Motamid, to whom they were loyal, Ibn Rashik had meanwhile taken measures to oust Ibn Ammar. Motamid having become convinced of the treachery of his Wizir, had him imprisoned and executed, and endeavoured to restore the Beni Tahir at the instance of the Beni Abi Amir of Valencia. Ibn Rashik declined to relinquish the government he had usurped, and retained it until shortly before the occupation of Andalucia by the Almoravides, employing himself in the meanwhile by intriguing with Ibn Somadeh (Motassim) against Motamid. Dozy, in his table of the rulers of the small states, expresses a doubt whether Motamid or Ibn Rashik ruled in Murcia at this time. Conde says that Ibn Rashik governed ostensibly on behalf of Motamid, but without paying tribute or in any way acknowledging his authority. Al-Marrakushi says that Motamid finally bought Ibn Rashik out after the first (or second) coming of the Almoravides (see pp. 251–2). Dozy gives the Beni Tahir as restored at this time.

ALMERIA was governed from 1010 to 1038 by two freedmen of Almansur in succession. The second was treacherously killed in a fight in which he was allied with Ibn Somadeh (Motassim), who betrayed him. Ibn Somadeh, who appears to have been a Berber, then assumed the government, and although nominally allied with Motamid and the Yemenite federation, intrigued with Ibn Rashik against Seville and the other loyal states. Coins have not been traced.

The origin of the Beni Somadeh of Almeria is not clearly stated by any authority we have been able to consult, but as the Berbers are extolled in poems addressed to the second of the line, Motassim, the presumption is that they were Berbers. It is probable at any rate that they were Sunnites, for Makkari in his summary of the Amirs of the eleventh century enlarged upon Motassim's good qualities, as "a wise and enlightened monarch," while the Amirs of Yemenite extraction are passed over without comment. Motassim married a daughter of Abdalaziz of Valencia, and thus became Motamid's cousin by marriage. He professed a warm attachment to the ruler of Seville, but secretly worked for his undoing, having begun to make mischief between him and Yusuf Ibn Tashfin even before the Almoravide's first visit to Andalucia. According to Al-Marrakushi, jealousy of Motamid was the motive of his treachery. Motamid to the last either did not suspect or chose to ignore Motassim's disloyalty towards him.

Certain minor states, consisting of little more than fortified towns and their immediate surroundings, were conquered by Motadid Ibn Abbad from Berber governors who had usurped rule there during the civil wars following the deposition of Hisham II. in 1009. Chief among these were ALGECIRAS, CARMONA, MORON, ARCOS, and RONDA. The population in each case was largely Yemenite and detested the Berber rule. After 1058 they were always loyal to the Abbadites. These cities, having been taken in war, were incorporated as part of the dominion of Seville. The other states mentioned never belonged to or were ruled by Seville, but only attached themselves to Motamid as the head of the federation to which they all subscribed for purposes of self-defence against Castile and Aragon.

TOLEDO, GRANADA, and MALAGA were ruled by Berbers, who were constantly at war with the Yemenite states, and occasionally succeeded in possessing themselves of one or another of them for longer or shorter periods. But on the first opportunity the populace rose against them and restored the rulers of their own race.

Toledo and Granada remained isolated and independent until 1085, for there was never any attempt at federating the Berber states. Then the Christians of Toledo forced their Moslem fellow-citizens to surrender to Alfonso VI., and that city ceased to play any part in the history of Moslem Spain. Granada not long afterwards came to terms with Motamid on the basis of a friendly alliance; and the last of her Berber princes, Abdullah Ibn Zehr, appears to have entered the federation of which Motamid was the head, with the conviction that loyalty to the Abbadite would be his best policy. The Berber governors of the minor states had all disappeared many years before. The population of Granada was largely Yemenite and Christian in origin.

Malaga seems to have had a larger element of Berbers and Sunnites among her population than any other of the minor states annexed or brought into the federation by the Abbadites; and as late as 1273 we find this city rebelling against the Yemenite king of Granada, Mohammed Ibn Nasr. There is no direct evidence, however, that her people took any part in the intrigues of Motassim and Ibn Rashik at the court of Yusuf Ibn Tashfin.

Another state governed by Berbers is mentioned by Dozy and others, but it seems to have played no important part at any time. This was AS-SAHLA, ruled by the Beni Razin from 1011 to 1090. Their territory seems to have lain between the then borders of Murcia and Valencia. The capital, Santa Maria de Ibn Razin, is now known as Albarracin. The chief interest of this little state lies in the name of its capital, which shows that the Christians had been numerous enough to maintain its Gothic name of Santa Maria. Señor Pons calls it Santa Maria del Levante.

Thus, so far as can be discovered from translations of Arabic writers accessible to us, Yusuf's distrust of Motamid, which led to the occupation of all Andalucia by the Almoravides, was brought about by the Sunnite governor of Murcia and the Berber Amir of Almeria alone, all the other states at that time either being loyal to the Yemenite federation, or already subject to the Christians. The oft-repeated accusation against Motamid, of having possessed himself of these states by force, is, we think, disproved by his personal and tribal relations with them, apart from the absence of records of campaigns during his reign, resulting in such conquests.

To give detailed references for the above statements would be tedious and extremely lengthy. The greater part of the data are arrived at by a comparison of the genealogical tables at the end of Gayangos' translation of Makkari and in Dozy's *Geschichte der Mauren* with statements in the text of those writers and in Conde, Dozy's *Abbadites*, Codera's *Estudios*, Pons' *Historiadores y geografos*, Al-Marrakushi's *Histoire des Almohades*, Simonet's *Historia de los Mozarabes*, and Idrisi's geography. The facts about the coins were supplied, as stated in the preface, by Mr. Longworth-Dames of the Numismatic and Asiatic Societies.

CHAPTER XV

SPAIN AND THE ALMORAVIDES

BY the end of the year 1085 the rapid advance of the Castilians was a grave and pressing danger to the whole of Moslem Spain. Alfonso VI., who had been harrying the country round Toledo for some time, laid formal siege to the city early in that year, and with the help of the Gothic Christians (Mozarabs) within the walls,[1] entered it as conqueror at the end of May. The Berber ruler, Yahya, the last of the Beni Dhinnun, who had seized the city after the fall of the Khalifate and had held it until now, made no long resistance, but stipulated as a condition of surrender that Alfonso should aid him to take the kingdom of Valencia, which for twenty years had been a bone of contention between the Beni Dhinnun and the Beni Abi Amir. This stipulation Alfonso carried out without delay, and sent Alvar Fañez with sufficient troops to force Yahya on the unwilling Valencians. Yahya, being unable to provide their pay, gave them land instead, on which they settled, and enriched themselves by raiding the country round. At the same time Zaragoza was undergoing a siege, and a body of Castilian troops had fortified themselves in the castle of Aledo, near Lorca, and were harrying Almeria.[2] Thus at

---

[1] The Chronicle (xi. 220) quotes a priest living in Toledo at the time, to the effect that in 1082 the Christians sent a deputation to Alfonso to beg him to continue the siege, and Yahya sent another deputation (also of Christians) asking him to desist.
[2] *Crónica general*, xi. 226–8; Makkari, ii. 257, 505, and genealogical tables; Dozy, *G. der M.*, ii. 352-3.

SPAIN AND THE ALMORAVIDES   245

the end of 1085 Alfonso was not only established in Toledo, but was in a position to annex Valencia, and possibly Zaragoza, whenever it might suit him to do so.

In addition to his advances in the east, Alfonso was also pushing forward in the south and west. Makkari says that no sooner was he master of Toledo than he began making incursions into the territories of the Kings of Seville and Badajoz, "taking so many of their towns and castles and causing such havoc and ruin, that these monarchs, together with many other petty princes, consented to pay him an annual tribute, rather than have their dominions continually exposed to his devastating fury."[1]

There was no power in Moslem Spain capable of opposing any effective resistance to the steady and alarming advance of the Christians. Seville, the strongest of the Moslem states, was far too weak to resist Alfonso single-handed, and Motamid's constant efforts to federate all the small principalities for self-defence failed through the inveterate jealousies of their rulers. Left to themselves, says Dozy, the Spanish Moslems had only two courses open to them: submission to Alfonso, or exile. Many of them indeed were of opinion that they should leave the country, and Dozy quotes a line of a poem advising the Andalucians to go, "for to remain here would be folly."[2]

Thus in their great straits an appeal to their co-religionists in Africa would seem to be the only resource left to the Andalucians; but the proposal was fraught with considerable danger. Yusuf Ibn Tashfin might indeed be capable of checking or destroying Alfonso, but he might also absorb Andalucia, as he had already absorbed the greater part of North Africa. Both Motamid and the rulers of the

---

[1] Makkari, ii. 270. The Chronicle (xi. 294) also says that Alfonso made war on Motamid after having conquered Toledo.
[2] *G. der M.*, ii. 353.

minor states were fully alive to this danger, but it seemed to be a choice of evils, and they did what they could to protect their own freedom by extracting from Yusuf a promise that he would not dispossess them of their territories.[1]

In addition to the general danger to which the whole of Moslem Spain was subjected, Motamid seems to have been in individual peril from Alfonso owing to some difficulty about the payment of his tribute. Makkari gives two long versions of this incident, taken from writers of the thirteenth and (probably) fourteenth centuries respectively, and observes that "the above is differently related by Ibn Lebbanah." It is to be regretted that he does not give Ibn Lebbanah's version, as he was a contemporary and a friend of Motamid. This latter fact is perhaps the reason why Makkari suppressed it. The details he gives are probably inaccurate, and in any case are of no great consequence; but they go to show that there was some kind of quarrel, and that this was one of the reasons which influenced Motamid in his decision to summon the help of the Almoravides.

According to all the accounts the idea of asking Yusuf Ibn Tashfin for help originated with Motamid; he communicated it to the Amirs of Granada and Badajoz, and on his invitation they sent representatives to a meeting at Seville, which was also attended by the Kadi of Cordova, by Ibn Zagut, Governor of Malaga appointed by Motamid, and by Motamid's own Wizir Ibn Zeidun. It was then decided to appeal for help to Yusuf, the only dissentient being the Governor of Malaga, who pointed out how dangerous such a step would be to the liberties of the country, and suggested that they had better forget their differences and unite as good Moslems against Alfonso, when they would be invincible. This wise reasoning, says the writer quoted by

[1] Makkari, ii. 277.

Conde, was badly received, and the others declared Ibn Zagut to be a bad Moslem and a confederate of Alfonso, and worthy of death. According to some accounts, Motamid himself was the bearer of the invitation.[1]

Yusuf landed at Algeciras in June 1086 : Radi, Motamid's son, who was in command, gave up that town to him, the fortifications of which he repaired ; he then went to Seville, where he was joined by the Spanish Amirs and their troops, and then moved on to the scene of the great battle. According to Conde, Motamid was placed in command of all the Andalucian forces. (ii. 130.)

Conde's is the only account in which we have found an indication of the site of the battle. The two armies encamped he says, on opposite sides of the " Nahr-Hagir " (? the Guadajra, a tributary of the Guadiana) " in the wood and plains called Zalaca, four leagues from Badajoz." (ii. 134.) [2]

The battle was fought on October 23, 1086, and resulted in an overwhelming defeat for Alfonso. But at one stage the issue seems to have been doubtful, for Conde says that the Amirs of Spain did not behave well, and that Motamid and the Sevillians alone fought bravely ; this Al-Marrakushi confirms, saying that Yusuf was taken by surprise, and that Motamid, who was posted in the rear, " was able that day to render the most signal service that had ever been seen.[3]

After their joint victory, Yusuf and Motamid went together to Seville, where Yusuf remained for a time as the guest of the Abbadite. Makkari, quoting from Al Himyari, says, in reference to this visit—

" Seville, as is well known, is one of the most splendid

---

[1] Conde, ii. 72, 97–8 ; Dozy, *G. der M.*, ii. 354 ; Makkari, ii. 274.
[2] Mr. Seybold, in his pamphlet *Die geographische Lage von Zallaka-Sacralias* (Paris, 1906), places the site on the R. Guerrero, about 15 kilometres north-east of Badajoz.
[3] Conde, ii. 146 ; Marrakushi, 114 ; Dozy, *G. der M.*, ii. 358, 416, where he says that there is no contemporary account of this battle, the earliest known being of the twelfth century.

and magnificent cities in the world. . . . On one side are the palaces of Motamid and his (late) father Motadid, both extremely beautiful in their proportions and most splendid in their decorations. In one of these palaces, which was furnished for the occasion with every requisite article, Yusuf Ibn Tashfin was lodged with his suite, Motamid taking care that they should be provided daily with food, drink, clothes, beds, etc., and appointing persons to see that all the wishes of his royal guest were fully gratified. Such, indeed, was the attention and courtesy which Motamid displayed on this occasion, that Yusuf could not forbear showing his gratitude and thanking him for his hospitality." [1]

Up to this moment Yusuf and Motamid seem to have been on the most friendly terms, and Al-Marrakushi says that Yusuf declared that he and his followers were Motamid's guests, and must not stay in Spain longer than he desired. But a hostile influence was at work in the person of Ibn Somadeh (Motassim) of Almeria, who had for long been excessively jealous of Motamid. The favour with which Yusuf regarded him he owed chiefly to Motamid's recommendation, "but as soon as his influence over Yusuf was assured, he endeavoured to prejudice him against Motamid and to destroy the harmony which existed between them. . . . Motassim began his manœuvres without foreseeing that he himself would fall into the well that he was digging, and would himself be a victim of the sword he had caused to be drawn from the scabbard." [2]

Yusuf was informed that Motamid led a dissipated life, thinking of nothing but amusement; that he obtained large sums unjustly from his subjects in order to spend the money on forbidden pleasure and frivolous pastimes; that instead of giving his attention to good administration and

[1] Makkari, ii. 289.
[2] Marrakushi, 115–7; *Abbadites*, i. 118.

defence of his kingdom, he only thought of gratifying his own desires ; that his friends, allies, and the high functionaries of his Court, instead of imitating his follies, disapproved of his conduct, and were displeased with him ; in short, no stone was left unturned to degrade the King of Seville in the estimation of the stern and ascetic Almoravide, whose own habits were so simple and self-denying. Al Himyari represents Yusuf as volunteering criticisms of Motamid's conduct, couched in these terms, to his own courtiers ; but this assertion is discounted by a passage in the same paragraph, saying, that "several courtiers daily called Yusuf's attention to these things."

On the other hand, Motamid was warned not to trust his guest, who, he was assured, "was filled with the desire to seize this happy and fertile kingdom " ; and he was pressed to secure the person of Yusuf and detain him as a hostage until every African of his army had left Andalucia and returned " to the deserts whence they came." [1]

Small wonder if either or both the men who were thus surrounded by traitors desirous of making bad blood between them, became suspicious and doubtful as to the truth of what was said ; for the intriguers did not stop at giving advice, but repeated what was said to the person calumniated, as though the words had been spoken by the one king of the other. Here is an example of how the mischief-makers went to work.

" One day when Motamid was absorbed in thought, one of his own courtiers remonstrated with a stranger who had been counselling ill-faith, saying—

" ' It is not for princes like Motamid, who is the pattern of every virtue, to commit such a treacherous act as to seize on the person of his guest.'

" ' No matter,' said the man [whose name is not given],

[1] Makkari, ii. 289–91.

it is always lawful to circumvent one who is trying to circumvent you.'

"'It is better to suffer injury in good faith,' said the courtier, 'than to act prudently with injustice.'"

Motamid dismissed the false counsellor after thanking him for his advice and giving him a present. But it appears that Yusuf was informed of what had passed, for when on the morning of the following day Motamid came to him as usual with valuable gifts, Yusuf took leave of him and departed on the same day.[1]

The conduct of the Sunnite and Berber Amirs was consistent throughout. Their one object was to destroy Motamid at any cost. They opposed the summons to Yusuf, hoping no doubt that if Motamid were left without support he would soon fall before Alfonso. Their behaviour at Zalaca may have been due to cowardice, but it is at least as likely, if not more so, that it was a treacherous endeavour to bring about the defeat of Yusuf and Motamid. Having so far failed in their attempts, they now set to work to undermine the good relations which at first existed between Yusuf and Motamid, and in this they were at length successful. Their blindness to the obvious fact that Motamid's fall must necessarily be followed by their own is extraordinary, and as we have seen was a source of some surprise to Al-Marrakushi.

Yusuf returned to Morocco not long after Zalaca,[2] but two years later he was again sent for.

The reason of this second invitation was the great weakness of the Eastern states, where Alfonso's garrison in Aledo was a source of trouble to the whole country side and a standing danger to Almeria, Murcia and Lorca. Murcia

[1] Makkari, ii. 292; cf. *Abbadites*, ii. 252 note.
[2] Some authorities say that he returned at once in consequence of the death of his son, but for our purposes the point is not important. See Codera, *Almoravides*, p. 2.

was under Ibn Rashik, a Mudarite Arab of a family which had been settled in the district for some four hundred and fifty years, who through an intrigue had seized and still held the state. The ruler of Lorca, the district in which Aledo lay, had not long before offered himself as Motamid's vassal, driven thereto by his hope of support against the Christians in Aledo. Almeria was under the Berber Motassim. Motamid himself went to Morocco to explain the situation to Yusuf, who came over in 1088 and met the Andalucian rulers near Aledo. At this meeting Motassim, Motamid's professed friend and secret enemy, appeared in a black burnus like that worn by Yusuf. This change in his usual dress was made a joke of by Motamid, who said that he looked like a crow among doves, for his party in Almeria always wore white. This trifling incident has a bearing on the situation, for the Shiites habitually wore black and the Sunnites white. Thus it is made clear that Motassim and Yusuf belonged to opposite forms of religion, and that Motassim was prepared to forswear the badge of his own sect in order to win the approbation of the Shiite Sultan.[1]

Discord immediately broke out between Motamid and Ibn Rashik. Yusuf, Motamid, and Ibn Zeyr of Granada were all of opinion that the best course for the Moslems to adopt was to attack the Christians on their frontiers, because Aledo was practically impregnable, and to besiege it would merely be a waste of time. Ibn Rashik opposed this idea, and wished that the siege should be proceeded with. The question was debated with a great deal of heat, Ibn Rashik drew his sword on Motamid, who accused him of advocating the prosecution of the siege in order to favour the Christians, and of having come to an understanding with Alfonso,[2] and

---

[1] Dozy, *G. der M.*, ii. 360-3 ; Conde, ii. 157.   Dozy puts the second coming of Yusuf in the year 1090 ; Codera (*Almoravides*, 226-7) dates it 1088, and the third coming in 1090.

[2] Conde, ii. 158-9.   There is presumptive evidence that about

Rashik was arrested and imprisoned. Peace seems to have been patched up between the disputants, and Al-Marrakushi says that thanks to Yusuf's good officers, Ibn Rashik after this agreed to give up Murcia to its rightful rulers, the Beni Tahir, in exchange for a sum of money and a governorship in the territory of Seville.[1]

But in the meantime serious trouble had been produced by the quarrel with Ibn Rashik. On seeing their leader imprisoned, the Murcian chiefs of his party retired from the camp with their troops, and not content with this, they placed themselves on the main road to Aledo and proceeded to stop the passage of provisions to the encampment, robbing the merchants of everything they brought. This caused famine among the besiegers, and when Alfonso heard what was going on he started with a flying column for Aledo, mobilising his allies in every direction for his support.

Conde says that Yusuf did not venture to await Alfonso, on account of the divisions in his camp, and retired towards Lorca, accompanied by or following Motamid and his troops. Al-Marrakushi also says that Yusuf went to Lorca, and although he only mentions his reviewing the troops there, and gives no information as to what had happened at Aledo, his whole account of this period confirms in the main what Conde tells us. Alfonso reached Aledo and released the Christian defenders, but made no attempt to hold the place, which was situated in the heart of the Moslem country.[2]

---

this time some of Motamid's enemies were treating with the Cid, among them one Ibn Labbun, son or brother of an Ibn Labbun whom, according to Conde, Motamid had appointed as Governor of Lorca, and who died in 1087, and was succeeded by Ibn al Yasa. Dozy, *Recherches*, ii. chap. iii.; *Abbadites*, i. 100; Conde, ii. 60, 151; but the history of this period is exceedingly tangled and obscure.

[1] P. 112; cf. Dozy, *G. der M.*, Chron. tables.

[2] Conde, ii. 159-60. Al-Marrakushi relates the incidents of Aledo as if they had occurred on Yusuf's first coming, before the battle of Zalaca: this seems an undoubted mistake, so we have transferred them to the second coming in 1088. Señor Codera says that Yusuf came to

Before continuing the history of the dealings of Yusuf with Motamid, which ended in his exile and imprisonment, we must give some account of an important episode in Motamid's career, about which there is exceedingly little information accessible, but which, if we are right in our conjectures, must have had very considerable influence on his destiny. This is his alliance with Alfonso. The Arabic historians say nothing about it; and the accounts given in the *Crónica general* are wildly confused in their chronology and difficult to reconcile with the events of Motamid's life as told by the Arabic historians. But in the midst of the confusion one or two facts stand out, which have to be taken into account.

In the Chronicle of Alfonso VI., we find the following passages:—

"King Alfonso had a great friendship with King Ibn Abbad of Seville, who had been his father-in-law and was the grandfather of the Infante Don Sancho, and they concerted together to make themselves the lords of all the Moslems of Spain ... who had a mortal hatred against Motamid of Seville, saying that although he was a Moslem in public, in secret he was a Christian and an enemy of Mahomet."[1]

On this follows an account of how Motamid recommended Alfonso to make an alliance with the Almoravides, and a description of their coming. The King of Morocco, we are told, was pleased with Alfonso's friendship, and sent over

---

Spain five times between the years 1086 and 1102 (*Almoravides*, 226), but from his account there is considerable difference of opinion as to what took place on the third coming, some authors saying that on that occasion Yusuf took Granada and Malaga, others that this was on his previous expedition; others again say that the third time he came it was with the determination to make himself master of Spain. We need not stop to discuss the various accounts, our only object in calling attention to them being to put on record the wide divergencies in the versions given by different writers of the same events.

[1] There is evidence that the relations of the Abbadites with the Mozarabs of their own dominions were uniformly friendly.

one of his captains, who rebelled and proclaimed his independence. Whereupon the Spanish Moslems rose, refusing the tribute and vassalage they owed to Alfonso.[1] The King of Seville tried to bring them to their senses, whereon they quarrelled with him and killed him for a secret Christian.[2]

It is impossible to make the Spanish narrative agree with the Arabic accounts, so far as we yet know them, and of course the statement that the Amirs put Motamid to death is quite incorrect. But there is a certain amount of confirmation of the allegation that dealings of some kind took place between Motamid and Alfonso, in an account of "secret treaties" negotiated between them by Ibn Ammar, given by Conde (ii. 62), although his narrative appears to refer to an earlier year. It also supports what is said by other writers about the hostile attitude of the Andalucian Amirs.

The one undeniable and very important fact which we learn from the Chronicle, is that Alfonso married Motamid's daughter Zaida. This is not mentioned by any of the Arabic writers to whom we have access, except for an obscure allusion in Conde,[3] and we must go to the Chronicle for such information as there is.

Sandoval, the writer of the Chronicle of Alfonso VI., discusses the date of the marriage, and is inclined to attribute it to the year 1097, because the Infante Sancho, the child of the marriage, was said to have been eleven years old when he met his death at the battle of Uclés. This we know is wrong, for Motamid was deprived of his kingdom and exiled in 1091. But it is quite impossible, on the data given in the

[1] Makkari says that almost all the Andalucian Amirs, including Motamid himself, paid tribute to Alfonso. (ii. 270; cf. Marrakushi, 113.)
[2] *Crónica general*, xi. 316 ff.
[3] In the passage about the negotiations of Ibn Ammar, referred to above, he says that in his dealings with Alfonso, "sacrificaba Aben Abed á su ambicion pueblos de Muzlimes, y su propria familia," which seems to allude to the marriage and dowry.

Chronicle, to arrive with any certainty at the true date of the marriage. Alfonso was married six times, and the dates have to be deduced from the occasional appearance of the signatures of his wives to various grants and privileges conferred by him. The confusion is increased by the fact that Zaida, on her marriage, was baptised by the name of Isabel, and that another of Alfonso's wives was also called Isabel, whose epitaph says that she died in 1107 and was the daughter of Louis, King of France.[1] An early writer quoted by Mariana cuts the Gordian knot by saying that Zaida was not his wife at all, but only his concubine; but this is disproved, not only by the extreme improbability that Motamid would have allowed his daughter to occupy such a position,[2] and by the dowry he gave with her, but by the epitaph on her tombstone, which distinctly states that she was Alfonso's wife.[3] Unluckily the epitaph does not mention the date of her death. The writer of the Chronicle describes the tomb in the Chapel Royal of San Isidro of Leon, in considerable detail.

The battle of Uclés was fought in 1108, when according to the Chronicle Sancho was "at most" eleven years old. But this Infante's signature is attached to a grant of his father's, made in the year 1103, when, according to the Chronicle he would have been barely six years old.[4]

Alfonso's second wife was Constance of Burgundy, whom he appears to have married in 1077, since her signature as queen is attached to a document dated at the end of that year, and she was alive in April 1087, when her name

[1] *Crónica general*, xi. 314. This makes confusion worse confounded, because Louis VI. did not come to the throne till the year after his alleged daughter's death.

[2] Cf. the Kadi's statement of the Moslem law about free women, p. 115.

[3] H. R. Regina Elisabet uxor Regis Alfonsi; filia Benavet Regis Sibiliæ; quæ prius Zayda fuit vocata. (*Crónica general*, xi. 296; Mariana, Book IX. chap. xx.)

[4] *Crónica general*, xi. 306, 317-8.

appears together with that of her husband in a grant of privileges to the clergy of Astorga. After this the Chronicle makes no further mention of her. Sandoval, who compiled it, says that she died in 1092, but gives no evidence in support; in that year Alfonso married Bertha, said to be of France.[1] Most likely Constance died in 1087, and Alfonso at once married Zaida. If so, her son Sancho would be nineteen or twenty at the battle of Uclés, and fourteen or fifteen when he confirmed his father's grant, which are more probable ages than those given in the Chronicle; while this date agrees with the statement of the Chronicle, that the negotiations for the marriage began "after the conquest of Toledo" (p. 294). The writer would not describe the events of 1097, the date he assigns to the marriage, as "after the conquest of Toledo," which took place in 1085.

The Chronicle tells us, then, that after taking Toledo Alfonso made war on Motamid and raided his lands. But Motamid desired his friendship, "and much more so his daughter," who had formed a romantic attachment for him, based on reports of his renown and his personal attractions. With her father's approval she sent word to Alfonso that she would like to see him, and was quite willing to marry him, he being now a widower, and would give him the towns and castles which belonged to her. A meeting was arranged at Ocaña; on seeing each other they fell in love, and the marriage was arranged. Zaida was baptised, and brought in dowry the towns of Cuenca, Huete, Ocaña, Uclés, Mora, Valera, Consuegra, Alarcos, Caracuel, "and many other places of great importance for the conquests the king proposed making." Most or all of these are in what is now the Province of Cuenca, and in the east of that of Toledo, and would extend and strengthen Alfonso's dominions towards the borders of Aragon and Valencia.[2]

[1] *Crónica general*, 166, 242, 275. [2] *Ibid.*, xi. 294–6.

SPAIN AND THE ALMORAVIDES

Only one child seems to have been born of the marriage, but this was a son, and all Alfonso's other children were daughters. No doubt the desire for an heir to the throne had something to do with his numerous matrimonial ventures.

According to Conde (ii. 62), Motamid made a secret treaty with Alfonso some time before the fall of Toledo, the immediate consequence of which was Alfonso's attack on the territory belonging to that city, "in order to further the plans of Ibn Abbad." Later on, "as Ibn Abbad observed that Alfonso had not only conquered the city of Toledo but . . . was taking towns and fortified places without resistance, he thought it well to put a limit to his conquests, fearing much from his aggrandisement. He wrote to him not to go on to occupy the towns of the kingdom of Toledo, but to be satisfied with that city, and to perform what he had offered when they made their alliance. King Alfonso replied that he was ready to help him in Andalucia with selected troops of cavalry, and to prove that he was mindful of his agreement he sent him five hundred horsemen with whom to invade the land of Granada," and explained that the towns he had occupied were his own and those of his friend and ally the King of Valencia.[1] This incident, as related by Conde, comes immediately before his account (or one of them, rather, for there are two) of the meeting of Walis which resulted in the invitation to Yusuf Ibn Tashfin.

The interest of these statements of Conde's is that they go to confirm the confused references in the Chronicle to an alliance between Alfonso and Motamid, although when this took place is quite uncertain.

It seems not unlikely, however, that it was made after Zalaca. This would agree with the date we have conjecturally assigned to the marriage of the Castilian king with

[1] Conde, ii. 71.

Zaida, and there would be a good reason for it in the fear which the battle must have instilled in both parties. Motamid, who had had forebodings of danger to himself from the intervention of the Africans, may well have had these increased by the immediate result of his appeal for help: Zalaca had crushed Alfonso for the time being, and there was nothing to prevent Yusuf from taking the whole of Moslem Spain if he so desired. And Alfonso on his part was looking round for support of some kind, and, according to the Chronicle, asked help from the Duke of Burgundy and the French Princes, saying that if they did not aid him he would have to come to terms with Yusuf and give him passage through his country to France.[1]

The closer relations between Motamid and Alfonso may no doubt have contributed to widen the breach between Yusuf and the King of Seville, which had been already begun by the machinations of Motassim and other of Motamid's enemies. Yusuf came over for the third time in 1090, and now without waiting for an invitation. He came on his own initiative, "in order to wage war against the infidels." On this occasion, says Makkari, "none of the Andalucian chieftains joined him, although they had been particularly requested to do so, which so incensed Yusuf that he decided to chastise them for their negligence and deprive them of their dominions." He seized Granada, and then returned to Africa, leaving one of his generals, Seyr Ibn Abi Bekr, to continue the war. Seyr presently reported that he was getting no help from the Andalucian kings, and Yusuf instructed him as follows:—

"Order them to accompany thee to the enemy's country (the Christian territory): if they obey, well and good; if

[1] *Crónica general*, xi. 241. The Chronicle adds that forces actually set out from France, and that Yusuf was afraid to wait for them, and left the kingdom.

they refuse, lay siege to their cities, attack them one after the other, and destroy them without mercy. Thou shalt begin with those princes whose dominions border on the enemy's frontier, and shalt not attack Motamid until thou hast reduced the rest of Mohamedan Spain to thy obedience."[1]

No reason is given for Yusuf's change of attitude towards Motamid, with whom two years before he had been on friendly terms; but if he was aware that Motamid had entered into a treaty with Alfonso, that would no doubt be sufficient cause for his resolve to dispossess him. It is however quite possible that Seyr exceeded or anticipated his instructions, for we find the following statement in Al Kortobi, as translated by Gayangos:—

"The Amir (Yusuf) then sent Seyr to Seville with instructions to take the command from the hands of Motamid, and if possible to secure his person; bidding him put to death such as should oppose him, whether citizens or soldiers. Some authors pretend that the Amir issued no such orders, as he had upon a certain occasion solemnly promised Motamid upon his oath never to dispossess him, unless the theologians, the Kadis, the officers of the troops, and the principal citizens should desire him to do so." [2]

There seems no doubt that when Motamid finally became convinced that Yusuf had turned against him and that Seville was to be attacked, he appealed to Alfonso for help, and that Alfonso actually sent troops. But Seyr met and checked the Castilians, and they were unable to advance beyond Almodovar del Rio, near Cordova. Seville was being attacked by land and water, says Al-Marrakushi, the galleys were burnt,[3] and there was no further possibility

[1] Makkari, ii. 294-6.
[2] In Makkari, ii. app. xli.
[3] P. 120. It seems probable that the "galleys" destroyed were a bridge of boats connecting Seville with the suburb of Triana and the Ajarafe on the opposite shore. We have nowhere found any definite

of holding out. Still, "the situation remained doubtful for a few days," until the arrival of Seyr Abi Bekr with reinforcements brought the siege to a close. No doubt the temporary uncertainty was whether Alfonso's forces would be able to relieve the town. Conde speaks of Alfonso's "strange generosity" in coming to Motamid's assistance, but his alliance and family connection with the Abbadite would be quite a sufficient reason for it, not to mention that self-interest would prompt him to take any available means to oppose and check the all-conquering Almoravides.[1]

statement of the existence of such a bridge, but we know from the history of the siege of Seville by Fernando III. that most of the provisions were brought from the other side of the river, and it is most unlikely that this necessary traffic was conducted by ferry boats under rulers so advanced in civilisation as the Abbadites. At least one of the Abbadite palaces was on the right bank of the river, and it is recorded that on one occasion (in the year 1063) when Motadid was staying in this palace, one of his sons rebelled, seized some treasures from his father's palace, "sank the boats used for crossing the river, which were arranged in the river before the palace" (quae ante palatium in flumine dispositæ erant) and made his escape. (*Abbadites*, i. 291-5.) Zuñiga tells us that there used to be a great chain of logs of wood linked with iron rings, extending from the Torre del Oro to a wall on the other side, the foundations of which existed in his day. (i. 22.) This chain of timbers might well have been the remains of Motamid's bridge of boats, and the position agrees with that of the "boats" sunk by the rebel prince, as the Torre del Oro was an outwork of the Alcazar.

[1] Conde, ii. 168; Makkari, ii. 297; Al-Marrakushi, 120.

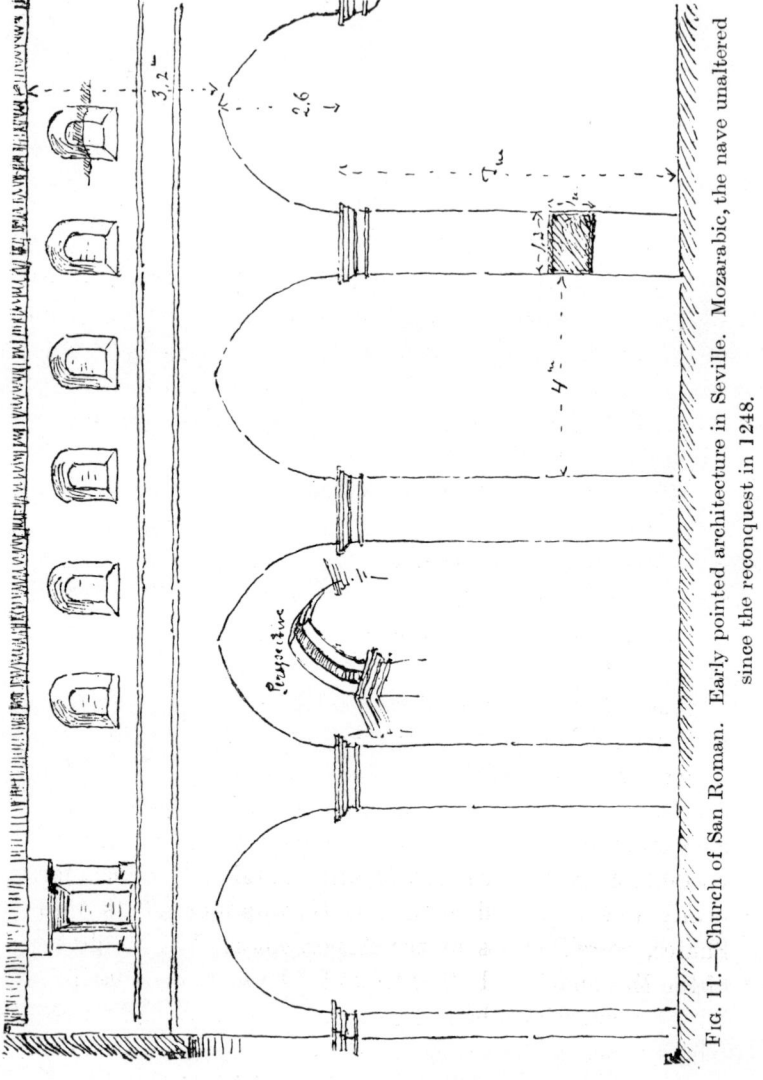

FIG. 11.—Church of San Roman. Early pointed architecture in Seville. Mozarabic, the nave unaltered since the reconquest in 1248.

CHAPTER XVI

THE BENI HUD AND MARDANISH

In 1106, when Yusuf Ibn Tashfin was dying at the age of a hundred years, his last advice to his son was that he should fix his Court at Seville, not Cordova; that he should not disturb the Masmudah and other tribes to the south of Morocco; and that he should conclude peace with the Beni Hud, Sultans of Zaragoza.[1]

Conde gives substantially the same account of Yusuf's dying advice, adding that he told his son not to make war unnecessarily (cf. the Law of Ali, p. 75). He adds that the mother of Ali Ibn Yusuf was a Christian named Comaica, and his secretary Abu Mohammed, one of the sons of Motamid of Seville.[2]

Yusuf Ibn Tashfin is often described as a fanatic whose first thought was the furtherance of his own creed, but his dying commands to his son hardly confirm that view of his character. The choice of Seville as the capital was, we conjecture, due to its value as a sea port far inland, its importance as having been the *de facto* capital of Andalucia for nearly a century, and to the fact that its inhabitants were Shiites, co-religionists of the Almoravides. Yusuf's dread of the Masmudah and other tribes to the south was justified all too soon, when those African Berbers, who really were fanatics compared with the Almoravides, dispossessed them of all their dominions both in Africa and Spain.

[1] Makkari, ii. 302.
[2] Conde, ii. 192–3. Codera says that the mother was a Christian slave. (*Almoravides*, 230.)

As for the Beni Hud, the advice to make peace with them was evidently dictated by Yusuf's knowledge of the power wielded by the only Yemenite dynasty now left in Moslem Spain, who were likely, were they inimical to the Almoravides, to collect under their banner all the mass of the population attached to their race and to the Shiite religion. Although Motamid was dead and gone, his memory remained alive in the minds of his people. And although the Beni Abi Amir, the Beni Al-Amiri, the Beni Tahir, the Beni Al-Aftas, and all the other Yemenite leaders had been defeated and dispossessed, the people were loyal to them, and only needed a leader to rise against the new comers, except where these had taken peaceable possession of the state by alliance with its original masters. Zaragoza was a case in point, and the Beni Hud remained on good terms with the Beni Tashfin down till 1126.

In that year Abdalmalek Ibn Hud was threatened with an attack from the Almoravides, on the ground of his inability to defend his capital, Zaragoza having been taken in 1118 by the Christians from the north, after a protracted siege.[1]

The real reason for the advance of the Almoravides against their old ally seems to have been the fear lest the submission of Ibn Hud to Alfonso I. of Aragon would injure the cause of the Moslems in Spain; for Ali Ibn Yusuf seems to have forgotten his father's warning that no ground of offence should be given to the Beni Hud, whose strength lay in their being on good terms with the Christians. Ibn Hud, after the fall of his capital, had retained the bulk of his dominions by the surrender of several border fortresses by treaty with his conquerers.

When he heard of Ali Ibn Yusuf's plans, he wrote him a

[1] Makkari, ii. 303.

long letter setting forth that Yusuf had made a treaty with his father Al-Mustain, by which the latter was to retain possession of his kingdom, and hinting that his dealings with the Christians had been misrepresented to his over-lord in Morocco.

"God forbid that we should come to the breaking off of our friendship and do ourselves injuries which would rejoice our common enemies; and since until now we have maintained in public and in secret the friendship of our fore-runners, do not give cause, through the evil intentions or the ignorance of counsellors, for this good harmony to be broken. . . . God is the judge and the avenger of those who do ill and of those who produce disagreements and discord between us; I repeat that God is the just judge."

Thereupon Ali changed his mind and ordered his commander not to disturb the dominions of the King of Zaragoza.[1]

Makkari does not mention this episode, but that is not surprising, for his account of the Beni Hud is compressed into the briefest possible space, as indeed is all that portion of his work which deals with the Almoravides. It would seem as though this nation, whether as "barbarous hordes from the African deserts," or as a cultured people more or less of Yemenite descent, and certainly Shiites in religion, had small interest for the seventeenth century historian of the Sunnites of Spain. He certainly was at no pains to elucidate their origin or any details relating to their rise or fall either in Africa or Spain.

It is assumed that the Beni Hud disappeared from history with the death, in 1146, of Ahmed, son of Abdalmalek—he who lost the city of Zaragoza. Three years after his father's death he is said to have ceded all the fortresses he still held on the eastern frontier of Moslem Spain to the Christians, and

---

[1] Conde, ii. 241–3.

Gayangos in his genealogical tables does not continue the dynasty beyond 1146.[1] But this was not their end, for the Beni Hud rose into power again ninety years after, and as late as 1255 we find Mohammed Ibn Mohammed Ibn Hud, King of Murcia, witnessing a grant as a vassal of Alfonso X.[2]

Passing over as foreign to our subject the overthrow of the Almoravides in Africa by the Almohades, and many abortive risings among the lesser chiefs in Moslem Spain, we will take up the story of the Yemenites in 1134, when on the defeat and death of Alfonso I. of Aragon, a Yemenite suddenly sprang into fame, and became before long the ruler of almost all these states in eastern Andalucia which had been included in the federation loyal to Hisham II. and Motamid.

This was Mohammed Ibn Sad Al-Jodhami, better known as Ibn Mardanish.

That he had some Christian blood in him seems certain. The northern Christians called him King Lope or Lobo, and various attempts have been made to prove that he himself was a Christian, though we cannot find anything in his history to explain why a Pope a century after his death should have called him "King Lope of glorious memory."[3] Dozy derives the name Mardanish from Martinez. This Señor Codera says he cannot accept, for reasons connected with Arabic orthography. He agrees with Dozy that the name Mardanish is not Arabic, but proposes Mardonius as its origin in preference to Martinez. He suggests that Mardanish might have been a descendant of the Byzantines of Cartagena, and brings forward in support of this view the fact that his daughters are spoken of as having golden hair and blue eyes.[4] Señor Codera does not give us his authority

---

[1] Conde, ii. 267; Makkari, ii. lxxxvii.
[2] Rodriguez, *Memorias para la Vida de Fernando III.*, p. 397.
[3] Codera, *Almoravides*, 115.   [4] *Ibid.* 113, 310–1.

for these physical attractions in the ladies of the Mardanish family, but we suggest that they might have been inherited equally well from a Gothic ancestry, which would be somewhat less remote than the Byzantine. Be this as it may, Ibn Al-Khattib distinctly states that Mardanish was a Jodhamite, while Makkari himself says that he was of Christian origin.[1] Al-Khattib, himself a Yemenite, would hardly have made a mistake in the genealogy of so renowned a ruler, which Makkari, writing some three centuries later, and unfamiliar with the Yemenite authorities, might very likely have done. We will take it, therefore, that Mardanish, who became king of all the Yemenite states in the east, was a member of the tribe of Jodham, like his neighbour Ibn Hud of Zaragoza. As for his personal connection with the Gothic Christians, that must be left an open question until we get a little more of the information relating to this period which has not yet been given to the world.

Sad,[2] the father of Mardanish, was an officer known for his courage and experience, who had been the principal instrument in the defeat and death of Alfonso I. of Aragon, in 1133. When Alfonso laid siege to Fraga, Sad, who was then its governor, made so stout a resistance that he gained time for Ibn Ghaniyyah, an Almoravide officer, to come to his assistance and engage Alfonso. The son of Sad, whom we know as Ibn Sad Ibn Mardanish, was trained to arms from early youth, and at the age of eighteen was already considered an accomplished captain. He became connected by marriage with the Amir of Murcia, Ibn Iyad, who appointed him Governor of Valencia, and on the death of Ibn Iyad Mardanish succeeded him as Amir or King of Murcia.[3]

[1] Makkari, ii. 314; Al-Khattib in *id.* ii. 519.
[2] This should be written Sa'd, but we have throughout omitted the breathings in the Arabic names.
[3] Al-Khattib in Makkari, ii. 519. According to Makkari, ii. 334, one of the Beni Abi Amir ruled Murcia before Ibn Iyad.

According to Al-Marrakushi, Ibn Iyad deliberately preferred the young officer to his own son when appointing his successor. When he was dying, the officers of his army and the leading men of the country who surrounded him suggested his nominating his son, and he replied—

"He is little fitted for that position, for I have heard it said that he drinks wine and neglects prayer. If you wish it I cannot refuse, but I advise you to take that man." (pointing out Mardanish); "He shows energy and is very rich. It is possible that through him God will extend his favour over the Moslems."

Ibn Sad Mardanish, adds Al-Marrakushi, actually did direct the affairs of his country until his own death in 1172.[1]

Before long Mardanish became over-lord of Jaen, Ubeda, Baeza, Baza, Guadix, and Carmona, all cities which had been struggling to secure autonomy, and all, or almost all, so far as can be discovered, rising under leaders of Yemenite extraction.[2] Before long he was master of the greater part of Eastern Andalucia, and laid siege to Seville and Cordova, both of which he nearly if not quite succeeded in subduing.[3] From the mention of Kings of Baeza, Murcia, etc., in Zuñiga's account of the conquest of Andalucia by Fernando III., we gather that Mardanish did not dispossess the rulers of these different states, but pursued the traditional Yemenite policy of federating them under his own banner, which explains his rapid advance in power and dominion.

One of his wives was the daughter of Ibrahim Ibn

---

[1] Al-Marrakushi, 180–1. This author's history of the period has the charm and the value of being contemporary, and he got the account of Ibn Iyad's appointment of his successor from people who had personally known Ibn Iyad.

[2] In Codera, *Almoravides*, names are mentioned in connection with these risings which suggest a Yemenite or Muwallad origin, although Señor Codera does not appear to appreciate the significance of the fact. Conde's accounts of the same risings confirm Señor Codera's as a rule.

[3] Makkari, ii. 519–20.

THE BENI HUD AND MARDANISH

Mufarraj, known as Ibn Hamushk. He was of Christian origin, and his great-grandfather had joined the Beni Hud of Zaragoza. Having lost an ear in battle, when the Christians met him in the field they derisively named him *Ha Meshak* (the one-eared man). Thus Mufarraj became known as Al-Hamushk in Arabic, because *al mushk*, according to Al-Khattib, means "in the Christian language," a man who has had his ears cut off; and the name was handed down to his posterity.[1]

Ibn Hamushk, during his alliance with his son-in-law Mardanish, took Granada by surprise from the Almohades in 1162, through the collusion of the Christians and Jews within that city. He was secretly admitted by a gate which his partisans opened for him, and held Granada without difficulty until a large reinforcement of Africans arrived from Morocco. Not disconcerted by the appearance of so powerful an army, Ibn Hamushk sallied out of Granada and defeated the Almohades, making great slaughter among them, owing to their becoming entangled among the trenches and canals into which the plain (*vega*) before the city is cut up, so that their flight was arrested. It was some months before the nominal rulers of Andalucia could dislodge this powerful ally of Mardanish. Eventually a large army was sent under the command of one of the Almohade sultan's own sons, and after a hardly contested battle on the *vega* between the hosts of Africans and those of Mardanish and Hamushk, fortune decided in favour of the former, and Mardanish fled to Murcia.

---

[1] Al-Khattib's etymology of "the Christian language" helps to account for many strange perversions of Gothic names.
Señor Codera gives what is no doubt the correct explanation, viz. that what the Spaniards said was *He mochico*, meaning *He aqui el mocho pequeño*. ("Here is the little *mocho*.") *Mocho* meaning whatever lacks its point or end, as a dishorned cow or a pollarded tree. (*Almoravides*, 116.)

Some time after this Mardanish repudiated his wife, and in the end, although not immediately, Ibn Hamushk quarrelled with him, and went over to the Almohades. He served against his son-in-law for a few years, but in 1175 he asked leave to retire to Africa with his family, where he died shortly after.[1]

Conde at this period frequently writes of the forces of Mardanish and the Almoravides as if they formed one party, as indeed towards the time of the Almohade invasion they apparently did. We may instance the taking of Granada by Ibn Hamushk. "The Almoravides took the city of Granada . . . and Mardanish set himself up in the city with the help of his relative Ibn Hamushk, Lord of Segura and Governor of Murcia, united with the Christians."[2] As for Seville, we have not succeeded in obtaining any definite information about Mardanish's reputed conquest of that city, but Al-Marrakushi says that she remained faithful to the Almoravides (p. 181), implying that her sympathies were, as ever, with the Shiite rulers; and Makkari mentions Mardanish having almost succeeded in taking Seville and Cordova by surprise, as well as Granada, which suggests that the Almoravides and Shiite Arabs were making common cause with Mardanish in all three cities. The date of these events is given by Codera and Conde as 1162–3, if, as we assume was the case, they formed part of one campaign.[3]

The following are mentioned by *e.g.* Makkari, Conde, and Codera, as among the most important centres of disaffection to the victorious Almohades in the twelfth century: Valencia, Murcia (Tudmir is no longer spoken of as a separate government, so presumably was now finally included in Murcia), Zaragoza, Almeria, Denia, Granada, Jaen, Baeza,

[1] Codera, *Almoravides*, 138–44, 147–8. Al-Khattib in Makkari, ii. 315–6 and 520–1.
[2] Conde, ii. 346.
[3] *Ibid.* ii. 362–4; Codera, *Almoravides*, 142–4, 316–8.

Baza, Guadix, Mertola, Carmona, the Algarbe, Silves, Niebla, la Rabida, Saltis, and, of course, Seville. The names will be familiar to our readers, for hardly one of them failed to figure in the civil wars either of the ninth or the eleventh century, or both, and always as supporting the Yemenite or Muwallad cause against the Sunnite or Berber party.

Among the Yemenite leaders descendants of the tribes of Jodham and Lakhm predominate. These two tribes, according to the genealogy given by Makkari, originated in two brothers, and although the close relationship was prehistoric, they clung together to the end as they had done in the beginning. Thus, while Motamid, the Lakhmite, was over-lord of the greater part of Moslem Spain, the Jodhamites acknowledged his supremacy. And when Mardanish, the Jodhamite, succeeded in establishing a kingdom in the eastern provinces as powerful as that of Motamid had been in the west, the Lakhmites of Seville and her territory stood by him.

The policy of Mardanish was, broadly speaking, that of all the great Yemenite statesmen before him. He aimed at federation within the Moslem borders and treaties of neutrality or alliance with the Christians from the north. Each successive revolution had made it more clear to the peace-loving Shiites that their trade, commerce, manufactures, and agriculture would be irredeemably destroyed unless some compromise with the Christians could be arrived at. The Almohades were comparatively few as yet, and the fact that they could only reach Spain by sea might render combined resistance on the part of the Andalucians possible. But the Christians had, so to speak, all Europe behind them, and as we know, fighting the Spanish Moslems had come to be considered little less of a holy war than was a crusade in the East, long before Fernando III. took Seville.

So Mardanish made treaties with all the Christians on his frontiers, and even sent presents of Murcian silks, and gold, horses, and camels, to Henry II. of England, from whom he received gifts in return. The Count of Barcelona, the King of Castile, and the Republics of Pisa and Genoa all entered into treaties with him. In 1149 an agreement with the two Republics provided that the Genoese should not interfere with the subjects of Mardanish in Tortosa and Almeria, in return for which Mardanish undertook to pay ten thousand morabitines in two years. The treaties were evidently purely commercial, for Mardanish further " offered to the Genoese living in Valencia and Denia a *fondak* or inn for trade with the prohibition to others to inhabit it." He seems to have desired to inculcate the Moslem virtue of cleanliness, not at that time much in vogue among the Christians, for he also gave the Genoese merchants a bath gratis once a week.[1]

From 1148 Mardanish paid tribute to his over-lords of Castile and Barcelona for his dominions of Murcia and Valencia, until 1168, when the treaty was renewed by Alfonso II. of Aragon, successor to Berenguer Count of Barcelona, for another two years. The tribute was a hundred thousand mitcals of gold, and very good gold, remarks Señor Codera, examples of which may be seen in various numismatic collections. He does not make it clear whether Mardanish paid this sum to each of the Christian kings, or half the amount to both. In 1154 he and Alfonso VIII. of Castile went together to the assistance of Almeria, which was besieged by the Almohades. Alfonso had 12,000 men and Mardanish 6000, but they could not raise the siege.

---

[1] Codera, *Almoravides*, 115, 123. Señor Codera translates *fondak* by *mesón*, an inn. In Belot's dictionary *fondak* is translated " registre des recettes et des dépenses." It may be conjectured that what Mardanish gave the Genoese was not an inn to live in, but something in the nature of a staple or exchange.

THE BENI HUD AND MARDANISH 271

This was their last campaign together, for Alfonso died three years later.[1]

We need not pursue the long record of the battles and the acts of prowess of Mardanish. That he suffered several defeats, and among them some very serious ones, is clear, and indeed it could not have been otherwise, surrounded as he was by enemies. But we so constantly read that this, that, and the other city in his dominions was besieged in vain, that we find it difficult to accept Señor Codera's estimate of his waning power when death cut short his career at the early age of forty-nine, in or about 1172.

Historians differ as to the cause of his death. Some say his spirit was broken by his realisation of the impossibility of holding his own against the Almohades after his father-in-law had allied himself with the enemy; others that Mardanish, like the veriest poltroon, fell ill and died of fear when he heard that a new Almohade Sultan was coming to Spain. Others again say that he was murdered by his mother, because, having severely reprehended her conduct towards her servants, her family, and the great men of the state, she feared his violence and gave him poison.[2] Al-Marrakushi, however, states that he died a natural death, young though he still was. He sustained a severe defeat at Al-Jellab, four miles from Murcia, retired to his capital, and there resisted the siege until death cut short his labours. They kept his death secret until the arrival of his brother, Abul Hejjaj, who hastened from Valencia, which state he was governing in the name of Mardanish.[3] Señor Codera says that Abul Hejjaj had rebelled against his brother and made himself master of Valencia, but Al-Marrakushi's statement contradicts this. Meanwhile the siege of Murcia must have

---

[1] Codera, *Almoravides*, 120–2, 136–7.
[2] Makkari, ii. 318; Codera, *Almoravides*, 151–2.
[3] Al-Marrakushi, 215–6.

been raised, for Abul Hejjaj seems to have had no difficulty in gaining access to his family within the city.

Murcia, Valencia, and Almeria were loyal to Mardanish throughout, and his rule extended as far north as Tortosa, Lerida, and Fraga, all powerful cities of great importance as border outposts of Moslem Spain. In the west he was over-lord of many of the cities in what was once the dominion of Prince Artebas, his frontier at one time extending to, if it did not include, Cordova and Seville. As for the southwest, the Algarbe, Niebla, and all the lesser states and cities populated by Yemenites and descendants of the Muwallads, they had little chance of seriously supporting his claims, for Seville was the centre of the Almohade Government during most of the time that Andalucia was under their dominion; but the fragmentary mention of efforts at rebellion in that part of the country shows that *force majeure* and not their own wishes kept them from joining the banner of Mardanish.

Many references are made to his alliances with the Christians. The King of Castile came to his assistance at the siege of Almeria, and the " Lord of Barcelona " sent him help in 1151. At his last fight with the Almohades, at Al-Jellab, the Christians formed the bulk of his army.[1]

Al-Kortobi [2] says that the last of the Beni Hud, for hatred of the Almohades, accepted terms from Alfonso VIII. of Castile, which included the exchange of the fortress of Roda or Rotalyehud in Aragon and all the cities on the frontier held by the Beni Hud, for "more extensive and better dominions in Castile," Alfonso's object in the barter being to have the frontier towns under his own control. This tallies with the author of the *Kartas,* who according to Señor Codera [3] says that in the year 1149 the Christians possessed themselves of . . . Almeria, Tortosa, Lerida,

---

[1] Makkari, ii. 313; Marrakushi, 215.
[2] In Makkari, ii., app. xlvi.   [3] *Almoravides*, 126 note.

THE BENI HUD AND MARDANISH

Fraga, Santarem, and Santa Maria (presumably Santa Maria de Razin, or Albarracin). It also agrees with Conde's statement that the last of the Beni Hud allied himself with Alfonso and ceded to him all his fortresses on the eastern frontier of Moslem Spain.

But these statements do not explain how Mardanish came to be ruling most if not all of these same cities during his reign, with the consent of, or as representative of the Christians to whom the Beni Hud had ceded them. As for Almeria, if it was taken by the Almohades at all, it must have been retaken by Mardanish very soon after, for his cousin, Mohammed Ibn Sad, was governing it in his name in 1168.[1] Señor Codera quotes evidence suggesting that Valencia also was under his rule in 1169. And Ibn Khaldun says that Abul Hejjaj Yusuf Ibn Sad besieged Valencia, and on taking the city, put the name of the Abbaside Khalif in the Khotba. This, however, was nothing new, for Mardanish appears to have made a practice of attributing the supreme power to the Abbasides on his coinage.[2]

Makkari's account of the vicissitudes of Valencia during the reign of Mardanish does not altogether bear out Señor Codera's, but he says that Abul Hejjaj Ibn Sad Mardanish governed the city of Valencia until, after his brother's death, he allied himself with the Almohades.[3]

All historians agree that the sons of Mardanish came to terms with the Almohades as their allies or over-lords in or about 1172, but they differ as to the manner of this submission. We will adopt Al-Marrakushi's version, as being contemporary.

When Mardanish was dying he said, among other things,

---

[1] Codera, *Almoravides*, 129. We accept Señor Codera's facts, confirmed by Makkari, but note that Mardanish himself was called Mohammed Ibn Sad Mardanish.
[2] *Ibid.*, 128, 130, 395.
[3] ii. 334.

to his children, whose names Al-Marrakushi gives, "As I think you may not be able to hold your own against the newcomers," (for he saw that the Almohades were rapidly extending their conquests and were supported by numerous adherents), "I advise you to recognise their authority of your own will, so that you may enjoy some influence with them; do not wait to suffer the same fate as others before you, for you are not unaware how they have treated countries conquered by force." And, says Al-Marrakushi, they followed the counsels of their father.[1]

This story seems to us very plausible, for, no matter how greatly their power was then increasing, the Almohades previous to the death of Mardanish had certainly been unable to deprive him of his kingdom. But his children must still have been quite young, and he may well have feared that they would not have strength to maintain the struggle.

Conde's account supports that of Al-Marrakushi, and adds confirmation to it.

He says that after the death of Mardanish "Lord of Eastern Spain, of Valencia, and of Murcia, and of many other cities, his sons took refuge with King Yusuf Abu Yakub of Africa, and handed all their dominions to him, fearing that they could not retain them, because on the one side the Christians made savage war on them,[2] and the African Almohades troubled them on the other. . . . And fortune gave him (Yusuf Abu Yakub) gratuitously that which he had not hoped to obtain by force; he gave the Beni Sad new titles and estates, and married a sister of those princes." A couple of pages later Conde adds another paragraph, from another writer, as follows:—

"In 570 (1174–5), being desirous of assuring the

---

[1] P. 216.
[2] This we have seen was not the case, since Mardanish was allied both with Castile and Aragon, but of course the dying father had no guarantee that the treaties would be renewed in favour of his children.

THE BENI HUD AND MARDANISH

peace and tranquillity of the Moslems of Spain, the Amir Yusuf Abu Yakub married the beautiful daughter of Ibn Sad Mardanish, sister of the lord of Denia and Jativa and of a great part of eastern Spain; and to receive her and do her honour he ordered a magnificent *miherghana* (*sic.*, ? a dower house) to be built, of which no tongue can describe the beauty and grandeur." [1]

Thus after they had, according to another authority, " handed all their dominions " to Yusuf, the brother of the bride was still " the lord of Denia and Jativa and a great part of eastern Spain." It is here made clear that the Beni Mardanish were not deprived of their dominions at all, but merely gave their allegiance to their brother-in-law, on their own terms, in accordance with the advice of their father.

The fact of the marriage, stated by Conde, is confirmed by others writers. Al-Marrakushi mentions two daughters, one of whom married Yusuf, and the other his successor Yakub.[2] Señor Codera tells us that Yusuf gave the government of Valencia to the bride's uncle Yusuf, " who had governed it a good many years before in the name of his brother King Lobo." [3]

In 1224 we again find a member of the Mardanish family holding Valencia against the Almohades, until the city capitulated to the Christians in 1238. As the name of Mardanish is not met with after that, we may suppose that it really was an unconditional surrender, otherwise we should have expected to find this Mardanish among the vassals of San Fernando, like his neighbour Ibn Hud.

The second of the eight sons of Mardanish became admiral of the Almohade fleet, and commanded an expedition against Lisbon in 1179.[4]

[1] Conde, ii. 380–2. The building is part of the Seville Alcazar.
[2] P. 216.   [3] *Almoravides*, 153.
[4] Makkari, ii. 334–5; Ibn Khaldun, in *id.* app. lxxvi.–viii.; Codera, *Almoravides*, 153.

Much though the information here set forth leaves to be desired as a coherent narrative, we think it proves that the Yemenites and Gothic Christians of Moslem Spain were playing as important a part in the twelfth century as in any of the preceding ones, being in fact, the one party in Andalucia with strength and statesmanship enough to realise that alliance with the Christians was the only safeguard against extermination at their hands. Had Mardanish lived longer, not Granada alone, but all the eastern provinces, if not the south and south-west also, might have existed another 250 years; for his policy was precisely that which enabled Al-Ahmar the Nasrite to carve out for himself a dominion solid enough to stand alone until 1492.

Little has been published relating to the fortunes of the Yemenites in the last quarter of the twelfth century. It is clear, however, that they did not voluntarily support the campaigns of the Almohades in any direction. Among the names mentioned by Conde in connection with the battle of Alarcos in 1195, at which Alfonso IX. of Castile was so signally defeated, there is not one which indicates a Yemenite ancestry.[1] And on the other hand he attributes the terrible rout of the Africans at Las Navas to the defection of the Andalucians, who must now have consisted almost entirely of Shiites, for the Mudarite Arabs, never very numerous, seem to have disappeared from Spain, and the Almoravides who had not fled to their own country had become amalgamated with the Yemenites of the peninsula.

The excuse for their desertion in the thick of the battle was the barbarous treatment meted out to one of their friends, Abul Hejjaj Ibn Kadis, who after gallantly defending the fortress of Calatrava on behalf of his masters, the Almohades, was forced to capitulate. He had sent many appeals

[1] ii. 401.

THE BENI HUD AND MARDANISH

for reinforcements to the "Amir Almumenin" (Abu Abdullah), but owing to an intrigue on the part of that king's Wizir, the letters had not reached their destination. When the defeated Abul Hejjaj arrived at the Almohade camp with his father-in-law, the two officers were arrested, and after brutal treatment in their confinement, were taken out and speared without being permitted to speak in their own defence, the accusation being that of treachery in the surrender of Calatrava.

The result was that the Andalucians openly protested, and after further strangely undiplomatic conduct on the part of the Wizir, who seemed actually desirous of provoking mutiny, the Andalucian commanders and their picked troops turned their horses and galloped off the field in the thick of the ensuing battle with the Christians.[1]

This Abu Abdullah seems to have been born under an evil star, for, regardless of the plain warning thus offered that the country was ripe for revolt, he proceeded to infuriate the Spanish Moslems still more against him.

"The conquered Prince An-Nasir, filled with anger, attributed that misfortune, not to the skill and strength of the Christians, but to the default of the Andalucian commanders; and when he reached Seville, he took cruel vengeance upon them, beheading some of the most important and depriving others of their government and offices. By that unjust satisfaction he left the nobility of Andalucia very much offended, and naturally desirous of revenge. Thus when occasion arose, these numerous honourable people were very ready to show the effects of their just indignation."[2]

Al-Marrakushi attributes this defeat at Las Navas to

[1] Conde, ii. 420; cf. Al-Marrakushi, 279; and Makkari, ii. app. lxviii.
[2] Conde, iii. 1.

the defection, not of the Andalucian commanders, but of the Almohade troops themselves. He says that since the time of Abu Yusuf Yakub they had drawn their pay regularly every four months, while under his successor it was often in arrears, and especially so in the course of this expedition, and as they held the Wizirs responsible they marched against their will.

"I have heard it said by many of them," he adds, "that they did not draw their swords nor strike with their lances, nor do any other hostile act whatever, and for that reason they fled at the first charge of the Franks."

He corroborates Conde's statement as to the Amir returning to Seville after the battle and remaining there for some little time, although he does not mention the execution of the nobles.[1]

Thus we find that the Almohade troops were as disaffected as the Andalucian, although for another reason. Concerning these Almohade troops Al-Marrakushi gives some information which is important as bearing on the prolonged resistance made later to San Fernando in and around Seville, when the power of the Almohades had been broken everywhere else. Particulars will be found in the next chapter.

The Almohade population in Spain seems to have consisted solely of the troops which garrisoned different cities, who throughout their occupation of the country were regarded as enemies by the mass of the people. Their religion alone would have been sufficient to cause this hostile attitude towards them, for although they had a special "reform" or schism of their own, it was on Sunnite lines, and wherever they took command the name of the Abbaside Khalif was at once banished from the Khotba.[2]

When the soldiery played their rulers false, therefore,

---

[1] Al-Marrakushi, 280.
[2] *Encyc. of Islam*, art. "Abd Al Mumin," p. 51.

THE BENI HUD AND MARDANISH 279

the end soon came within sight; and a Yemenite was not wanting to avail himself of the opportunity thus offered for revolt against the savage and tyrannical Africans.

Although the Beni Hud had become vassals of the Christians in 1145-6, and their dominions had been apparently administered by Mardanish after that, the dynasty was by no means extinct, and as the result of the battle of Las Navas " a noble knight descended from the Kings of Zaragoza, seeing the opportunity that offered itself of avenging himself upon the Almohades and recovering the ancient rights of his family, with his eloquence and generosity and through the industry of his followers, gathered together a large number of valiant gentlemen who declared themselves for him and offered to die in his service." [1]

Makkari confirms Conde's story, adding a long and tedious account of how Ibn Hud's rising was brought about by the prophecies of an astrologer, which we need not pause to discuss. The important part of Makkari's narrative is the list of cities he gives as immediately sending in their adherence to the Jodhamite leader. These were—our readers will know what is coming—Murcia, Denia, Jativa, Granada, Malaga, and Almeria, followed not long after by Cordova, Jaen, and others, the names of which Makkari omits.[2]

Then comes a passage of great interest, as showing how the Andalucians rebelled against the form of religion imposed upon the country by the Almohades.

" Seeing himself sole master of Andalus, Ibn Hud hesitated not to assume the title of Amir al-Moslemin (Commander of the Moslems) and to despatch an embassy to Al-Mustanser Al-Abbasi, the reigning Khalif at Bagdad, requesting him to be allowed to hold his dominions from him and to mention his name in the public prayers. Ibn al-Khattib relates that the ambassadors returned to Andalus in 631

[1] Conde, iii. 4.   [2] ii. 327.

(1233–4), bringing a favourable answer from the Khalif, together with a letter granting Ibn Hud the investiture of all the dominions which he then held or might acquire in the future. Ibn Hud was then at Granada, and he ordered that the letters of the Khalif should be read to the people, which was done in the principal mosque of the place. Ibn Hud himself was present at the ceremony and he stood dressed in the sable uniform [of the Abbasides], and holding in his hand a black banner." [1] In this connection it is worth noting that some years before Ibn Hud had thought it necessary to "purify" the Almohade mosques, and had dyed the arms and banners black.[2]

The Abbasides had no political influence in Spain at this period, and could give Ibn Hud no material aid whatever. It is clear, therefore, that this proclamation of the Shiite Khalif as his over-lord was a purely religious act, intended as a public protest against the form of religion which had been forced upon Andalucia at the point of the sword by the Africans, who prayed for their own Mahdi or Imam in the Khotba from end to end of their empire. The restoration of the Abbasides to the place they had held for generations in public prayer wherever the Yemenites held sway was like a clarion call to the scattered forces of the Shiite persuasion in Spain, and probably was what caused the immediate success of Ibn Hud in his assumption of the sovereignty over the Yemenite states above-mentioned.

For a while it seemed as though he might create a strong Yemenite monarchy, and if he had been more of a statesman and less of a fighter, possibly he might have united those of his own religion under his banner. But he was a warrior pure and simple, not a statesman like Mardanish and Motamid, who came nearer to success under far more discouraging conditions. The Almohade power was broken

[1] Makkari, ii. 327–8.   [2] *Primera Crónica*, p. 721.

by the defeat at Las Navas, and had ceased to be acknowledged save in isolated cities where Almohade princes or governors held their own by force against the will of the inhabitants. And the Christian King Fernando of Castile would have been ready enough to enter into an alliance with the Yemenite with a view to driving the Moors out of the country, as he afterwards did with Al-Ahmar of Granada. Even in Seville, the capital of the Almohades, they were so hated that the people rose independently and invited one of the Beni Hud to assume the government.[1]

Everything was in his favour, but he failed to rise to the situation, and in 1237 he was assassinated by one of his own captains, while his son was reduced to accepting the overlordship of Al-Ahmar of Granada. Other members of the family tried for a time to support themselves in Murcia and Almeria, but in 1242-3 they submitted to Fernando of Castile; Alfonso, his son, " visited the land as his own without offending the inhabitants, and the day of his entry into Murcia was a day of great rejoicing. And with this good treatment he pacified and subjugated many other places which at first had not wished to make their submission." [2]

[1] Conde, iii. 9 ; Makkari, ii., app. lxxix., and p. 530 note 26.
[2] Makkari, ii. 337-8 and 530; Conde, iii. 24-5.

CHAPTER XVII

SAN FERNANDO AND AL-AHMAR

VARIOUS accounts are given in the guide-books of the rise and origin of the Nasrite dynasty of Granada, and of the relations of Al-Ahmar, the founder of the family, with San Fernando of Castile. But it is, we believe, not mentioned by the writers upon whom tourists depend for historical information touching the Alhambra, that Al-Ahmar was not a "Moor" but a Yemenite Arab who claimed descent from the tribes of Khazrej and Ansar.[1]

In 1232, when Moslem Spain was in bad case, distracted between the attacks of the Christians and her own struggles against the hated Almohades, there arose upon her darkened horizon like a new star, this man who was destined to found a kingdom which should endure for two hundred and fifty years after all the rest of Andalucia had come under Christian domination—Mohammed Ibn Nasr Al-Ansari, usually known at Al-Ahmar.

Desiring to perform some signal service on behalf of his uncle Yahya, who had brought him up to be an ornament to the profession of arms, in the year mentioned he attacked the city of Jaen and took it. His uncle, who was present at the siege, was seriously wounded and soon afterwards died of his injuries, but not before he had bequeathed to his nephew all his estates and pretensions. Al-Ahmar concealed his uncle's death from his partisans until he had secured in the old man's name the cities of Guadix and Baza, and then,

[1] Makkari, ii. 341.

finding himself acceptable to their inhabitants, he announced that Yahya was no more, and was thereupon proclaimed King of Arjona, Jaen, Guadix, and Baza, and, according to Makkari, of Jerez also.[1]

Al-Khattib says that Al-Ahmar was born in 1195 at Arjona, in the province of Cordova, where he inherited extensive estates which he cultivated himself, after the custom of the Yemenites. He was a valiant and skilled commander, and distinguished among the Andalucian youth of his station for his courage and *gentilesse*. It is curious how often this latter quality is mentioned in connection with Yemenite celebrities.

He assumed the royal title at Arjona soon after he took possession of Jaen, but historians are at variance as to the cause that impelled him to do this, some saying that it was in consequence of some injustice done him by the governor of the district that he revolted against that authority. After securing the allegiance of the people of Jaen Al-Ahmar took Granada. Then he entered Seville, and remained there for nearly a month. From the confused statements made by different writers, it seems probable that the *plebs* of Seville invited him to come to their aid in an endeavour to throw off the yoke of the Almohades. The relations of Al-Ahmar and Ibn Hud, who was master of a great part of Andalucia when the Nasrite first came to the fore, are not at all easy to disentangle, nor does it appear why they, being both Yemenites, should have been always at enmity. It is asserted that both Cordova and Seville, after acknowledging Al-Ahmar's supremacy, returned to their allegiance to Ibn Hud. Al-Khattib says that Seville and Cordova were taken by Al-Ahmar in 1231-2, and that five years later Ibn

[1] This we take to be an error of Makkari's, for at that time Jerez was occupied by the Almohade *jond*, or militia, strong fighting men, and hostile to the Shiites of Andalucia. (See Conde, iii. 11–2; Makkari, ii. 339-40.)

Hud was again defeated with great loss by Al-Ahmar in the district of Elvira near Granada; and this brings us somewhere near the submission of Ibn Hud to Prince Alfonso of Castile, afterwards Alfonso X.[1] Ibn Khaldun says that Al-Ahmar caused himself to be proclaimed Sultan of Andalucia in 1231, Jaen and Jerez (?) submitting to him in the following year. Al-Khattib, however, distinctly states that it was not until 1238 that he was proclaimed at Granada, which city he entered as king in May of that year.

"Ibn-al-Ahmar arrived at Granada in the evening," says this writer, "and encamped outside the walls. The ensuing morning, at dawn of day, he entered the city, and rode to the castle towards sunset. Abu Mohammed Al-Basti (from Baza) who saw Al-Ahmar ride through the city, says he was dressed in a striped tunic of the stuff called *milaf*,[2] the sleeves of which were open at the sides. Just as he arrived at the gate of the *kassabah* the voice of the muezzin was heard in the distance, calling the people to the prayer of the setting sun, upon which, without going any further, Al-Ahmar went into the *mihrab* of the mosque and recited the first chapter of the Koran, and then went into the castle of Badis, preceded by men bearing wax tapers."[3]

Al-Ahmar sent in his allegiance to the Abbaside Khalif as Ibn Hud had done on the day when he in his turn was proclaimed Sultan of Andalucia at Granada. "At the beginning of his reign Al-Ahmar caused Al-Mustanser Al-Abbasi of Bagdad to be proclaimed in his dominions."[4]

---

[1] Makkari, ii. 341–3, and app. lxxix.
[2] The word translated "tunic" is "shayah" the Spanish *saya*, a skirt. The translation of *milaf* is not given by Gayangos; Dozy gives *milhaf* and *milhaffah*, which he says meant in Spain a woman's veil and sometimes a horse-cloth; and *milaffah*, part of a woman's head-dress. (*Dict. des Vêtements*, 401–3.)
[3] Al-Khattib in Makkari, ii. 344. Badis was one of the Berber Amirs of Granada, which he ruled from 1038 to 1073.
[4] Al-Khattib in Makkari, ii. 532.

SAN FERNANDO AND AL-AHMAR

Once firmly seated on the throne of Granada, Al-Ahmar set to work to strengthen his frontiers and repair the walls of his fortresses. In Granada he erected beautiful buildings, including hospitals for the sick, asylums for old men and for pilgrims, colleges, schools, bake-houses, baths, butchers' shops, and excellent granaries for the storage of provisions.

These works compelled him to impose various temporary taxes over and above those common to Islam, but when the people saw the frugality with which his own establishment was conducted, and that he employed all the money collected from them for the common weal, they made no objection to paying these new duties.

He built fine public fountains, supplied by the mountain streams which flow past the city, and he largely developed the existing irrigation channels in the Vega. He also took care that all the necessaries of life should be abundant and cheap. It was hardly surprising, therefore, that it became necessary to augment taxation.

His own life was that of a model ruler. He constantly attended the Council meetings of his Sheikhs and Kadis, gave audience to rich and poor two days in the week, visited schools, colleges, and hospitals, personally informing himself of the services provided by the doctors, and enquiring of the patients themselves how they were attended to. In the management of his private house he was no less admirable. He had but few women in his harem and visited them seldom, although always careful that they were well waited upon. They were daughters of the principal lords of the state, and he treated them with much affection and kept them contented and friendly with each other, using all his tact and good temper to attain that end.

He also cultivated the friendship of the Amirs of Africa, and sent envoys to the King of Tunis, Ibn Hafss, and to a Christian whose name is given by Conde as "Yugomarsan"

(? Hugo of Lusignan, Count of La Marche) as well as to the Beni Merin, who were at war with the Almohades.[1]

We now come to what is, to our mind, one of the most interesting and instructive passages in the whole history of Spain, namely the relations between the wise and beloved Yemenite King of Granada, and Fernando III. of Castile, known to posterity by the name bestowed on him out of the love of his people, which is " San Fernando."

Setting aside all the exaggerated praise lavished upon this monarch by priestly chroniclers, and discounting to the utmost the florid periods of ecclesiastical historians, there yet remains no room for doubt that Fernando III. of Castile was one of those truly saintly souls who appear on earth at long intervals and leave the world better than they found it.

He was not canonised by the Church until four hundred years after his death, but already on the first anniversary of his funeral, his subjects, Christian and Moslem alike, had given him the name by which he is called in Spain to this day, and had begun to worship at the shrine of their " Sainted King " (*Rey Santo*).

Al-Ahmar's submission to him is generally represented by popular writers as a proof of the decline in " Moorish " power, but in this, as in every other stage of Yemenite history, there is another side to the story. The Sunnite writers naturally condemned an alliance with a Christian and said as little as possible about it. Indeed Makkari dismisses the whole rise of the Nasrite dynasty in a couple of pages or so, grouping the King of Granada with the various unsuccessful rebels against the Almohade dominion, as if

---

[1] This description of Al-Ahmar's rule is abbreviated from Conde, iii. 26–7. Cf. Makkari ii. 340, and Gayangos, *ib.* 532. The improbable statement of Ibn Khaldun that Al-Ahmar ordered the name of Ibn Hafss, Sultan of Eastern Africa, to be mentioned in the public prayers, as well as that of the Abbaside Khalif, may have been suggested by some incorrect account of the embassy here recorded.

he had been of no more account than they. And the early Christian chroniclers made as little as possible of the alliance, which they thought derogatory to the Christian monarch. Happily the standard authority on the history of Seville, Ortiz de Zuñiga, in his account of the political conditions of Andalucia during the reign of San Fernando, and Conde in his volume on the Kings of Granada, confirm each other in ascribing a greater importance to the friendship of Al-Ahmar and Fernando than writers outside of Spain have done. Thus between the two we are able to extract a fairly convincing narrative of the policy pursued by the Christian and the Yemenite in their joint endeavours to procure peace and prosperity for their respective dominions.

As we have shown, Al-Ahmar thought more of increasing the material prosperity of his people by good government at home than by attempting to enlarge his borders by force, thus maintaining the traditional principles of his race. He was far-sighted enough to realise that resistance to the whole might of Christian Spain could have but one conclusion, and he seems to have avoided coming into conflict with Fernando as long as he possibly could. Nevertheless the two rulers were not so unequally matched as appears at first sight. True, the Castilians were steadily increasing their dominions by the conquest of fresh territories, but it was practically impossible for a king continually on the march to effect more than a military occupation of the cities which fell to his arms. He could not colonise the conquered states with Christians, for Castile had never had any population to spare, and the lamentations of contemporary chroniclers over the deserted towns and abandoned villages of Andalucia in the thirteenth and fourteenth centuries show clearly enough that if the Moslems were evicted there was no one to replace them. San Fernando, who combined the qualities of a statesman and a mystic, fully appreciated this, and partly because he saw it was the wisest course, partly because his innate gentleness forbade him ever to commit acts of unnecessary cruelty, he was always ready to treat with the enemy on terms of surrender followed by alliance in preference to taking possession of Moslem states or cities by main force.

It has been said that his son Alfonso X., "had a noble ambition to call kings his vassals," and certain it is that several Moslem Amirs swore allegiance to him. But what is not generally realised is that this had been his father's policy before him, steadily pursued at a time when the way was far less open than after the fall of Seville, which deprived the militant Moors of their last great stronghold. It was easy for Alfonso, who inherited the vast dominion won by San Fernando, to make his own terms with such Moslem princelings as remained, but it was another matter for his predecessor.

In 1216, when Fernando came to the throne at the age of eighteen, Castile and Leon were divided and constantly at war, the friendship of the King of Aragon was not to be depended on, and practically the whole of Andalucia was under the rule, more or less acknowledged, of Ibn Hud, who had severely shaken the nominal dominion still claimed by the Almohades, and was ready at any moment to unite with Aragon against Castile or Leon or both. When Fernando died in 1252, thirty-six years later, Castile and Leon were united, never again to be separated; the daughter of the King of Aragon was the wife of the heir to Fernando's throne, and all Andalucia, except the kingdom of Granada and a few scattered cities held by Almohade commanders, had come under his over-lordship. The Amirs of Baeza and eastern Andalucia retained their states as vassals of the King of Castile, and Al-Ahmar of Granada was not only his vassal but his loyal ally and intimate friend.

SAN FERNANDO AND AL-AHMAR

In 1243 the continual advance of the King of Castile became a source of great anxiety to Al-Ahmar, although down to that date he had suffered no serious reverses at Fernando's hands. Even then he seems to have had no desire to resist encroachments by force, but in that year he strengthened the garrisons of all his frontier fortresses, and provisioned them with extra care, foreseeing that a trial of strength was at hand.

Jaen was included in these preparations, and one day a convoy of 1,500 transport animals left Granada for that city, laden with arms and food, and escorted by 500 horse. The Christians having been informed of the convoy, laid wait for it with a large body of troops on the road it had to follow. Some of the fighting men discovered the trap laid for them, and having warned their commanders, they effected a successful retreat to the capital. The desirability of this course was for some time debated by members of the expedition, certain adventurous spirits declaring it was their duty to go forward at all costs, and a disgrace not to risk a fight in the service of their king. But Al-Ahmar approved of the prudent counsels which eventually prevailed, although he praised the courage of the young men who had been so eager to fight their way to their destination.

Prudent counsels, however, now no longer availed, for, as Al-Ahmar had feared, the Christians after this disappointment laid siege to Jaen. They found that no easy task lay before them, for the Governor was a good soldier, and the siege promised to be a long one. But meanwhile the Castilian troops, which were very numerous, over-ran the district, destroying farms, vineyards, and olive-groves, robbing cattle-grounds and villages, and killing and taking prisoners men, women, and children. When they occupied the fortress of Alcalá de Ibn Said [1] and burnt and destroyed the

---
[1] Now known as Alcalá la Real.

town of Illora, Al-Ahmar felt the time had come to give them battle, but he went out unwillingly, for his army was chiefly composed of hastily collected volunteers from among the agricultural and manufacturing classes who composed the bulk of the population of the new Yemenite dominion, all unaccustomed to the terrors of war and the use of arms.[1]

A hotly-contested battle took place at Hisn Bollullos, twelve miles from Granada, to which point San Fernando had advanced. But the ill-organised and untrained country people lost courage and turned to fly. This caused confusion and alarm among the few skilled fighters, and before long Al-Ahmar saw that he had no choice but to retire from the field, which he did, losing many men in the retreat.[2]

This misfortune was followed by heavy rains and great storms, and only those who live in Andalucia can appreciate the influence exercised by stormy weather over even the ordinary actions of life in that part of Spain. So many months in every year go by without a drop of rain falling that the great mass of the people are unprovided with clothing fit to resist so much as a shower. In a few hours roads become bogs knee-deep in mud, and dry channels are converted into raging torrents. This is the case in the great flat plain surrounding Seville, and much more so in the mountainous region of Granada. Still fresh in memory of Andalucians is the sudden tempest of October 10, 1906, which flooded the bed of the river Guadalhorce, and within four hours had inundated a large portion of Malaga to a depth of twelve or thirteen feet. We may imagine, therefore, the effect that prolonged bad weather would have on the campaign in the Vega of Granada in 1243, with an army of

---

[1] This statement supports our contention that Al-Ahmar's root-policy was the development of his kingdom by peaceful methods rather than by aggression or resistance to aggression.

[2] Conde, iii. 28-9.

Andalucian agriculturists unused to war, suddenly exposed to the miseries of camp-life in a flooded country.

Nor was it necessary to apply the epithets of weakness and effeminacy to the Moslems, as modern writers so often do, in order to explain the ignominious conclusion of the fighting. The impression that each nation in turn which invaded southern Spain became demoralised through the languorous climate and luxurious life of Andalucia has probably been created by the frequent reference of Moslem and Christian writers to military expeditions being postponed or abandoned in consequence of bad weather. Why should Orientals or North Africans, whose progenitors were bred in climates at least as enervating as that of southern Spain, have suffered a constitutional change in a generation or two because they had crossed the Mediterranean? Northern nations, used to and forearmed against wet, cold, and winds, have no conception what these imply in a semi-tropical country where they are of comparatively rare occurrence. The conditions we observe to-day must have been present to a still greater extent in medieval days; yet apart from indirect suggestions such as the above that the Andalucians were susceptible to bad weather, there seems no particular evidence that they were less virile at one period than another, nor can we discover that the revolutions which on stated occasions transferred the nominal government of the nation from one race to another, were ever the result of the physical decay of the defeated party. In the case of the Granadine army under Al-Ahmar, the reverse must have been the case, since, notwithstanding their retirement in confusion from their first encounter with San Fernando, this Yemenite nation was vigorous enough to maintain itself as a race apart for some ten or twelve generations to come.

The storms which crushed the resistance of the lightly clad army of Granada in 1244 seem to have exercised no ill effect upon the hardy Castilians in their coats of mail. They continued the siege of Jaen with unabated energy, and neither day nor night was there any rest for the garrison of that beleaguered city.

At length Al-Ahmar, distressed beyond measure at the suffering inflicted upon his people, who in the great majority were peaceful farmers and merchants dreading the call to arms, resolved for their sakes to set aside his own pride as soldier and as monarch, and to humble himself before the Christian to plead for those whom he had sworn to protect and defend. We must remember that he, as a Shiite, was bound by his religious principles to show consideration for the women, children, old people, and all non-combatants, who were the worst sufferers from the incursions of the Castilian troops. But on the other hand, he must have had reason to believe that Fernando held the same views as himself on these matters, otherwise he would never have acted as he did. Indeed the historian from whom Conde drew his account of the first interview between the two kings, although he does not say it in so many words, implies that Al-Ahmar had grounds for counting upon a worthy reception from Fernando, whose dealings with the Amirs already subject to him had proved that he was no ungenerous enemy.

"Al-Ahmar, knowing the decision and determination of King Ferdeland," says Conde, "who had sworn not to raise the siege until he held that city in his power, took a strange resolution, and went with great confidence to the camp of the king of the Christians, and threw himself upon his honour and his protection,[1] telling him who he was, and that he put himself into his hands with all that he had, and he kissed his hand in token of obedience."

Fernando proved worthy of the trust thus shown in his honour. "He did not choose that Al-Ahmar should

[1] *Se puso bajo su fé y amparo.*

SAN FERNANDO AND AL-AHMAR

excel him in confidence and generosity, and he embraced him and called him his friend, and would accept nothing that was his, content only to accept him as his vassal, and to be over-lord of all his lands and cities." [1]

It seems strange that this dramatic episode has not attracted the attention of English writers, for one would have expected it to appeal to the popular taste in Spanish history. Probably it has been passed over as unworthy of note because it is Conde who records it, but it is amply corroborated not only by Zuñiga's reference to the incident, as " in which " he says " San Fernando was assisted by heaven," but by various after events in the siege of Seville referred to by the Sevillian and other Christian annalists.

The terms of the treaty thus auspiciously entered upon included the payment of " a certain quantity " of gold *mitcals* every year, and the service of " a certain number " of horsemen, when called upon for any enterprise. Finally it was agreed that Al-Ahmar should attend the Cortes of Fernando when summoned to them. This clause in the treaty was not intended in any way as a derogation of Al-Ahmar's dignity. On the contrary, it was the greatest compliment that could be offered in those days, when the Cortes was composed of great nobles and *Ricos Omes*.[2] Not only that, but the invitation of Fernando to attend the deliberations of the Council showed that he considered the Moslem's views of government valuable to the monarchy, which now contained almost as many Moslem as Christian subjects; for, as we shall see, the King of Castile was well aware that a difficult task lay before him ere he could reduce the rest of Andalucia to his obedience.

---

[1] Conde, iii. 29–30; cf. Zuñiga, i. 139. The *Primera Crónica General* adds that Al-Ahmar was required to pay an annual tribute of 150,000 maravedis. (p. 746.)

[2] These are continually referred to in the Archives of Seville as if the name of *Rico Ome* was equal to a title of nobility.

One of the conditions of the surrender appears to have been that Fernando undertook to restore Jaen to Al-Ahmar when he should ask for it. Fernando mentioned this promise to his son Alfonso on his death-bed, and urged him to keep it.[1]

It is as strange that historians have not realised the importance of this alliance between the two strong men of the time as that romancists have overlooked the picturesqueness of the meeting in the royal camp at Jaen. Possibly documents relating to it lie buried in the archives of that city, but we have so far been unable to find any publication on the subject.

As soon as the alliance was concluded a garrison of Christians was put into Jaen, and the city placed under the government of Fernando's commanders as a guarantee of Al-Ahmar's good faith. The treaty was signed in the camp before Jaen in April 1246, according to Zuñiga,[2] and Al-Ahmar returned to Granada, Fernando treating him up to the moment of his departure with great honour. With him went the Governor of Jaen, to whom, as a reward for his defence of that city, he gave the command of his cavalry.

Soon after the surrender of Jaen Fernando announced his strong desire to proceed immediately towards Seville, but his counsellors were by no means unanimous in supporting the proposal. Some, it is true, were of opinion that the army should invest the stronghold of the Almohades at once, but others were in favour of previously subduing all the surrounding country, and especially the ports in which munitions and provisions were received from Africa for transport to Seville. This party argued that once outside support was cut off, the city would sooner or later be com-

---

[1] Pineda, *Memorial para la canonizacion del Rey Fernando III.*, Seville, 1627, p. 118, quoting a manuscript *de las antigüedades de España*. Señor Ballesteros tells us that he has found independent confirmation of this statement.

[2] i. 1, 138; cf. Conde, iii. 30, and Makkari, ii. 344.

SAN FERNANDO AND AL-AHMAR

pelled to surrender, either without resistance or at worst after a short siege, because the immense number of people within her walls, if the food supply were obstructed, would inevitably bring about the end.[1]

How much wiser were those who recommended the latter course than the knights who merely thought of gratifying the King's personal wishes, was seen when the Christian army found itself compelled to retire before the gallant resistance and desperate sallies of the besieged. But before entering upon the narrative of the investment of Seville, we must retrace our steps for some years, in order to show why a city which had been for so many centuries a stronghold of the Yemenites should have resisted for eighteen months a Christian king supported by one of the race to which so many of its own people belonged.

Valencia, Murcia, Baeza, Baza, Guadix, Jaen, and Granada, among other strong places ruled by men of Yemenite descent, had all submitted to the over-lordship of Fernando III., and still Seville held aloof. True, she had been the capital and court of the Almohades for a good many years, but their power was so shaken here, as everywhere else, in the first quarter of the thirteenth century, that one after another of their representatives had been overthrown and compelled to retire elsewhere. What then enabled her to make so stout a defence when the Castilian army invested her?

The clue to the situation is found in the chance statement made by Al-Marrakushi,[2] that the first Almohade ruler established a militia of horsemen in the environs of Seville.

[1] Zuñiga, i. 4.
[2] Al-Marrakushi was able to detach himself from the party point of view sufficiently to give us an obviously unbiassed picture of the Almohade dynasty under whose ægis he wrote in 1224, notwithstanding that he was (apparently) a Shiite living among Sunnites. His dispassionate comments upon the persons and events of his time are of especial value to students dependent upon translations for their facts.

He says that when Abd Al-Mumin, the Almohade Sultan, first went to Spain, he called upon all the people of the Moghreb to accompany him, and among those who responded were the descendants of Hilal Ibn Amir, who had made themselves masters of the kingdom of the Beni Ziri. These Arabs had been in the habit of paying tribute of half the harvest of wheat, dates, etc., in their dominion, but when Abd Al-Mumin conquered them he enrolled them in his service as a kind of militia (*jond*), giving their chiefs part of the land as his vassals. Many of his *jond* answered the call to invade the peninsula, and when he himself returned to Africa, he left a number of them installed in the neighbourhood of Seville on the Jerez side of that district. They were still there when Al-Marrakushi visited Seville in 1224, and, he says, formed an important group, for they had increased in numbers through births and reinforcements sent over by Abd Al-Mumin's successors, Abu Yakub and Abu Yusuf, so that early in the thirteenth century there were, besides foot soldiers, about 5,000 Arab horsemen in the service of the Almohade governors of Seville, Jerez, and any other fortified place within reach of a flying squadron.[1]

Ibn Khaldun gives us an interesting sidelight on the position of parties in the city at this time.

There were in or about 1233 two influential (Yemenite) citizens of Seville, one named Abu Merwan Al-Baji, who was a descendant of Abul-Walid Al-Baji,[2] and the other Abu Amru Ibn Al-Jadd, a descendant of the celebrated traditionist, Abu Bekr Ibn Al-Jadd. Both these men,

---

[1] Al-Marrakushi, 192–3. Cf. article "Amir," *Dict. Islam*, p. 329. We hope in a subsequent volume to show the curious mark made upon the artistic tradition of Jerez and its district through the influence of these African Arabs upon the Yemenite styles of design.

[2] Of the tribe of Tojib. (Cf. Gayangos in Makkari, i. 508).

SAN FERNANDO AND AL-AHMAR

whose ancestors had enjoyed great favour with the Khalifs, had inherited considerable property and influence. They were held in great estimation and respect by the people of Seville, who never failed to consult them and look up to them in every emergency. Not only the people but the Almohade rulers had shown them deference, for all the princes of the house of Abd Al-Mumin who had held command in Andalucia had appointed them (the ancestors of the Al-Baji and Al-Jadd now in question) to offices of trust, and had given them places on their Council.

After the death of Al-Mustanser the Almohade princes of that sultan's family had thrown the country into confusion, each one appropriating a part of the dominion for himself. Then Ibn Hud and Ibn Mardanish raised the standard of revolt in the eastern provinces (see pp. 275 and 279) while Al-Ahmar rose in the west.

In November, 1228, Ibn Hud, who was everywhere successful against the disunited Almohades, possessed himself of Seville, but three years later the people expelled his brother, whom he had placed there as governor, and overthrew his authority.

Seville and her neighbour, the strongly fortified city of Carmona, then proclaimed as their lord the Yemenite noble, Al-Baji, and he proceeded to form an alliance with his fellow-Yemenite, Al-Ahmar of Granada. Al-Ahmar gave him one of his daughters in marriage, and promised to defend Al-Baji against Ibn Hud provided he would acknowledge himself his vassal, which Al-Baji agreed to do, and Al-Ahmar entered Seville as its over-lord in 1234.[1]

What happened after this in Seville is uncertain, for the accounts given by different writers are so confused and contradictory that it is not possible to obtain anything

[1] Makkari, ii. 340, lxxviii.–lxxix.

coherent from them. *E.g.* Ibn Khaldun goes on to say that Al-Ahmar, apparently without any particular purpose, presently made a sudden and unexpected attack upon Al-Baji, and put him to death outside the walls of Seville. Such a course, if Al-Baji was his own son-in-law,[1] could only have been dictated by some powerful motive, but no motive at all is given beyond a hint at Al-Ahmar's vaulting ambition. According to this story the individual chosen by Al-Ahmar to put Al-Baji out of the world was one Ashkilulah, a Tojibite like Al-Baji's companion in the government of Seville, Al-Jadd, and also a son-in-law of Al-Ahmar's, to judge from the inscription on the tomb of Ashkilulah's son at Granada, which states that his mother was a sister of Al-Ahmar's son. Thus the family as well as the Yemenite connection would have been outraged by the event, if Ibn Khaldun's account were correct.

We feel little doubt that Ibn Khaldun, who lived in the fourteenth century, confused two incidents in this troublous period, and attributed to Al-Ahmar what was really the work either of the Almohades or of Ibn Hud, who seems to have made great efforts to recover Seville.[2]

In spite of all the turmoil of the succeeding years, it appears that Ibn Al-Jadd retained the practical if not the ostensible control in Seville after the death of his colleague, Al-Baji, for in 1238 we find him appointing Muhammed, son of Sid Abu Imran, a youth of the Almohade royal family, as a figure-head in the government, and maintaining this young man on his uneasy throne until 1242. And again in 1245 Al-Jadd appears, this time as the sole master of Seville.

He then made peace and contracted an alliance with San Fernando, according to Ibn Khaldun, and in order to

---

[1] As Ibn Khaldun himself says he was (quoted in Makkari, *loc. cit.*).
[2] Makkari, ii. 340, 532.

conciliate the Christian king, he struck off from the rolls his best Almogavares.[1] Gayangos gives Almogavares (*Al-mughawar*) as " a soldier employed in frontier warfare," and there can be little doubt that these were the *jond* or militia established in the Seville district by Abd Al-Mumin. The Almohades were in no position now to maintain troops exclusively devoted to the care of their ever varying and diminishing frontiers, although the *jond* might have been given the name of Almogavares because they had their headquarters in and near Jerez de la Frontera.[2]

The Almogavares were a strong force still in 1245, when Al-Jadd was proclaimed ruler of Seville. It is difficult to understand his having "struck them off the rolls of his army " if they were men upon whom he could depend, for we cannot imagine that he would willingly have deprived his weak state of any elements of defence. We take it that although themselves of Arab extraction, the African militia were of the opposed religion, and therefore declined to submit to a Yemenite governor. No doubt Al-Jadd had excellent reasons for the course he took, but unfortunately for the peace of Seville, the militia was too strong for him. They revolted against him and put him to death, at the instigation of their captain Sakkaf—the Axataf of the Christian chroniclers—and once more Seville was dragged into war with the Christians. This time the city came under the administration of a council composed of six individuals,

[1] Makkari, ii. app. lxxix.-lxxx.
[2] There are several towns in this district still called de la Frontera (of the border), of which Jerez is the chief. The others are Bejer, Chiclana, Arcos, and Moron. They all appear to have been border towns delimiting the kingdom of Granada in the thirteenth century, with Christian troops garrisoned in them under the terms of Al-Ahmar's alliance with San Fernando. Before the fall of Seville, however, it seems probable that they were held by the Almogavares or Almohade militia, and if this were so, the term " de la Frontera " and " frontier soldiers " as applied to them and their Almohade defenders is accounted for.

chiefly of African origin. The only Arab seems to have been Yahya Ibn Khaldun, grandfather of the historian from whom this account is extracted,[1] another was a representative of the new African dynasty of the Beni Hafss, who had put an end to the Almohade dominion in that continent; and another was the Almohade commander Sakkaf himself. The one party not represented on this curiously mixed council was that of the people of the city, the Yemenites who formed the bulk of the population. But they were helpless, for both their chosen leaders had been put to death, and there seems to have been no one left to replace them.

Although the fact that the historian was closely related to one of the council may seem to give considerable weight to his account of the events of the period, the contradictions and discrepancies with which it abounds are explained when we discover that he was born nearly ninety years after the fall of Seville, and appears never to have visited Spain.

A curious remark of Ibn Khaldun's may or may not be based on fact. We have, so far, found no corroboration of it in Christian writings. He says that San Fernando took offence at the murder of his ally Al-Jadd at the hands of Sakkaf, and made it a pretext for declaring war on the Almohade party, took Carmona and Marchena, and then laid siege to Seville. The people sued for peace, but he "arrogantly refused to grant it," and this was the beginning of the siege which lasted for nearly two years.

We may discover as our knowledge of the period increases that there is a measure of truth in this story. But it is evident that the historian relied solely on oral tradition for this part of his work, for he does not once refer to any

---

[1] Gayangos considers him to have been a descendant of the Beni Khaldun who intrigued against Ibrahim Ibn Hejjaj in order to bring him into discredit with the Sultan Abdullah at the close of the ninth century. (See p. 90; Gayangos in Makkari, i. 311-2.)

earlier authority. Probably he put together the narrative as his grandfather had handed it down to his family. He could not have had it at first hand, for Yahya Ibn Khaldun of Seville would have been at least a hundred when the grandson was born in 1332. Thus many errors in chronology would be likely to creep in, for we all know how difficult it is to repeat the same story twice in precisely the same words; and a very large number of names and dates are recorded in Ibn Khaldun's chapters relating to the fall of Seville.[1]

The same historian says that in 1227 or 1228 Al Bayesi (the Amir of Baeza) and "his ally the King of the Christians," were compelled by the Almohade Governor of Seville to retire from an attack on that city. The Amir of Baeza had sworn allegiance to San Fernando previous to 1227.[2] We also are told that Al-Ahmar entered Seville as its overlord in 1233 or 1234, and that he had under his command a division of Christians.[3] These may have been descended from the Gothic Christians of the territory of Granada, of whom we have already heard, or they may have been troops supplied by San Fernando to help his Yemenite allies in Seville against the Almohade party, supported by the Almogavares, or militia. If, as these fragmentary allusions seem to indicate, San Fernando had held friendly relations with the Yemenite Amirs who were struggling to drive the Almohades out of Andalucia ten or a dozen years before the final siege of Seville, we can understand why Al-Ahmar felt sufficient confidence in the Christian monarch to throw himself on his generosity when the war was carried into his own country.

[1] Practically all the above narrative is taken from the portion of Ibn Khaldun translated in Makkari, ii. app. D, the only comparatively detailed account of the period that we have been able to find.
[2] *Op. cit.* Makkari, ii. lxxiv; Zuñiga, i. 109, 110.
[3] Makkari, ii. 340-1, app. lxxix.

So little has been done yet to disentangle and connect the accounts of the Christian conquest as given by the historians of the opposed races, that Al-Ahmar's alliance with San Fernando has been completely misunderstood. Limited as is our knowledge of the details of events, one thing at least stands clearly forth from the mists of the centuries. The compact between the Yemenite of Granada and the Christian of Castile was based not only upon mutual respect but upon mutual interest, for the Almohades against whom Al-Ahmar bound himself to fight when called upon by San Fernando were the enemies of both.[1]

[1] Mariano Gaspar Ramiro, in his *Murcia musulmana* (Zaragoza, 1905, p. 272), says that when Al-Mamun, the last of the Almohade rulers, left Spain for Morocco in 1228, the Spanish Moslems rose as one man against the Almohades and drove them out, or slew them wherever they could reach them.

CHAPTER XVIII

YEMENITES AND ALMOHADES IN THE TERRITORY OF SEVILLE

In 1245, eight months after the meeting of the two kings at Jaen, San Fernando wrote to Al-Ahmar to tell him he wished to open the campaign against Seville and hoped Al-Ahmar would accompany him in the expedition against "their common enemies."

According to Conde, the King of Granada as well as the five hundred cavalry whom he took in his train were all very willing (*todos dispuestos*) to go, and early in the autumn of 1245 the allies met on the road from Cordova to Alcalá de Guadaira, a great Arabic castle, the ruins of which tower above the river Guadaira, some nine miles from Seville.

This castle was the scene of much fighting in the civil wars of the ninth century. It was called the "key to Seville," and certainly was of great strategical importance in the Middle Ages. One only needs to see the castle to understand why this was so, for it lies high above the Roman road from Cordova to Seville, with a sheer fall of some two hundred feet to the river on two sides, and of the two gates giving on the keep, one is protected by a deep moat, and the other is approached by a narrow path which runs for a quarter of a mile beneath the ramparts, while the gate itself commands a sudden turn and such a steep incline directly before it, that an attack from that side could have been resisted by a couple of men in the doorway of the tower.

It is difficult to imagine any attempt at assault being

made here, for beyond the gate a wall runs almost perpendicularly down to the river, so there would be no possible escape for a defeated enemy. A fellow wall, with an equally sharp descent, protects the approach to the outer keep on the other side of the bend of the river. Between the two lies the Roman mill on the river bank, from which subterranean stairs and passages led to granaries excavated under the inner keep, and gave the defenders control of an unlimited supply of water. To these advantages may be added the enormously strong outer walls, of which many vestiges still exist, and the commanding situation on an eminence whence to the west the plain of Seville is seen with the city in the distance, through the opening in the hills cut by the river, and the roads to the neighbouring towns of Utrera, Osuna, and Carmona are visible for miles to the south and east.

Adequately fortified, it might even now have some strategical value, and in the thirteenth century, if loyally defended, it must have been almost impregnable. According to Ibn Khaldun, Abu Yakub the Almohade had the castle repaired, because it had been in ruins since the civil wars of the ninth century.[1]

The broad road down the pass from the hills and the rich table-land of the Alcores—a corn-district of such productive quality that from Iberian times it has never been manured,—has been used daily for a couple of thousand years or so for the conveyance of bread from Alcalá to Seville. Something in the chemical constituents of the water which bubbles up from subterranean caverns and passages to fill the Roman aqueduct known as the Caños de Carmona gives a specially agreeable flavour to the bread made at Alcalá. These inexhaustible springs serve also for turning the many water-mills which grind the flour to make the

---

[1] In Makkari, ii. app. lx. (We think this is an error.)

bread. So Alcalá lives by her bread as Seville lives upon it; and when the supply to the city was stopped in 1245 it brought the surrender of Seville appreciably nearer.

Notwithstanding the immense importance of Alcalá to the rulers of Seville, and the fact that "thanks to art and nature they could have resisted a long time," its defenders made no serious attempt to hold out against the united army of San Fernando and Al-Ahmar. Conde and Zuñiga agree in this, and Zuñiga seems rather puzzled at their prompt surrender. To us it appears quite natural. The people were Yemenites, and seized the opportunity of overthrowing their Almohade commander or governor in favour of a Christian allied with one of their own race. With little or no fighting, they accepted the advice of Al-Ahmar to submit to San Fernando and obtain all the advantages of vassalage instead of undergoing the miseries of a siege. They at once surrendered to the King of Granada, who gave the castle to Fernando.[1]

San Fernando then divided his army into two detachments, and while he remained in Alcalá, strengthening the fortifications and provisioning the place, he sent one division under the Infante de Molina and the Grand Master of the Order of Santiago to harry the Ajarafe, and the other with the Grand Master of Calatrava and the King of Granada to invest the country round Jerez; both these districts being, it appears, defended by the Almohade militia referred to in the last chapter. Although the cutting off of the bread supplies from Alcalá was a serious loss, Seville was by no means distressed for provisions as long as she had free access to the great plain which extends from San Juan de

---

[1] Los moros de Alcala de Guadera, quando lo sopieron que el rey de Granada yua y, salieron et dieronse a el, et el dio luego el castiello a su sennor el rey don Fernando. *Primera Crónica General*, p. 748; cf. Zuñiga, i. 5, and Rodrigo Caro *Antigüedades de Sevilla*, fo. 151, v.; who repeat this.

Aznalfarache on the Guadalquivir to Niebla, a walled city which was at that time almost as strong as Alcalá itself. All this tract of country was still dominated by the Almohades, with Niebla as a base at one end and Jerez at the other. Except for the bridge of boats at Seville there was (and is) no bridge across the Guadalquivir nearer than Cordova, nor was there any ford below the city. So that the Ajarafe at that time was as safe as if Alcalá had not been taken.

Meanwhile the Almohades were concentrating their forces in Seville. The people of Carmona and Constantina, left under the command of subordinate officers, refused to obey them and compelled their commanders to send messengers to San Fernando, offering themselves as his vassals on condition that he should respect their farms and estates. Al-Ahmar persuaded those of Lora and Guillena to follow suit, but not until after a serious reverse had been inflicted upon the Christians at Cantillana, for which a savage revenge was immediately taken.

Cantillana is a hill town in a commanding position above a Roman weir on the Guadalquivir, ten miles or so above Seville, and at that time was strongly fortified. The river has here cut itself a deep and narrow channel between a high bank of clay on one side and the outcrop of rock on which Cantillana is perched on the other. There is, however, at a short distance below the weir (relics of which can still be seen) a great bend in the river, where in winter the stream overflows and creates acres of marsh, intersected with channels and pits deep enough to drown a horse. Here the Christians got entangled, owing to their ignorance of the district and lack of guides, and the garrison of Cantillana, seeing their distress, came down upon them and handled them severely, for the heavily armoured cavalry were unable to extricate themselves from the bog. The infantry came to the rescue, and the Cantillana people had to retreat to their fortress. Then the Christians, furious at the ridiculous as well as tragic plight into which they had fallen, besieged the town, and taking it by storm they made a terrible slaughter among the unhappy inhabitants.[1]

Al-Ahmar, who doubtless felt that if he had been beforehand with the Christians he could have prevented all this waste of life, was much distressed to learn what had occurred, and at once went to take counsel with Fernando as to avoiding unnecessary bloodshed for the future. The two kings, who were always of one mind when it was a case of the welfare of non-combatants, agreed that the troops should be ordered to try persuasion and use gentle measures in the first place with every city and fortress they came to, and ordered that force should only be employed if the Moslems would not come to terms nor listen to reason. And in no circumstances were old men, women, or children, or any others who submitted unarmed, to be included in violent reprisals. Thereupon Al-Ahmar wrote letters and sent them by his own knights to the different towns in the sphere of action, telling them of the terms proposed, and recommending them to surrender without resistance. By this means much bloodshed was avoided; and once more we see how pacific a people the Yemenites really were, and how ready to choose vassalage in preference to war.

Guillena, which lies on the Huelva river to the southwest of Cantillana, and northward of Seville, was the first to submit to Al-Ahmar's persuasions, and San Fernando in person conducted his troops into this town. Thence he went on to Gerena, another of the numerous towns scattered about the foot of the Sierra de Huelva; where fragments of strong walls still testify to their medieval fortifications. Here the Almohades seem to have been in force, for

[1] Zuñiga, i. 5, 9; Conde, iii. 31-2.

notwithstanding that it was a place of small importance, a vigorous resistance was made, and not until the whole garrison seemed threatened with destruction did they come to terms. Al-Ahmar's good offices were of no avail at Gerena, although they had been so effectual at Guillena, only a league or so away.

It seems to have been considered inadvisable to continue the march in that direction, for San Fernando retraced his steps to Guillena, and here he became very ill and was compelled to remain for a time. He was doubtless already in the grip of the internal disease which a few years later proved fatal to him; and probably the knowledge that his life was unlikely to be much prolonged helped him so heartily to respond to the desires of Al-Ahmar, that the campaign should be conducted mercifully. It was not usual at that time for a Christian conqueror to accept advice from one of the other religion, as the accounts of these events, whether written by Christians or Moslems, show that San Fernando did. Nor does he ever appear to have experienced himself, or to have permitted his counsellors to express, the slightest suspicion of Al-Ahmar's good faith. Theirs was a real friendship based on mutual admiration and respect, and it is clear that Fernando, wise in his generation, appreciated the immense advantage to himself of the Yemenite's influence with those of his own race and religion throughout the whole of the two years in which they fought side by side.

Reading still further between the lines, we discern clearly that Al-Ahmar was never asked to take part in active fighting against places peopled by the pacific portion of the community. We hear of him at Alcalá de Guadaira, at Carmona, at Guillena, and so forth—all of which surrendered peaceably—but he is not mentioned in connection with the siege of Gerena, and he does not seem to have been at Cantillana. He was, however, sent against Jerez, which was garrisoned by his own enemies, and he was also at Alcalá del Rio, whither Sakkaf, the Almohade leader, had come from Seville to take command of the defence, as that riverside town was the gate through which provisions entered from the Sierra for the use of the capital, to which they were thence conveyed by boat.

Sakkaf was inflicting a reverse on the Christians here, without the walls, when the Granadinos opportunely arrived. By a rapid manœuvre Al-Ahmar flung his cavalry between the Almohades and the fortress; and then charged them so determinedly that they turned and fled to Seville. After this Al-Ahmar without difficulty induced the people of the town to put themselves into San Fernando's hands, assuring them that they would be protected and safe-guarded by the Christian king; and thus this fortress also was won to Castile through the intervention of the Yemenite monarch.

While Fernando was at Alcalá del Rio, after the surrender, news reached him that Admiral Ramon Bonifaz had arrived at the mouth of the Guadalquivir with his navy, consisting of thirteen large ships and various smaller vessels, had engaged the enemy there, and now was master of the approach to Seville from the sea. A force of Almohades, sent to the assistance of their own ships, had been overtaken and defeated among the marshes of Lebrija by a party sent out from Alcalá de Guadaira, and San Fernando was so encouraged by the double success that he determined upon investing Seville without further delay.

On August 20, 1247, the Christian army camped outside the city, so near to it that the royal quarters were on what is now known as the Prado de San Sebastian, the scene of the great Seville Fair. The army, says Zuñiga, was exceedingly limited although formidable in training; but the exaggerated confidence of the king, or of his militant counsellors, was the cause of "irreparable ills." It is difficult, he adds, to discover the precise facts, for the historians are silent about them, but it is known that it became necessary before long to beat a retreat from the Prado of San Sebastian to Tablada, the angle formed by the junction of the Guadaira with the Guadalquivir, where at the time of writing a great new canal is being cut to avoid the shallow bend of the river at San Juan de Aznalfarache and permit ocean-going steamers to come up to Seville on one tide.

The navy under Bonifaz had by this time got up the river to San Juan, and was probably stationed near Tablada. The Christians now commanded the road from Seville to Dos Hermanas and Utrera, as well as that from Alcalá de Guadaira and Carmona, and the road into the Sierra to the north as well as the river above Seville right up to Cordova. Thus the city had become entirely dependent for supplies upon the Ajarafe, whence, protected by the militia, they were brought in daily without difficulty across the bridge of boats. The bridge was guarded by the strong castle of Triana, into whose walls the chains holding the boats together were built. True the cultivators and farmers were in the majority opposed to the Almohades, but the latter were in command and the peaceful people dared not refuse their demands.

From Seville right away to Niebla the whole country was, and is, richly cultivated, and Niebla was still in the hands of the Almohades, under one Mohamad, whom we take to have been the Mohammed Ibn Imran set up by Al-Jadd as governor of Seville, and overthrown when Al-Jadd was murdered by Sakkaf.[1] Mohammed, son of Sid Abu Imran, is not mentioned as having been killed together with his protector Al-Jadd in Seville, and Mohammed King of Niebla certainly was an Almohade, whence we argue that

---

[1] See p. 298. Conde calls him "Mohammed, lord of Niebla" (i. 33), and Zuñiga (i. 27, 402) "Aben Amafon," and "Aben Mahfot."

YEMENITES AND ALMOHADES IN SEVILLE

he escaped from the revolution of 1242 with his mother, who appears to have been a competent woman; and set up his rule at Niebla. Mohammed is not mentioned by Ibn Khaldun as having offended the Almogavares, so it is possible that they supported him, after the death of the Yemenite, to secure a base of operations at the head of the Ajarafe, on account of the great importance to Seville of keeping that road to the city open.[1]

Niebla lies, like Alcalá de Guadaira, on a steep hill, above a sharp bend in the Rio Tinto—a quiet stream with waters of a strange bronze-green colour derived from its source among the copper-mines. On one side the walled city commands the road over the plain to Seville and on the other a rocky pass, through which the river winds down to the sea below the port of Huelva. The situation is not so strong as that of Alcalá, but it is clear that a determined resistance might have been made here in the Middle Ages, for the city wall, which still is almost complete, runs down to the edge of the river, so that it was hardly possible for the enemy to cut off the water except by diverting the course of the stream, a measure which we seldom or never read of as adopted in Andalucia. San Fernando seems to have left the place alone, no attack on Niebla being referred to under his rule, and when Alfonso X. besieged the city with Al-Ahnar's help nine years after the fall of Seville, it was ten months before the allies could reduce it. Gibraleon, Serpa, Mora, Faro, and several other towns, with almost the whole of the Algarbe, were still under the dominion of the Almohades and their Amir Mohammed, and all submitted to the Christians, together with Niebla, in 1257.[2]

Early in the siege—apparently even before Fernando

IbnKhaldun in Makkari, ii. app. lxxix.-lxxx.
[2] Corde, iii. 41 ff.; Zuñiga, i. 221 ff. The great majority of the population were Mozarabs and Yemenites.

had sat down before Seville—the Master of Uclés crossed to the west side of the river with 280 knights "between friars and seculars," and camped before Aznalfarache, where he held his own with difficulty until Fernando sent him reinforcements. These forces remained on the west bank during the whole of the siege, fighting with the garrisons of Aznalfarache and of the Castle of Triana.[1] The besiegers were unable to make any impression on the Castle of Triana, which held out even after the bridge of boats was broken, and only capitulated with the surrender of the city.

About this time the Archbishop of Santiago, following the example of other militant prelates, came to assist at the siege with a company of Galician knights. They encamped near the Tagarete, a sluggish stream which winds outside the eastern walls of the city, embouching into the Guadalquivir below what is now the wharf known as the *Muelle Mineral*. But the noxious smell of the pestilent brook poisoned the Archbishop and all his men, and while they were feeling very ill the Moslems, aware of their condition, came out and attacked them. To avenge themselves, sundry knights laid a trap, baited with a flock of sheep without a shepherd, and when the Almohades attenpted to catch the animals, the Archbishop's party killed five hundred of them. At least so says Zuñiga, but without mentioning his authority for the story. That the Galicians got a fever from the smell of the Tagarete is easy to believe, for any one who camped on its banks would do the same now. But we doubt if the Moslems risked five hundred of the garrison to secure a few sheep, for in the scarcity of provisions prevailing in both armies they must have known the flock would not be left unguarded without a purpose. The

---

[1] *Primera Crónica*, 750-1. Zuñiga, i. 11, who gives the command to the Master of Santiago, not of Uclés.

Archbishop did not recover from his sickness, but became so ill that San Fernando sent him back to the north.[1]

Zuñiga, as already mentioned, says that Fernando first pitched his camp in the Prado de San Sebastian, just outside the walls. The *Primera Crónica* does not say this, but tells us that he went to Tablada, where, his force being small, he entrenched himself as strongly as he could.[2] Possibly he only stayed a short time under the walls, but there seems no doubt that he encamped there first. The Chronicle says that, " being much harassed by the Moslems where he was," he moved on to Tablada. Alfonso X., with filial respect, always minimises his father's reverses if possible.

San Fernando had to send for his son from Aragon, where he had gone for his wedding with the princess Violante, daughter of Jaime I.; and although the prince came unwillingly, he brought with him an army from Murcia—whose Amir, Ibn Hud, was Fernando's vassal—besides many Aragonese soldiers sent by his father-in-law.

Reinforcements were no doubt needed, for reading between the lines we can see that matters were not going so well for the besiegers as the Christian chroniclers try to make out. The work of the foragers especially was one of peril, yet it obviously could not be neglected for a day. It was when escorting one of the foraging expeditions that Garci Perez de Vargas first sprang into fame ; putting to flight " seven Moors " single-handed, with the great sword now in the Columbus Library at Seville, arrogantly inscribed " With this sword and Garci Perez Seville was won." But Zuñiga and the Chronicle, however unwillingly, make it evident that neither Garci Perez nor his companions invariably came off victorious in these encounters, for on more than one occasion the whole of the escort were killed.

[1] Zuñiga, i. 26.   [2] P. 751.

Both by land and river the Almohades made repeated sallies, and they even tried to burn the Christian ships with "a great fire raft," all Admiral Bonifaz's courage and talent being needed to frustrate the endeavour. He seems to have got his fleet up the river as far as San Juan de Aznalfarache, and it appears that after the attempt to burn his ships Fernando fixed a couple of stout logs or stakes in the stream to block the fairway.

One thing certain is that the river was not won or held by the Christians without much sharp fighting. Eventually, however, Bonifaz "took by force some military vessels called Zambras,"[1] and after that nothing more is said about encounters on the Guadalquivir until the breaking of the bridge of boats, which introduced the last act of the prolonged drama of resistance.

The most frequent actions by land were on the banks of the Guadaira. The Moslems came out by a gate of the Alcazar and crossed the bridge over the Guadaira a couple of miles from Seville. In Zuñiga's time the remains of the fortifications[2] of this bridge were still to be seen, and it seems that the river could only be crossed here, for by leaving a guard at the approach to the bridge the Almohades were always able to get back to the city in safety after a sally into the Christian encampment.

We must not forget that the historians of the Court of Granada, upon whom Conde depended for his account of the siege (no particulars of which are to be found in Makkari), were as much interested as the author of the Chronicle of Alfonso in minimising reverses with which their own king Al-Ahmar was connected, so we get no help from the Moslem writers there translated towards verifying the facts.

As a rule the Christians are asserted to have followed

---

[1] Zuñiga, i. 17.
[2] These have now disappeared, but the bridge still stands.

the Moslems to the very gates of Seville after reducing them to flight in their frequent sallies. One day Garci Perez and Lorenzo Suarez desired to make an example of the "infidels," who were so unduly bold, and they laid an ambush in a secret place, Lorenzo warning his men that when the Moslems "as usual" fled, they should not follow them over the bridge on account of the risk involved. The Moslems fell into the snare and fled in confusion, leaving the field covered with their dead. The Christians, obedient to orders, paused in their pursuit at the end of the bridge. Not so Garci Perez. Forgetting what had been agreed upon, he rushed across the bridge alone. Don Lorenzo thereupon said to his men:—

"Gentlemen, Garci Perez de Vargas has deceived us. See where he goes among the Moslems! He will get us into a place where we shall have the full need of our hands."

All followed, flying to the bold adventurer's help, and after killing "more than three thousand," [1] they pursued the routed Moslems to the very gates of the Alcazar.

"That day," says the Chronicle, "Don Lorenzo Suarez confessed himself excelled in courage by Garci Perez," and the result was that the sallies of the garrison became less frequent. [2]

San Fernando, however, disapproved of these exhibitions of fool-hardiness on the part of his knights, and on one occasion ordered the arrest of both Garci Perez and Suarez for having risked a serious catastrophe by riding up alone to hammer at the gates of Seville with the butts of their lances—a proceeding which brought out such a large

[1] The Chroniclers of the Middle Ages in Spain, whether Christians or Moslems, never condescended to deal with less than "thousands" of the enemy on occasions such as these. Nor is this characteristic entirely wanting among certain Spanish journalists of the present day.

[2] Zuñiga, i. 21.

force of the enemy that practically the whole army had to go to the rescue of the two adventurers. He pardoned them, but turned them into ridicule by asking who had given proof of the greatest courage, the one who had first hazarded his life, the one who had stayed longest at the gate, or the one who had had the self-restraint to keep still instead of inviting attack. The decision was put to the vote, but we are not informed which came out highest, neither are we given, in the Chronicle, the name of the knight who restrained his martial ardour rather than bring the enemy out upon the camp. Zuñiga tells us his name, from another source. The story indicates that San Fernando was born in advance of his time, for even Zuñiga half apologizes for the king's view of what was then considered courage.

Notwithstanding—possibly indeed in consequence of—these ill-judged feats of arms, the besiegers made no real progress, and at length it became evident that Seville was and would continue practically impregnable as long as communication with the highly cultivated Ajarafe remained open. But it was exceedingly difficult to cut off supplies on that side; for the Castle of Triana was impervious to attack, its garrison made numerous sallies, and in every quarter of the city the defence continued to be conducted with unabated vigour.

At length, about nine months after the investment of the city, Al-Ahmar suggested to Fernando that it would be well to destroy the bridge of boats, and thus deprive the garrison of their only means of access to the Ajarafe, on which they now entirely depended for food supplies. His plan was to prepare fire ships to burn the boats, and two great vessels to break the chain which held them together, and to set them adrift on the river when the wind and tide were favourable.[1] Neither the Chronicle nor Zuñiga mention

[1] Conde, iii. 33-4.

the fire ships, and the writer quoted by Conde may possibly have confused the breaking of the bridge with the previous attack, by fire ships, on Fernando's navy, although it is quite possible that Al-Ahmar recommended their use, for it is clear that the stratagem was familiar to the Spanish Moslems at this time.

Zuñiga says that the king proposed the scheme to Bonifaz and "other experts of the naval ministry," and makes no mention of any suggested use of fire ships. The Castilians were not a maritime nation, as indeed they hardly could have been considering the situation of their country, and the first mention of a Castilian navy is the account of the thirteen ships built at Santander, by San Fernando's order, for the siege of Seville. The Moslems, on the other hand, were familiar with the use of Greek fire, which the Chronicle mentions as a source of terror to the Christians, adding that in Arabic it was called "tar-fire."[1] Very possibly Al-Ahmar's advice was rejected because the besiegers had no ships to spare; San Fernando possessed at this time no ports in the south, and as we have seen, Bonifaz had to go to the north to procure any ships at all.

The bridge of boats made by the Almohades was somewhat higher up the river than that which had been destroyed by the Almoravides when they besieged Seville and overthrew Motamid in 1091. The remains of the chains used for the former bridge were still visible when Zuñiga wrote, fixed into the foundations of great walls close to the Torre del Oro and opposite to it.

The attempt was made on May 3, 1248. Two large ships were prepared, the bows being strengthened with iron plates, and were taken some way down stream, with their crews on board, Bonifaz himself being in command. They came

[1] Et dizenle en arauigo fuego de alquitran. (*Primera Crónica*, pp. 754, 756.)

up on the flood tide, with a strong wind behind them, through a storm of missiles from both sides of the river; the first of the ships shook the bridge, and the second, on which Bonifaz was, " gave such a blow that it passed clear through to the other side " amid the triumphant shouts of the Christians and the bitter lamentations of the Moors.[1]

After this success the end of the siege ought to have been in sight, but we doubt whether the destruction of the bridge was quite as complete as the Chronicle would have us believe, for the city held out for over six months longer.

Zuñiga at any rate had no doubts as to the satisfactory result of the attempt. He says that the famous vessels " are more worthy of eternal fame than the much-sung Argo of the Greeks." The city of Santander, he tells us, " placed the ship on its arms because they were justly proud of its having been built in their port, and the Cathedral of Seville put the same ship on the first seal of the Chapter, with an image of Our Lady in the stern, and the Holy Cross on the sail," and this statement is doubtless true, for he gives us a wood-cut of the seal, dated 1256, from the Archives of Seville. He does not say, however, why only one ship was considered worthy of commemoration, when we are distinctly told that two were used to break the bridge.

[1] *Primera Crónica*, 761.

CHAPTER XIX

THE FALL OF SEVILLE

THE destruction of the bridge of boats was the first important advantage gained by the Christians; but they were still a long way from the final victory.

"The soldiers," says Zuñiga, "were wearied owing to the lack of provisions and the inclemency of the season, and dangerous murmurings began, for through lack of money the pay was in arrears, although in order to obtain it the coinage had been debased under promise to redeem it at the expense of the Treasury when present difficulties were overcome. . . . The king was saddened by the general discouragement, while at the same time his spirit was raised up in more fervent prayer, which he accompanied by fastings, disciplines, and hair shirts." [1]

Still, the besiegers were encouraged by occasional minor successes. "They entered Goles," says Conde, "and burnt the suburb of Ben Alfofar, and sacked that of Bab Macarena." [2]

Immediately after the bridge was broken, San Fernando attacked the Castle of Triana by land and water. First

[1] i. 27–8.
[2] iii. 35. Goles in the sixteenth century was still a plot of garden land outside the walls, between the gate then called by that name and the river. In Zuñiga's time it belonged to the heirs of the Columbus family. It is now a manufacturing suburb flanked by the railway to Madrid. The suburb of Ben Alfofar, which the Chronicle calls Benaliofar and Zuñiga Venahoar, is now, he says, known as San Bernardo, which lies between the Prado de San Sebastian and the Macarena Gate. (*Primera Crónica*, p. 758; Zuñiga, i. 19.)

the besiegers tried to carry it by storm, but failed for want of ladders and picks; then they made an unsuccessful attempt to undermine it: then Fernando laid siege to it in form, with engines made in haste, with no further result than heavy losses to the besiegers from the powerful catapults or cross-bows (*ballestas*) used by the garrison; the *cuadrillos* [1] which they discharged, passed, it is said, right through an armoured knight, and buried themselves in the ground, and no progress seems to have been made until further reinforcements came from Cordova and camped near the walls. Now, says the Chronicle, the Moslems were shut in, and could only go in and out by water, in a boat or swimming, and at great risk. Yet, in spite of all the efforts of the besiegers, they could not prevent the besieged from crossing to Triana or bringing supplies into the city.[2]

Two miraculous incidents of the siege, recorded not in the Chronicle but by Peraza and Juan de Pineda, are related by Zuñiga; we will repeat them here, because to this day memorials of them exist in Seville.

The Master of Santiago,[3] after taking the little town of Gelves on the right bank of the river, several times attacked the Castle of Triana, which was so strong that its possession was disputed to the end of the siege. "From here [4] he made sallies against the Moslems of the Sierra Morena, further to bridle their pride. One day, when light failed for the fight, because night was rapidly unfolding its shade and was favouring the escape of the enemy, like another Joshua he made the sun to stay its course, invoking Our Lady with the celebrated words :—' *Santa Maria, deten tu dia!* '

[1] An arrow-like missile, the familiar " quarrell " of the cross-bow, quadrangular in shape.
[2] *Primera Crónica*, pp. 761–5. Conde also mentions the powerful missiles used by the garrison. (iii. 35.)
[3] The *Primera Crónica* says it was the Master of Uclés. (P. 753.)
[4] Presumably from Gelves; the Castle of Triana was never taken; see below.

THE FALL OF SEVILLE

(Holy Mary, detain thy day), which the Divine pity granted, so that the light supernaturally endured until he had completed his triumph, while in his prayers San Fernando helped him better by appeals to Heaven than he could have done with the bravest troops; a miracle vouched for by the Church of Our Lady of *Tentudia*, founded afterwards by this same Master." [1]

The other miracle evidently has a basis of fact, and as this has a direct bearing upon the history of Seville under the Yemenite dominion, it is worth discussing at some length.

We have already shown how the descendants of the Princess Sara, a noble caste of mixed descent, part Gothic and part Yemenite, ruled Seville for many generations, and how wide was the liberty permitted to the offspring of the Gothic Christians who formed so large a part of the population of the *tierra de Sevilla* in the eighth century and later. This liberty was apparently continued, for there is no evidence that the Christians of Seville were persecuted by the Almoravides, nor that the Almohades interfered seriously with them. The fact that the Church of San Lucar la Mayor was built in 1214 (see p. 18), and that the Mozarabic Convent *de la Luz* at Moguer was undisturbed down to the Christian re-conquest (see appendix), is of itself sufficient evidence that the Almohades did not treat the Christians in this district with excessive intolerance.

It is true that no distinct mention is made in the Chronicle of the Christian churches existing in Seville when San Fernando took possession of it. But Simonet (see appendix) refers to no less than six Christian churches in the twelfth century, all of which still exist in Seville,

---

[1] Zuñiga, i. 11–2. Although the church no longer exists, its site is marked by a little street called Tentudia, on the outskirts of Seville near the Prado de San Sebastian.

with their primitive advocations. And there are many legends of the miraculous preservation of pictures and images of saints, which have an undoubted basis in fact. These legends have sprung up especially round certain mural paintings, which would long ago have created interest among foreign students of early Christian art, were their existence in Seville generally known.

The particular mural painting which forms the subject of the legend we are about to relate, ruined though it is by numerous restorations and re-paintings, would at once be recognised as of great age, by any student who really examined it. But as the chapel containing it is kept locked and the guide-books lay no stress on its interest, few amateurs of medieval art take the trouble to look at it.

With this preface we will give Zuñiga's narrative of the occurrence in question.

"From the time of the Goths there had been in the great Mosque a painted effigy of Our Lady, larger than life, a custom of the primitive Church, signifying that the subject was superhuman. The Divine Providence did not permit the Moslems to efface it, although they attempted to do so, for it remained in their despite always more beautiful and resplendent. Therefore, not being able to destroy it, they hid it, raising another wall in front of it,[1] although the faithful who lived in Seville never forgot it, and worshipped it without seeing it, until a few years before the conquest it suddenly became visible and shed rays of light, which the Moors interpreted as a presage of their ruin: . . . and they never again could conceal it; and every time they ventured to look at it it compelled them to kneel, an impulse which they did not resist.

"San Fernando had heard of this sovereign image, and

[1] This shows that it was a mural painting, a fact not previously stated by Zuñiga.

with a lively desire to worship it he entered Seville one night in search of it, and, carried away by ecstasy, lost consciousness in profound contemplation; and having worshipped it he returned, escorted by a divine guard, to leave by the Gate of Jerez,[1] when his sword fell, and stumbling over it he came to himself and knew where he was and the sovereign favour which he had received. At this moment he was missed by Don Rodrigo Gonzalez Giron, who was one of his nearest attendants, and by Fernan Yañez and Juan Fernandez de Mendoza, brothers of his most intimate friends, who anxiously went to look for him. . . . These gentlemen, with others, entered Seville in search of him, and near the Mosque they had a terrible fight with the Moors, after which they left the city with good fortune equal to their temerity. . . . We know," says Zuñiga, "that in the conquest of Granada Fernando del Pulgar attempted and achieved a similar act of daring. And," he concludes, "the image is that which is still in the holy Church [the Cathedral of Seville] under the advocacy of *la Antigua*." [2]

The whole story of this "miraculous" entrance of San Fernando into the beleaguered city under cover of night, with the incidents of his stumble over his sword and the fight near the Mosque, is obviously the record of a venturous secret entry, facilitated by Yemenites or Christians of Muwallad descent within the walls, who had access to the concealed image and offered to show it to the Christian king as a pledge of their good faith, with the object of hastening the surrender of the capital. One can understand the interest that the sight of this ancient image would have for the pious king, while the apposite arrival of his knights when his sword clattered on the ground and woke the

---

[1] This was the nearest city gate to that in the Alcazar, by which the garrison generally went out to attack the Christian camp.
[2] i. 28–9.

suspicions of the garrison may have been a preconcerted part of the scheme. From the Jerez gate (still so called, although the walls have long been pulled down and the gate replaced by the palace of a Sevillian nobleman) to the Cathedral (converted not long before into a Mosque), is quite a short distance, and if the party on the watch for Fernando was a strong one, they might easily have penetrated thus far, once the gate was opened by his Christian friends within, before the garrison was aroused.[1]

At a previous period of the siege, certain of those within the city had approached Prince Alfonso through a Faqui called by Zuñiga "Orias," recently arrived from Africa to visit the mosques of Andalucia—"sanctuaries according to their way of thinking," says Zuñiga—with a proposal which that historian characterises as a snare designed to bring about the death of the Infante or his capture as a hostage. The "Moro Orias" on behalf of "several of the chief Moors" offered to deliver to him two towers from which, once in his possession, he could quickly take the city. "The wise prince feared the treacherous proposal, and, although they begged that he would go in person, sent Don Pedro de Guzman [2] . . . who escaped from the treachery with the death of only one knight." [3]

It is impossible from the materials at our disposal to discover the truth about this "plot," and Zuñiga of course had no idea that there was any distinction between the "Moors" or Almohades and the Arabs and Muwallads in the beleaguered city. But it is possible that Alfonso was unduly cautious in the matter, and that if he had gone in

---

[1] It is possible that the intention may have been to admit a sufficient number of men to overpower the guard of the Jerez gate and open it to the besiegers, and that the plan went wrong.

[2] Founder of the great house of Guzman, from which sprang the dukes of Medina Sidonia and other noble families.

[3] Zuñiga, i. 26–7.

THE FALL OF SEVILLE

person, instead of alarming the Faqui and his party by sending a man whom they did not know, he might perhaps have had his two towers and a good deal more besides.

A writer was born at Ceuta in 1260, who, as he afterwards became director of the prayers and preaching in the great mosque of Granada, was presumably of Yemenite extraction and certainly of Shiite religious views. He was known as Ibn Roshaid, the diminutive of Roshd, which Pons (p. 317) translates as "a preacher." If, as is suggested by the name, his father Roshd too was a preacher, he might possibly have been the "Orias" (Ar-Roshd or Ar-Rosh) of Zuñiga, in which case the possibility of communication between the Shiites in Seville and the Shiite followers of Al-Ahmar in the Christian camp would be established. Orias was evidently a person of some importance in Seville, for he "with other of the best Moors of Seville" took a leading part in the *pour parlers* which preceded the surrender of the town.[1]

We hear of him once more in Zuñiga, who, quoting from "an ancient memorial," says that after the surrender Sakkaf went from Seville to Africa, "where, as long as he lived, his name was always abhorred, and was made more odious by the execrations of the Faqui Orias."[2] If Orias or Ar-Roshd had been within measurable distance of coming to terms with Fernando on the basis of an alliance with the Yemenites instead of a complete surrender of the city, we can imagine how his compatriots would curse the name of the Almohade whose obstinate resolve to fight to the last resulted in the loss of Seville to Islam.

That San Fernando felt no great confidence in his prospects of ultimate success is suggested by the readiness with which he agreed to the terms of capitulation proposed by the besieged, which certainly were exceedingly liberal for a city conquered after a resistance of a year and a

[1] *Primera Crónica*, p. 766.   [2] i. 42.

quarter. Indeed the whole course of the siege and surrender of Seville differs in important respects from that of other cities falling to the Christian arms at that period, in which stern treatment was meted out where there had been active or prolonged resistance. Nor can we attribute San Fernando's action in this case entirely to the influence of Al-Ahmar, although it is clear that the Christian king treated his advice with respect. It is possible that the final capitulation was forced upon the Almohades of the garrison by the peace-loving and practical Yemenites, who formed the majority of the population. If their chosen leader Ibn Al Jadd had lived, the siege might never have taken place, for it is safe to assume that the Yemenites, had they alone been concerned, would have allied themselves with San Fernando as Al-Ahmar did, and Seville, with the Ajarafe and the Algarbe, might like Granada have paid tribute to Castilian kings as her over-lords for many years before they became her actual rulers.

We will now go on to the closing scene of the long siege, which the Chronicle relates as follows:—

"The king was vexed because neither with machines nor by fighting nor in any way could he take the Castle of Triana or prevent the Moslems from crossing." He tried to land troops at the Arenal [1] in order to bar the passage across the river, but was driven off. At length one day, when Orias and several of the chief men of the garrison had crossed over to Triana, Bonifaz brought up a number of ships and managed to cut them off. Now the garrison of Triana, being shut in on both sides and hopeless of succour, asked a parley and came out to see Fernando. Having seen him they went to Seville, and Sakkaf then offered terms.[2]

---

[1] A sandy portion of the river bank outside the walls on the city side; now the Paseo de Colon.

[2] *Primera Crónica*, p. 766.

THE FALL OF SEVILLE

The first proposals made by the garrison were to hand over to San Fernando the Alcazar and all the tribute of the town " as was paid to the Commander of the Faithful when he was lord of it." To this Fernando refused to listen, and Sakkaf then offered a third of the town, with the Alcazar and all the rights of lordship. This also Fernando refused. Then they proposed to give up half the town, making a division wall between Moslems and Christians; some of San Fernando's people advised him to accept this, but he declined, and then at length Sakkaf agreed to evacuate the city, the king to give him and the Arraez (chief) " Aben Xueb " permission on payment of tribute to go to Niebla, Aznalfarache, or San Lucar.[1]

The Moslems stipulated for the removal of their arms and property. This was agreed to, and San Fernando took possession of the Alcazar on November 23, 1248. But he did not yet make his formal entry into the town, for the Moslems asked for a month in which to sell such of their property as they could not carry away with them. At the end of that period, having sold all they wanted, they gave up the keys, and San Fernando entered the city on December 22nd, 1248, the day of the translation of St. Isidore.

To those of the inhabitants who wished to depart by sea, says the Chronicle, the king gave five ships and eight galleys; to those who went by land he gave beasts of burden and a guard; numbers of them went to Jerez (which was in the

---

[1] *Primera Crónica*, 766-7; Zuñiga, i. 29-30. Zuñiga adds that Sakkaf wanted to pull down the Giralda, and that Alfonso replied that if a single brick of it were removed he would massacre them all. Both the proposal and the terms of the refusal are clearly a late fabrication.

" Aben Xueb " must stand for Ibn Shoayb, one of the Almohade Council of Administration appointed after the murder of Al Jadd; see Ibn Khaldun in Makkari, ii. app. lxxx. It is not clear whether the San Lucar is San Lucar la Mayor in the Ajarafe or San Lucar de Barrameda at the mouth of the river; for " San Lucar " Zuñiga substitutes Tejada. It is not said when Aznalfarache fell, but Niebla was not taken until 1257, five years after the death of San Fernando.

hands of the Almohades), escorted by the Master of Calatrava.[1]

The Chronicle makes special mention of the sufferings of the besieging army from sickness, from which many died, and from a wind, "as hot as though it came from hell," and says that "all the men were dripping all day, in the shade and out of it, as though they were in a bath."[2] This must have been the scourge which we now call the levanter.

The camp of the besieging army, the Chronicle goes on to say, was like a great and noble city, with streets and squares. There was a street of cloth merchants and money changers, another of dealers in spices and drugs needed for the sick and wounded; another of butchers and fishmongers, and so on. There was great abundance of food and merchandise, and the men settled down with their goods and their wives and children, "as though they were going to remain there for ever," for the king had promised not to raise the siege until he had taken the town, and this certainty of having possession of it caused them to come from all parts.[3]

The Chronicle describes the strength and greatness of the walls of Seville and the beauty and costliness of the Torre del Oro and that now known as the Giralda—"who is there who can say what it cost the king who had it made?" "Ships," the writer goes on to say, "used to come up the river every day, to within the walls, bringing merchandise from all over the world: from Tangier, Ceuta, Tuniz, Bugia, Alexandria, Genoa, Portugal, England, Pisa, Lombardy, Burdel (? Bordeaux), Bayonne, Sicily, Gascony, Cataluña, Aragon, and even from France, and many other places over sea, from the land of Christians and of Moors." In the Ajarafe

---

[1] *Primera Crónica*, 766–7; cf. Conde, iii. 36–7. The Chronicle says that 120,000 went to Ceuta (in five ships and eight galleys!) and 300,000 to Jerez; such statistics hardly require comment.
[2] P. 767–8.
[3] P. 768.

there were fully 100,000 farmhouses (*alquerias*). "So great was the city," the Chronicle adds, "that only by divine help could it have been won in so short a time."[1]

Conde adds one or two details. "The Wali Abul Hasan," he says,[2] gave up the keys of the city on Shaban 12, 646 (November, 1248), and on the same day took ship and crossed over to Africa. "King Fernando occupied the Alcazar, and his captains the fortresses of the town and neighbourhood. At once the Moslems began to leave that populous city;

[1] P. 769. The places named, which conclude the narrative of the taking of Seville, are clearly those with which the city traded in Moslem times. Seville continued commercial relations with many if not all of these countries down to the end of the reign of Henry IV., brother and predecessor of Isabel the Catholic. He protected and was on friendly terms with the Moslems and Moriscos in his dominions, and although in many respects he was a bad ruler, there is no doubt that in his reign trade flourished, and especially so in the beautiful silken textiles illustrated under the heading of "Saracenic" in the great work of the late Frederick Fischbach on textile ornaments. Relics of mediæval Arabic art exist, inscribed with names, or dates, or both, which show them to have been connected with Seville. The relationship between these and several of the designs in the "Saracenic" *Textile Ornaments* leaves no room for doubt that the latter originated in Seville. From the time that Isabel and Fernando began to pursue their relentless war against the Moslems, who were the chief workers at all the textile industries of the time, manufactures of silken fabrics and those of gold and silver thread rapidly declined. Seville, whose population was largely Morisco, felt the change of policy severely. Notwithstanding the apparent prosperity which resulted from her privileged trade with the New World in the sixteenth century, her manufactures, and with them her real prosperity, began to decline under the Catholic Kings, and continued to do so, in fact if not in appearance, until the expulsion of the Moriscos by Philip III. completed the destruction begun by Isabel in the supposed interests of religion. It is significant that Zuñiga, writing towards the end of the seventeenth century, complains that the silk-weavers of Seville were steadily losing their trade because it had become the fashion to import cheaper and inferior fabrics from Italy, with which the Sevillian manufacturers could not compete: (iv. 120–1), the fact being that skilled labour had become so scarce in default of the exiled Moriscos that materials of the traditional Seville standard could not be produced at a profit. Hand-loom weaving is even now carried on at Seville and Granada, and in certain country places fine cloth, silk ribbons, and damask linen of excellent workmanship are produced, but only in minute quantities, because of the national preference for cheap machine-made stuff.

[2] Probably this should be Abu Faris, President of the Almohade Council of Administration. (Makkari, ii. app. lxxx.)

many accepted the protection of King Al-Ahmar and went to the land of Granada, others to Jerez and other towns, and to the Algarbe, and a few crossed to Ceuta with the Almohades.[1] Thus ended the empire of these princes (the Almohades) in Seville, and the Moslems lost that beautiful city, her towers and mosques were filled with crosses and idols, and the sepulchres of the faithful Moslems were profaned." [2]

The sepulchres here mentioned were not those of the Yemenites, who were generally buried before the doors of their palaces, or, if poor men, in the public cemetery without the walls. The reference is to a custom introduced about the twelfth century from Egypt, of erecting a mausoleum alongside of the mosque, to serve both as a sepulchre and a private chapel for the great man who built it. Most of the churches in Seville which are named as having been mosques in the thirteenth century have these mausoleums on the north or south of the nave, towards what is now the chancel, and frequently on both sides.

These, no doubt, were the sepulchres which the Christians are said to have profaned when they converted the mosques to Christian uses in 1248. There is no evidence that the Christians profaned the Moslem burying grounds, for which act of sacrilege they could have had no motive. On the contrary, there are indications that they adopted and continued to use them for centuries after the conquest.

San Fernando made his triumphal entry into Seville on December 22, the day on which is commemorated the removal of the relics of St. Isidore to Leon (see p. 27). That saint, says Zuñiga, is believed to have revealed his victory to San Fernando; and the pious king converted the triumphal march into a religious procession. "The army marched

---

[1] This passage shows how small the Almohade population was.
[2] iii. 36-7.

THE FALL OF SEVILLE

first in military order, waving the banners of the victors and tearing down those of the vanquished,[1] the universal rejoicing being heightened by the sound of a thousand sonorous military instruments. The procession was headed by the principal commanders, the nobility (*infanzones*), *Ricos Omes*, Grandmasters of the Military Orders, and a numerous concourse of priests, secular and regular, with the Archbishops and Bishops escorting a portable throne on which was borne a sovereign image of Our Lady."

"I do not venture to decide," continues Zuñiga, "whether this was the image 'of the Kings' or that 'of the *Sede*,' for either conjecture is equally probable, but the one generally accepted is that it was that of the Kings, which we see majestically placed in the Royal Chapel. Yet that of the *Sede*, titular and tutelary Saint of our Cathedral, is placed on the High Altar, and has been the object of devotion for so long, that it seems as though it could never have been given the second place.

"Bringing up the rear came San Fernando and his wife [2] and sons, his brother, and various royal personages."

The procession passed between the Torre del Oro and the river to the Gate of Goles (now the Puerta Real), pausing at the Arenal to receive the keys from Sakkaf.

When the king reached the great Mosque, which had been previously "purged of the filthiness of Mohammedan impiety," one or more Archbishops said Mass, and "the temple being thus *restored*[3] to Christian worship with the title of St. Mary of the See (*de la Sede*), San Fernando left in it the before-mentioned image, called *de la Sede*, which is all of silver, and is placed on the great Altar. And the image

---

[1] So says Zuñiga, but such an ungraceful act is improbable, seeing the consideration with which Fernando treated the Moslems of Seville.

[2] Joan, Countess of Aumale and Ponthieu, whose daughter Eleanor married Edward I. of England.

[3] Italics ours. See p. 398.

of the Virgin of the Kings was placed in that which was at once marked out as the Chapel Royal, in the most easterly part of the Mosque. And at the same time the royal standard of the Cross was raised on the top of the lofty tower of the Mosque." [1]

The image of the Virgin of the Kings in the Chapel Royal is pronounced by all competent authorities to be undoubtedly of the period here ascribed to it, and the fact that the Lilies of France form part of the design on the silver shoes—the image is life-size—seems confirmation of the tradition that it was a gift to San Fernando from his cousin St. Louis of France.

In connection with this event the editor of Zuñiga quotes a curious prophecy which the "Moors" of Seville are said to have preserved touching the approaching loss of that city. It is said to have been found by the Catholic Kings among the archives of Granada when they conquered it.

It is to the effect that when the Almohades possessed Andalucia a young knight named Abenhuc (Ibn Hud) who was the richest and most powerful man in the kingdom of Murcia, rose against them and vanquished them, bringing under his lordship all the "Alarabes" of those parts.[2] "And in order to establish his kingdom he put to the sword all the Almohades under the pretext of ceremonial and superstition (*sic*), saying that they had offended God with their sins and vices. He ordered his priests to clean and wash with water their mosques, and to dye black the shields and banners on which were the arms of the Almohades, and when this was being done, a Moorish wizard (*hechichero*) whom they held for a great prophet, lamented loudly [literally ' emitted great howlings '] when he saw those shields dyed, and

[1] Zuñiga, i. 39–49.
[2] The word Alarabe here evidently means the Shiite Arabs who followed Ibn Hud. The Spanish writers do not as a rule distinguish between the Arabs and the Moors or Almohades.

THE FALL OF SEVILLE

calling together the principal Moors he told them that the kingdom of the Moors in Spain was at an end, and that in vengeance for the death of the Almohades the King Abenhuc would have an evil death ; and that on the day he died all those shields and black ensigns would fall to the ground, and that there would never more be a Moorish king in Seville. After this occurred the death of Abenhuc who was made drunk by a confidential friend at a banquet in Almeria, who when he was unconscious drowned him in a tank of water, and the same day those shields and standards fell in the mosque of Seville, and the Moors considered the loss of the city certain ; and never more was there a king after Abenhuc, for Axataf (Sakkaf), who was in Seville when the sainted king won it, was no king, but a captain." [1]

The account of the dyeing of the banners by Ibn Hud, and of his subsequent death, is in the main correct, but the story is probably a Christian version of the incidents, for no Moslem would have confused Murcia with Seville (cf. p. 280).

[1] Zuñiga, i. 48–9.

CHAPTER XX

THE PASSING OF SAN FERNANDO

AL-AHMAR returned to Granada after the surrender of Seville, "more sad than satisfied" at the victories of the Christians, for he could not fail to foresee that sooner or later their aggrandisement must bring about the downfall of Islam in Spain. But this did not diminish his affection for and admiration of their monarch.

During the brief respite from warfare he devoted himself to the encouragement of manufactures and commerce among his own people, giving exemptions from taxation and prizes to the best farmers, horse-breeders, armourers, weavers, and harness-makers. Thus these arts flourished in his states, and the land, which is naturally fertile, became doubly so under good cultivation. He especially protected the silk-worm industry and the manufacture of silk, with the result that the silks of Granada competed successfully with those of Syria.[1]

He improved the coinage, and worked gold and silver and other mines, and began building the Alhambra—the palace, for the fortress had been in existence for centuries—and himself directed the work and frequently went among the architects and workmen. His chief amusements were reading history, and gardening.

Most, if not all, of his Wizirs, Kadis, etc., were Yemenites,

[1] Conde, iii. 37–8 ; cf. Williams, *Arts and Crafts*, iii. 49, and Gudiol *Arqueologia sagrada*, 408 note.

THE PASSING OF SAN FERNANDO 335

among them being one of the Beni Abi Amir, who had ruled for so long in the Eastern provinces of Andalucia.[1]

Thus Al-Ahmar, like all the great Yemenite rulers before him, devoted himself to strengthening his kingdom by encouraging and developing the arts and industries known at the time, within his own borders, instead of trying to extend them at the expense of continual war with his neighbours.[2]

San Fernando meanwhile was occupied with the settlement of Seville, and with the subjugation of the surrounding country. He acquired, says the Chronicle, Jerez, Medina (Sidonia), Alcalá (this must have been Alcalá de Ibn Said, afterwards la Real, for Alcalá del Rio and Alcalá de Guadaira were already in his hands), Bejer, Puerto de Santa Maria and Cadiz, " Salucar d'Alpechyn,"[3] Arcos, Lebrija, Rota, and Trebujena. "He gained everything from the sea here, part by fighting, part by agreements," save only Niebla and Aznalfarache, which latter was afterwards surrendered. Then, "there being now no more enemies to triumph over in Spain," he built a number of ships with a view to a campaign against the "Morisma" of Africa, "Christian and gallant plans which," says Zuñiga, "his death cut short."[4]

---

[1] Conde, iii. 38–9.
[2] Cf. Al Hakem's advice to his son, p. 160.
[3] A part of San Lucar (? de Barrameda), see the Repartimiento in Espinoza's *Historia de Sevilla*, pt. II. fol. 2.   There are three San Lucars in S.W. Andalucia: San Lucar de Barrameda and San Lucar la Mayor in the Province of Seville, and San Lucar de Guadiana in that of Huelva. The name is a corruption of Solucar, the origin of which is, we believe, unknown.
[4] Zuñiga, i. 85 ; *Primera Crónica*, 770–1. Some of the places referred to, if subdued by San Fernando, must shortly have rebelled again, for they are mentioned later as having been conquered by Alfonso. The annexation of Alcanate or Puerto de Sta. Maria (not mentioned in the Chronicle) is described at length in the *Cantigas* of that King, and no suggestion is made that it had already been conquered. On his return from an expedition to Africa against the Moors of Salé, Alfonso put in at the "Moslem port" of Alcanate, and was so delighted with the scenery and pleasant air that he remained at anchor some days. While there a Moslem Alguazil of Jerez came to him and told him the Moslems

The year 1252 was ushered in with great preparations for an over-seas campaign, but they were quickly nipped in the bud and replaced by general anxiety, for San Fernando fell dangerously ill with dropsy, and it became evident that his end was near. His strength was wasted by the fatigues of war and the austerities of his life, and flattery could not conceal his danger. He himself, perfectly aware of his condition, prepared for death, offering an example of patience and resignation.

He made his will, richly endowing the Chapter of Seville, and the document was kept in the archives of the Cathedral for many years, until Philip II. asked the Chapter to let him see it, on the ground that he had forgotten the contents, and took it with him to Madrid, whence it was never returned. The indignation with which Zuñiga describes this act of pillage is hardly concealed by his extreme respect for the king.

Finding his end approaching, San Fernando desired the

were much annoyed at some audacious person having changed the name to Puerto de Santa Maria, and that serious disturbances might result. The King ordered severe punishment to be meted out to those who had dared to alter the Arabic name, but in vain, the Christians could not be prevailed upon to call it anything but Puerto de Sta. Maria. Eventually, says Alfonso in the hymn relating to the event, the Queen of Heaven prevailed upon the Moslem Alguazil to come again to the King of Castile and offer voluntarily, in the cause of peace, to hand over not only the port itself, but all that coast of the ocean. *Cantiga*, cxcvii.) There is internal evidence that the Christians maintained a small church here from Visigothic times, portions of the Roman columns on which it was built still remaining with Arabic work superimposed, in a ruined chapel under a castle built round it early in the fourteenth century (see p. 137). There is also an ancient image of the Virgin, now in the parish church, which was found at the reconquest in what is now the castle, and the *Cantigas* are full of stories of the miracles effected by this "Virgin of Puerto de Santa Maria." Probably the Christian name had never been forgotten in that of Alcanate, and the desire of the descendants of the Gothic Christians to throw off the yoke of the Almohades of Jerez in favour of Alfonso was the real reason for the Alguazil's "miraculous" meekness. This seems the more probable, because according to the *Cantiga* relating the event, there were at the time no Castilian Christians there except those who came with Alfonso in his ships.

last offices of the Church. When his confessor, the Bishop of Segovia, came to him with the viaticum, escorted by all the Court, the king threw himself from his bed before the Host, made his attendants put a halter round his neck as a symbol of the criminal he felt himself to be before his God, and prepared to receive the Sacrament. From that moment he put away all the signs of majesty. He then called for his wife and children to take leave of them. He gave them documents increasing their inheritance, and recommended the younger ones to the care of his eldest son, to whom he read so wise a lesson that if he had been able to follow it he would have succeeded in being truly wise.[1]

" And now, feeling the last moment approaching, he asked for the lighted candle, the symbol of faith, and humbly prayed those present to pardon him, in the name of his subjects, for his faults in his governance of them; they broke into sobs and tears," and the king fell into a swoon which seemed to be the end. But he spoke once more, asking those present to sing the Te Deum, " and while they were singing he gave up his happy soul to God." [2]

He died on May 30th in the fifty-fourth year of his age, and the thirty-fifth of his reign, and, says Zuñiga, the people immediately canonised him, after their fashion, by general acclamation, giving him the title and worship of a saint.[3]

He died in the Alcazar of Seville, but " it is not known," says Zuñiga, " in what room, which devotion would consecrate as a chapel, or whether it was one of those pulled down by Pedro the Cruel for his new building." This last conjecture we hope to show was ill-founded, the Alcazar of

---

[1] This is an allusion to Alfonso's nickname of *El Sabio*, the Wise or the Learned.
[2] Zuñiga, i. 85-8.
[3] In the account of the closing scene in the Chronicle, written by order of his son, he is for the first time spoken of as " Saint " Fernando; up to that point the Chronicle always refers to him as " Don."

Motamid Ibn Abbad still standing substantially as he left it, and tradition points to the position of San Fernando's death-chamber.[1]

San Fernando had Norman blood in his veins, his mother Berengaria being the daughter of Alfonso IX. of Castile and Eleanor, daughter of Henry II. of England. The princess Berengaria married Alfonso IX. of Leon, and thus the two states became united under the monarchy of her son Fernando III.

The place of his birth had not been discovered down to the end of the eighteenth century, for although it was known that he was not born in his father's capital of Leon, none of the early historians mentioned his birth-place. But the editor of the second edition of Zuñiga's *Anales*, published in 1795, gives the following narrative.

In 1755 Don Diego Alejandro de Galvez, who was travelling all over Spain, France, Germany, and the Low Countries, chanced to call at a Cistercian monastery near Zamora, called the Monastery of Val-Paraiso; a building which lay deep in woods. After Mass was over Don Diego was invited to breakfast with the Abbot. While they were at breakfast the Abbot, on learning that his guest was a Sevillian, and attached to the Cathedral of that city, remarked that although Seville had the glory of being the place where lay the body of San Fernando, their Monastery had the equal glory of being built on the spot where he was born. And he proceeded to relate that the Monastery was originally founded by the "Emperor" Alfonso (VI.) close to a place called Peleas de Arriba, and that San Fernando, desiring to benefit the Monastery and to leave a memorial of his birthplace, had rebuilt it where it now stood, on the spot

[1] In the Seville Art Gallery there is a fine painting by Señor Mattoni of the death of San Fernando, based on a careful study of illuminations and monuments of the period. It gives an interesting idea of the dramatic scene depicted by Zuñiga and the Chronicle.

where he was born, endowing it with various estates in addition to the property it held from its founder. The Abbot added that all the documents relating to both foundations were in the archives of the Monastery, and Señor Galvez deeply regretted that want of time prevented his going through them. The next year he wrote a full account of his discovery, which at the urgent request of the Librarian of the Royal Library of Fernando VI. he was obliged to send to Madrid. It was never published, and in 1795 Espinosa found it impossible to trace the manuscript.[1] He adds that tradition had always said that San Fernando was born in a wood, but as the tradition had never been verified during the five centuries since his death Señor Galvez had not dreamed that a chance *détour* in his European journey could result in such a discovery.

The manner in which Madrid took possession of historical documents of interest, such as this account of Galvez and San Fernando's will, and then lost them, is thoroughly characteristic of Spanish official methods, both in the centralisation which draws everything to the capital and in the carelessness and neglect which loses or destroys what it has taken possession of.

Oddly enough there is no detailed account of the funeral of San Fernando. Zuñiga, whose examination of all existing records was most exhaustive, only tells us that the king was buried on June 1st in the Royal Chapel of Seville Cathedral, and that the coffin was placed at the feet of the image of Our Lady of the Kings, in accordance with his desire. On the mausoleum erected over the coffin his epitaph was inscribed in Hebrew, Arabic, Spanish, and Latin.[2]

The body, says Zuñiga, was miraculously preserved from corruption. No doubt it was embalmed, for to this day it preserves a semblance of humanity.

[1] Zuñiga, i. 91 note.   [2] *Ibid.*, i. 140.

The robe in which the king was wrapped for his burying was of Moslem manufacture. It is a mantle of silk woven in squares of red and white, forming a chess-board pattern of lions and castles;[1] a fragment of it is preserved in the Archæological Museum at Madrid, where it was sent by order of Charles II. when, on the rebuilding of the Chapel Royal, the coffin was opened. The corpse was then attired afresh in the seventeenth century costume which it still wears, and placed in the silver casket in which it lies to-day. A ring from the dead hand and other relics, sent with the fragments of the robe, have disappeared, with many more art-treasures lost and destroyed in the Royal Museums of the Capital. But the precious relic of thirteenth century textile work was rescued from oblivion some years ago by Señor Gestoso, a popular writer on Sevillian art, who found it in a packet thrown away as rubbish in a dark corner. The writing on the wrapper placed beyond a doubt the fact that this was what remained of the burial robe of San Fernando.

Not only was San Fernando buried in a silken robe of Moslem manufacture, but occasionally in life he seems to have worn the Moslem dress. Señor Gestoso, while collecting materials for a monograph on the Christian textile arts of Seville, came across the ancient banner of a Guild known as that of the *Sastres* (Tailors), which claims to have been founded by San Fernando and to have possessed a banner given by the king himself. Señor Gestoso found the tattered relics of their sixteenth century banner in the " rag-drawer " in the sacristy of the Church of San Ildefonso, among many scraps of vestments thrown away from generation to generation. Beneath an embroidered presentment of Charles V. which formed the centre of the banner he found another

[1] Alfonso X. is several times depicted in robes of this pattern in the illuminations to his *Cantigas* and *History of Chess*.

embroidered figure representing San Fernando. We have examined this banner as closely as is possible through the glass which protects it, and have no doubt that the figure formerly covered by the sixteenth century over-laid work representing Charles V. is the original portrait of San Fernando. In this portrait the king wears a Moslem turban and a flowing robe, but the features, except the pointed beard, are entirely worn away.[1]

The Guild was originally called that of *San Mateo de los Menestrales* (mechanics) *de Sevilla*, and the tradition is that San Fernando had done it the honour of becoming a member and presenting it with this portrait of himself. In memory of the king's connection with it the Guild, as long as it existed, retained the privilege of mounting guard over the body of the king on the days when this was displayed to the public. So clearly was their right established that once when some richer and more influential confraternity tried to oust the *Sastres* in order to appropriate to themselves the honourable guardianship of the coffin, the *Sastres* took their case before the Ecclesiastical authorities and won it in virtue of the documents they possessed showing the origin of their claim.[2]

Presumably they mounted guard from the beginning. If so, they stood alongside the Moslems of Granada, who came to offer the same tribute of respect to the dead king of Christian Spain.

As soon as Al-Ahmar received the news of San Fernando's death he ordered a general mourning throughout his kingdom, and sent messengers to express his grief to King Alfonso, with letters proposing to renew with him the treaties of peace and alliance on the same terms as he had made them

---

[1] Gestoso, *Noticia historico-descriptiva de la bandera de la hermandad de los sastres*, Seville, 1891.
[2] *Ibid., op. cit.*; Zuñiga, i. 145.

with his father,—" terms to which King Alfonso agreed, thanking Al-Ahmar for his courtesy." [1]

He did more to testify his admiration than this brief paragraph suggests; for we find that eight years later Al-Ahmar was still sending representatives to do honour to his dead friend on the anniversary of his funeral.

On May 30 (1260), King Alfonso was in Seville for the anniversary of San Fernando, " and as he was already acclaimed as a saint there was more celebration of his glory than prayer for his rest. . . . The day and its eve were kept as festivals, in which no shops whatever were opened and no mechanics made anything. A magnificent catafalque was erected in the Cathedral, and the towns of the district (*comarca*) attended with their banners . . . so that it looked more like a pilgrimage than a funeral, and some of them brought such great candles that they burnt the whole day. And Ibn Al-Ahmar, King of Granada, who was most attached to the sainted king in life and greatly honoured his memory in death, sent a number of Moslem nobles and a hundred foot soldiers with as many candles of white wax, which they placed around the pyre.

"Those were the days of the greatest concourse and rejoicing which in those times Seville knew; her knights celebrated them with military exercises, the public with dances, and all with joyful shouts of *Santo! Santo!* through which piety and devotion miracles occurred, particulars of which have been forgotten through the lapse of time, although it is known that prodigious events happened." [2]

When we remember that the population of Seville was still largely Moslem at this time,[3] while the towns in the

---

[1] Conde, iii. 39; *Primera Crónica*, 774.
[2] Zuñiga, i. 233.
[3] A grant to the Cathedral, dated 1263, contains the following passage: "For we found that the noble city of Seville was being depopulated and was falling into ruin, and that many houses were

THE PASSING OF SAN FERNANDO

neighbourhood can hardly have had any Castilian inhabitants at all beyond the troops in the service of the noble or *Rico Ome* in command, this description of the general celebration of the anniversary of the death of the Christian who had conquered the country speaks eloquently of the political conditions of the time. Instead of regarding the king who had driven out their Almohade rulers as an enemy, the Moslems of Seville worshipped him as a saint.

If we only had the word of the Christian chroniclers for the feeling shown by his Moslem allies and subjects, we might attribute something of San Fernando's reputed popularity to the natural exaggeration of pious writers. But every mention made of him by the Arabic writers quoted by Conde confirms the facts as stated by the Christians. It is impossible to doubt that San Fernando won his canonisation at the hands of the people he had recently conquered, by his just and generous treatment of those of alien faith who had surrendered peaceably through the mediation of Al-Ahmar. These, with certain exceptions, included the whole population of what is now the Province of Seville and part of that of Cadiz, and consisted of the descendants of the Yemenites and Gothic Christians who had for so many generations acknowledged the dominion of the offspring of Witiza.

By the time that San Fernando died all that tract of country which had been ruled in turn by the Princess Sara and her descendants the Beni Hejjaj, and by their fellow-tribesmen the Abbadites of Seville, had contentedly accepted the domination of the first Christian king who had ruled in Seville since the death of Witiza. The only towns of importance yet to be subdued were Jerez, Niebla, and Tejada,

being destroyed through the fault of those [Christians] to whom they were given, and through the men who left them empty and ill-kept." (Zuñiga, i. 260.)

which were still occupied by Almohade governors and commanders. San Fernando left the *tierra de Sevilla* in peace and prosperity. It is no wonder that after so many years of unrest and misrule at the hands of their racial and religious enemies the Moors of Africa, these peasants and labourers blessed the name of the Christian king who had emancipated them from their tyrants the Almohades.

More than six centuries and a half have elapsed since San Fernando was gathered to his fathers, but still every year the silver casket in which his body lies is opened, the brocaded curtains are drawn aside, and the face of their saint is shown to his people, as it has been shown on the anniversary of his death every year since he died.

And although the kingdom built up by Al-Ahmar was destroyed and his subjects persecuted and banished many centuries ago, and there is now no Moslem guard of honour to keep watch over the coffin, strangely enough Granada is still represented in the ceremonial of the day. For it is the privilege of the regiment of infantry called after that city to keep guard in the Royal Chapel when the casket is opened and the people file by to look at the mortal remains of San Fernando, and lest their connection with the fall of Islam in Spain be forgotten, the memory of the conquest of Granada is perpetuated by the gloves worn by the troops, which are green like the banner of the prophet.

But it is not the conquest of Seville nor the victory over the "infidel" that has been celebrated by nearly thirty generations on the festival of San Fernando. It is the gift of peace to the poor and needy, and of the even-handed justice which made peace possible, which are commemorated in the worship offered up at the shrine of the warrior-saint, "the most true, the most generous, he who most feared God and who did God most service," who won the people to his God, not by force, but by example.

CHAPTER XXI

ISLAM UNDER CHRISTIANITY

THE most noticeable feature in the policy adopted by Fernando after the surrender of Seville is his insistence on the absence of distinctions between the members of the two religions. In addition to Al-Ahmar of Granada, whose forces formed part of Fernando's army, the Kings of Murcia, Baeza, and Valencia were his vassals or allies, and appear to have taken part in the siege.[1]

Al-Ahmar is named before any of the Christian knights as receiving honours for his services, and from that moment until San Fernando's death four years later, the monarch seems to have been at special pains to secure even-handed justice for his new subjects, not only as to rewards for services rendered in the field, but in all the common details of daily life.

San Fernando knighted Al-Ahmar on the day of his entry

[1] The King of Valencia, Sid Abu Zeyd (Zuñiga calls him Seit Abuceit), one of the Beni Hafss (see Gayangos in Makkari, ii. 528), was afterwards baptised, took the name of Vicente Velbis, and is known in Spanish history for a miraculous appearance of the Cross which is worshipped at Caravaca. It is a double cross with four arms, supported by cherubim, and is to this day reputed to exercise a miraculous effect upon the diseases of cattle. The King of Baeza also became a Christian under the name of Fernando Abdelmon, and was buried in the Cathedral of Seville (Zuñiga, i. 50). The author of the *Memorias para la vida de Fernando III.*, who refers to a papal rescript in confirmation, says that both "Zeyt Abenzeit" and his son were baptised and professed the rule of the Knights of Santiago, to whom the son "gave all the kingdom of Zalé in Africa, which was his by right of succession" (p. 562).

into Seville, and, says Zuñiga, gave him for blason " on a field gules a band or with dragons' or serpents' heads at the extremities ; the reward of his loyalty and services." The band issues from the mouths of dragons or serpents, and it is worth noting that in a Spanish translation of Mariana (ii. 625) there is a wood-cut representing a sword in the Royal Armoury of Madrid, said to have belonged to the last of the Nasrites of Granada, in which the guard is formed of two dragons' heads with their tongues hanging out.[1]

Conde confirms Zuñiga's description of Al-Ahmar's arms, though without mentioning Fernando's grant of knighthood, as was perhaps natural in a quotation from an Arabic writer. He says :—

"He (Al-Ahmar) took for arms on a field argent a diagonal band azure, and on it written in letters of gold, ' *La ghalib ila Allah,*'—' There is no conqueror but God,'—because his people used to salute him with the title of *Ghalib* (conqueror) and he replied, ' There is no conqueror but God.' The ends of the band of the shield issue from the mouths of dragons. This same blason his descendants always used, though varying the colours of the shield, which was commonly red, blue, or green, and in the same way they altered the band ; but all preserved the motto of Al-Ahmar."[2]

Apart from the warriors, *Ricos Omes*, noblemen, priests, and religious orders, to whom were granted the dwellings and estates left vacant by the emigrants to Granada, Jerez, etc., and by the Almohades who went to Africa, the mass of the population—of the working population at any rate—must have consisted mainly of Moslems. The Chronicle, it is true, speaks of the numbers of camp followers, tradesmen, and so forth, present with the besieging army (see p. 328) ; but clearly these attendants on an army which was at no

---

[1] Zuñiga, i. 49–50 ; cf. Williams, *Arts and Crafts*, i. 230.
[2] Conde, iii. 38.

time excessively numerous, can have done little towards populating a large town, to say nothing of the highly cultivated suburbs and country districts surrounding it.

Early in 1250 the king proposed to go to Castile, but his son and some of his gentlemen pointed out to him the risks of leaving the city. San Fernando seems to have been somewhat unwilling to relinquish his plan, but was finally dissuaded, according to Zuñiga, by his jester. The jester, who was called Paja (Straw) was so discreet yet so cheerful that the king took pleasure in hearing him talk. While San Fernando was still wavering about the Castile expedition, Paja invited him to an entertainment on the top of the tower (the Giralda). San Fernando accepted, and when they got up the jester told him that the banquet he wished to serve was the beautiful view of the city the king had won, the extensive walls of which were marked by the banners of the *Ricos Omes* appointed to guard them. But he also pointed out how large a portion of the quarters bestowed upon the Christians were empty of inhabitants, and how thickly populated were those of the Moslems. In both conditions alike, argued the jester, there would be inevitable perils should the monarch absent himself, even the risk of losing the city again. San Fernando listened and agreed. " Such," concludes Zuñiga, " ought to be the jesters of all princes." [1]

The importance of the story lies in the indication it gives f the smallness of the Christian population over a year after the surrender of Seville, and it shows how wise was Fernando's policy of not distinguishing against or placing disabilities on his Moslem subjects.

In 1250 Fernando granted to the city of Seville the privileges (*Fueros*) given to Toledo. But whereas the *Fueros* of Toledo were granted to " the Mozarabs, Castilians, and

[1] i. 61.

free men (*Francos*), that to Seville was given to " all the inhabitants " (*todos los vecinos*): as Zuñiga says, " the privilege granted to all the inhabitants of Seville, gentry, citizens, merchants, sailors, and workmen in common, all the rights, franchises, exemptions, and prerogatives which Toledo enjoyed . . . without reserve of any and with the addition of many." The grant encourages horse-breeding, and gives important privileges to "those connected with the sea " (*los del mar*), who were exempted from military in exchange for naval service, and for whom special courts and special legislation were provided.[1]

Not only the Moslems, but the Jews, were treated by San Fernando and his son with favour. They continued to reside in the large Jewry that they had previously occupied, and three mosques were given them for synagogues. They

[1] Zuñiga, i. 62–7. There is a whole series of enactments, from the time of Henry III. to the beginning of the nineteenth century, for the encouragement and regulation of horse-breeding (*Novisima Recopilacion*, Bk. VII. Tit. 29), and to-day the State owns several stud farms, and maintains a staff of experts and attendants to look after them.

The stud-farm system was developed in Moslem Spain as early as the ninth century. In the reign of Al-Hakem I. (822–852), there was a large horse farm and cavalry training school on the banks of the Guadalquivir at Cordova, belonging to the Amir. There were two thousand horses housed in two stables. Each stable was under the charge of ten instructors, and each instructor was responsible for a hundred horses. He had to take care of them, see them fed in his presence, and replace those that became useless, and they had to be always ready to take out each one his hundred horses, at a moment's notice. Only one instructor, however, had to appear at a time to the king's call. On one occasion Al-Hakem, on hearing of a rising at Jaen, secretly despatched one of them after another, each with his hundred horses, and so complete was the organisation of the farm, or school, that no instructor knew another had gone out until one detachment after the other fell upon the enemy. (*Akhbar Majmua*, 116–7, and note.) Nor was it only the Sultan who bred horses, for Ibn Hayyan in his history of the civil war which occupied the whole reign of Abdullah, mentions that in 889 a Yemenite leader who had built himself a strong castle in the territory of Seville not far from Lebrija, made an incursion into a neighbouring island (Lebrija is near the Guadalquivir) where Al-Mundhir, the Sultan's uncle, kept his stud, and having put to death the director of the establishment, carried away all the horses and mares that he found to another strong castle about ten miles from Seville. (Makkari, ii. 449.)

continued to pay the same tribute as they had paid to the Moslem kings, and were favoured by the Jewish Treasurers and Accountants, the king's servants, who had come with him from Castile, "and they settled in this city, as being the general port of the universe, and the most appropriate market for their traffic." Another edict permitted the inhabitants of Seville to purchase real estate from the Moslems, but forbade any attempts to compel a sale, towards which some tendency had begun to appear.[1]

Mention is frequently made in the various grants and privileges of a tax called the *Almojarifazgo*, which was an import and export tax on merchandise. It had been imposed by the Moslems of Andalucia, and San Fernando left it in Seville as he found it.[2] Fernando granted to the Cathedral a tenth of the product of the Seville *Almojarifazgo*, which Alfonso afterwards commuted for an annual payment of 5300 maravedis.[3] This *Almojarifazgo* developed later on into the Customs' dues. On the first Custom House built in Seville, in the year 1587, was an inscription recording that "Seville made this Custom House to serve His Majesty, having in its charge the *Almojarifazgos*." [4]

Argote de Molina, in his introduction to the *Repartimiento* (the record of the grants of houses and land made by Fernando and his son after the conquest of Seville), comments on the value of the document as containing "notices of all the Infantes, Grand Masters, Counts, *Ricos Omes*, and Esquires, *Hijosdalgo* of all the kingdoms of Castile, of Leon, and of the French, Aragonese, Navarrese, Portuguese, Italian, and Moslem knights (*caballeros*) present at the conquest; the names of the settlers, and the grants made to them," etc. These Moslem knights who were given property in Seville were, as Zuñiga tells us, partly those who remained, partly

---

[1] Zuñiga, i. 194–6, 208. [2] *Dict. of the Academy*, s./v.
[3] Zuñiga, i. 349–50. [4] *Ibid.*, iv. 120.

those " who lived with the King of Granada, and inhabited the quarter known as the Aduarejo and the Moreria, where they remained until their expulsion " (in the seventeenth century).[1]

The son of the King of Baeza (see above) was given a house in the parish of Santiago. After the fall of Niebla, in 1257, the ruler of that little state (see p. 310) received a farm or country house (*alqueria*), which was called the Algarbejo in memory of his former domain of the Algarbe, and the garden (*huerta*) of Ben Alhoar, close to Seville, called after him the king's garden (*huerta del rey*) with certain rights in the tithe of oil of the Ajarafe and the tribute of the Jews.[2] This land, which is just outside the line of the old city walls, is now part of the grounds of the Alcazar, and is still called the *huerta del rey*.

The King of Granada received, it would appear, one of the finest houses in Seville, for we read that about 1251 an embassy was sent from Morocco to congratulate Fernando on his victories, and Fernando, in order to honour the ambassador, gave him as a guest to the King of Granada, who was in Seville at the time.[3] Conde does not mention this embassy or the entertainment of the ambassador by Al-Ahmar, but Makkari [4] says that all his life Al-Ahmar was on terms of amity and friendly correspondence with the Beni Merin, from whom no doubt the embassy came. Zuñiga's account, which is confused, suggests that the embassy came from the Almohades; but they would hardly congratulate Fernando on having turned them out of the last of their Spanish possessions.

[1] Zuñiga, i. 195. "Aduarejo" is not in the *Dictionary of the Academy*, but "Aduar," from the Arabic "ad-dawar" means a camp or settlement of Bedouins. Did the Moors or Almohades call the Yemenite Arabs Bedouins ? The distinction of name is curious.
[2] *Ibid.*, i. 182, 222; Conde, iii. 42.
[3] Zuñiga, i. 85.
[4] ii. 344.

In the abstract of the *Repartimiento* printed in Zuñiga,[1] there are some names which appear to be of Arabic origin, such as Alarcon, Aznar, Tafur, Torcat (?), "Venavet" (? Ibn Abbad), whom Zuñiga conjectures to have been one of the "ten most illustrious gentlemen" appointed as a tribunal for certain judicial purposes; and no doubt a careful search through the whole document would reveal plenty more. Zuñiga only mentions persons of high standing. Of lesser people who received small grants of land, the *Repartimiento* mention a number who have Arabic names.[2]

There is an interesting note of Zuñiga's on the use of the word "vassal" at this time. The *Infanzones* who drew pay from the *Ricos Omes* were, he says, called their vassals and belonged to their private forces or guard (*mesnada*); and the members of the king's *mesnada* were called the king's vassals.[3] The *Infanzones* were a class of *Hijosdalgo* with limited powers in their territories. This would account for the fact that on at least one occasion (in 1255) the Viscounts of Bearn and Limoges witnessed a grant of Alfonso's as "vassals of the king."[4] Zuñiga transcribes another grant which these nobles also witness, but not as vassals.[5] As this document was signed before the election of Alfonso as Emperor, they certainly did not sign as vassals of the empire (if those lordships were imperial fiefs), nor were the two Viscounts tributaries or vassals in the ordinary sense of the word. The presumption, therefore, is that they formed part of his guard of honour. The three Moslem Kings of Granada, Niebla, and Baeza, whose signatures are frequently attached as witnesses to documents signed by Alfonso, were no doubt vassals in the ordinary meaning of the word, although they may well have formed part of the guard of honour as well.

[1] i. 162–88.   [2] Espinoza, Pt. II. fo. 14 r.   [3] i. 180.
[4] *Memorias para la vida de Fernando III.*, p. 397.   [5] i. 202.

A good water supply, both for irrigation and domestic use, was as we know a matter of the first necessity to the Moslems, and Fernando III., Alfonso X., and Sancho IV., the first three Castilian Kings who ruled in Seville, having appreciated the virtues of cleanliness in a way that some of their successors did not, all took measures to maintain the supply.

The Council of Seville received a grant in perpetuity of the mills on the Guadaira, with all their houses, rights, and appurtenances, in return for which they were to supply water from the aqueduct known as the *Caños* to "the king's palaces of the Alcazar, the Huerta of Ben Alhofar, and to two fountains in Seville." They were also to keep in repair the pipes of the town, of "Santa Maria" (the Cathedral) and of the Alcazar. In addition to the grant of the mills, which were of great value, the Council received 1000 maravedis a year to meet these charges.[1]

This water is brought to Seville from Alcalá de Guadaira by a Roman aqueduct, it is supplied to most of the large old houses in Seville, either by original grant from the crown or by subsequent purchase, and is now a part of the freehold. Thus these water rights, which are very ancient and excessively intricate, make it almost insuperably difficult for the Council to take over the whole supply from the *Caños* for the use of the town, as has often been proposed with a view to bringing the water supply of Seville up to present needs.

The Council, so far as can be judged, has at no time carried out its share of the bargain by keeping the pipes in order. The leaden and earthen pipes which carry the water through the town have been reduced by the incrustations of centuries to half or a quarter of their original diameter, and there is leakage all the length of the aqueduct, besides a large hole in it close to Seville, through which thousands

[1] Zuñiga, i. 358-9.

of gallons a day have been going to waste for no one can say how long. Thanks to this characteristic neglect, there is now a shortage of water in Seville in spite of the further supply brought by the English Water Co.: yet in Moslem times the *Caños* sufficed not only for the domestic needs of a populous town, but for numerous bath-houses, which must have been of considerable size and importance, for they were the subject of special grants in the *Repartimiento*.

Of these baths, three, together with an immense amount of other property, had been owned or held by one " Don Zulema." This man, whose name appears frequently in the *Repartimiento*, but who is not named elsewhere in Zuñiga or in the Chronicle, was the King's Commissioner. There is a letter from Fernando to " *vos Don Zulema, mio mandadero*," informing him that he (Fernando) has given to the Church of Toledo 1000 marevadis from the annual tribute of the King of Granada, and ordering Don Zulema, while he has to collect the rents, to pay this sum to the authorities at Toledo or their representatives.[1] This Don Zulema, we are informed by Don Antonio Ballesteros, who is making a special study of the period, was a Jew, and Fernando's principal man of business.

The royal baths were given to Joan of Ponthieu, widow of San Fernando. How many of them there were Zuñiga does not say, but he mentions that two of them still retained their original form and use when he wrote. One was in the parish of San Juan de la Palma (the building added to by Queen Itimad in 1086, see p. 217), and this stood, tradition says, in the street still called Alcázares (Palaces). Another was in the parish of San Ildefonso. The third in Zuñiga's time had been converted into a convent for nuns of the Order called the Name of Jesus. This was in the district of San Vicente, and until quite lately the street in which it

[1] *Memorias, etc.*, 537–8.

stood still bore the name of "the street of the bath-houses of the Moslem queen" (*calle de los baños de la reina mora*). Indeed to this day the street, now officially re-named Marques de Tablantes, is never called by rich or poor anything but the *Calle de los Baños*. There were other royal bath-houses, but these three are the only ones of which details are given.[1]

A bath-house in San Salvador is granted by Alfonso to the Chapter of Seville, and another one is specified in a further donation to the Cathedral of the country estate of Rianzuela, with various appurtenances, and the *atahona* (which means a horse-power mill or a public bakehouse), "all of which were formerly the property of the Infante Don Fadrique."[2]

Alonso Morgado, who wrote towards the close of the sixteenth century, mentions some of these bath-houses, and says that "in the great rooms where people bathe are pipes running with hot and cold water, with which, and with a certain unguent which is given them, they refresh and clean their bodies; nor is any one in Seville surprised that ladies should go to the bath openly, this being the custom there from time immemorial."[3]

Public bathing places for the use of the poor are placed every summer on the banks of the river by the Town Council, and hours are assigned for their use by men and women respectively, as was done in the public bath-houses described by Morgado in the sixteenth century. Tradition says that these date from time immemorial. They certainly were not instituted since the Inquisition, and we feel no hesitation in affirming that they are a heritage from Moslem times.

We hope in the future to refer to the personal cleanliness of the Andalucians. The surprising thing is that it should

---

[1] Zuñiga, i. 162.
[2] *Ib.* i. 352–3. The building which is now the convent of Santa Clara was the palace of this prince, and a tower bearing his name still stands in the convent garden.
[3] Quoted in Palomo, *Riadas*, p. 144.

have persisted for so many centuries, in spite of the opposition of the Church and the persecution of the Inquisition.[1]

Not only drinking water and bath rights were carefully legislated for by San Fernando, but the Moslem rules as to dredging the Guadalquivir and other tidal waters were adopted and insisted upon in the case of Christians taking up business on such rivers. There was a tax on the boats "which went to and fro to Cordova" from Seville, and there is mention of royal dues on "porterage" payable by vessels going up the Guadalete to Jerez. For many centuries now these valuable waterways have been closed to all but rowing boats owing to the silting up of their streams for lack of attention. But under the Moslems the water mills above Seville were rented upon terms of dredging the channels which supplied the mills, and the earlier Christian kings granted leases from the Crown on similar conditions.[2]

Throughout his legislation San Fernando's aim seems to have been even-handed justice to all his subjects alike without distinction of religion, for the Moslems are relieved of certain taxes, and it is set forth that they are to pay only what before the capitulation they paid to "the Miramolin Menin."

And Alfonso X., in concluding a privilege in which he recapitulates clauses drawn up by "the very noble, very elevated, much honoured and well-fortuned King Don Fernando" his father, charges all whom it may concern faithfully to keep the law:—

"And let no one to dare to go against this my privilege, nor to contravene it, nor to diminish it in any way. For he who shall do or wish to do that shall incur the ire of the Omnipotent God, and shall descend with Judas the traitor

[1] On one occasion a gardener was tortured for having washed himself at his work; and in 1566 the use of baths was forbidden under severe penalties. (Lea, *Moriscos*, pp. 129, 229.)
[2] Zuñiga, i. 200.

to the bottom of hell, and shall besides open my wrath, and pay me in penalty a thousand pounds of gold, and to them [the injured persons] they shall pay all the damage doubled ; and because this is my privilege of this my gift, and that these my liberties shall be more firm and abiding, and stand for ever, I order it to be sealed with my seal of gold." [1]

Then the king signs the deed, and has it witnessed by three Princes of the Blood Royal, three Archbishops, three Moslem Kings, two French Viscounts, twenty Bishops acting and elect, the Grand Masters of two Military Orders, and thirty-five Knights and *Ricos Omes* of the most distinguished in the State.

Thus it was made manifest that the conquered Moslems of *la tierra de Sevilla* were to be treated with as much dignity as their Christian fellow citizens, if San Fernando and the wise Alfonso could secure justice for them. Had their descendants employed the same wide charity and broad statesmanship in their dealings with the alien race, Spain might have kept through all the centuries the place she then held as the most enlightened and most prosperous nation in Europe.

[1] Zuniga, i. 201. It is interesting to observe that the seals are attached to one of San Fernando's privileges with ribbons of red and yellow, showing that these colours were adopted by the Kings of Castile over two centuries before the discovery of America and the fighting in that continent gave the Spanish banner the name of "a river of blood between two streams of gold."

CHAPTER XXII

EGYPT AND THE CHURCH IN SEVILLE

IN Chapter VII. we have traced the influence of the Copts in the arts and crafts of Seville; and we shall now give some account of a dogma of the Roman Church which colours and is intimately connected with the daily life of the Sevillians, and which, unless we are mistaken, has certain features which are more or less directly traceable to Coptic influence. This is the dogma of the Immaculate Conception of the Virgin, with its curious symbol, ubiquitous in local art, of the Virgin's " heraldic arms."

In his *Foundations of the Nineteenth Century*, Mr. Chamberlain says :—

"It is an old idea that God becoming man was born of a virgin, but the worship of the 'mother of God' was taken from Egypt. . . . In the history of mythological dogma, nothing can be so clearly proved as the direct, genetic connection of the Christian worship of the 'mother of God' with the worship of Isis. In the latest times the religion of the chaos that dwelt in Egypt had limited itself more and more to the worship of the 'son of God'—Horus and his mother Isis. Concerning this the famous Egyptologist, Flinders Petrie, writes: 'This religious custom had a profound influence on the development of Christianity. We may even say that, but for the presence of Egypt, we should never have seen a Madonna. Isis had obtained a great hold on the Romans under the earlier Emperors, her worship was fashionable and widespread; and when she found a place in the other great movement, that of the Galileans, when fashion and moral conviction could go hand-in-hand, then her triumph was assured, and as the Mother Goddess she has been the ruling figure of Italy ever since.' "[1]

The orthodox doctrine of the Incarnation was denied by the Copts at the cost of centuries of persecution on the part of the Byzantine Church, because to the mystical mind of the Egyptian it was a degradation of the Divinity to attribute to God the weaknesses of humanity. To them the Son of God was Horus, symbolised by the rising sun, born of the Almighty, Osiris, the midday sun, the source of all life, and of Isis the eternal Mother; engendered by Khem, the Holy Spirit, the divine libation poured out by Osiris to create new life. All Egyptian symbolism circled, under one name or another, about these four persons, each of whom was perfect individually, yet formed an indivisible part of the other three. Thus the Christian doctrine of the Trinity and of the motherhood of Mary was readily accepted by the Egyptians, since to them it was little more than calling their old gods by new names. Then came the schism on the question of the nature of Christ, and, as Gibbon says, persecution converted a sect into a nation.

The Copts never depicted the dead Christ, and, as Dr. Butler says, to speak of a Coptic crucifix is to speak of what was never found. At the same time the idea that the Copt strictly observed the prohibition of " graven images " is not tenable, in view of the many Coptic tombstones carved with birds, beasts, and human beings, the cedar panels from the Church of Mohallakah at Cairo (now in the British Museum) and the innumerable designs representing men, women, and animals, on the woven and embroidered fabrics found in Coptic tombs.

One striking characteristic is to be noticed in all this

[1] *Foundations of the Nineteenth Century*, ii. 28.

Monophysite art. However rude it may have been in its earlier stages, the idea represented is invariably one of happiness and content, never of pain and sorrow. The Copt deliberately closed his eyes to every suggestion of suffering in the Christian creed, and dwelt only on the beautiful and the divine.

Among the various images and paintings which tradition and technique alike lead us to attribute to the Christians who maintained their religion in Seville previous to the reconquest, representations of Christ as man are very rare. For medieval crucifixes and paintings or sculptures of the dead Christ we must go to northern Spain. Survivals of this early art in Seville (which, few though they are, are more numerous than is generally supposed) represent the Mother and Child alone, every suggestion of pain or grief in connection with them being studiously avoided, just as such suggestions are absent from the sculptures which have been found in Coptic churches and monasteries dating from the third to the thirteenth century.

We have already related the legend of San Fernando's "miraculous" vision of the mural painting known as the *Virgen de la Antigua*. Other images of great antiquity also exist in Seville, which we hope to discuss fully in a subsequent volume; for the present we need only say that although the *Virgen de la Antigua* has been so often repainted that much of its original character is lost, another picture of the Virgin, known as the *Virgen del Corral*, which must be at least a century earlier than that of the *Antigua*, bears an unmistakably Egyptian stamp. The eyes are those of Egypt, the head-dress is Egyptian, the mouth is that which one sees in Coptic women to-day—a mouth which no one who has attempted to draw the outlines of the rounded lips will mistake for a Greek or Latin type. The height of the figure, much greater than life, and the position of the Child, pressed close to the Mother's breast, might be Byzantine, but the draperies, like the head-dress, have no semblance of the Greek. The Virgin of the Corral is instinct with the spirit of ancient Egypt, and the eternal motherhood of Isis looks out of the oval Egyptian eyes.

This painting (of which it is impossible to obtain a reproduction) was "miraculously" discovered in a church which was said to have been converted into a mosque not long before the reconquest of Seville. The traditions of all similar images run on the same lines, and all the images said to have been found in the thirteenth and fourteenth centuries bear indications pointing to an earlier date than that of the reconquest of Seville. Were there any doubt on this point, it would be at once removed by comparing these Copto-Gothic Virgins with two images given by San Fernando to the Cathedral of Seville between 1248 and 1252, the genuineness of which is not open to question.

Another important feature, which can hardly fail to carry conviction of the Egyptian origin of this school of art, is the drawing of the eyes. Whether the figure is depicted in wood, stone, paint, or embroidery, the eyes are drawn full face, whatever the position of the head may be. Down to the thirteenth century we practically never find the eye drawn in profile. This curious reminiscence of ancient Egypt is well seen in an early sepulchral stone, carved in low relief and painted, from the district of Zaragoza, which was a stronghold of Yemenite Arabs and Gothic Christians for centuries. The head-dress of the moon shows that the stone is not earlier than the Moslem invasion.[1]

Had the continued existence of the Gothic Church in

---

[1] This sculpture is the property of Don Francisco Anaya of Seville, and may be seen at his house, Calle Lepanto 9. We think the stone image of the *Virgen del Carmen*, also in Seville, bears signs of being a finished product of the same school, with three centuries of development in between.

EGYPT AND THE CHURCH IN SEVILLE

Seville been realised earlier, the provenance of these images would never have been in doubt. The controversy which has been carried on for the last thirty or forty years with so much bitterness between the "Mudéjarites" and the "traditionalists" of Seville on this point has arisen from the ignorance of both parties of the true history of the Moslem occupation. The traditionalists are perfectly right in classing the images as belonging to the Gothic Church in Seville, while the Mudéjarites are equally right when they say that such work cannot by any stretch of probability be assigned to the Gothic Church of the seventh century.[1]

Nowhere else in Spain are there, in comparison with the total number of saints, etc., represented, so many medieval representations of the Virgin as in Seville. However connoisseurs may differ about the paintings and statues in question, the fact that they present artistic features which cause such disputes goes far to prove that they do not date from the reconquest or later, as the Mudéjarites maintain. And there is certainly no small weight in the argument of the traditionalists, that the history of so many and such remarkable representations of the Virgin, whom Sevillians

---

[1] Another ancient image has been the subject of more heated discussion than any of the rest. This is the *Virgen de la Hiniesta* (the genesta or broom) so called because it is said to have been found by a knight named Bernard de la Tous in a copse of broom in Cataluña in 1380. We have no hesitation in saying that this tradition is based on fact, and that the image is the work of a Gothic Christian, produced in some village where Romano-Gothic art traditions survived through the Moslem occupation, as in many places they survive to-day in certain local industries. The drapery is Roman, as is the one sandal visible. The pose of the body, thrown slightly back to counterpoise the weight of the Child on the left arm, is entirely classic, and might have been copied from a Roman statue, while the rounded contours of the head and face, the simplicity of the Virgin's expression, and the arrangement of the hair, have a curious suggestion of Teutonic matter-of-factness and stolidity. The image is of wood, and the right arm has been cut off (!) at an unknown date, to facilitate the dressing and undressing of the image in the silks and brocades with which the pious ladies of Sevillo to-day like to decorate the images they worship. It is in the ancient basilican church of San Julian, and can only be seen disrobed by favour of the parish clergy.

worship with extraordinary devotion, could not have passed unrecorded in the archives of the City and the churches, were they not anterior to the reconquest. It is worth mentioning that the date of the earliest known Sevillian painting of the Crucifixion is the fourteenth century, only one of that date existing, and that in a missal belonging to the Cathedral Chapter.[1]

San Fernando was a devotee of the Virgin all his life, and, as we are told in one of the *Cantigas* written by his son, he placed her image in the mosque and over the gate of every town he won from the Moslems.[2] The Sevillian Church has always been pre-eminent in her cult. The newly-conquered region was, and is, called "The land of the most blessed Mary" (La tierra de Maria santisima), and "the sweet mystery of the Immaculate Conception," or, as the mass of the people call it, "the Mystery," was soon the object of a passionate devotion, giving rise in later years to strange acts of self-abnegation. Thus in 1618 two negroes, named Domingo de Molina and Pedro Moreno, and in 1653 another, unnamed, actually put themselves up to auction in order to pay for Masses for the Feast of the Conception. Whatever may be thought of the motive, it would be difficult to imagine a more complete sacrifice of self on the altar of religion.[3]

The Immaculate Conception has always been the most popular of the many festivals of the Church in Seville, and there is not a church in the city where an altar to "the mystery" is not found. Seville was the first city to solicit from the Pope the declaration of the dogma of the Immaculate Conception, and threw herself so energetically into the prolonged controversy between the Franciscans and the Dominicans,—the former of whom maintained while the latter denied the miraculous birth of the Virgin,—that Sevillian

---

[1] *Glorias Sevillanas*, pp. 45–6. [2] Zuñiga, i. 303.
[3] *Glorias Sevillanas*, 501–2, 531.

ecclesiastical writers claim that the declaration eventually was due to this city. In 1613 a Dominican preached a sermon in Seville impugning the popular belief, which threw the whole town into an uproar, and processions headed by a Franciscan bearing the banner known as the *Sin pecado* [1] took place daily and were attended by thousands of persons. Their object was to make amends to the Virgin for the " insults " levelled at her by those who refused to accept the belief in the " mystery."

These functions of *desagravio* to the Virgin (compensation for an injury inflicted) still take place on occasion. So recently as March, 1911, they were organised all over the country by her worshippers, as a protest against certain irreverent expressions used by a deputy to the Cortes in an attack on the Religious Orders. The life-size image of the Virgin given by San Fernando to the Cathedral, and known as the Virgen de los Reyes, was carried in procession from the Chapel Royal to the High Altar, amid the prayers of a great crowd of men and women of all classes.

In 1615 a Sevillian named Miguel del Cid composed and a priest named Bernardo del Toro set to music some verses, of which the refrain is—

> " *Todo el mundo en general,*
> ' *A voces Reina escogida*
> *Diga que sois concebida*
> *Sin pecado original.*' "

(Let all the world in general shout aloud, " Chosen Queen, you are conceived without original sin.")

The hymn, and especially the refrain, achieved instant and immense popularity in Seville, which has never decreased from that day to this. The original air, however,

---

[1] " Without sin." The full title is " the banner of Mary most pure, born without spot of original sin." The *Sin pecado* is much in evidence in Seville during the processions of Holy Week.

does not seem to have lived in the public memory, and the refrain has been adapted to endless different hymns to the Virgin during the three hundred years that it has been sung. It will be observed that the poetical gifts of the worthy Miguel were not commensurate with his piety.

It became the custom at that time in Seville for the supporters of the miraculous birth of the Virgin to place her monogram, the interlaced A.M., on the fronts of their houses. It was adopted as the badge of the Franciscan party in the controversy, and was introduced into all sorts of artistic design in the sixteenth and seventeenth centuries: so much so, indeed, that it practically dates certain developments, especially in what we should now call " art needlework " and in pottery.

The night watchmen of Seville, who until quite recently used to cry the hours, invoked the Immaculate Conception, for their cry was—

"*Ave Maria purisima, la una ha dado y sereno*"

(Hail, Mary, most pure! One o'clock has struck and a fine night.) From this cry the watchmen get their popular name of *Sereno*.

Every child is taught as soon as it can speak, to invoke the Immaculate Conception in its prayers, in the words *Bendita sea la inmaculada Concepcion de la Virgen Maria* (Blessed be the immaculate Conception of the Virgin Mary). The great majority of Sevillian women bear the name of Mary with one of her attributes, as, *e.g.*, Mary of mercy (Mercedes), Mary of pain (Dolores), Mary of help (Amparo), of the rosary (Rosario), of the pillar (Pilar), and so on. And perhaps the most curious of the many local customs arising out of the cult of the "mystery" is that of invoking the purity of Mary when changing the underclothes. This is done by both men and women, the putting on of clean linen being held to symbolise the limpid whiteness of the soul wrapped in the contemplation of Mary's sinless birth.

In Seville there are more altars erected to the Virgin than in any other city of the same size. Between thirty and forty of her images are brought out in procession every Holy Week, besides which there are a great number which are never moved from the chapels dedicated to them in parish and convent churches.

And now we must draw attention to the special feature in the art history of this Sevillian cult which seems to link it closely with Egypt.

From early days we find here the design which is called the heraldic arms of the Virgin; the pot or jar from which springs a plant with a flower symmetrically placed on either side. Elsewhere, *e.g.* in Italian art, the lily is held by the Angel Gabriel or is placed in a pot beside Mary, and has come to be looked upon merely as a poetical suggestion of the virginal purity of the maid to whom the angel announced the birth of the Saviour.

But in Seville the symbolism refers to the conception of the Virgin herself, for in the church of the Convent of Santa Clara is a bas relief forming part of the reredos of the high altar, in which the figures of St. Anna and St. Joachim are represented with a stem springing from the breast of each, whose extremities unite in a flower like a water lily, and seated within that flower is the Virgin Mary. We have found a similar conceit in more than one church in the rural districts of the province of Seville.

From the time of Ferdinand and Isabella onwards we continually find the design known as the *Jarra* (jar or vase) of the Virgin: but that the idea is of much earlier date is shown by the fact that by the end of the fifteenth century the flowers had become so conventionalised as often to resemble no known botanical type. And there is historical evidence that the symbol was a good deal older, for in 1403 an Order of Knighthood is recorded to have been founded by Fernando of Antequera, afterwards King of Aragon, "in honour of Santa Maria de la Antigua de la ciudad de Sevilla," which was known as *La Orden de la Jarra de Azucenas* or *de los Lirios* (the Order of the Vase of Lilies or Irises), the heraldic device of which the Chapter of Seville took as its coat of arms in honour of the image of the *Antigua*.[1]

The jar of lilies is to be seen in many places in Seville Cathedral. It figures in large medallions in the marble pavement of the transept immediately below the high altar, and it is displayed in wrought iron over the gate of the chapel *de las doncellas* (of the maidens), which was founded early in the sixteenth century and endowed with funds to provide dowries for poor girls. Over this gate is a representation in iron of the Annunciation, with the jar of lilies between the Angel and the Virgin. It also appears in one form or another in all the beautiful seventeenth century lace albs which are used in the cathedral at great festivals.

Why should this symbolism have been referred in Seville to the Immaculate Conception, while elsewhere the lily is merely introduced as a picturesque adjunct in representations of the Annunciation?

In Egypt the lily of the Nile, which poets if not botanists call the lotus, pervades every class of ornament. It is, says Professor Flinders Petrie, "so widely spread that some have seen in it the source of all ornament."[2] The lotus in ancient Egypt was one of the symbols of Khem, the element of life, the libation with which Osiris fertilised the world. It was therefore placed on Egyptian altars, where its pointed petals rose up like flames towards the

---

[1] Chronicle of Aragon, quoted in Serrano, *Tradiciones Sevillanas*.
[2] *Egyptian Decorative Art*, p. 61.

object of worship; and thus it came to be adopted as the
"altar lamp," emblem of the eternal fire wherewith Osiris
regenerates the earth.[1]

Probably the adoption of the lotus or water lily as
the emblem of the fertilising spirit gave rise to the ancient
Andalucian tradition that a woman who ate of the root
of the lily would become miraculously pregnant. Therefore, says tradition, the lily was adopted as the arms of
Mary, the virgin mother, who was herself conceived without
human agency.[2] But whence could have come this essentially Egyptian tradition of the lily and the Khem, unless from
the Copts, who brought here their old Egyptian beliefs
thinly disguised under Christian names?

This is not the place to show how the historic lotus of
the Nile, the altar-lamp of the Egyptian, gradually became
conventionalised into the jar of lilies of the fifteenth century,
and thence into floral forms resembling no flower that ever
grew: in the future we hope to give designs showing this
evolution from the lotus of the head-band of Nefert to its
descendant in Andalucian handicraft to-day. But we may
mention, as an instance of the extraordinary persistence
of tradition, that we recently heard a flower-form of the
eighteenth century confidently called " the lotus " by a
Sevillian gentleman who on inquiry told us that he had not
the remotest idea why he gave it that name. It was quite
unlike any real flower, but certainly a sport from what
Fischbach calls a lotus in his "Saracenic" examples.

We may be wrong in thinking that the heraldic arms of
the Virgin, as symbolising her immaculate conception, are

---

[1] Gayet, *L'Art Copte*, pp. 73, 104–5.
[2] One would suppose that this symbolism would be taken to refer
more especially to the miraculous birth of Jesus; but Lady Day,
although of course a festival of the Church, is not observed with anything like the same general interest and devotion as that of the Immaculate Conception.

peculiar to this part of Spain, for we cannot obtain in Seville access to works on Christian Iconography and Symbolism. But we feel safe in assuming that the Egyptian origin of the *Jarra* design in lace and textile work is not generally recognised, for none of the accepted authorities that we have been able to consult mention it as such, while its origin is discussed and admitted to be unknown. The strong resemblance between the seventeenth century Antwerp Potten Kant design with its two widely separated branches, and the fifteenth and sixteenth century *Jarra de la Virgen* so constantly seen in Seville, seems clear evidence that the earlier idea was introduced into the Low Countries while they were under the dominion of Spain. Miss Sharp [1] mentions that some authorities have considered the Potten Kant to be " a survival from an earlier design including the figure of the Virgin and the Annunciation," but adds that " it is not known that any such larger composition has ever been seen." It is undoubtedly, as Miss Sharp suggests, a traditional design relating to the Virgin, but in Seville it takes a far more important place as a symbol of Mary's own miraculous birth than as an adjunct in pictures of the Annunciation.

The " Lily of the Nile " is not commonly seen in this part of Andalucia. The little yellow water-lily grows wild, to a limited extent, in the Guadaira, two or three miles from Seville, but the white water-lily is not, we believe, indigenous to this region, nor is it cultivated in gardens here. Thus we cannot attribute to any local influence the traditional employment of the flower in design. Nor must it be supposed that its original significance is present in the minds of those who still reproduce the graceful outlines of the Egyptian altar candle. To them it is merely " *la flor*,"—" the flower " *par excellence*. Why it should be so they never dream of

[1] *Point and Pillow Lace*, p. 158.

inquiring. They introduce "the flower"—often now a flower only by courtesy—into their work because their fathers and mothers did so before them. The respect of the Andalucian peasant for tradition is immense. He is Egyptian in his reverence for the dead.

Our readers, few of whom probably have any intimate acquaintance with Sevillian traditional design, may think we are inclined to labour this Lotus or Lily-of-the-Nile idea. But those who have seen our collection of examples of the Lotus, "Lotus-tree" and Lotus "Altar-candle" designs, numbering over a hundred of all varieties, are impressed, like ourselves, with the amazing persistence of the tradition. For it is not one among many floral types, conventional or otherwise. It is hardly too much to say that "*la flor*" forms some 95 per cent. of all the flower forms represented in the provinces of Seville, Huelva, and Cadiz, and in the district of the Algarbe, whatever the material in which the design is found, and in modern and antique work alike. In its purest forms it is always the Egyptian lotus, never the Greek, and the strangest fact in this continual reproduction of the ancient symbol of life is that we find it in work—*e.g.* furniture—produced some fifty or a hundred years ago, perfect in outline but placed upside down, proving that the artist had no idea what was represented by the form which he delighted to produce. We doubt if in any other country there is so persistent a tradition of the kind, always excepting Egypt, where, as we began by saying, the lotus seems to be the basis of almost all decorative art.

CHAPTER XXIII

THE INDUSTRIES OF ANDALUCIA UNDER ISLAM

In conclusion we will give a list of towns and cities colonised by Yemenites and Egyptians in the eighth century or later, or retaining their Christian population by treaty or alliance with the Moslems, many of which are recorded by Moslem writers as noted for art or industries.[1]

In several cases the tribal or family names are not given, and in many cases special industries carried on in minor places populated by Yemenites or Muwallads are not named. Further research, however, will certainly strengthen the evidence that the Yemenites, Egyptians, and Gothic Christians living under the Moslem dominion, were the manufacturers, artizans, and mechanics who provided not only the articles of luxury used in the Court of Cordova, but also the materials for the extensive export trade with the East which so greatly enriched the Khalifate of Cordova under Abderrahman III.

ALCALÁ DE GUADAIRA (*Kalat Yahsob*). Tribe of Yahsob. Dominion of Princess Sara. *Industries*: Bread for the consumption of Seville, from Roman times. Horticulture.

ALCALÁ LA REAL (*Kalat Said*. The *Alcalá de Aben Zaide* of the thirteenth century chronicles). Beni Said, descendants of Princess Sara.

---

[1] We do not include industries of to-day, unless they have some apparent relation to the traditional Arabic work.

INDUSTRIES OF ANDALUCIA UNDER ISLAM

ALGECIRAS. Khamdani. Maaferi. The Castle of Torrox, part of the estate of Almansur, was here. A tower still stood in the seventeenth century, which appears to have belonged to Almansur's Castle of Torrox.

ALICANTE. Territory of Tudmir. Retained by the Christians by treaty with Abdalaziz, son of Musa Ibn Noseir, in 714. Always Christian and Yemenite. *Industries:* *Esteras* (reed mats), which are still made in different districts where the Christians were numerous under Islam, and have always retained the Latin name employed by the Goths. Horticulture, especially grapes for the raisin industry.

ALMERIA. Tribes of Jodham and Ansar among others. Always Yemenite, although in the eleventh century the government was usurped by a Berber, who retained it for many years. *Industries :* Shipbuilding (there was a celebrated dockyard here from the tenth century, if not earlier); brocade, damask, *tiraz*, utensils of glass, iron, copper ; candied fruits. Horticulture. According to Ash-Shekundi, who wrote previous to 1231, factories were established here by Christian merchants under the Yemenite Amirs, who traded largely with Italy. (Cf. p. 270, dealings of Mardanish with Pisa and Genoa). Señor Gudiol, in his *Arqueologia Sagrada* (p. 409, note), mentions silken fabrics purely Arabic in style called *drap d'aur de Spanya, ceda de Spanya,* and *ceda girasol de Spanya*,[1] which he has found named in early Catalonian inventories. These probably were produced in the Spanish-Christian factories established in Almeria and elsewhere under Mardanish in the twelfth century.

BADAJOZ. Tribes of Hadramaut, Tojib. The Beni Moslemah, descendants of Princess Sara, founded the dynasty of Beni Al-Aftas in eleventh century. *Industries :* Horticulture, fine woodwork, and pottery.

BAEZA, Christian, part of the territory of Prince Artebas.

[1] Spanish cloth of gold, Spanish silk, and Spanish shot-silk.

Many Yemenites, tribal names not stated. *Industry:* Saffron.

BALEARIC ISLES. Tribe of Jodham. *Industries:* Horticulture, fine pottery.

BEJA, now in Portugal, but formerly included in the boundaries of Andalucia, which extended as far north as Coimbra. Colonised by Egyptians and Yemenites, including the tribe of Yahsob. *Industries:* Tanyards, manufactures of cotton materials, silver mines. Pillow lace and needlework with designs of a strong Copto-Arabic flavour are still produced all over this district.

CALATRAVA. (Province of) Tribe of Jodham. The town of Almagro in this province is the centre of a pillow-lace-making industry, the origin of which is lost in the mists of antiquity. The earliest examples known imitate the technique of pillow-lace found in the tombs of Antinoë.

CINTRA. Tribe of Lakhm. *Industry:* Horticulture. Enormous water-melons are recorded as having been grown here in the eleventh century. From the Arabic name *sindi* or *sindiyyah* is derived the Spanish *sandia*.

CUENCA. Early history as yet undiscovered. *Industry:* Woollen carpets. In the eleventh century the city belonged to the Lakhmite dynasty of Seville, and was given as part of the dowry of Princess Zaida on her marriage with Alfonso VI. It then had an advanced school of ivory carving, the designs of the earliest existing examples being markedly Copto-Arabic in style. One of these is in South Kensington Museum, another in Pamplona Cathedral. In 1373 Cuenca was claimed by the Countess Mary of Alençon, in right of her descent from Fernando de la Cerda, son of Alfonso X. of Castile. A lace industry was established at Aurillac in the fourteenth century. We are not able to say whether Aurillac was a part of the possessions of the Count of Alençon (brother of Philip VI. of France) at that

INDUSTRIES OF ANDALUCIA UNDER ISLAM

period, but it is worthy of note that Cuenca is mentioned in connection with the fashionable Point d'Aurillac and the enormously costly Point d'Espagne in the seventeenth century, shortly before Colbert set up his factory of Point d'Alençon. It is suggested that Aurillac sent teachers of lace-making to Cuenca, but as Cuenca was then a moribund city, and has steadily declined ever since, until it is now no more than a village, it appears to us more probable, given the connection with the Countess of Alençon, that teachers of lace-making were procured from instead of sent to Cuenca. (This question will be dealt with in our essay on Point d'Espagne, vol. ii.)

DENIA. Yemenite and Christian (Territory of Tudmir). *Industry*: Glazed pottery. The iridescent glazing of pottery in Seville may date from the marriage of Motadid Ibn Abbad with the daughter of Mujahid, Amir of Denia and the Balearic Isles, in or about 1048, although the industry is of immemorial antiquity here.

ELVIRA. Jews and Yemenites. *Industry*: Horticulture.

GRANADA. Largely Christian. Tribes of Hadramaut, Azd, Madhaj. *Industries*: Horticulture, silken fabrics, and many others.

GRAZALEMA. (Province of Sidonia; now Province of Cadiz) Yemenite. *Industry*: Woollen cloth. Still woven here by hand.

IVIZA. Balearic Isles. Yemenite. Salt industry.

JAEN. One of the chief towns in territory of Prince Artebas. Christian, Egyptian, and Yemenite. Its silk-worm industry was of such proportions that the city was called by the Moslems "Jaen of the silk-worms."

JATIVA. Territory of Tudmir. Christian and Yemenite. *Industries*: Linen manufacture and linen-paper.

LISBON AND SANTAREM. Yemenite, but tribe not

mentioned. Internal evidence that Lakhmites predominated.
Industries: Gold and honey.

LORCA. Province of Tudmir. Christian and Yemenite. *Industry:* Mines of lapis-lazuli, the stone being worked and cut on the spot for the export trade to the East.

MALAGA. Tribe of Azd. *Industries:* Mines (metal not named) silks, brocades, *tiraz*, "golden pottery," saffron, raisins, and figs celebrated for their quality all over the East.

MEDINA SIDONIA. Christian and Yemenite throughout history. *Industries:* Pottery of a peculiar dark clay, still found in the Medina claypits, and still dug and worked by hand here. *Esteras,* still made by the Gitanos (Egyptians) of the place, in designs more strongly Arabic than any others we have met with. Agriculture.

MURCIA. (Territory of Tudmir.) Christian and Yemenite. *Industries:* Silken fabrics, carpets, *esteras,* "and other manufactures too numerous to mention" (Ash-Shekundi, writing early thirteenth century). Horticulture, especially fruit.

SALTIS. (Now Province of Huelva.) Muwallad rulers from ninth to thirteenth century. Family of Bekr.[1] The Copto-Arabic flavour in traditional design in all this district is very marked still, as is the Teutonic type among the people. *Industries:* Salt fish for the Seville market, where the consumption was very large: pottery in Roman forms.

SANTA MARIA DE OCSONOBA. (Between Huelva and Faro. The town has disappeared, but the site is marked by the Cape of Santa Maria.) Colonised by Egyptians and Yemenites, eighth century. (See Saltis.)

---

[1] Makkari says the Bekrites of Saltis, Niebla, and Sta. Maria de Ocsonoba, who figure largely in the wars of the ninth and eleventh centuries on the Yemenite or Muwallad side, belonged to a Mudarite tribe, but Señor Pons shows that they were Muwallads, and they seem to have been of the ruling caste, descended from Princess Sara, and related to the Abu Bekr who was an ancestor of Al Kuttiyyah.

INDUSTRIES OF ANDALUCIA UNDER ISLAM

SEVILLE. Tribes of Hadramaut, Hawazen, Khaulani, Morad, and Lakhm. The Christians remained in Seville and the surrounding country undisturbed by the Moslem invasion. It was the Court of Princess Sara, granddaughter of Witiza, after the death of her father Prince Almond.

FAMILIES DESCENDED FROM THE GOTHIC PRINCESS.

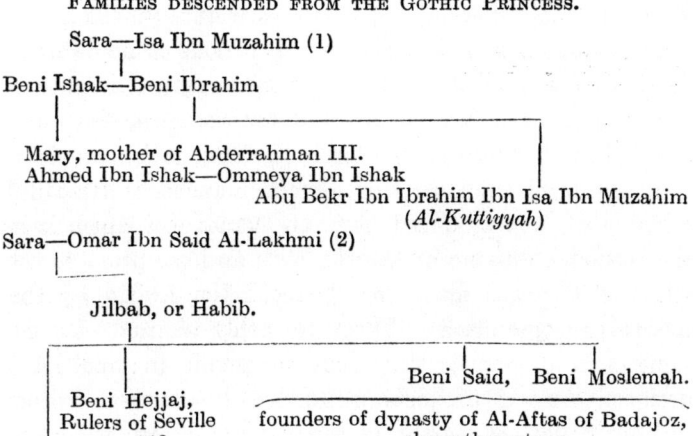

Beni Jurz, or Jorj (George), Christians who held several strong fortresses in the Civil War of the ninth century (St. George was a favourite Coptic saint). It seems probable that the Castle of St. George at Triana was named after them. It bore that name before the reconquest.

The descendants of Sara who adopted the religion of Islam appear to have adopted also the Arab nomenclature. Those who retained the religion of their maternal ancestress may be traced by having held to Christian names. The Beni Hejjaj were people of importance in Seville down to the last quarter of the eleventh century. The name does not appear during the Almoravide occupation, but further research will probably produce evidence of their continued existence here.

As late as 1263 the persistence of the name Alcalá de Ibn Said shows that that branch of the Gothic-Yemenite

Royal family still existed in the district where they had held estates at least two centuries earlier, just as the mention of "Venabet" in the *Repartimiento* of the thirteenth century shows that descendants of the Beni Abbad were yet recognised as persons of importance in Seville at that time. *Industries* of Seville mentioned by different Arabic writers: Shipbuilding and architecture (Seville is the only city mentioned by writers of all periods as noteworthy for the beauty of its buildings in general, and architects were taken from Seville to build for the Almohade and other Moorish dynasties in Morocco), silken fabrics, musical instruments, horticulture in all its branches. Beautiful inlaid work was produced here, an example of which is in the National Museum of Madrid, with an inscription to the effect that it was made for Motamid Ibn Abbad by Ibn As-Seraj (his grandson). Furniture richly adorned with the same class of inlay is still made in Seville in traditional designs. Among products mentioned by Eastern writers visiting Seville as worthy of especial praise, are wine, oil, olives, oranges, limes, citrons, a rare fig called *al-Kutti* (Gothic), and vegetables of every description, including cucumber and lettuce. Cochineal was largely cultivated, also a kind of yew-tree of which bows were made, "which grew here in greater profusion than anywhere else in the world." Dried fruits and cookery are singled out for praise. *Esparto* and *junco* (reed and grass) work was (and is) the occupation of many Gitanos (Egyptians) in Triana, a quarter largely populated by this race. Pottery from time immemorial.

TOLEDO. Capital of the Territory of Prince Romulo, youngest son of Witiza. The population was mainly Christian throughout the dominion of Islam, until reconquered by Alfonso VI. in 1085, in response to urgent appeals made to that monarch by the Christians of the city.

INDUSTRIES OF ANDALUCIA UNDER ISLAM

They were known as Mozarabs, and corresponded to the Gothic Christians of the region of Seville, the dominion of Romulo's eldest brother. The Yemenite tribe of Azd was established at Toledo with the Christians, while the Mudarite tribe of Kenanah, which had a branch here, was settled chiefly in the districts outside of the city. Toledo was always celebrated for its armour and inlaid metal work, an art industry which survives to-day.

UBEDA. Yemenites. Tribe not named. *Industry:* Vine-growing.

VALENCIA. No special mention is made of the tribes which settled here, but they were mainly Yemenite, and Valencia had Yemenite rulers unless they were temporarily overthrown by the opposition party. It has always been renowned for horticulture, and especially for flowers. Arabic writers gave it the names of "the scent-bottle of Andalus" and "the bundle of sweet-smelling herbs." Saffron and an especially fine kind of pear are mentioned as grown there. Ash Shekundi, writing in the thirteenth century, said that Valencia was a garden of delight and the only annoyance was "that the fleas were always dancing to the music of the mosquitos." Valencia is still celebrated for its horticulture and its flowers are still renowned, while excellent pears are grown there and sent for sale all over southern Spain.

ZARAGOZA. Tribes of Hamdani, Tojib, and Khazrej predominated from the time of the Moslem invasion. The industries were salt, horticulture generally, preserved fruits, and *garbanzos*—the Egyptian "chick-pea," which is still the staple food of the peasantry all over Andalucia.

The cities in which Mudarite tribes preponderated were few, and of these the Arabic writers do not mention a single one as noted for any special industry. Mudarite families were, of course, to be found in some of the places named above, but always in a minority. The leather-work, silver-set diamond jewellery, and silver and gold filigree-work of Cordova, although they became celebrated under Christian rule, are not referred to by Arabic writers.

Many other places are named as populated by tribes and families of Yemenite descent, but we have only included in this list those mentioned in connection with arts, crafts, or industries. Although the final expulsion of the Moriscos in the seventeenth century has resulted in the stagnation and decay of almost all the trades and manufactures for which Andalucia was once so celebrated, few of her Coptic or Arabic arts and crafts have entirely died out even now, and were there any demand for such products there is perhaps hardly one of the above industries which could not be revived, by employing, as teachers, men and women who mastered their local industry in their youth. Hand-woven silk ribbons and linen and baskets of Arabic design are still made in Seville and Granada, Grazalema half lives upon her hand-woven woollen cloths, which have the credit of never wearing out; Arabic sweetmeats are made from traditional Arabic recipes in Medina Sidonia and in Gibraleon; stamped leather-work is produced in Seville, where also exquisite embroidered leather-work is still occasionally seen; the Arabic *artesonado* (inlay of woodwork) and *alicatado* (mosaic of hand-cut glazed tiles) are part of the stock-in-trade of every master-carpenter and master-mason in the province of Seville; hand-shaped pottery is made in every village that boasts a clay-pit; and *esteras* are found wherever there is a colony of Gitanos. As for the pillow-lace, netted laces, and embroideries—which were introduced by the Copts and carried to such a pitch of perfection that edict after edict was issued to suppress them as articles of undue luxury from the fifteenth century—they are to be seen in every household. They are only not found in the market because every woman does so much work of the kind that no one requires or desires to purchase it. In one or two of the larger towns the making of "English" lace composed of machine-made braid has become the mode among the leisured class, but off the beaten track *malla* or fish-net, elaborate drawn-thread, the curious pin-lace called "suns," "wheels," and "webs" (*soles, ruedas* and *randas*), and pillow-lace with Arabic and Egyptian suggestions in the design are the chosen employment of all women, gentle and simple.

Unfortunately these things are no longer purchased by wealthy Spaniards, preference being given to foreign machine-made articles in every branch of domestic economy. Stamped tiles are imported at great expense from France notwithstanding the cheapness and singular beauty of the native *azulejos* and *alicatados;* splendid *artesonado* ceilings are pulled down to make room for plaster replicas of Italian pseudo-classic models; beautiful stamped and embroidered leather and rich local brocades are discarded in favour of brand-new satin or plush for the upholstery of mansions and palaces; and imitations of "Louis XV." furniture have ousted the characteristic Spanish cabinets, chairs, and tables of cedar, lignum vitæ, and mahogany inlaid with orange-wood, which formerly held places of honour in kings' houses.

In another generation or two all such arts and crafts will have died out for want of a market, but to-day the work would be forthcoming were it appreciated by the wealthy. A gallant effort to revive and develop the ancient *azulejo* and faïence industry of Seville is being made by the present Director and Secretary of the School of Art there, Sres Pitalugo and Mattoni, but the admirable work turned out by their students meets with small encouragement from the wealthy householders of the city. Great new houses are yearly being built here at the cost of millions of pesetas; but—although cultivated Americans consider the Seville craftsmen good enough to engage as teachers for American Schools of Art—the men who preserve Copto-Arabic traditions have to spend their lives setting up machine-made products manufactured in London, Paris, or New York, instead of continuing to produce the beautiful manual work which they have kept alive for a thousand years.

Fig. 12.—*Convento de la Luz* (No. 3). Arabic arches in "the modern part."

APPENDIX

NOTE TO CHAPTER I

CHAMBERLAIN, in the introduction to his *Foundations of the Nineteenth Century*, remarks that "in Spain it was the Western Goths who formed the element of life." [1] The vitality of this race is evinced by the fact that for nearly seven hundred years they maintained their religion, their customs, even their family names, amid an alien race of hostile creed. From 711 to 1390, when as we have seen the descendants of "the good Goths" were permitted to return to Seville, they held their own not only in their native land, but also in Morocco, when war and persecution drove them out of Andalucia to take refuge with the Moslem rulers who some three hundred years later commended them to the monarch of Castile in the complimentary terms quoted on p. 33.

The history of Andalucia from the coming of Musa to the fall of the Almohades of Seville in 1248 has been so misread that the part played by the Gothic community has not been recognised. It is said that the Goths during their three centuries' occupation of Spain, before the Moslem conquest, had "sunk in the same slough of sensuality that had proved the ruin of the Romans" . . . "gave a fresh licence to the general corruption," and "rivalled if they did not exceed the polished wickedness of the pagans." [2]

The Goths on their arrival in Spain seem to have assimilated the Roman culture as completely as did the Arabs after them. "From the time of the Visigoths" says Dozy, "Seville had been the home of the sciences and the Roman civilisation, and the residence of the noblest and wealthiest families. The Arab conquest had brought about hardly any change in the social conditions." [3] They adopted as their own the Roman style of house-building, which has prevailed in Seville ever since, and carefully preserved and repaired the Roman roads, aqueducts, bridges, and fortresses. The Arabic historians write with admiration of the fortified cities which they found in the south-west of Andalucia, as, *e.g.*, Carmona in the province of Seville, "which

---

[1] i. lxvi.
[2] S. Lane Poole, *Moors in Spain*, pp. 7–8. This writer attributes to the same cause—demoralisation brought about by unaccustomed luxury—the downfall of the Almoravides, but in this case he allows only twenty years for the loss of their martial habits and pleasure in the hardships of war (pp. 183–4).
[3] *G. der M.*, i. 392.

although strong by reason of its situation and its ancient walls, surrendered after the example of Seville and others of Andalucia." On his march from Merida to Toledo, Musa and his forces found " wonderful bridges " the like of which they had never seen, " for they seemed to be the work not of men but of divine Jinns." Among the strong cities which surrendered to him were Niebla, which is still completely surrounded by its Roman walls, Ocsonoba, Mertola, and Beja, which still retains vestiges of Roman walls and a Roman gateway. The surrender of these places without fighting must have been due to Musa's alliance with the Gothic princes, for their strength is not only commented upon by the chroniclers of the invasion, but is confirmed by the resistance some of them were able to offer at a later date. When Niebla, for example, became the head-quarters of the Almohades after the fall of Seville in 1248, she withstood the whole strength of the Castilian army during a siege of several months, thanks to the immense strength of her walls.

The only city that gave Musa any trouble was Merida, where the leaders of Roderick's party had fled, and where his widow was residing. The description of the city quoted by Conde is fully borne out by recent excavations.

"When Musa saw that magnificent city he said to his captains, 'It seems that all men have united their art and power to exalt this city; fortunate is the man who succeeds in subduing it.' He sent to summon the city to submit under the usual conditions; but the citizens, trusting in their lofty and towered walls, replied with disdain." And when at length Merida was starved out and surrendered, and Musa entered it, he " marvelled greatly at its grandeur and its magnificent buildings."[1] Makkari says much less about the siege than Conde, but remarks that "This city was of considerable size; in it were the remains of palaces, temples of vast size and exquisite workmanship, and other public builings."[2]

These " palaces, temples, and other public buildings " are now in course of excavation, and not only bear out all that the Arabs say of them, but prove that the Goths, far from destroying or even neglecting the architectural triumphs of their predecessors, must have been at pains to preserve them; for the amphitheatre, the Temple of Vesta, and other remains recently brought to light are as fine and in as good condition as any known buildings of their date.[3]

Personally we are convinced that rude buildings such as the hermitage of Santiago at Medina Sidonia (see pp.136-7) must not be accepted, as seems hitherto to have been the case, as fair examples of Visigothic architecture. In no country do we find the fine flower of the art

---

[1] Conde, i. 41, 44.
[2] i. 284.
[3] Compare the action of Theodoric, the Eastern Goth, " whose first care it was to take strong measures for the protection and restoration of the Roman monuments " which the Christian fanatics of Rome had been doing their best to destroy. (Chamberlain, *Foundations*, i. 322.)

of a race or a period in remote villages or mountain chapels. Why then assume that such relics of the Gothic dominion in Spain represent the highest art of which the Spanish Goths were capable?

We are inclined to think that as time goes on it will become evident that a good deal of what has been accounted late Roman architecture in Spain is really Visigothic. If it were indeed Roman, some of it would be very decadent. But regarded as the work of a new nation, recently emerged from barbarism, it has features of peculiar interest. This is not the place to go into details of the kind of work we have in mind, the importance of which can only be shown by numerous illustrations; but we hope to deal fully with it in the future.

Wren attributed the pointed architecture commonly known as Gothic to the Arabs, "refined by the Christians:" and we believe it is now generally admitted that the pointed arch came from the East, although the origin of the term Gothic, as applied to the style of which this arch is a leading feature, seems never to have been satisfactorily explained. We therefore venture to hazard the suggestion that the name originated in the style of building developed, under Coptic influence, by the Gothic Christians of Southern Spain. The Gothic tradition has never died out in South-west Andalucia, and the adjective *gótico*—gothic—is still used here in a sense different from that assigned to it elsewhere. Illiterate peasants in the mountains, who certainly know nothing about the terms and periods of European art, apply that adjective to buildings and sculptures of much earlier date than anything that would be called "gothic" in the ordinary sense of the word.

The suggestion that the term "gothic" was applied in derision by cultured Italian architects to early pointed architecture may have had its origin in fact, although at an earlier date than is usually attributed to it. The foreign knights who accompanied the Castilian army in the wars of Fernando III. and his son Alfonso X. in the thirteenth century, may well have been struck by the rudeness of the Christian basilican churches they found in Seville, which, as they were the churches of the Goths, would naturally have been described to them as Gothic.

For at least a hundred years before the reconquest, the primitive pointed architecture of Seville and the neighbouring districts had been restrained from its natural development by the fondness of the Almohades for the horse-shoe arch and the filigree stucco work then in vogue in Moslem countries in the East. The destructive effect of this school upon the Copto-Gothic taste of the territory of Seville may be studied in the Church of San Lucar la Mayor, already referred to as finished in 1214. Here Moorish arches and Moorish decoration are mingled with the purer Gothic work, producing that perplexing combination which the local Mudéjarites have described as "a foreign style produced by Moorish artisans for their Christian masters after the reconquest." This was not the style preferred by the Andalucian Spaniards after the reconquest, for every cathedral, church, and castle recorded to have been built or rebuilt between the thirteenth and the fifteenth centuries conforms to the "Gothic" style then prevalent in Europe.

From the middle of the thirteenth to the beginning of the sixteenth century we can find nothing but Gothic work, and no building of any importance appears to have been constructed in the "Moorish" style in any part of the territory of Seville. Then two famous palaces were built or rebuilt in Seville by the Riberas, one of the leading families in that town in the sixteenth and seventeenth centuries. One was the Casa de las Dueñas, now the palace of the Duke of Alva, which was sold to the Riberas by the original owners to raise money for the ransom of their head, Juan de Pineda, who had fallen into the hands of Moorish pirates, and the Riberas restored and re-decorated it. The other was the so-called House of Pilate, now belonging to the Duke of Medina Celi, a descendant of the Riberas. The decorations of both these houses are a copy of the style affected by the Almohades, and both are of the same period, although that of the Duke of Alva contains traces of an earlier origin, and is doubtless a survival of the Moslem dominion. But they both merely represent the artistic tastes of a single family. Other fine buildings described by the guide books as "Mudéjar" date from the Almohade occupation or earlier, although in some cases decorations and inscriptions of a much later date have been added. The magnificent palace of the Dukes of Medina Sidonia, the surviving portion of which is now a wholesale draper's shop, was redecorated probably in the late fourteenth or early fifteenth century, on the old Moorish lines, but still retains some of the beautiful twelfth century *alicatado* or mosaic of tiles on the ground floor. It was one of the Roman-Visigothic palaces, and has a Roman fishpond and a Roman fountain with a Latin inscription in the garden.

There was never any deep-rooted or general feeling for "Moorish" art in Seville, and it seems quite possible that the rebuilding of the Cathedral, begun in 1401, was decided upon rather because the Chapter wished to be rid of the Moorish aspect of the transformed mosque than because it really was in a ruinous condition. A building erected little more than two centuries before (1175–81) would hardly have been already in ruins.[1] When the whole trend of the period was towards Gothic architecture, it is easy to understand how offensive to Sevillian Churchmen must have been the horse-shoe arches and filigree ornament of the Moors, and how both their artistic taste and their religious prejudices would have impelled them to get rid of everything that could recall the former dominance of the hostile religion.

CHURCHES, IMAGES, ETC., IN ADDITION TO THOSE NAMED IN THE TEXT AS EXISTING DURING THE MOSLEM OCCUPATION.

SEVILLE.—The *Compas de San Miguel* was the dwelling of the Bishops " during the captivity," and at the time of the reconquest was inhabited

---

[1] This may well have been the case, however, it if were—as we now have evidence that it was—the ancient Gothic Cathedral, merely enlarged and adorned by the Almohades.

by Christians. In memory of the Bishops San Fernando gave it to the Cathedral. It is still the residence of the inferior clergy and the choir school of the Cathedral, and is still known as the *Colegio de San Miguel*.

The present Church of *San Nicolas* was used for Christian worship under Islam, and was known as *Santa Maria soterranea*. The (probably Roman) vaults or catacombs which gave it this name are mentioned by Abad Gordillo in the sixteenth century.

Santa Marina had, down to the sixteenth century, an inscription with the date 607 or 670 A.D. ;—one authority giving one and another the other year. Santa Marina (to whom another ancient church in Cordova is also dedicated) has no day allotted to her in the long list of present-day Spanish festivals. This Church, like San Nicolas and many others in Seville, is of the basilica form with Roman columns and capitals, and has Moslem additions in the roofs and side chapels. The west front is adorned with eleventh-century images of Egyptian inspiration, including the Kha as a female figure supporting a bracket, on which sits the Virgin with the Child in a position common in sculptures of Isis and Horus.

San Lorenzo, previous to the reconquest, was a hermitage and hospital dedicated to Santa Barbara. Here is the mural painting known as the Virgin of Rocamador, which is attributed by connoisseurs to not later than the twelfth century.[1]

In the *Cantigas* of Alfonso X. we have found the following references to early churches, etc.

There was an ancient Christian Church in Murcia " in a sacred place of the Mohammedans," which their king (name not given) refused to destroy for fear of the vengeance of " Mariame " (Mary).

Puerto de Santa de Maria, opposite to Cadiz, was called by the Moslems Alcantir, Alcanatir, and Amaria Alcanter. The Al-canter refers to the Roman bridge, of which a vestige is even now visible in the river at low tide, but the Amaria can only be a corruption of the Gothic name. Alfonso X., in a privilege dated at Seville, orders that the place is to be known as El Gran Puerto de Santa Maria, and we find in the *Cantigas* that there was ill-feeling between the two races because the Christians resident there before the place surrendered to Alfonso persisted in calling it Santa Maria, while the Almohades of Jerez desired it to be known only as "Alcanate." When Alfonso finally obtained possession of the town an image of the Virgin was discovered in the moat of the Castle of San Marcos, and the king at once ordered a new church to be begun to receive the image, to which highly miraculous powers are ascribed in the *Cantigas*.[2] (For a description of the primitive church under this castle, see p. 137.) This is now the parish church. It may have been the principal or only mosque, converted to Christian

---

[1] See Zuniga, i. 57–8, and iii. 262–9, and Serrano, *Glorias Sevillanas*, 158, 163, 167.

[2] Idrisi, p. 47. *Cantigas, passim*. Pelayo Quintero y Atauri, in an article on Mozarabic Churches in *Diario de Cadiz*, July 30, 1910.

uses, rather than built, by Alfonso X., for it possesses certain features unlike the generality of thirteenth-century churches here or elsewhere. The fifteenth-century west front is so similar to that of Seville Cathedral on a small scale as to suggest both being the work of one architect. There is no resemblance between this church and that of Santa Ana in Triana, altered by Alfonso in 1282. The Virgin found in the Castle moat is still preserved here as the *Patrona* (patron image) of the town. It is quite small, and is almost black with age.

At Faro, in the province now called the Algarve (the southernmost part of Portugal), there was an image of the Virgin on the seashore "in the time of the Moros." The "Moros" (Almohades) threw it into the sea, and thenceforth not a fish was caught there until the Christians recovered the image, when the fish again became abundant; vide the *Cantigas*.

Santa Maria de Ocsonoba appears to have been the same as the Santa Maria de Al-gharb, both being frequently referred to by Moslem and Christian writers. According to Idrisi, this town was situated somewhere near Silves, on the sea-shore. "It was built on the edge of the ocean, and its walls were washed by the high tide. It was fairly large and very pretty, there was a cathedral mosque, a parish church, and a chapel. Ships landed and arrived and departed from it." (Idrisi, p. 16.) There is a Cape of Santa Maria close to Faro. Many of the landmarks described by Idrisi have long disappeared, but it seems practically certain that this was the place referred to in the *Cantigas*, although, owing to its being very difficult of access, we have not yet been able to visit it ourselves to form a definite conclusion.

At Alcalá del Rio on the Guadalquivir, near Seville, there is an ancient basilican church with pointed arches built into the structure, not added at a later period like many in the early churches in Seville. This retains its primitive dedication to San Gregorio, and it is known to have existed in its present form long before the reconquest.

We feel little doubt, from our own experience, that when all the places named as Christian either by Arabic or Christian writers have been carefully examined, and, if necessary, the remains of their ruined churches excavated, it will be proved that the Christian communities referred to were far larger and more important than is at present imagined. The precise meaning of the term "*mezquita catedral*" in the Spanish translation of Idrisi is not very clear, but the fact that he found at Sta. Maria de Al-gharb two Christian places of worship and only one for the Moslems, is significant, especially as he wrote during the Almohade occupation, when the Christians, if ever, were under the ban of the ruling race.

Before concluding this note, rendered necessary by fresh evidence which has come to light in the years since the first part of our book was begun, we must add a few words about ceremonies used in religious worship in Andalucia which are not, we believe, common to the Roman Church elsewhere.

A wooden bell—really a kind of clapper—called a *matraca*, is used n many churches in Seville and elsewhere on Holy Thursday, when

APPENDIX

no bells are rung. This is Oriental in origin, and therefore cannot be posterior to the Christian reconquest, but must be a survival of Christian usage under Islam.

A very singular ceremony known as the "Display of the Banner" (*Ostentacion de la bandera*) takes place in Seville Cathedral on Holy Thursday. It consists in waving a huge flag of green *tafetán*[1] over two priests who prostrate themselves on the altar steps. It is impossible to obtain any official explanation of this extraordinary rite, which the Cathedral employees describe as "*cosas de la Pasion de nuestro Señor*" ("Something to do with the Passion of our Lord"). We take it to be the survival of some ceremony of submission to the banner of the Prophet imposed upon the Christians by the Almohades as a condition of retaining their religious usages in their primitive Cathedral, after it had been in part, but not in whole, transformed into the principal mosque of the Andalucian capital in the fourth quarter of the twelfth century. There is now incontrovertible evidence, recently brought to light, that the mural painting of the Virgin *de la Antigua* was permitted to remain in its chapel in the south wall of the new mosque, where it was treated with superstitious reverence by the Moslems down to 1248, when San Fernando secretly visited and worshipped at the shrine during the siege of Seville. It is commonly said that the Cathedral was rebuilt from its foundations in the fifteenth century, but a comparison of the ground plan of the wall of the south side with the evidence, written and traditional, makes it certain that a part at least of this wall was left untouched by the rebuilders from the same motives of respect to the chapel and image of *la Antigua* which had induced the Almohades to leave the shrine undisturbed.

The curious "*ostentacion de la bandera*" survives also in the neighbouring town of Alcalà de Guadaira, but here it takes place in the street during the Holy Thursday procession to the Stations of the Cross, and is repeated three times on the road to a steep hill, half a mile away, known as Calvary, which is visited by the whole population in the night previous to the Crucifixion. Another ceremony, that of fanning the officiating priest and the elements during the elevation of the Host during the summer months, is believed to be peculiar to Seville, and undoubtedly dates from before the reconquest. It may have been introduced into the Gothic ritual by the Coptic Christians who came here from Egypt with the Arabs, or may have had an earlier origin. In any case it evidently was carried on here through the domination of Islam.

Note to Chapter II

The various accounts given of Tarik's movements after the fall of Toledo are hopelessly contradictory. Gayangos examined with great care all the evidence available at the time he wrote, with the object,

---

[1] An antique silk material of Oriental origin.

if possible, of identifying the town called Maya, or Medinat-al-Meydah, where Tarik is said to have found the famous table of Solomon. Some of the Spanish writers, according to Gayangos, say that when Sindered, Bishop of Toledo, heard of the approach of the Arabs, he fled to Galicia, taking with him the ornaments and jewels of his church, and that most of the inhabitants followed his example. Isidorus Pacensis says that Sindered went to Rome ("Romanae patriae sese adventat") if that is the meaning of "Romana patria," but says nothing about the jewels. The situation of Maya, however, seems to have been cleared up by the accidental discovery, in 1858, of the celebrated collection of jewels among the ruins of a Visigothic church dedicated to St. Mary, near the little town of Guadamur, Province of Toledo. The collection is preserved in the Museums of Madrid and Cluny.

In a work on the conquest of Spain in the possession of Gayangos—of doubtful authorship, but probably contemporary—there is an account of Musa's expedition to Toledo. He found in that city "a palace called the Beyt-al-Moluk (the mansion of the kings), so named from the circumstance of twenty-four gold diadems, one for each of the kings who had reigned over Andalus, being found in it. Each diadem had an inscription bearing the name of the king to whom it had belonged, and stating the number of children the king had left, the days of his birth, accession to the throne, and death; for it was a custom among the Gothic sovereigns of Andalus that the diadem worn by each of them during his life should after his death be deposited in that mansion. Besides these treasures, Musa found in the same palace a table on which was the name of Suleyman, son of Daud (on whom be peace!) and another table of onyx."[1]

Previous to 1858 such a description as this of the jewels possessed by the Gothic kings of Spain must have seemed a romantic exaggeration, but the treasure of Guadamur shows that the Arabic writer was stating little beyond the bare facts.

The discovery was made by a poor ignorant peasant woman one day when the swollen waters of the little river Guarrazar had gone down after a great storm, leaving exposed to the light of day that which had lain buried alongside of the bed of the stream for over eleven hundred years. She and her husband, all unconscious of the historical importance of their treasure-trove, only thought of selling it as speedily as possible to the jewellers of Toledo, before the authorities could claim it on behalf of the State. Thus various articles of incalculable archæological value were broken up and melted before any one capable of appreciating them knew they had been found. Indeed, but for the fortunate chance that a teacher in the primary school of Guadamur was sufficiently educated to recognise their immense age, when he happened to see one of the jewels in the hands of the finders, the world would have been the poorer by the loss of what even now is probably the most complete collection of seventh-century Christian ornaments in existence.

---

[1] Makkari, i. app lxxii.

We need not give particulars of everything that was discovered, but the note of the Arabic historian quoted above acquires singular interest when we learn that among the objects found on the banks of the Guarrazar were crowns bearing, in letters composed of precious stones, the names of Recesvinth, Svinthila, Sonnic and the Abbot Theodosius, besides a votive cross with the name of Lucetius. There were also many ecclesiastical ornaments which had lost the names of those who gave them to the Church.

The crown of Theodosius bears the following inscription, not formed of pendent gems like that of Svinthila, but engraved on the gold itself—

OFFERET MUNUSCULUM SCO STEPHANO THEODOSIUS ABBA,

while those of the kings only display their own names and the words—

REX OFFERET.

Thus the Arabic historian is shown to have had good reason for his statement that the votive crowns of the Gothic kings were inscribed with their names, and we can hardly wonder if the Arabic historians, who probably knew little or no Latin, should have taken long inscriptions such as that of the Abbot Theodosius to be a condensed record of their whole family history. The crowns were not, however, those worn by the kings and given to the Church after death, but votive offerings presented during life. Every pious Gothic king added two such crowns to the collective treasure of the country;—the one he wore himself, and that which he had made for the Church: a fact which offers a simple explanation of the great number of such ornaments said to have been found by the Moslems when they invaded Spain.[1]

Julian, Archbishop of Toledo in 684, in his history of the rebellion of Paulus against Wamba, apparently refers to some of these treasures, including the crown of Reccared, in a passage quoted by Señor Sentenach, but so full of misprints as to be barely intelligible. We give it here, from the text in *España sagrada*, vi. 554. After remarking that Paul had added sacrilege to tyranny, by stealing the Church treasures, Julian says, "Unde factum est, ut vasa argenti quamplurima de thesauris Dominicis rapta, et coronam illam auream, quam divae memoriae Reccaredus Princeps ad corpus beatissimi Felicis obtulerat, quam idem Paulus insano capiti suo imponere ausus est, tota haec in unum collecta studiosius ordinaret (sc. Wamba) secernere, et devotissime prout cuique competebat Ecclesiae intenderet reformare."

NOTE TO CHAPTER V

CONDE must have used some account of Abdullah's reign to which neither Makkari, Dozy, nor Gayangos had access. The whole of the

---

[1] For a full description of the Guadamur treasures, see *Bosquejo historico sobre la orfebreria española* by N. Sentenach, in the *Revista de Archivos* for 1908, p. 225, and Williams, *Arts and Crafts*, i. 15 ff.

chapters from which we have drawn the above account are written in a style which forbids any doubt as to their being a literal translation. Gayangos, while criticising Conde's work with extraordinary acerbity, and continually calling attention to his mis-spellings and mis-translations, makes no allusion to the passages from which our narrative is largely taken. We cannot suppose that so careful a commentator would have passed over in silence Conde's use of a work with which he himself was acquainted, dealing with a period which he found "despairingly" difficult to understand. Either he would have quoted the author or he would have been careful to explain that the author was not worth quoting. In other chapters Conde mentions Hayyan, and in these we find the same contradictions as in the work of Hayyan himself. But the story of Prince Mohammed and his son, with Abdullah's devotion to Abderrahman in his adolescence, we have not found anywhere except in Conde, and since no one goes so far as to suggest that Conde deliberately invented his history, we are driven to the conclusion that he had lighted upon some Shiite MS. giving all these details of a period which the Cordovan Court chroniclers had left wrapped in obscurity. Considering that even now there are many Arabic MSS. in Madrid and the Escorial not edited, there is nothing improbable in this.

As an example of Hayyan's methods in writing of the Muwallads, his account of the Beni Khaldun incident may be given.

In 889, "the power of the Muwallad faction becoming greater, Abdullah was advised by some of his Wizirs to grant liberty to the Arabian chiefs [including Ibn Hejjaj] who were prisoners in Cordova, and to employ them. They were accordingly conveyed to Seville and set free, after they had severally taken a most solemn oath never again to rise against their lawful sovereign, but to employ all their energies in reducing the Muwallad faction. No sooner had they returned to their respective districts than they again declared themselves in open rebellion and refused to pay the customary tribute. Abdullah, however, having through his Wizir Abdullah Ibn Mohammed Ibn Abi Abdah [Ibn Gamri] succeeded in dividing them, the rebels made war upon each other until Ibrahim Ibn Hejjaj took both Khaled and Koreib [Ibn Khaldun] prisoners and put them to death, by which means the Sultan's authority was re-established in Seville." [1]

If the Muwallads were increasing in power, why did Abdullah permit the great chief of their party to return to his own people instead of holding him as a hostage for the good behaviour of the rest? Our view is that this "imprisonment" was the euphemism employed by Hayyan to describe a visit to Cordova of Ibn Hejjaj, who went from Seville to treat with the Amir as one potentate with another. Elsewhere Omar Ibn Hafsun is also represented by Hayyan as having been in the hands of Abdullah against his will, while another account shows that he was entirely master of his own movements. We can imagine how little the client and chronicler of the Ommeyads would

---

[1] Hayyan in Makkari, ii. 450.

like to admit that such conferences were possible with opponents whom he regarded as contemptible, and how he would think it a duty to his race to distort the facts for the misleading of future generations.

The paragraph following that quoted above is still more unconvincing.

"Ibrahim," proceeds Hayyan, "wrote to announce his victory to Abdullah, and asking to be appointed Governor of Seville. The Sultan granted his request, on condition that he should yearly remit to Cordova the sum of seven thousand dinars, after defraying all the government expenses in the province. Ibrahim consented, and Kasim Ibn Walid Al-Kelbi was given him as lieutenant, but some time after, at the solicitation of Ibrahim, Kasim was recalled and that chieftain remained sole governor of Seville and its district."

The conduct of Ibrahim, who "writes announcing his victory" to the Sultan against whom he had been fighting, and whose clients he had put to death by way of establishing order—for we are told that he had killed the brothers Koreib and Khaled Ibn Khaldun "because they opposed the rebellion and preached obedience to King Abdullah," [1] is hardly that of a prisoner set free on condition that he should never again dispute the authority of the person he addresses. Neither is Ibn Hejjaj's demand to be appointed sole governor of Seville precisely the act of a conquered man appealing to an offended ruler. Conde, as usual, does not give the authority for his account of the episode, but it ends with a vague reference to mischief made at Cordova through the unfair use of letters written by Ibrahim Ibn Hejjaj to Ibn Khaldun in which the poet Kalfat (" a man as malignant as he was clever," see p. 74) was concerned, so the passage is probably taken from the author quoted by Dozy in regard to the betrayal of Ibrahim through letters written to Khaldun.

NOTE TO CHAPTER X

ON THE ALLEGED DESTRUCTION OF THE CORDOVA LIBRARY.

THE principal authority for the story that Almansur destroyed the great library of Cordova is Ibn Said of Toledo, a writer who died in that town in 1069 at the age of forty, and who therefore wrote some eighty or ninety years after the date of the alleged occurrence. His account is as follows.

After relating the formation of the library and the progress of learning under Al-Hakem, which went on until the death of that Khalif in 976, he goes on—

"However, when the Wizir Mohammed Ibn Abi Amir usurped the empire, as is well known, and took the direction of public affairs entirely into his hands, he followed a different course, and in order to conciliate the favour of theologians and other austere men who were averse to the cultivation of the philosophical sciences, commanded a search to be

---

[1] Conde, i. 337.

made in Al-Hakem's library, and all works on philosophy and astronomy and other similar subjects treated by the ancients, with the exception of books on medicine and arithmetic, were by his orders removed, and either burnt in the squares of the city or thrown into the wells and cisterns of the palace. . . . This act of Almansur has been attributed by the historians of the time to his desire of gaining popularity with the multitude, and thereby finding less opposition to his ambitious views, and casting a sort of stain upon the memory of the Khalif Al-Hakem, whose throne he sought to usurp. . . . Whoever, therefore, had formerly studied and taught the philosophical sciences publicly, had now to conceal his learning from his most intimate friends, for fear of being denounced. . . . This state of things lasted until the overthrow of the Beni Ommeyah dynasty, when the dominions of that powerful family fell to the share of the rebels who rose against them."

Makkari, who has given the history of Almansur's rule at some length and in considerable detail, and who certainly shows no disposition to minimise or gloss over anything to the Yemenite's discredit, says not a word of this. Quoting Ibn Khaldun, also a Sunnite, he says, "This immense collection of books remained in the palace of Cordova until, during the siege of that capital by the Berbers, the Hajib Wahdeh, who was a freedman of Almansur, ordered them to be sold, the remainder being shortly after plundered and destroyed on the taking of that city by the Berbers." He adds that "Ibn Hazm was told by Talid, who was the keeper of the library," that the catalogue consisted of forty-four volumes.

Ibn Hazm, who was of Spanish descent, was born in Cordova in 994, and therefore must have been a boy when Talid told him about the catalogue. But he became in after life a devoted servant of the Ommeyads, and it is inconceivable, if the library had been already destroyed, as Ibn Said says, that he should not have mentioned the outrage on the memory of one of the dynasty to whom learning owed such a debt.

Not only does the silence of Ibn Khaldun and Ibn Hazm contradict the allegations of Ibn Said, but Makkari devotes several pages to a description of the flourishing state of literature and the sciences in Cordova under the administration of Almansur. "Even the Slavonian eunuchs of the palace cultivated it with great success," he says, and after mentioning some names he adds, "We forbear mentioning the poets, theologians, orators, and rhetoricians who flourished under this reign, for they were as numerous as the sands of the ocean. Many men, too, distinguished for their talents or renowned for their proficiency in some department of science or literature, visited Andalus under this reign, and were induced, through the liberality of Almansur, to fix their residence in Cordova."

Dozy gives the story of Almansur's alleged vandalism substantially as related by Ibn Said, to whom he refers. He also quotes Makkari and Ibn Adhari. The reference to Makkari we cannot verify, as he quotes his own edition of the Arabic text, and the passage is not in Gayangos' translation. Ibn Adhari wrote about the middle of the thirteenth century, and according to Dozy's own criticism, quoted by Pons, he is nearly always lacking in judgment and historical instinct.

Apart from the evidence, both positive and negative, of the falseness of Ibn Said's accusation, it is incredible that a man of liberal and enlightened views, and a patron of literature, should have been guilty of an act so contrary to all that we know of his character, in order "to conciliate the favour of theologians and other austere men." The fact that he only gave up drinking wine two years before his death (see p. 179) shows how little he troubled about conciliating the Sunnite theologians, as this practice, above all others, was the continual mark of their invectives and attacks. Ibn Said's story may, we think, be relegated to the limbo of exploded fables.[1]

Note to Chapter XIV

Alphabetical List of Towns and Fortresses held by Yemenites, Muwallads, or Christians in the Civil War of the Ninth Century; with Names of Provinces as given by Idrisi in the Twelfth Century, and as named now.

Places which apparently no longer exist are marked with a star.

*Al Ashad.
*Alava.
Albalate, Province of Valencia.
*Al Barr.
Alborgelat or Alpujarras, Province of
Algeciras, Province of Lago, now Cadiz.
Alhama la Seca, Province of Almeria.
*Al ghalyah.
*Al hadrah.
Alanje, Province of Merida.
*Al foseca.
*Al fanateyne.
Alicante, Province of Tudmir, now Murcia.
*Al havia.
*Al kutt.
*Al kanatt.

Alcala,
Kalat Yahssob
Alcala de Ibn Said
} Some authorities give this as Alcalá la Real in the Province of Jaen, others as Alcalá de Guadaira in the Province of Seville. Alcalá de Ibn Said in the thirteenth century certainly seems to have been known also as de la Real.

---

[1] See Makkari, i. App. c.; ii. 169, 199 ff.; Pons, 130, 139, 414–5; Dozy, *G. der M.*, ii. 109–10.

*Al isannah.
*Al ijjah.
*Asher.

Badajoz, Province of Castillo, now Estremadura.
Baeza, Province of Farmera or Paramera, now Jaen.
*Balagi.
Beja, Province of Al gharb, now Algarve, Portugal.
*Begrah.
*Bejannah.
*Birtannieh.
*Beni Tarik.
Bishter. (See p. 105 ff.)
Borja, Province of Zaragoza.

Cabra, Province of Campania, now Seville.
Calatrava, Province of Las Cuevas, now La Mancha.
Callosa, Province of Tudmir, now Murcia.
Cazlona (Kashtulah, the Roman Castulo), Province of Jaen.

Ecija, Province of Campania, now Seville.
Elvira, Province of Elvira, now Granada.
Estepa, Province of Seville.

*Finnilejat.

Gibraleon, Province of Ajarafe, now Province of Huelva.
Guadajoz, Province of Seville. There was a Roman town here, whence the olive oil of the wealthy Vega de Carmona was exported to Italy. The marks of potters of Guadajoz have been found in excavations in the Monte Testaceo, near Rome, the top of which is composed exclusively of the remains of great amphoras from the Iberian Peninsula. (George Bonsor, *Los Pueblos antiguos del Guadalquivir, Revista de Archivos, Bibliotecas, y Museos*, Madrid, 1902.) In the second half of the eighth century, Guadajoz was the property of Prince Artebas, second son of Witiza. (See p. 54.)

*Hansah.
*Hisn Amarina, Province Lago, now Cadiz. On the Guadalekke (miscalled Guadalete in the accounts of the invasion of Tarik) now known as the R. Barbate.
*Hisn Belay.
*Hisn Jerishah.
*Hisn Harkabah.
Huete, Province de las Sierras, now Toledo.

Jerez, Province Lago, now Cadiz.
Jodar, Province Jaen.
Jubiles.

*Karbar.
*Kalsannah.
*Kora, Province of Lago, now Cadiz. The Sultan Abdullah's stud, which was kept there, was looted by Muwallads from Lebrija.

*Lakmesh.
Lebrija, Province of Seville.
Lerida, Province de las Olivares, now Lerida.
Lorca, Province of Tudmir, now Murcia.
Loja, Province of Elvira, now Granada.

Malaga, Province of Raya, now Malaga.
*Matalanata.
Medina Beni Selim (Medina Celi), Province of Arnedo, now Soria (Castile).
Medina Sidonia, Province of Lago, now Cadiz.
Merida, Province of Castillo, now Badajoz.
Mertola, Province of Al gharb, now Alemtejo, Portugal.
*Monte Alesa.
*Montefique, on the Guadaira, Province of Seville.
*Monteleon.
Monte Mayor.
Mora, or Morad, Province of Campania, now Moratalla, Province of Cordova.
*Morana.
Murcia, Province of Tudmir, now Province of Murcia.
*Murlianah.

Niebla, Province of Ajarafe, now Huelva.
*Nixam.
*Nokur.

Ocsonoba, Province of Al gharb, now Huelva.
Osuna, Province of Osuna, now Seville.

Purchena, Province of Pechina, now Almeria.

Raya, Province of, now Malaga.
Roda. Said by some authorities to be Rotalyehud in the district of Zaragoza. There is a place named La Roda in the Province of Seville.

Santa Maria de Al gharb. This place, frequently referred to by historians, appears to have been situated at the Cape of Santa Maria, near Faro, in the Portuguese province of Algarve.
San Esteban, Province of Jaen.
*Sahnah.
*Santiberia.

Silves, Province of Al gharb, now Algarve. When Idrisi wrote Silves and the neighbouring towns were still populated by Yemenites.
*Somonton.

*Talheyrah.
Toledo.
Torrox, Province of Raya, now Malaga.
Tudmir, Province of (Theodomir), now Murcia.

Uclés, Province de las Sierras, now Cuenca.
*Umm Ja'afer.

*Ward, Province of Lago, now Cadiz.   (Ward was near Medina Sidonia.)

*Yemes.

Zaragoza, Province of Arnedo, now Zaragoza.

TOWNS AND PROVINCES MENTIONED AS EITHER OCCUPIED BY YEMENITES, OR LOYAL TO THE DEPOSED KHALIF HISHAM II. UNTIL HIS DEATH IN 1059, OR ALLIED WITH ABBADITES IN THE SECOND HALF OF THE ELEVENTH CENTURY. IN MANY CASES THE THREE CONDITIONS OCCURRED.

At this time many of the Provinces here named were governed by independent princes under the over-lordship of Seville, for longer or shorter periods; but we use the term Province for convenience, following the example of Idrisi.

Algeciras.
Almeria, Province of.
Al gharb, Province of.
Alarcos.
*Auriola.

Balearic Isles.
Badajoz, Province of.
*Bardania.
*Bala.
*Balaguer.
Baeza, Province of.

Calatrava.
Cartagena.
Castillon.
Cuenca.

Denia, Province of.

Gandia.

Huelva.
Huesca.

*Jabora.
Jaen, Province of.
Jativa.

Leiria.
*Lenant.
Lerida, Province of.
Lorca.
Lusitania, Province of.

Martos.
Medina Sidonia.
Merida.
*Murbiter.

APPENDIX 397

Murcia, Province of.

Niebla, Province of.

*Ocsonoba, Province of.

Rotalyehud.
Ronda.

Saltis, Province of.

Santa Maria de Al gharb, Province of.
Silves, Province of.

Tortosa.

Valencia, Province of.

Xelba.

Zaragoza, Province of.

Among the most important of the districts which rose against the Almohades in the twelfth century under the Christian-Yemenite [1] dynasty of Beni Mardanish, were Albacete, Baeza, Denia, Fragar, Granada, Jaen, Murcia, and Valencia.

Among the principal towns and provinces which rose against the Almohades under the Christian-Yemenite Beni-Hud were—the whole of the Al gharb, Almeria, Badajoz, Cáceres " and other towns of that district" (Makkari, ii. 329), Denia, Granada, Jaen, Játiva, Malaga, Mérida, Murcia, Seville, and Zaragoza. Those which had been under the dominion of the Beni Mardanish went over to the Beni Hud on the extinction of the Mardanish influence owing to their alliance with the Almohades.

Among the first places which submitted to or invited the aid of Al Ahmar, when he founded the Yemenite dynasty of Nasr of Granada, were Arjona, Almeria, Granada, Jaen, Jerez, Lorca, Málaga, Ronda, and Seville. Towards the end of his life the last ruling prince of the Beni Hud allied himself with Al Ahmar.

Thus we find that throughout the history of Islam in Spain the districts, cities, and towns which were held by descendants of the Gothic Christians allied with the Arabs of Yemen in the eighth century, never failed to unite with the Yemenite or Christian-Yemenite leaders who, century after century, rose in rebellion against the government of races alien in nationality or religion; until finally Fernando III. in the second quarter of the thirteenth century, with the help of his Yemenite ally, Al Ahmar of Granada, contrived to bring all the Christian-Yemenite districts outside of the new kingdom of Granada more or less peaceably under his own dominion.

Note to Chapter XIX

Simonet mentions the Mozarabic churches of Santa Marina, S. Pedro, S. Andres, Santiago, S. Lorenzo, and La Magdalena, which he says were in Cordova: we think, however, for the following reasons,

---

[1] The term "Christian-Yemenite" does not refer to the religion of the families in question, but to their being of mixed Gothic and Yemenite descent.

that they were not in Cordova, but in Seville. There are, it is true, churches dedicated to S. Marina, S. Pedro, and S. Lorenzo in Cordova, but none to the other three saints named. In Seville there are churches dedicated to all the six named by Simonet, and five of them have archæological features showing the Mozarabic influence, while all six have traditions or records of Christian worship during, if not previous to, the Almohade occupation. It would be stretching the long arm of coincidence too far to assume that Cordova and Seville each had six Mozarabic churches dedicated to the same six saints, while we should have further to assume that all trace of three of them had disappeared from Cordova since the reconquest, while all six still exist in Seville.

Simonet also mentions a record of "the basilica of Santa Maria" in Cordova, where free worship was still permitted in 1147, in which year a funeral service for a Portuguese "martyr" was held there. But here too we think that Seville, not Cordova, is the city referred to, for the Cathedral of Seville is said to have been "restored" to its primitive advocation to the Virgin on the reconquest (see p. 331), whereas the primitive Cathedral of Cordova, which appears to have been dedicated to St. Vincent, was bought from the Christian community by Abderrahman I. in 785 (Makkari, i. 218).

The archives of Seville Cathedral were lost in the first half of the thirteenth century, when the last Bishop-elect was driven out of Seville by the Almohades: and from then to 1248 there are no records. But it is known that there were always many more Christians in Seville than in Cordova. (Simonet, pp. 778–9.)

The *Convento de la Luz* at Moguer, Province of Huelva.

WHILE this book was in the press we discovered a building which strengthens our conclusion that a hitherto unrecognised Christian art existed in the south-west of Andalucia under Islam. This is the fortified convent known as the *Convento de la Luz* at Moguer,[1] in the heart of what was the Muwallad territory of Saltis, governed down to the invasion of the Almohades by the family of Bekr, descendants of Princess Sara and Omar Ibn Said al Lakhmi. The Arabic castle, the walls of which are still seen close to the convent, shows the importance attached to the defence of Moguer when the Muwallads and Mozarabs ruled there.

Until 1911 the Convent belonged to the Order of Poor Clares (Clarices), and as long as one of them remained alive the whole place was rigidly closed to the public. But some twelve months ago the last of that Order died, and now the whole of the great building has

---

[1] See illustrations facing pp. 132, 237, 381, and 398.

Fig. 13.—*Convento de la Luz* (No. 4). The Arabic Infirmary of the Poor Clares.

APPENDIX

been taken over by a teaching branch of the Conceptionists, who offer no obstacles to its investigation by serious students. It so happened that we were the first foreigners to obtain admittance for the purposes of study, and a few hours within the walls sufficed to prove that we had found one of the finest examples in existence of a Mozarabic *ribat* (see p. 227, note), overlooked until now alike by artists and historians.

Indeed, this fortress-convent suggests the interesting question whether the *ribat* were not generally of Christian rather than Moslem origin. La Rabida, famous in the annals of Columbus, has been supposed to take its name from an Almohade *ribat* of which one or two (horse-shoe) arches still remain. But in the course of restoration, extending over many years, a Christian fresco has recently been discovered beneath the Moorish work, showing that this *ribat* was Christian before the Moslems made it their own. There are one or two horse-shoe arches of the Almohade style in the *Convento de la Luz* also, but only in what is locally called "the modern part." This was the Poor Clares' infirmary (now class rooms) which has beautiful marble columns and Arabic capitals with the characteristic extension in brick-work above, so constantly observed in Moslem architecture here. The immense central court, on the other hand, which is about 150 feet square, has an arcade formed of primitive pointed arches opened in six-foot thick walls, and is entirely unlike any recognised Moslem work in Spain. The refectory has tall and bluntly pointed arches in pairs, and a crude vaulted roof which connects with but does not spring from the coupled arches. This lofty hall is lighted only by a circular window on each side, not more than eighteen inches in diameter, and high up under the roof: a small square window in the west end is obviously a modern addition. Stone seats are built in all along the walls, and an archaic pulpit of brick carved with cherubs' heads in relief (thickly whitewashed) springs from a spiral column of red marble, Arabic in technique.

Both the court and the refectory impress one by their immense strength; they look as if they would stand for ever. Not so the arcade above the court, which appears to have been added in the fourteenth or fifteenth century by the family of Portocarrero, maternal ancestors of Martin Alonso Pinzon, the companion of Columbus.[1]

Beautifully sculptured effigies in alabaster of nine Portocarreros lie at the east end of the convent church, and the Pinzons, still the leading

---

[1] This family bear on their shield, by special grant of the Emperor Charles V. to the son of Martin, three caravels, with the same motto as the descendants of Columbus, but with the name changed: *A Castilla y á Leon, nuevo mundo dió Pinzon.*

family of Moguer, inherit from them the right to be buried at the foot of the altar. The Portocarreros raised the roof of the convent, the line of their addition being clearly marked by the more modern brick-work superimposed on the primitive walls, built an immense dormitory for the hundred nuns of the Order, and considerably altered the interior of the church. It is curious to see Gothic vaulting and capitals of that period supported by tenth or eleventh century piers of masonry, with rough fragments of the original work projecting here and there at haphazard from the walls.

One part of the interior of the church, however, is in some respects unchanged since the eleventh century. This is the choir, which internal evidence shows to have been converted into the nuns' chapel somewhere about the end of the thirteenth century, by the addition of large doors adorned with paintings of the Virgin of Guadalupe, the Annunciation, and the Nativity. The costumes are of that period, as shown in the *Cántigas* and the *Book of Chess* of Alfonso X., and all the faces are of the Teutonic type, as indeed are almost all the paintings in this convent, not excluding one of the Virgin in faience, restored in 1621.

The choir stalls are of the utmost interest. The arm-rests end in archaic lions' heads, one of which is represented on the cover of this book. These are supported on columns with Arabic capitals, above which are inscriptions in the Kufic script used down to the end of the eleventh century in this region. The character is rather more decorated than that of, *e.g.*, the inscription, dated 1085, referring to the wife and son of Motamid Ibn Abbad (see p. 217), and suggests a tendency towards the more flowing Karamatic which one sees alongside of the Kufic in the Seville Alcazar. Unfortunately the bad light prevented our obtaining photographs, and the inscriptions, which occupy the front and both sides of the arm-rests beneath the lions' heads, are too much worn to allow of rubbings being made. An outling drawing was all that could be got. No inscription is found complete in all its three faces, those on the inner face being badly injured by so many centuries of use. But the mere existence of Arabic inscriptions on the choir stalls of what evidently was never other than a Christian church bears out the statement of Alvarus (p. 26) that the Mozarabs forgot their own language while remaining faithful to their religion.

To describe all the points of interest in the *Convento de la Luz* would require a long chapter rather than a necessarily brief appendix, and we must cut our account short. The ante-choir leading into the church from the great central court has a dome and cupola in the Arabic style, with a magnificent *artesonado* ceiling, contrasting curiously with a dado of sixteenth-century tiles. Over a massive grille which shuts off the nuns' chapel there is a circular light on to the nave, filled with *artesonado* in a primitive geometrical design. The apse has thirteenth-century lancet windows, but they are blind, and the immense buttresses, which divide each window from the next, are connected by a broad rampart to which access is given by archways through the buttresses. We have seen many fortified churches in the S.W. of what was Moslem Spain, but none to compare with this in strength, for not only is the actual building fortified, but a wall fully twenty feet high still surrounds it on three sides, the fourth having been removed to make a public square. It is only from this gap in the defences that we are able to see the outline of the church, which was originally completely shut in. To the south of the High Altar the wall is over six feet thick, and a narrow tunnel-like opening through it gives access to what seems to have been a guard room, although the staircase to the ramparts has disappeared, having probably been bricked up in comparatively modern times. On the north side of the apse the ramparts connect with the upper arcade of the central court by a narrow passage in the thickness of the wall. From the rampart here we obtain a view of the convent garden, some acres in extent, provided with numerous wells, and secured from attack by the lofty outer walls. Here tradition says that everything necessary for the victualling of the convent used to be grown, including wheat for making bread. In the whole structure there were originally no exposed windows of any kind save the tiny circular light in the south wall of the refectory; and as long as the single entrance was guarded the convent must have been practically impregnable.

In 1257 or thereabouts Alfonso X. conquered the Amir of Niebla, and according to some accounts he then became ruler of the district known as the kingdom of Saltis, which included Moguer, Palos de la Frontera, La Rabida, Gibraleon, and various other towns and villages in that region. At the earliest date of which we have record the Lordship of Moguer belonged to the family of Tenorio, and probably it was they who bestowed the Mozarabic convent *de la Luz* on the Order of Santa Clara. About 1335 this lordship passed by marriage to the Portocarreros, connections both of the Tenorios and the Pinzons. These last are markedly Teutonic in type, all the present generation, even to collaterals, having grey eyes and many of them brown hair. The Tenorios, like the Portocarreros, claim Gothic descent, and Argote de Molina and Pifferer profess to trace both families back to one Juan Alfonso de Benavides, whom both authors describe as descended from one of the early kings of Leon. They differ as to whether it was

Alfonso VII. or IX.; but they agree that the founder of these families was an *hijo d'algo notorio de sangre* (an hidalgo of well-known nobility). We think that this *hijo d'algo* was certainly of noble Gothic descent, but that he sprang not from the stem of Roderick or of the mythical Pelayo, but from that of Witiza.

Montemayor, now a mere hamlet with a much-visited hermitage, about a mile from Moguer, is mentioned as a Muwallad stronghold in the civil war of the ninth century,[1] and the Virgin of Montemayor is the patron saint of Moguer.

In 1349 Alvaro Pelaez, Bishop of Silves (a Mozarabic diocese now long extinct), made a bequest to the convent of Moguer,[2] and perhaps this was employed to alter the church as above described. But no official records of the convent are accessible, for our friend the Archdeacon of Seville, after inquiring of the Keeper of the Archives at the Archbishop's palace, told us that nothing was known there of the foundation or the history of the place, and that no information on the subject was to be had. Having regard to the careful records kept of every religious establishment founded after the reconquest in 1248, the lack of any document relating to the *Convento de la Luz* goes far to establish its Mozarabic origin, apart from the history carved on its wood and graven on its stones.

---

[1] Makkari, ii. 448.   [2] Zuñiga, ii. 120.

GENEALOGICAL TABLES

GENEALOGICAL TABLES

OF THE

DESCENDANTS OF WITIZA,

THE LAST LEGITIMATE KING OF THE GOTHS OF SPAIN.

TABLE I.

DESCENDANTS OF PRINCE ARTEBAS.
DESCENDANTS OF PRINCE ROMULO.

N.B.—Genealogies which are doubtful or based on presumptive evidence only, are marked by a note of interrogation.

WITIZA I. c. 701–11.

ALMAND (Seville). (See Tables II., III., IV., and V.)	ARTEBAS (Jaen). The first Count of the Christians. Treated by the Moslems as a ruling Prince. Held property from Guadajoz to Jaen and Almodovar. (See p. 57.)	ROMULO (Toledo).
	?	?
	? Abu Said al Kumis, (Makkari, ii. 415.)	*Jaafar Ibn Alfor, or Alfaro*. Judge of the Christians at Cordova. (Makkari, ii. 415.)
	?	?
		Family of Alfaro, who had the oldest chapel in the Visigothic church of St. Vicente in

GENEALOGICAL TABLES

Count Alphons.
(Dozy, *G. der M.*, i. 366.)
|
Jaafar al Islami.
|
Omar Hafs.
|
Omar Ibn Hafsun Ibn Jaafar Ibn Arius.
"King" of Kashtelah and of Toledo, 913.
Possessed Archidona and Jaen. (Dozy, i. 366;
Makkari, ii. 439; Conde, i. 295, 309, 332.)

Suleyman.	*Jaafer.*	*Abderrahman.*	*Hafs.*
Submitted to Abd. III.	Held Toledo, c. 930.	Submitted to Abd.	Killed, c. 927.
Killed in a skirmish,	(Makkari, ii.	III., 913. Settled in	(Dozy, i. 464.)
927. (Dozy, *G. der M.*, i. 463.)	135, 462.) Escaped when Abd. III. took city, and joined Christians of Galicia. (Conde, i. 377 ff.)	Cordova, and became a writer.	

Seville. (Zuñiga, iii. 264.) A sepulchral stone in Seville Cathedral is inscribed, "Los de Alfaro Son hijos de Algo." A Plaza de Alfaro until recently was attached to the walls of the Alcazar, where the Sta. Cruz gate has been opened.

|
?
|
Gonzalbo Ibn Yoannex (Joannes).
Ibn Sebryanes Ibn Hafzón.
|
Aurea.
A nun.

Witnessed sale of a vineyard at Salancas, near Toledo, 1212.
(Pons, *Escrituras Mozarabes Toledanas*, p. 223.) Ayala says that all the Christians in Toledo, *hijos d'algo* and men of every other condition, were exempt from tribute throughout the Moslem occupation. (*Cronica del Rey Don Pedro*, i. pp. 62–3.) Ayala says this was a condition of the capitulation of the city to the Moslems, but probably it refers to the treaty made with Al-Walid in 711, by which Prince Romulo and his descendants were given Toledo for ever.

GENEALOGICAL TABLES

TABLE II.

DESCENDANTS OF PRINCE ALMAND THROUGH HIS DAUGHTER SARA AND OMAR IBN SAID AL LAKHMI.

THE BENI HEJJAJ.

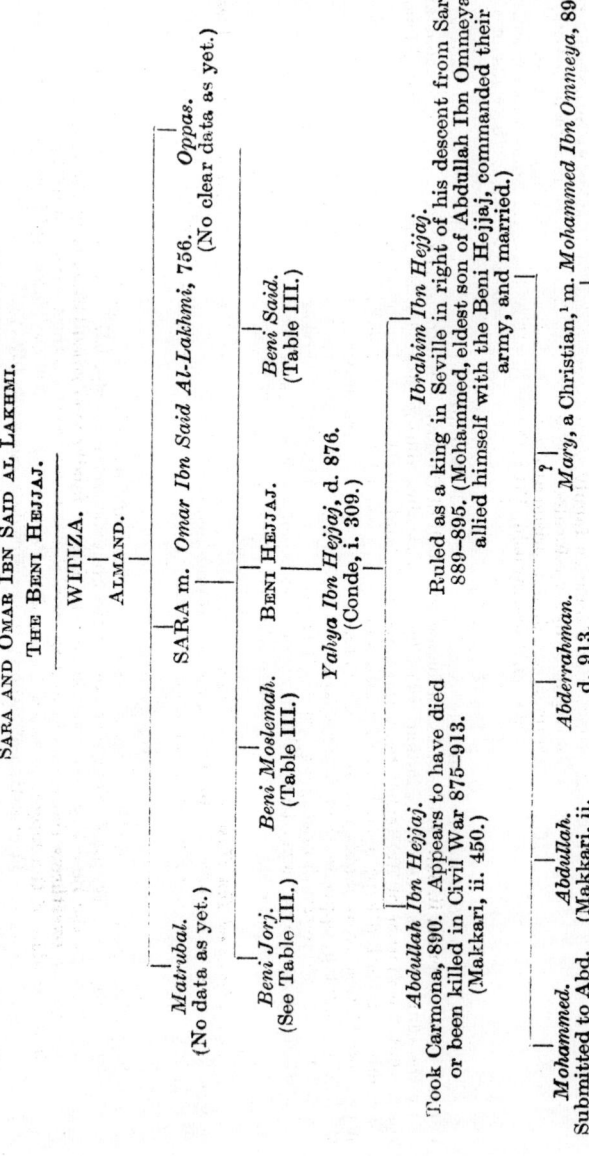

WITIZA.
ALMAND.

SARA m. Omar Ibn Said Al-Lakhmi, 756.   Oppas. (No clear data as yet.)

Matrubal. (No data as yet.)   Beni Jorj. (See Table III.)   Beni Moslemah. (Table III.)   BENI HEJJAJ.   Beni Said. (Table III.)

Yahya Ibn Hejjaj, d. 876. (Conde, i. 309.)

Abdullah Ibn Hejjaj. Took Carmona, 890. Appears to have died or been killed in Civil War 875–913. (Makkari, ii. 450.)   Ibrahim Ibn Hejjaj. Ruled as a king in Seville in right of his descent from Sara, 889–895. (Mohammed, eldest son of Abdullah Ibn Ommeya, allied himself with the Beni Hejjaj, commanded their army, and married.)

Mohammed. Submitted to Abd. III. with all the Yemenites and Muwalllads, 913. (Dozy, i. 456–7.)   Abdullah. (Makkari, ii. 450.)   Abderrahman. d. 913. (Dozy, i. 456–7.)   Mary, a Christian,[1] m. Mohammed Ibn Ommeya, 890.

ABDERRAHMAN III.
(Makkari, ii. 145, 439, 448–9; Dozy, G. der M., i. 393–4, 399; Conde, i. 358; Al Kuttiyyah in J.A., pp. 432–4.)

GENEALOGICAL TABLES

```
?                                    ?
|                                    |
Isa Al-Estád Abu-l-Hejjaj.           Romaik Ibn Hejjaj
Alime of Motamid, 1086.
(Conde, ii. 70.)
                                     |
                    ┌────────────────┴─────────────────┐
           Saïd Cubra Romaikkiyyah  m.  MOTAMID IBN ABBAD
           A member of Romaik's family, exact relationship   AL LAKHMI, king of
           uncertain. Highly educated. Was exiled with       Seville, 1064–91.
           Motamid, and died in prison at Agmat, Morocco,
           c. 1095. (Al Marrakushi, 131; Conde, ii. 169.)
                                     |
        ┌────────────────┬───────────┴──────┬──────────────────┐
                                                        Several
                                                        other sons and
                                                        daughters.
Obeidallah Ibn Hassan Ar-Rashid.              Seraj-ad-Daulah.
Cadi of Seville (Conde, ii. 64). An inscription formerly   Wali of Cordova. Killed at Medina
on the Church of St. Juan de la Palma in Seville           Az-zahra during siege by Berbers
states that the mother of Ar-Rashid built the tower        and Mudarites under the Beni-
for him. Ar-Rashid kept open house for rich and            Dhinnun of Toledo,
poor every Thursday, probably at a magnificent man-        c. 1084.
sion, still inhabited, opposite the church where a rag-
market is still held every Thursday, and called " The
Fair of the Thursdays," after the Arabic custom.

                                                    And six other children.

Mohammed Ibn Hassan Fakr-ad-daulah Ibn As-Seraj.
Earned his living as a goldsmith in Africa during the imprisonment of his
                    grandfather, Motamid.²
```

The Beni Seraj.

The "Abencerrajes," of the Christian writers. This family settled at Granada, and were loyal to the legitimate kings, the Beni Nasr, who were Yemenites like themselves. The endeavours of the so-called "Zegris" (the Beni Zeyr, descendants of the Berber family who ruled Granada in the eleventh century) to overthrow the Nasrites, and their intrigues and quarrels with the Beni Seraj, caused the final downfall of the kingdom in 1492. (Abbad., i. 109, 372; Al Marrakushi, 119; Conde, ii. 65; Fernandez y Gonzalez, *Museo Esp. de Antiguedades*, i. 67.)

¹ That Mary was of the Sevillian royal family appears probable; but as yet we have only presumptive evidence, set forth in Chapter IV., that this was so.

² Maker of the jewelled casket on which his name and that of his grandfather appear, now in the National Museum of Madrid (see p. 139).

408 GENEALOGICAL TABLES

TABLE III.

DESCENDANTS OF SARA AND OMAR IBN SAID AL-LAKHMI.

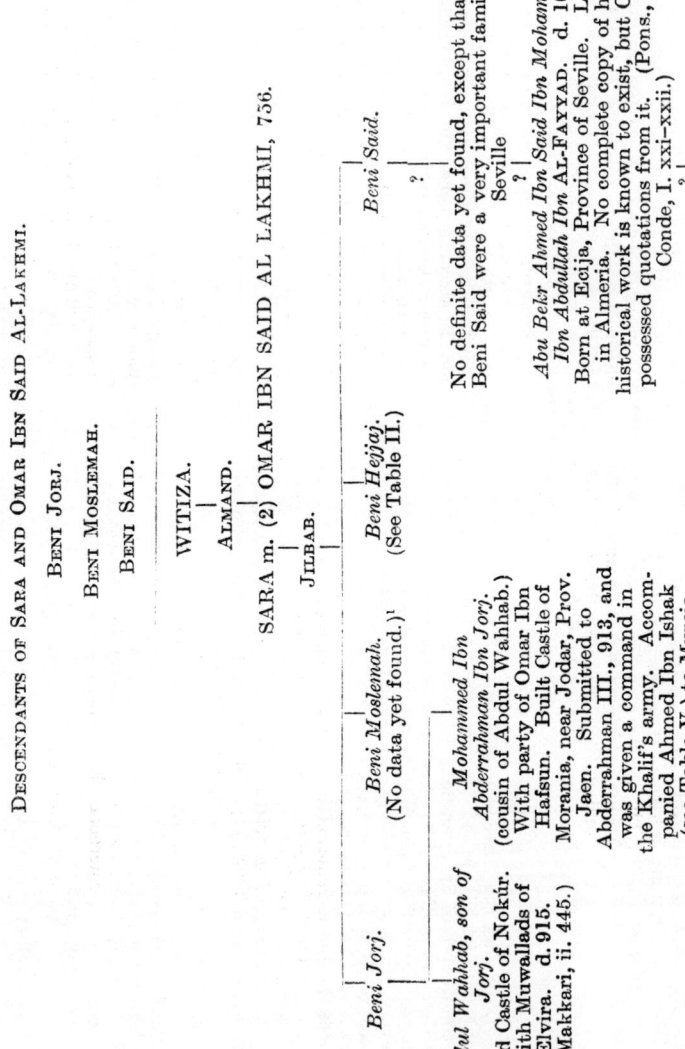

BENI JORJ.

BENI MOSLEMAH.

BENI SAID.

WITIZA.
ALMAND.

SARA m. (2) OMAR IBN SAID AL LAKHMI, 756.

JILBAB.

Beni Hejjaj.
(See Table II.)

Beni Said.

?

No definite data yet found, except that the Beni Said were a very important family of Seville

?

Abu Bekr Ahmed Ibn Said Ibn Mohammed Ibn Abdullah Ibn Al-Fayyad. d. 1066. Born at Ecija, Province of Seville. Lived in Almeria. No complete copy of his historical work is known to exist, but Conde possessed quotations from it. (Pons, 138; Conde, I. xxi–xxii.)

?

Beni Jorj.

Beni Moslemah.
(No data yet found.)[1]

Mohammed Ibn Abderrahman Ibn Jorj. (cousin of Abdul Wahhab.) With party of Omar Ibn Hafsun. Built Castle of Morania, near Jodar, Prov. Jaen. Submitted to Abderrahman III., 913, and was given a command in the Khalif's army. Accompanied Ahmed Ibn Ishak (see Table V.) to Murcia,

Abdul Wahhab, son of Jorj. Held Castle of Nokúr. With Muwalleds of Elvira. d. 915. (Makkari, ii. 445.)

and was killed at siege of Alicante. (Makkari, ii. 445.) The Castle of St. George at Triana, which bore that name under Islam, may have been built by this family.

The Beni Said in the thirteenth century were an important family established since 1106 at Alcalá la Real (called Alcalá de Aben Zaide in the Cron. of Alfonso X.), and appear to have been closely connected with the Beni Said (Bekrites), who governed Silves in the eleventh century. Their genealogy, however, is not given in full in any chronology as yet translated.

There is an important tribe in the Spanish zone in Morocco, called the *Beni Said*. They are fair-skinned with brown or chestnut hair, and pride themselves on being descended from the Goths of Spain. It appears probable that they were among the Yemenites driven out of Andalucia in 1009 or in the twelfth century. (Letter from Colonel Rabadán, Sanidad Militar, for several years editor of the *Boletín Hispano-Marroquí* of Ceuta.)

The chief of this tribe, which numbers about 25,000 members, was in 1893 *Sî Mahommed Ar Raisuli*, a relative of the Sultan Muley Hafid, and of the Shereef of Wazan, whose mother is an Englishwoman. He had about 1000 soldiers of the Beni Said around his residence on the Wady Siffelán. (Gonzalo de Reparaz, *Politica de España en Africa*, pp. 123, 130.) Some of the Beni Said near the frontier of Algeria have shown hostility to the Spanish troops at Melilla; but Ar Raisuli and the majority of his people have long been friendly to Spain.

[1] The Emirs of Badajoz in the eleventh century were known as of the family of *Al Aftas*; but their full names suggest that they were related to the Beni Moslemah, who sprang from the marriage of Sara with Omar Ibn Said Al Lakhmi. Gayangos gives them as follows (in Makkari, i. p. 369), but without mentioning their tribal name:—

Abdullah Ibn Moslemah.
Ruler of Badajoz and part of the Algarbe.

Abu Bekr Mohammed Ibn Abdillah Ibn Moslemah.
Succeeded his father, 1060–1.

Abu Mohammed Omar Ibn Mohammed Ibn Moslemah.
d. 1094.

(Cf. Tables, Makkari, II. lxxxvii. Dozy, *G. der M.*, ii. 422.)

TABLE IV.

DESCENDANTS OF SARA AND HER FIRST HUSBAND, ISA IBN MUZAHIM.

```
ISA IBN MUZAHIM.
        │
    AL KUTTIYYAH.
        │
    THE BEKRITES.


WITIZA.
  │
ALMAND.
  │
  ├─────────────────────────────────────┐
SARA m. (1) ISA IBN MUZAHIM.
  │
  ├──────────────────────────┬────────────────────────────┐
Ibrahim.                ? Zadlaf, a Christian.       Ishak. (See Table V.)
  │                           │
Abdalaziz Ibn Ibrahim.   Yahya Ibn Zadlaf.
  │                      Lord of Oesonoba. Leader of Christians.
Omar Ibn Abdulaziz Ibn Ibrahim        │
Ibn Isa Ibn Muzahim.             Bekr Ibn Yahya Ibn Bekr,
  │                         Governor of Silves, 875–913. Leader of
Abu Bekr Mohammed Ibn Omar Ibn    Christians and Muwallads. (Makkari, ii. 440.)
Abdalaziz Ibn Ibrahim Ibn Isa
Ibn Muzahim AL KUTTIYYAH, d. 977.
  The celebrated author.
(Pons, 83; Makkari, i. 460; ii. 415.)
```

Abu Said Mohammed Ibn Ayub al Bekri.
Lord of Huelva, Oesonoba, and Sta. Maria de Algarbe;
Kadi of Niebla, Governor of Saltis before 1009.
(*Dict. Islam,* 607.)

Abu Said Abdalaziz al Bekri.
Lord of Saltis and Huelva. Sold his heritage at
Saltis to Motadid. (Conde, ii. 32.)

Abu-l-Mosab Abdallah Ibn Abdalaziz, d. 1064. A captain in
Motamid's cavalry. Was by him made Governor of Niebla. (Conde, ii. 34;
Pons, 160; Dozy, *G. der M. Chron. Tables.*)

Abu Bekr Mohammed Ibn Isa Ibn Mohammed al Lakhmi Ibn al Lebbanah, d. 1113.
Brother of the geographer. Court poet and devoted adherent of Motamid Ibn Abbad. Resided in Almeria, but accompanied Motamid into exile in Africa, 1091. Died in Mallorca. (Pons, 172; Al Marrakushi, 126.)

Abdallah Ibn Abdalaziz Ibn Mohammed al Bekri, d. 1094.
The celebrated geographer. Lived in Almeria. Attended Motamid as Ambassador of the Amir of Almeria on his African Expedition, 1085–6.
(Pons, 160; *Dict. Islam,* 607.)

Note to Table IV.—It may be worth remarking that two of the first chiefs of the Almoravides figuring in history—who, according to some authorities, claimed descent from the Arabs of Yemen—were called Abu Bekr Ibn Omar and Yahya Ibn Omar. The *Dict. of Islam* (p. 318) gives the Sanhaja, founders of the Almoravide kingdom, as a Sahara tribe from the Sudan, and the chief who first sought education for his tribe was called Yahya Ibn Ibrahim. In the uncertainty that still prevails as to the antecedents of these rulers, it is interesting to note that the first four names we meet with among them are among those of Al Kuttiyyah, also of Yemenite extraction.

TABLE V.

DESCENDANTS OF SARA AND HER FIRST HUSBAND, ISA IBN MUZAHIM.

THE BENI ISHAK.

```
                                SARA = m. (1) ISA IBN MUZAHIM, d. before 756.
                                │              (Tribe not stated, but apparently a
                    ┌───────────┼───────────┐  Lakhmite.  See Table IV., Al Lebbanah.)
                 WITIZA.     ALMAND.      ISHAK.
                                            │
                                    Deysam Ibn Ishak
                                            │
                                       Ibrahim.
                                      (See Table IV.)
```

Ruled Lorca and Murcia and rebelled against Abdullah Ibn Ommeya in the Civil War, end of ninth century. Praised by the poet Obaydis. (Makkari, ii. 439.)

Ibn Ishak.
Wizir of Cordova under Abderrahman III. d. 915–6. Referred to by Abderrahman in terms which suggest that his wife may have been a Copt of Seville. (Dozy, *G. der M.*, ii. 34–5.)

{ Spoken of as related to the Royal house of Ommeya. This connection must have been through Mary, a Christian of Seville, mother of Abderrahman, as the father was not an Ommeyad. }

Ommeya Ibn Ishak.
A distinguished military commander. Taking offence at his brother's execution, he joined the Christians of Galicia under Ramiro V., and routed the Moslems at Zamora. Then offered his services to the Beni Idris of Africa against Abd. III. Finally returned to his allegiance, and was made Governor of Santaren. (Makkari, ii. 135–7; Conde, i. 429.)

Ahmed Ibn Ishak.
Field-Marshal, and Governor of the Upper Thagher. Proposed that his cousin the Khalif should name him heir to the throne. Executed for a civil offence. (Dozy, ii. 34–5; Makkari, ii. 136.)

Ommeya Ibn Ishak.
Appointed Governor of Cordova by his cousin Mohammed al Muhdi when he usurped the throne in 1009. (Makkari, ii. 488.)

INDEX

(*The places named in the Appendix, pp. 393-7, are not indexed.*)

ABBADITES, the, 14, 190 ff. (see also Ismail, Karis, Mohammed, Motadid, Motamid)
Abbassides, the, 55, 59, 87, 130, 225, 239, 273, 278-9, 284
Abdalaziz (of Valencia), 239, 241
Abdalmalek, 169 note, 173, 177-8, 181, 232
Abderrahman I., 52, 58, 61, 64 ff., 67-8
Abderrahman II., 22, 25, 70, 137
Abderrahman III., 10, 12, 28, 77; birth, 83; early life, 85, 89, 94; dealings with Christians, 115 note, 146; pacification of country on his accession, 116-8; commerce with Egypt under, 129-30; accession, 144 ff.
Abderrahman V., 198
Abderrahman, son of Almansur (*see* Sanchol)
Abdullah, the Sultan, 71, 78 ff., 86, 97-8, 110, 389-90
Abu Abdullah (the Almohade), 277
Abulola, 175
Aduarejo, the, 350
Aghmat, 216, 218, 222
Aguilar, castle of, 114
Ahl-adh-dhimmah, the, 110
Ahmar, Al, 276, 281; his rise, 282 ff.; rule in Granada, 284-5; relations with Fernando, 286 ff., 307 ff.; at siege of Seville, 316-7; after conquest of Seville, 334; is represented at Fernando's funeral, 342; renews alliance with Alfonso X., 341-2; his coat of arms, 346.
Ajarafe, the, 305, 310-1, 316, 328
Ajem, the, 101 note, 110
Akhmin, monastery of, 133

Alarcon, 104
Alarcos, 256; battle of, 276
Alava, 104
Albarracin, 243, 273
Alcalá de Guadaira, 303 ff., 308, 310, 352, 370, 387
Alcalá la Real, 289, 335, 370
Alcalá del Rio, 309, 386
Alcanate (*see* Puerto de Santa Maria)
Alcazar, the (Seville), 2, 3, 139-40, 202, 209, 212, 219, 232, 235, 275, 327, 337
Aledo, 244, 250-2
Alfons, Count, 100
Alfonso I. (Aragon), 28, 262, 264-5
Alfonso II. (Aragon), 270
Alfonso III. (Leon), 86, 88, 150 note
Alfonso VI., 239; takes Toledo, 242, 244; alliance with Motamid, 253 ff., 257, 259; marries Motamid's daughter, 254 ff.; his wives, 255-6
Alfonso VIII., 270, 272
Alfonso IX., 276, 338
Alfonso X., 15, 133, 140, 264, 281, 288, 311, 313, 324, 335 note, 351, 401
Alfonso XI., 2
Algarbe, the, 18-9, 113, 127, 237, 269, 311, 330
Algeciras, 88, 106, 241, 247, 371
Alhambra, the, 334
Ali, Law of, 75
Alicante, 371
Almand, 40, 47, 48 note, 51-2.
Almansur, rise to power, 160 ff.: dealings with the Christians, 169 ff.; Sunday a day of rest in his household, 174; death, 180-1; builds chapel in Fez, 236

INDEX

Almeria, 11, 130, 213, 241, 244, 251, 268, 270, 272–3, 279, 281, 371
Almodovar del Rio, 56, 259
Almogavares, the, 299
Almohades, the, architecture of, 138–9; centres of disaffection to, 268–9; relations with Mardanish's family, 274–5; population in Spain, 278; mosques of, "purified" by Ibn Hud, 280, 332; establishment of militia near Seville, 295 ff.
Almojarifazgo, the, 349
Almoravides, the, 29; origin, 225 ff.; employment of Andalucians by, 234; coinage, 234–5; various invasions of, 251 note, 252 note; in Spain, 246 ff.
Alpujarras, the, 107
Alvarus, 23, 26, 400
Ammar, Ibn, 213, 218, 240, 254
Andres, San, church of (Seville), 134
Antequera, 106–7
Arabic historians, their bias, 6
Arabic, prevalent use of, by Christians, 26
Arch, the pointed, 15–6, 383, 399
Archidona, 106
Arcos, 210, 241, 299 note, 335
Argentea, 107–8
Arjona, 283
Artebas, 24, 40, 47, 49, 51, 52 ff., 272
Artesonado, 131, 401
Asbagh, Al, 81
Ashkulilah, 298
Assido, site of, 45 note
Aurillac, 372
Averroes (*see* Roshd, Ibn)
Axataf (*see* Sakkaf)
Azaque, the, 87
Azhar, Al, mosque of, 140
Aznalfarache, San Juan de, 306, 310, 312, 314, 327 note

BADAJOZ, 14, 150 note, 235, 237, 246, 371
Baeza, 12, 107, 266, 268, 288, 295, 301, 337, 345 note, 350–1, 371
Baji, Al, 296–7
Balearic Isles, 238, 372
Barbastro (in Aragon), 104

Barcelona, Bishoprics of, 239 note; Count of, 270
Baza, 266, 269, 282–3, 295
Bearn, Viscount of, 351
Bedr, 91–2
Beja, 127, 372, 382
Bejer, 299 note, 335
Bekr, Abu, "Instructions" of, 75–7
Bekr, Abu (the Almoravide), 227–8
Birtannieh, 104
Bishops, Christian, 18, 22, 24, 238, 239 note
Bishter, 82, 99, 101–3, 104 note; discussion of site, 105–9
Bobaster (*see* Bishter)
Bollullos, Hisn, 290
Bonifaz, Ramon, 309–10, 314, 317–8, 326
Book of Chess, the, 140, 400
Borja, 104
Burgundy, Duke of, 258
Burials, Moslem, 330

CABRA, 106
Cadiz, 335
Calatayud, 238
Calatrava, 158, 276, 372; "Matmaker of," 188–9; Master of, 305, 328
Cantillana, 306, 308
Caracuel, 256
Caravaca, Cross of, 345 note
Carmona, 20, 44, 46, 72, 82–3, 132, 241, 266, 269, 297, 300, 306, 308, 310, 381
Carrion, Count, 184 note
Casa de las Dueñas, 384
Castulo (*see* Cazlona)
Cazlona, 9, 50, 68, 107, 118
Ceuta, 330
Chiclana, 299 note
Christians, deported to Morocco, 28–9, 31–5; in Granada, 28, 30; in Mardanish's army, 272; in Al-Ahmar's army, 301
Churches, Christian under Islam, 18, 20, 384 ff., 397 ff.
Cid, the, 252 note
Cintra, 372
Coimbra, 18, 21
Columbus, 227 note, 399
Conde's history, value of, 7–8, 68, 104 note
Constantina, 306

Consuegra, 256
Copts, the, 119 ff.; theology of, 358
Coptic churches in Egypt, 123; influence in architecture in Andalucia, 15–6, 131 ff.
Cordova, mosque, 3; arts and sciences, 10–1; Khalifate of, 12; churches, 18; monasteries, 20; bishops, 24; anarchy in, 186–7; in eleventh century, 239, 279; alleged destruction of library, 391–2
Cordovan governors and the Muwallads, 78
" Counts, Christian " join Almansur, 172–3
" Count of the Christians," the, 21–4, 57, 109
" Crow, church of the," 18–9
Cuenca, 104, 116, 256, 372

DAMASCUS, 16, 58
Daroca, 238
Denia, Princess of, 208; State of, 14, 238, 239 note, 268, 270, 275, 279, 373
Dhinnun, the Beni, 189–90, 194, 239, 244
Dredging of rivers, 355

ECIJA, 18, 46, 165
Egypt, connection of Andalucia with, 16; commerce with, 129–30; conquest of, by Arabs, 119 ff.
Egyptian fleet and troops, 125–6; influence in textiles, design, etc., 121–2, 127, 135
Elvira, 25, 81, 373
Enrique III., 33
Estepa, 81–2
Eulogius, 20, 22, 25
" Exceptor," the, 24–5

FADRIQUE, DON, 354
Fañez, Alvar, 244
Farfanes, the, 32–4
Faro, 311, 386
Fayik, 163
Fayyad, Al, 8, 163
Fehri, Yusuf Al, 61, 63
Fernando I., 27
Fernando III. (San Fernando), 83, 281; mortuary robe, 140, 340; relations with Al-Ahmar, 286 ff.; siege of Jaen and fighting near Granada, 289 ff.; treaty with Al-Ahmar, 293; entry into Seville, 330 ff.; illness and death, 336 ff.; birthplace, 338; banner and burial robe, 340; his jester, 347; grants to Seville, the *fueros* of Toledo, 347–8
Fez, 173; Andalucians in, 231 ff., 236
Fraga, 265, 273
Francis, St., 31
Frontera, de la, towns so called, 299 note

GAMRI, IBN, 86–9, 115, 146, 390
Garcia Fernandez, 173
Gayangos, P. de, his writings, 7
Gelves, 320
Genoa, treaty of Mardanish with, 270
Gerena, 307–8
Ghalib, Ibn, 80–1
Gibraleon, 237, 311, 378, 401
Giralda, the, 139
Granada, 28, 39, 242, 246, 258, 267–8, 279, 283–5, 295, 330, 350–1, 373
Grazalema, 373, 378
Greek fire, 317
Guadamur, treasure of, 388
Guadix, 266, 269, 282–3
Guillena, 306–8
Guinea, slave trade to, 230
Guzman, 28 note, 137 *and* note, 324

HAFSS, IBN, 285, 286 note, 300, 345 note
Hafsun, Jaafar Ibn, 116–8, 173
Hafsun, Omar Ibn, 9, 82, 86, 91, 390; parentage, 100–1; career, 110 ff.; death and fate of his sons, 116
Hakem II., Al, 24, 155 ff., 348 note
Hammud, the Beni, 188, 191, 193
Hamushk, Ibn, 267
Hayyan, Ibn, 6, 9, 13, 65, 193, 196 ff., 389–91
Hazm, Ibn, 193, 197–8, 392
Hejjaj family, the, 10, 14, 24, 63, 71 ff., 82, 85–6, 88, 90–2, 144–5, 214

2 E

INDEX

Henry II. (England), 270, 338
Hisham II., events after deposition of, 12–3; youth, 161 ff.; story of, 180 ff.; story of the false, 192 ff.; death, 202, 204
Hisham III., 195
Hisham, Khalif of Damascus, 58
Horse-breeding, 348 *and* note
"House of Pilate," the, 384
Hud, the Beni, 195, 211, 238, 261ff., 272–3, 279, 281, 283, 297, 313, 332
Huelva, 135, 237
Huesca, 104, 117, 238
Huete, 104, 256

IDRIS, the Beni, 236
Illora, 290
Immaculate Conception, dogma of the, 357 ff.
Imran, Mohammed Ibn, 298, 310
Infanzones, the, 351
Iñigo Arista of Navarre, 79 note
Ishak, Ahmed Ibn, 80, 128, 147 ff.
Ishak, Ommeya Ibn, 147, 149 ff., 152
Isidro, San, removal of relics of, 27; monastery of, 28 note
Ismail Ibn Abbad, 152–3, 190–1

ITIMAD, 213 ff.
Iviza, 373
Ivory carving, examples of, 372
Iyad, Ibn, 265–6

JACOBITES, the, 128
Jadd, Al, 296, 298–9, 310
Jaen, 9, 12, 81–2, 117, 266, 268, 279, 282–3, 289 ff., 295, 373
Janda, La, battle of, 45
Jativa, 12, 275, 279, 373
Jehwar, Ibn, 193–5, 197–8, 239–40
Jellab, Al, battle of, 271–2
Jerez 81, 210, 283, 296, 299, 305–6, 309, 327, 330, 335, 343, 355
Jews, at time of Moslem conquest, 38 note; under Fernando III., 348
Joan of Ponthieu, 331 note, 353
Jond, the, 127, 296
Juan I., 32–3
Juan de la Palma, San, church of (Seville), 217
"Judge of the Christians," the, 24

Justa, St., 27

KALFAT, 74
Kamar, 73
Karis Ibn Abbad, 190
Kasim, Al, 81, 83–4, 87
Khaldun, the Beni, 85, 90, 300, 390–1
Khalifate, downfall of the Cordovan, 12–3
Korra, Ibn Abi, 209–11
Kusair Amra, portraits at, 48 note
Kuttiyyah, Al, 40, 71–2

LABBUN, Ibn, 252 note
Latin, decay of, 26
Lebbanah, Ibn, 215, 246
Lebrija, 309, 335
Leon, siege of, 169; Church of S. Claudio, 170
Lerida, 103, 195, 239, 272
Limoges, Viscount of, 351
Lion, symbolism of, in Seville, 223 note
Lisbon, 18, 373
Lora, 306
Lorca, 251–2, 374
Lorenzo, San, church of, in Seville, 385
Lotus, the, in ornament, 366–7
Lucar, San, 327; three places of the name, 335 note
Lucar la mayor, San, church at, 18, 321, 383
Lucena, 81
Luz, Convento de la, 321, 398 ff.

MAIL, plate, worn by Moslems, 151
Makkari, Al, 7, 14, 65
Malaga, 18, 29, 39, 101, 242, 246, 279, 374
Marchena, 300
Mardanish, Ibn, 30, 264 ff.; policy, 269; treaties of, 270; death, 271; extent of dominions, 272; alliances with Christians, 270, 272; submission of his sons to the Almohades, 273–4
Maris Padilla, baths of, 212
Marina, S., church of (Seville), 133, 385
Martyrdom, epidemic of, at Cordova, 21–2
Martyrs and saints, relics of, given up by Moslems, 27

418 INDEX

Matraca, the, 386
Medina Celi, 181, 185 note, 384
Medina Sidonia, 18, 45 note, 81, 132, 136–7, 335, 374, 378
Merida, 18, 44, 47, 88, 382
Merin, the Beni, 286, 350
Mertola, 269, 382
Mesnada, the, 351
Miguel del Cid, 363
Miguel, San, College of (Seville), 132, 384
Moguer, convent at (*see* Luz, *Convento de la*)
Mohallakah, church of, 123, 358
Mohammed Ibn Abbad, 191
Mohammed Al Muhdi, 184–6
Mohammed (father of Abderrahman III.), 78–80, 83, 390
Mohammed (Sultan of Cordova), 102
Moizz-ad-Daula, 129–30
Monasteries under Islam, 20, 398 ff.
Montemayor, 402
Moors and Arabs, confusion between, 8 *and* note
Mora, 256, 311
Morocco, Bishopric of, 34; Christians deported to, 28–9, 31–5; foundation of city, 228–9
Moron, 46, 209, 241, 299 note
Mosalimah, the, 111
Motadd, 222
Motadid Ibn Abbad, 27, 202–3, 206 ff., 208 ff., 238, 240
Motamid Ibn Abbad, 14, 209 ff.; marriage, 213 ff.; death, 217; protection of Christians by, 224 note; relations with Niebla, 238; with Murcia, 240; with Almeria, 241; with Granada, 242; invites Almoravides to Spain, 246; at Zalaca, 247; dealings with Ibn Tashfin, 248 ff.; alliance with Alfonso VI., 253 ff.
Môtassim (*see* Somadeh)
Motref, Al, 73–4, 77, 81, 83–5, 88–9, 116–7, 151
Mozarab, meaning of, 19; applied to Christians of Toledo, 113
Mozarabic ritual, 19; churches in Seville, 397; convent at Moguer, 398 ff.
Mudarite Arabs, 8, 61–3
" Mudéjar " school, the, 2, 3, 14, 361, 384

Mugheyrah, Al, 161, 163
Mujahid, 208, 238
Mulamis, Ibn, 60, 62
Mumin, Abd al (the Almohade), 296, 299
Mundhir, Al, 70, 78, 99, 100, 102, 104–5, 348 note
Muradiin, the, 111
Murcia, 9, 12, 14, 30, 127, 176, 240, 251, 265, 268, 272, 279, 281, 295, 337, 371, 374, 385
Musa, 31, 46, 48, 50–1, 125–6, 206, 381–2
Mushafi, Al, 163–164
Muwallads, the, 4, 49–51, 71; rising of, against Cordova, 80 ff.; application of name to Sara's descendants, 113
Muzahim, Isa Ibn, 58, 63

NASR, Mohammed Ibn, 242
Nasrites, the, 75
Navas, Las, battle of, 276 ff.
Negroes in Seville, 129 note
Negroid race at Niebla, 129 note ?
Nicolas, San, church of (Seville), 385
Niebla, 14, 18, 82, 88, 113, 129 note, 198 note, 269, 306, 310–1, 327 note, 343, 350–1, 382, 401
Northmen, invasions of the, 70 note, 83 note
Nubians, 129

OCAÑA, 256
Ocsonoba, 127, 135, 153, 237, 374, 382, 386
Odhri, Abu Mohammed, 73
Omar, Yahya Ibn, 227–8
Oppas, Bishop, 48, 51
Ordoño of Leon, 24
Orias, 324–6
Ostentacion de la bandera, 387

PALOS de la Frontera, 227 note, 401
Paño de la Monteria, 141–2
Paper, manufacture of, 12
Pedro the Cruel, 2, 3, 15, 206, 337
Pinzon family, the, 399, 401
Pisa, 270
Portocarrero family, the, 399, 401
" Potten Kant," 368
Puerto de Santa Maria, 137, 335–6, 385–6

INDEX 419

Rabat, 32 note
Rabida, La, 227 note, 269, 401
Radi, Ar, 212, 222, 247
Ramiro II. of Leon, 149 ff.
Rashid, Ar, 217–8
Rashik, Ibn, 240–1, 251–2
Rayah, 39, 81, 105–6, 115
Recafred, Bishop of Seville, 22
Relics of saints given up by Moslems, 27
Repartimiento, the, 349, 351
Reyes de Taifa, 12 note
Ribat, the, 227 note, 399
Ricos omes, 293
Roda (Aragon) (*see* Rotalyehud)
Roderick the Goth, 30–1, 36 note
Romaikiyyah (*see* Itimad)
Romulo, 40, 47, 49, 51, 100, 103
Ronda, 81, 102, 132, 212, 222, 241; murder of chiefs of, 209 ff.
Roshaid, Ibn, 325
Roshd, Ibn, 29
Rota, 227 note, 335
Rotalyehud, 103–4, 272

Sabah, Abu-s-, 59, 61, 65
Safaya-l-Moluk, the, 43
Sahla, As, 243
Said, Ibn of Toledo, 391
Said, Omar Ibn, 59, 64, 113
Sakkaf, 299–300, 309–10, 325, 331
Salamanca, 20
Saltis, 237, 269, 374, 398, 401
Samil, As, 61
Sampson, Abbot, 20, 109
Sana, Cathedral of, 122–3
Sancho, the Fat, 27
Sancho, the Infante, 253–5
Sancho Garcia, 182 note
Sanchol, 21, 181 ff., 238
Santander, 317–8
Santarem, 147, 273, 373
Santiago, church at, 128; taking of, by Almansur, 170–1; Master of, 305, 312, 320; Archbishop of, 312
Sara, granddaughter of Witiza, 10; journey to Damascus, 57 ff.; her husbands and children, 58–9; founded a ruling caste, 113; relations with Abderrahman I., 59 ff.; in Seville, 71; her descendants, 113
Sassanides, textiles of the, 142
Sastres, Guild of the, 340–1

Secunda, 114
Seraj, Ibn, casket of, 139
Sergius, St., monastery of, 123
Serpa, 311
Serpent, symbolism of the, 223 note
Servandus, 22–4, 109
Seville, Bishops of, 18; convents, 20; new mosque at, 25; Franciscan mission to, 31; attacked by Northmen, 70 note; relations with Cordova before A.D. 888, 70; residence of Gothic families, 71; churches in, 132–4, 384–5, 397–8; Christian art in Moslem times, 136; symbolism in textiles, etc., 135; siege of, by Almoravides, 219 ff.; 259 ff.; bridge of boats, 220 note, 259 note, 317; description of, in eleventh century, 248; relations of, with Al-Ahmar, 283–4; condition of, immediately before siege by Fernando III., 295 ff.; siege by Fernando III., 305 ff.; suburbs of, 319 *and* note; terms of surrender, 327 ff.; trade of, 328, 329 note; distribution of Moslem inhabitants after the reconquest, 330; *Fueros* of Toledo granted to, 347–8; water supply and baths, 352–4; worship of Virgin in, 361 ff.; industries of, 375–6, 378; early churches, images, etc., in, 384 ff. 397–8
Seyr Ibn Abi Bekr, 258–60
Shabur, 237
Shaliyyah, Ibn Ash, 107, 117
Shiites, the, 5, 66 note, 75
Shoayb, Ibn, 327 note
Silves, 237, 269, 402
Sobeya (Sobha), mother of Hisham II., 162, 164–5, 167
Sobrarbe, Sierra de, 103
Somadeh, Ibn, 213 note, 240–1, 248
Somail, As, 55
Spain, Moslem, divisions of, 9
Suleiman, 186–8, 192
Sunnites, the, 5, 66 note, 75
Sunnite historians, their bias, 6–7, 9, 14, 65, 196–7

Tablada, 83 note, 310, 313
Tagarete, the, 312

INDEX

Taira, 208
Talavera, 117
Tarifa, 106
Tarik, 39 note, 41–3, 45–6, 48, 387–8
Tashfin, Yusuf, Ibn, 14, 220, 225, 228 ff., 234–5, 241, 245 ff., 247 ff., 257–8, 261
Taxes of Christians, 21, 25
Tejada, 327 note, 343
Tenorio, family of, 401
Textiles in Spain, 11, 140 ff.; in Egypt, 121–2
Thagher, the, 47, 49
Tiraz, 11, 71, 140, 162
Toledo, 9, 18, 20, 40, 81, 101, 104, 116–7, 150 note, 158, 242, 244, 388
Tolox, castle of, 115
Torrox, castle of, 371
Tortosa, 239, 270, 272
Tradition, persistence of, 369
Trebujena, 335
Triana, 310, 312, 316, 319–20, 326
Tudela, 238
Tudmir (*see* Murcia)
Tunis, 126

UBEDA, 377
Ucles, 104, 254–6; Master of, 312
Utrera, 304, 310

VALENCIA, 12, 14, 19, 20, 238–9, 244, 265, 268, 270, 272–3, 275, 295, 337, 345 note, 377
Valera, 256
Vallecos, 172
Vargas, Garci Perez de, 313, 315
Vassal, use of the word, 351
Vilches, 106
Violante of Aragon, 313
Virgin de la Antigua, 321 ff., 359, 366; del Corral, 359; del Carmen, 360 note; de la Hiniesta, 361 note; de Rocamador, 385; worship of, in Seville, 361 ff.; in every-day life, 364; heraldic arms of, 365 ff.
Viseu, 18
Visigothic architecture, 381; treasure of Guadamur, 388

WAHDEH AL AMIRI, 185, 187
Walid, Al, Khalif, 9, 30, 46–8, 51, 67
Water supply in Seville, 352–3
Wine, use of, 155–7
Witiza, character and legislation, 36–8; sons of, 9, 36 ff., 41 ff.; grant of estates to, 43, 46–7
Women, employment of educated, 74

YABASTER (*see* Bishter)
Yasin, Abdullah Ibn, 227–8
Yemen before Mohammed, 122–3
Yemenite Arabs, 10; quarrels with Mudarites, 61, 63, 75; ancient civilisation, 72; followers of Ali, 74–5; relations with Christians, 112
Yusuf Abu Yakub (the Almohade), 274–5, 304
Yusuf, Ali Ibn, 261 ff.

ZADLAF, Yahya Ibn, 152
Zagut, Ibn, 246–7
Zahira, Az, 177, 185, 187
Zahra, Az, destruction of, 187
Zaida, 254–5, 258–9
Zalaca, battle of, 247, 250, 257
Zamora, fortifications and battle of, 150–1
Zaragoza, 14, 104, 117, 147, 194, 238, 244, 261–2, 268, 377
Zawiya, the, 178
Zehr, Ibn, 242, 251
Zobaidi, Az, 159, 166, 191
Zohr, Ibn, 217
Zulema, Don, 353–4